Divided Nation

Divided Nation

Analyzing Policy, Behavior, and Institutional
Challenges in Modern American Democracy

Edited by
Jamie L. Carson and Ryan D. Williamson

DE GRUYTER

ISBN (Paperback) 978-3-11-159167-4
ISBN (Hardcover) 978-3-11-159204-6
e-ISBN (PDF) 978-3-11-159190-2
e-ISBN (EPUB) 978-3-11-159197-1

Library of Congress Control Number: 2025944741

Bibliographic information published by the Deutsche Nationalbibliothek
The Deutsche Nationalbibliothek lists this publication in the Deutsche Nationalbibliografie;
detailed bibliographic data are available on the internet at http://dnb.dnb.de.

© 2026 Walter de Gruyter GmbH, Berlin/Boston, Genthiner Straße 13, 10785 Berlin
Cover image: mustafabilgesatkin/iStock/Getty Images Plus
Typesetting: Integra Software Services Pvt. Ltd.

www.degruyterbrill.com
Questions about General Product Safety Regulation:
productsafety@degruyterbrill.com

Preface and Acknowledgments

The study of American government is at a crossroads. In an era marked by heightened polarization and institutional dysfunction, students entering the classroom are often confronted with a political landscape that feels increasingly complex, contentious, and disconnected from traditional narratives of democracy. This book was conceived out of a pressing need to provide a resource that both captures the urgency of these contemporary challenges and remains accessible to students encountering American government for the first time. It seeks to bridge the gap between a rapidly evolving political reality and the foundational knowledge essential to understanding it.

Over recent decades, the United States has witnessed a series of profound shifts that have reshaped its democratic institutions and practices. Partisan divides have widened to historic levels, public trust in government has plummeted, and the nationalization of politics has eroded localism in governance. At the same time, external pressures, such as the politicization of media and the judiciary, the growing influence of outside interests in Congress, and contentious debates over election administration, have placed unprecedented strain on democratic norms. These dynamics demand closer scrutiny, especially in the context of an introductory American government curriculum.

Most recently, the 2024 election of Donald Trump to a second term has intensified concerns about the boundaries of executive authority and the resilience of American democracy. His unprecedented efforts to consolidate power, challenge institutional norms, and sideline political opposition have deepened debates over the constitutional limits of the presidency. As Trump asserts greater control over federal agencies, undermines independent oversight, and reshapes the judiciary with loyalists, scholars and citizens alike are grappling with fundamental questions about the durability of democratic institutions. Will the system of checks and balances withstand these challenges, or are we witnessing a shift toward a more unconstrained executive? Several of the contributing authors explore these pressing issues within the broader context of American government, providing students with the tools to analyze how institutions, political actors, and the public shape—and are shaped by—the evolving nature of presidential power and democratic governance.

This book brings together the expertise of leading scholars working at the cutting edge of political science research to provide that scrutiny. Each chapter delves into a key issue shaping American democracy today, offering in-depth analysis of its causes, mechanisms, and consequences. From the role of partisan media in shaping public opinion to the structural factors driving gridlock in Congress, this volume unpacks the forces underlying contemporary polarization and

https://doi.org/10.1515/9783111591902-202

dysfunction. The contributors also explore potential reforms and solutions, encouraging readers not only to understand the current state of American democracy but also to think critically about its future.

Unlike traditional textbooks that often skim over or oversimplify pressing national debates, this book emphasizes salience and accessibility. It covers topics that resonate deeply with students—issues they encounter daily in the news and in their communities—while presenting them in a manner that is clear, engaging, and suitable for those with no prior background in political science. This approach ensures that readers gain both the theoretical foundations and the practical insights necessary to navigate and analyze today's political environment.

The versatility of this text makes it an invaluable resource for courses across the spectrum of American government studies. Whether the focus is on voting and political behavior, the inner workings of Congress, the executive branch and federal bureaucracy, or judicial politics and democratic reform, this book provides students with the tools to connect foundational concepts to real-world challenges. By integrating policy, behavioral, and institutional perspectives, it fosters a holistic understanding of the interplay between governance and societal trends.

Ultimately, this book is an invitation to engage with the complexities of American democracy at a pivotal moment in its history. It seeks to inspire a new generation of students not only to grasp the challenges before them but also to envision a path toward a more resilient and responsive political system. In doing so, it aims to cultivate informed citizens who are equipped to participate meaningfully in the ongoing project of democracy.

We are indebted to a number of individuals who helped us bring this project to realization. First, we want to thank each of our contributing authors who kindly agreed to write a chapter on their specialized topic. All of them did an outstanding job in that capacity. We also want to thank Ze'ev Sudry, the American Politics acquisitions editor at De Gruyter, who immediately recognized the potential of this project and encouraged us to submit it sooner rather than later. His encouragement and guidance along the way has been instrumental in the development of the book you are currently holding in your hand. We also wish to thank Michaela Göbels for her invaluable assistance with the production of our edited volume as well as John Ryan who did a fantastic job copyediting the chapters.

Contents

Jamie L. Carson and Ryan D. Williamson

1 Introduction

In recent decades, American politics has been characterized by growing dysfunction and polarization, posing significant threats to the democratic process. Polarization fosters an "us-versus-them" mentality that divides citizens and impedes productive discourse among policymakers across all branches and levels of government. As political groups become more entrenched in their positions, the willingness to engage in meaningful compromise diminishes, leading to increased fragmentation of the political landscape. This often results in partisan loyalty taking precedence over national interests, making it difficult to address critical and pressing issues effectively.

This divisive environment often results in partisan messaging and stalemate, hindering the resolution of pressing national concerns. Essential policy areas including education, healthcare, and infrastructure are caught in ideological battles, where pragmatic decision-making takes a backseat to partisan agendas. These impasses not only stall progress but also exacerbate existing societal problems, leaving citizens feeling neglected and dissatisfied with their leaders' performance. The lack of effective governance exacerbates and contributes to a growing sense of frustration among the public.

As political leaders focus more attention on party loyalty, opportunities for bipartisan collaboration decrease significantly. This entrenchment in partisan ideologies limits the potential for innovative policy solutions that require cross-party support. Consequently, the absence of bipartisan efforts leads to inaction, further deepening public frustration. This gridlock is particularly damaging when urgent challenges, such as economic inequalities, climate change, and public health crises such as the COVID-19 pandemic, demand swift and cooperative responses.

The persistent stalemate within all of politics fosters a widespread sentiment of disenchantment and cynicism among voters. Many citizens perceive their elected officials as being either unable or unwilling to deliver the reforms and policies they promised, intensifying disengagement as citizens lose faith in the political system. With voter turnout declining and public apathy increasing, the democratic process is undermined, raising significant concerns about the future resilience and functionality of democratic governance in the United States.

Adding to these challenges, the nationalization of politics has strengthened existing political rifts. Local and state issues are increasingly overshadowed by overarching national agendas and narratives, resulting in a discourse dominated by national party agendas. This often reflects priorities and concerns of a limited

https://doi.org/10.1515/9783111591902-001

set of interests rather than the diverse needs of local communities. As a direct result, the representation of local interests is marginalized, leading to a one-size-fits-all approach in policymaking that fails to address the unique challenges that different communities face.

This shift away from localized representation leaves many citizens feeling disconnected from their elected officials, perceiving their concerns as sidelined by the national agenda. Local and state governments often hold critical insights into the cultural, economic, and social contexts of their regions, but these are increasingly being ignored in favor of policies more national in scope. When overshadowed by national priorities, policies become mismatched with community needs, leading to ineffective or detrimental outcomes that entrench existing inequalities.

As this disconnect widens, citizens experience a growing sense of disenfranchisement, feeling their ability to influence change is diminishing. The erosion of locally focused governance contributes to the perception that individual and community voices are eclipsed by a larger, seemingly indifferent national dialogue. This sense of alienation poses serious risks to democratic engagement, diminishing voter motivation and trust in the political system and making citizens less likely to participate in elections or civic activities.

The widespread alienation of a significant portion of the electorate further divides an already polarized society. When large swathes of the population feel their voices are going unheard or their opinions undervalued, it affects their willingness to engage with political processes, challenging the legitimacy and efficacy of the democratic system. Addressing this disconnect requires empowering local and state governments and ensuring national politics is inclusive of diverse community needs, fostering a sense of involvement and representation for all citizens.

One significant consequence of these political trends is the erosion of public trust in political institutions, a fundamental pillar of democracy in any setting. As governmental bodies become more polarized, their efficiency and effectiveness are compromised, leading to gridlock. This inefficiency reinforces a cycle of mistrust among citizens, who view these institutions as incapable or unwilling to address their needs, undermining the legitimacy of current political leadership.

Growing dissatisfaction and disillusionment profoundly impact civic engagement, as individuals become less inclined to participate in processes they view as futile or ineffective. Low trust in government means citizens are less likely to vote, engage in debates, or join community organizing, all critical for a vibrant democracy. This leads not only to lower voter turnout but also reduces the diversity of voices in public discourse, weakening democratic governance. Moreover, the pervasive sense of disillusionment can give rise to populist movements and demagogues who exploit public frustration by promising rapid solutions. This type of behavior further strains democracy, as such movements often promote divisive rhetoric that exacerbates polarization. To rebuild public trust, governments need transparent governance and accountability, actively addressing citizens' needs to foster a participatory political environment.

Dissatisfaction with political institutions is also driven by a perceived lack of electoral or political accountability. When politicians prioritize party loyalty over constituent needs, it creates a sense of betrayal. This misalignment leads to declining public approval and a growing disillusionment with the political system, further eroding trust in government. The perception that political leaders are detached from citizens' everyday challenges intensifies this dissatisfaction. Many citizens believe politicians are insulated from economic hardship and job insecurity, questioning their commitment to representation. This disconnect further provokes feelings of cynicism and apathy, as participation feels pointless and unlikely to produce meaningful change.

Voter cynicism is exacerbated by perceived governmental inaction on pressing national issues like income inequality and climate change. Failure to address these challenges convincingly deepens skepticism about government efficacy, alienating citizens from voting or civic engagement. This further perpetuates the cycle of frustration and weakens democratic processes. Diminished civic engagement is both a symptom and cause of political dysfunction, undermining democracy's health over time. Disenchanted citizens withdrawing from participation reduces the diversity of perspectives, leading to policies that benefit only engaged minorities. This exclusion further weakens democratic institutions, harming their ability to adapt to population needs.

Ultimately, these issues highlight the urgent need for a concerted effort to address growing political dysfunction and alienation of citizens who feel marginalized by the current state of governmental affairs. Encouraging dialogue, transparency, and civic engagement can help restore faith in democratic processes, but it is not without its share of challenges, given the level of dysfunction in politics. By prioritizing inclusivity and enhanced levels of civic participation, we can foster a political environment that better serves all society members, reinforcing democracy's health.

This edited volume plays a crucial role in addressing these pressing challenges by bringing together the expertise of a diverse array of scholars, each contributing valuable insights into the underlying causes and consequences of political dysfunction and polarization. By drawing upon specialized knowledge across various subject areas, the book provides a multifaceted examination of how these trends impact American politics and governance. Its comprehensive approach offers readers a deeper understanding of the complexities involved, making it a valuable resource for anyone interested in the future of democracy. Covering a wide range of topics from electoral dynamics to legislative behavior, this volume equips readers with the analytical tools needed to navigate and understand intricate political landscapes. These insights can inform strategies to mitigate the harmful effects of current political trends and contribute to more informed public discourse.

Moreover, this volume delves deeply into contemporary issues poised to significantly influence the political landscape in the coming decade. Themes such as nationalization, polarization, and representation are thoroughly examined, revealing their intricate roles in shaping modern governance. By addressing these critical topics, the book seeks to enhance our understanding of the evolving dynamics within American government and democracy. It provides a comprehensive analysis of how these forces intersect and impact the democratic process, thus serving as an essential resource for those examining the future of political systems. This volume also helps readers appreciate the complexity of these issues and their far-reaching implications, offering insights critical for navigating the challenges posed by a rapidly changing political environment.

Furthermore, the book actively invites students and scholars to engage with pressing questions around electoral dynamics, media influence, and judicial impacts on society, each of which plays a pivotal role in contemporary politics. By fostering a space for critical reflection and dialogue, this work equips readers with the knowledge and analytical tools necessary to participate effectively in shaping a more responsive and resilient political landscape. It not only provides a solid foundation for academic inquiry but also acts as a catalyst for public engagement, encouraging a renewed interest in civic participation. Through its advocacy for informed debate and discussion, this volume aims to inspire the development of more sustainable reforms and policies. These reforms are envisioned to mirror the diverse needs and aspirations of the populace, ensuring that governance practices evolve in a way that is inclusive and representative of all societal sectors. This book ultimately empowers individuals to become active contributors to a healthier and more equitable democratic process.

1.1 Outline of the Book

The book begins with a broad discussion of attitudes towards political institutions. Specifically, in Chapter 2, "Affective Polarization: Decline in Approval and Trust in American National Institutions," Steve Nicholson and Tabitha Lamberth explore the impact of affective polarization on public trust in government. The authors analyze how negative sentiments towards opposing political parties decrease institutional approval and trust. Their findings underscore the dangers of deepening polarization, affecting governance and civility in political discourse. Understanding this phenomenon is necessary for devising interventions that can restore trust and enhance democratic resilience amidst partisan divides.

Part I of the book examines Congress and legislative politics. This begins with Stephanie Davis and Charles Finocchiaro's chapter, "Compromise and Consequence: The Impact of Institutions on American Representation," which explores the enduring features of the U.S. Constitution and the unique institutions it established, such as the Electoral College and the Senate. This chapter delves into how the Constitution was born out of compromise, which explains the creation of institutions like the Senate that wield unequal influence across states due to its representation system. Understanding these foundations is crucial for comprehending current policy debates and governance challenges in the United States. Reflecting on the historical role of the Senate provides valuable lessons for analyzing power dynamics in contemporary American politics and assessing proposed reforms.

Next, in chapter 4, Ryan Williamson and Jordan Windham ask, "Is the Legislature Broken? The Evolving Dysfunction of Congress and Paths to Reform," which sheds light on the dysfunctions in Congress marked by increased partisanship and decreased productivity. The analysis of recent congressional developments, including broken traditions in leadership elections and legislative proceedings, presents a critical view of how Congress's effectiveness has waned. This exploration is essential for grasping why public approval is so low and for considering strategies that might reinvigorate Congressional operations. The insights provided are important for proposing reforms that could restore confidence and improve legislative functionality.

Part II of the book looks at the executive branch, the bureaucracy, and the judiciary. To begin, Jamie Carson and Stewart Ulrich's work, "Disrupting the Norm: Redefining Presidential Nominations in Modern Politics," investigates the evolution of presidential nominations during the past few decades. Beginning with the 2008 election where Barack Obama built up a powerful campaign organization to successfully wrest the nomination away from establishment candidate Hillary Clinton, this chapter reveals the strategies candidates have employed in their attempt to win the presidency. The chapter's dissection of electoral trends from 2008 to 2024 underscores significant shifts in the political fabric, impacting both major parties. Understanding these changes is pivotal for forecasting the future of presidential elections and the political messaging that resonates with the electorate, thereby shaping American democracy.

In Chapter 6, "Peeking Behind the Curtain: The Federal Bureaucracy, Transparency, and Judicial Oversight," Gbemende Johnson, Yao Yao, and Hannah Lee examine the effectiveness of federal policies intended to ensure government transparency amidst various political and bureaucratic challenges. This analysis highlights the importance of transparency for accountable governance, delving into how judicial oversight can offset transparency deficiencies exacerbated during the Trump administration. Understanding these dynamics is vital for proposing solutions that enhance government openness, ensuring informed citizenry, and reinforcing democratic accountability.

Kirk Randazzo, Abigail Hassett, and Anna Puente analyze the ideological leanings of the U.S. Supreme Court and explore its potential impact on American politics in the seventh chapter, "The Judicial Balancing Act: Ideology, Law, and Legitimacy in Supreme Court Decisions." This chapter evaluates the increasing conservatism of the Court and its ramifications on legislative actions, public perception, and institutional legitimacy. Understanding these trends is crucial for anticipating shifts in policy and gauging the long-term influence of judiciary decisions on the political landscape, as well as maintaining a check on ideological extremes in governance.

Building upon the discussion emphasizing the three branches of government, Part III turns to an examination of political parties and interest groups. James Curry's chapter, "Capitol Gains and Losses: Navigating Leadership in Today's Polarized Congress," explores the complexities party leaders face in today's political environment. The chapter discusses how leaders can navigate challenges and opportunities, revealing the conditions under which significant legislative successes and failures occur. This understanding is vital for comprehending the extreme outcomes seen in Congress today and for formulating suggestions to improve decision-making efficacy and legislative outcomes.

In Chapter 9, "Voices of Influence: Outside Interests and Surrogate Representation," Lindsey Cormack evaluates how congressional communications represent outside interests. The chapter's analysis of profession-specific mentions and their implications provides insights into the intersection of public perception, policy, and media. Recognizing these elements is important for understanding how representation occurs and assessing the influence of various interest groups on legislative priorities and public opinion.

Next, we arrive at Part IV, which focuses on campaigns, elections, and voting. Bridgett King's chapter, "The Politics of Running Free and Fair Elections," examines the complexities of election administration at state and local levels against the backdrop of partisanship. The chapter addresses key debates about voting policy changes and their potential to suppress voter turnout or invite fraud. By scrutinizing these aspects, King highlights the critical role of public trust in the integrity of electoral processes and the impact of perceived partisan biases. Understanding these dynamics is pivotal for future election reforms and in maintaining a healthy democracy, as they shape citizens' perceptions of and engagement in electoral politics.

In Chapter 11, "National Waves in Local Waters: The Impact of National Issues on Down-Ballot Elections," Joel Sievert, Stephanie Mathiasen, and Abby Miller examines the profound impact of national issues and politics on elections at all government levels. This chapter highlights the dwindling separation between local and national political agendas, even in nonpartisan elections. Understanding this trend is crucial in dissecting voter behavior and election outcomes in the modern era, which suggests strategies for maintaining the health and diversity of local political ecosystems in a national context.

Enrijeta Shino and Seth C. McKee's chapter, "Voting Behavior and Participation: What Drives Us to the Polls," examines the myriad factors influencing election participation in America. By analyzing historical patterns, individual characteristics, and contextual features, this work provides a comprehensive overview of what drives or hinders voter turnout in federal elections. Recognizing these factors is essential for developing policies to increase voter engagement and ensuring a representative electoral process that accurately reflects the diversity of the American populace.

In the last section, Part V, authors explore issues related to mass media and public policy. Specifically, in Chapter 13, "From Local News to Polarized Views: The Nationalization of the American Media," Joshua McCrain investigates the increasing national and political focus of media coverage. The analysis of economic and political drivers presents a critical view of current media dynamics and its implications for democracy. Understanding these trends is crucial in addressing the media's role in public discourse and fostering environments that support democratic engagement and informed citizenry.

In "Redefining Reproductive Rights: Policy Evolution from *Roe* to *Dobbs*," Teena Wilhelm discusses the evolution of abortion politics in the U.S., beginning with *Roe v. Wade* and culminating in the recent *Dobbs* decision. This chapter explores the polarizing effects of *Roe* on American politics and the significant shift that Dobbs represents in legal and political discourse. Wilhelm's analysis of state policy reactions and public opinion in the post-Dobbs era is crucial for understanding how states navigate contentious moral and legal issues. Furthermore, the examination of broader implications for related policies offers insights into the future of reproductive rights and gender health policy in America.

In the final chapter of the edited volume, "Democratic Backsliding in the United States," James Druckman and Dot Sawler address the erosion of democracy in the twenty-first century and its specific manifestations in the U.S. This chapter highlights the processes and actors involved in democratic backsliding, providing a framework for understanding and counteracting democratic decay. Their analysis is crucial for identifying threats to democracy, envisioning preventive measures, and ensuring the stability and resilience of democratic institutions in the face of contemporary challenges.

In summary, the challenges highlighted here underscore the critical need to address political dysfunction and the alienation felt by many citizens in today's polarized environment. Restoring faith in democratic institutions will require deliberate efforts to foster dialogue, transparency, and civic engagement. These efforts must prioritize inclusivity and participation to rebuild trust and create a political system that is more representative and responsive to society's diverse needs. While the obstacles to achieving these goals are significant, they are not insurmountable if approached with a commitment to collaboration and reform.

This edited volume serves as an essential resource for understanding the complexities of political dysfunction and polarization. By bringing together a diverse group of scholars, it provides a multidimensional analysis of the forces shaping contemporary governance and democracy. Covering themes ranging from electoral dynamics to representation and media influence, the book offers a comprehensive exploration of the factors driving current trends. Its insights not only deepen our understanding of these issues but also equip readers with the tools to critically engage with them, fostering more informed public discourse and strategies for meaningful change.

Ultimately, the book seeks to inspire both scholarly inquiry and public action, encouraging readers to participate actively in shaping a more inclusive and resilient democratic system. By addressing pressing questions and proposing pathways for reform, it offers a vision for governance that reflects the aspirations of all citizens. This work stands as a testament to the power of informed dialogue and collective effort in navigating the challenges of a rapidly evolving political landscape. It empowers individuals to contribute to a healthier, more equitable democratic process, ensuring that the principles of democracy remain robust and adaptive in the face of future challenges.

Tabitha Lamberth and Stephen P. Nicholson

2 Affective Polarization and Public Trust in Government

Growing out-party sentiment in the United States has ushered in an era of affective partisan polarization, the emotional estrangement between Democrats and Republicans. Americans have increasingly divided into partisan teams that do not like each other. This circumstance has negatively affected public evaluations of American political institutions and has grave implications for governance. Across the three branches of government, approval has declined as partisans are increasingly unwilling to positively evaluate a branch of government controlled by the out-party. For instance, upon assuming office in 2021, President Biden had an approval rating of 98 percent among Democrats and 11 percent among Republicans, a whopping eighty-seven percentage point gap. In 1977, more than forty years prior, President Carter had an approval rating of 77 percent among Democrats upon entering office and 49 percent among Republicans, a gap of only twenty-eight percentage points.

Although the partisan differences in presidential approval ratings have changed considerably, the implications for trust in government are even more dramatic. At the beginning of Biden's presidency, 36 percent of Democrats and 11 percent of Republicans expressed trust in government, a gap of twenty-five percentage points. In contrast, at the start of Carter's presidency, 37 percent of Democrats and 34 percent of Republicans expressed trust in government, a difference of only three percentage points. In other words, whether a Democratic or Republican identifier trusted government back in the 1970s had little to do with the occupant of the Oval Office. Today, it matters a great deal as partisans have become less trustful of government when the out-party controls the presidency or Congress. In this chapter, we will discuss the rise of affective polarization in American politics and its consequences for public trust in government and the ability of political leaders to effectively handle the nation's problems.

Tabitha Lamberth, **Stephen P. Nicholson**, University of Georgia

https://doi.org/10.1515/9783111591902-002

2.1 The Ideal Citizen Is Not Partisan

In a democracy, the ideal citizen is well-informed about politics (Berelson et al. 1954).[1] Being well-informed requires citizens to be aware of current political issues and events, along with knowing the pertinent facts and history behind them. Drawing on this knowledge, citizens should weigh each political party's handling of, or solution to, a problem in light of their own policy preferences. The ideal voter is a rational being that approaches politics retrospectively, looking back at the performance of elected officials and rewarding them at the ballot box for good times and punishing them for bad times (Key 2013). In between elections, public evaluations of government should be informed by how well government operates and performs.

Unfortunately, the American public falls far short of the "ideal citizen," since most Americans are ill-informed and biased. It is hard to make an informed evaluation if you don't know much. This does not mean that the public is incapable; the time and effort required to be a fully informed, much less actively engaged, citizen is incompatible with the everyday lives of most people (Achen and Bartels 2016). The public knows, "jaw-droppingly little about politics" (Luskin 2002, 282) because it takes time, effort, and resources to be politically informed. Although one might assume an ill-informed public wouldn't possess strong opinions, once a question becomes partisan, they become highly opinionated. This is to say that the average American is not an impartial observer of political life.

Campbell et al. (1960) were the first political scientists to flesh out the notion of partisanship as an identity with a strong group attachment. Their "sociopsychological" approach to voting characterized party identification as a psychological attachment acquired early in life through political socialization (e.g., the family). As a stable orientation, party identity acts as a lens through which people perceive the political world, shaping political attitudes and, ultimately, voting behavior. Later conceptualizations of party identification borrowed from Social Identity Theory (SIT), a theory that emphasizes that in-group members are highly motivated to favorably differentiate themselves from the out-group, leading to in-group bias and out-group ostracization (Tajfel and Turner 1986). The motivation to protect the in-group stems from the strong sense of value and emotional ties that come from linking group membership to sense of self (Tajfel 1978).

---

1 Another component of being an ideal citizen is being politically engaged (Dahl 1992). Politically engaged citizens partake in multiple modes of political participation ranging from engaging in important political discussions with other citizens to actively working to influence representatives through direct communication and attendance at public meetings and city halls.

Although party has long been a salient political identity (Campbell et al. 1960; Green et al. 2002; Huddy et al. 2015), it is now among the most salient social identities in the United States (Iyengar and Krupenkin 2018). As political elites have become increasingly polarized, it clarified the ideological positions for ordinary Americans, leading to a resurgence of party identity (Hetherington 2001). This process brought about a stronger alignment between a person's ideology and party identification, a process known as partisan sorting (Levendusky 2009). Whereas substantial portions of each party used to include people with unaligned ideological beliefs (conservative Democrats or liberal Republicans), the ideological polarization of elites produced a shift such that most partisans now have aligned ideological beliefs (liberal Democrats and conservative Republicans). In addition, other social identities such as race, religious affiliation, and urban versus rural have sorted along party lines. As this social sorting has increased, partisanship has become more of a "mega-identity" strengthening emotional ties and reactions to partisanship (Mason 2015, 2018).

Mason (2015) likens the attachment of partisanship to that of a lifelong sports fan, instead of the reasonable and rational participant in the political system we would expect to see in the ideal voter. This social and emotional connection to partisan identity may account for its stability and salience throughout life (Sears and Funk 1999). People also view the political parties as opposing categories, meaning that if someone is viewed as highly typical of one party they are also perceived as highly atypical of the other (Heit and Nicholson 2010). This perception further undermines the ability of government to problem solve. As Heit and Nicholson (2010, 1513) conclude, "if a person knows that a Republican is sponsoring a policy proposal, Democratic Party identifiers may oppose it since they understand that a proposal backed by a Republican is likely the opposite of the Democratic proposal." Although partisanship has positive effects such as motivating political engagement (Campbell et al. 1960; Huddy et al. 2015) it also has negative consequences, motivating biased political perceptions (Bartels 2002) and opinions (Nicholson 2012).

The problematic aspects of partisanship have grown over the last fifty years as ordinary Americans have polarized. Much of it is driven by a growing disdain for the out-party. While partisanship is primarily conceived as a positive association between the self and party affiliation, recent research has focused on negational identity. Negational identities are social identities defined by a person's *opposition* to another identity (Zhong et al. 2008). In politics, this is what scholars refer to as negative partisanship, a partisan identity rooted in opposing a political party rather than a positive attachment to one (Abramowitz and Webster 2018; Bankert 2024). By using survey measures of how warmly (or coldly) respondents feel towards political parties, scholars have found that negative feelings towards the out-party have grown over time whereas feelings towards the in-party have remained relatively stable (Abramowitz and Webster 2016; Iyengar et al. 2012). For example, Democrats' positive feelings towards their own party haven't changed much over the last fifty years but their negative feelings towards Republicans have grown. Some scholars have pointed to this change as evidence of increased negative partisanship (Abramowitz and Webster 2016) whereas others have labeled it affective polarization, the growing negative feelings between Democratic and Republican party identifiers (Iyengar et al. 2012).

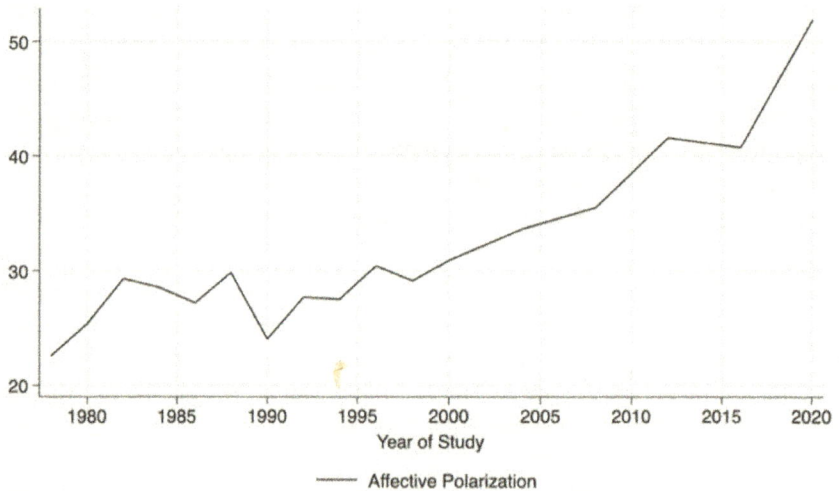

Figure 2.1: Affective polarization, 1978–2020.
Source: American National Election Study Cumulative File, 2022.

Figure 2.1 depicts the increase in affective polarization over time. Borrowed from Iyengar and colleagues (2012), the affective polarization measure is the difference between how warmly (or coldly) respondents rate the Democratic and Republican parties. In separate questions, the survey asks respondents to rate how warmly or coldly they feel towards each party on a 100-point scale. Scores above fifty represent warm feelings and scores below fifty represent cold feelings. As one might imagine, partisans typically rate their own party warmly (e.g., 75) and the opposing party coldly (e.g., 25). To produce the affective polarization measure (a measure of emotional distance), we subtract the two scores. Someone who rates their own party very warmly and the out-party very coldly will have a large affective polarization score whereas someone who rates the two parties similarly will have a low affective polarization score. The point estimates in the graph represent the average (mean) affective polarization score by election year. The graph shows that from the beginning of the time series until the early 2000s, affective polarization hovered in the thirties. From the mid-2000s to 2020, the score steadily increased, nearly doubling in size.

One might think that the growing animosity between Democratic and Republican identifiers relates to heightened policy differences, what scholars refer to as ideological polarization. Although ideological polarization among elected officials between the two major parties has been widely documented (McCarty et al. 2008), the policy and ideological differences between ordinary Democrats and Republicans are evident (Levendusky 2009) but much less pronounced (Fiorina, Abrams, and Pope 2005). The growing divide between Democratic and Republican identifiers therefore is not primarily about policy differences (ideological polarization) but instead is steeped in affective polarization where the in-party is favored and the out-party is loathed. Scholars have even found that partisans, especially the most affectively polarized, dehumanize the other side, viewing them as less human and evolved (Martherus et al. 2021). Such hyper-partisanship cannot be overcome by moderating policy positions and results in an unwillingness to compromise and, at worst, an acceptance of political violence.

Partisan biases are exacerbated by affective polarization. If polarization is about public policy differences such as conservative or liberal positions on issues such as taxation or immigration, it can be narrowed by one or the other party moving closer to each other. The disagreement is not personal and there are opportunities for compromise and finding common ground. Furthermore, if policy is what matters, it might even be the case that partisans, while disagreeing with the inputs, may acknowledge favorable policy outputs brought about by the other side. Although the electorate can reward or punish political parties for how well (or poorly) they do in office (Fiorina 1981; Mackuen et al. 1992; Nadeau and Lewis-Beck 2001), an increasingly partisan electorate—especially one increasingly characterized by disdain for the out-party—is less likely to do so. Rather than giving credit where credit is due, most Americans now perceive the world through partisan lenses, attributing blame or praise depending on whether it advantages their party or disadvantages the out-party. Although GDP growth, unemployment, and inflation are objective indicators of the nation's economy, for instance, partisanship biases economic evaluations (Bartels 2002; Evans and Anderson 2006).

Approval of the president is a prime example of how hyper-partisanship has severed the relationship between economic conditions and political evaluations. Since the 1950s, pollsters have routinely asked Americans about whether they approve (or disapprove) of the job performance of the president. The economy has consistently been a strong predictor of the time series wherein approval ratings would rise with a strong economy and fall with a weak economy. Using data on economic perceptions, Donovan and colleagues (2020) found that the effect of economic perceptions began to weaken with growing partisan polarization such that economic perceptions became divorced from approval after the presidency of George W. Bush. Beginning with the Obama presidency, Donovan and colleagues found that both Democrats and Republicans were immune to economic considerations when evaluating the president. With increasing partisan polarization, which party is responsible for the state of the economy often says more about the party a person identifies with than economic reality.

The heightened effects of party identification from affective polarization are not limited to the political sphere. Partisanship now plays a much larger role in our social relationships. Perhaps one of the most interesting findings reported in the work of Iyengar et al. (2012) is how someone would feel if their son or daughter married a person from the out-party. In 1960, when the question was first asked, only 4–5 percent of partisans expressed concern. In 2010, fifty years later, nearly half of Republicans and a third of Democrats expressed concern. Prejudice against those who identify with the out-party is widespread and deeply ingrained, even surpassing the influence of racial prejudice (Iyengar and Westwood 2015). Other studies have also shown how partisanship has become central to our nonpolitical lives by affecting a range of personal choices including dating (Huber and Malhotra 2017), who one finds physically attractive (Nicholson et al. 2016), roommate selection (Shafranek 2021), and the neighborhood one lives in (Hui 2013).

In sum, public attitudes towards government increasingly have more to do with party than what government does. Since ordinary Americans are much more likely to occupy the role of a cheerleader than a referee, there is little chance that they acknowledge a good performance from the other side and, on some occasions, proclaim that their opponent cheated. Indeed, partisans may even be worse than sports fans given that majorities of Democrats and Republicans disagree about who rightfully won the 2020 presidential election (Arceneaux and Truex 2023). This circumstance is troublesome since evaluations of government, especially trust in government, are essential to a functioning democracy, as discussed by Druckman and Sawler in the final chapter of this volume.

2.2 Political Trust

Political trust (or trust in government) is a general evaluation of how well government meets expectations for competent, fair, efficient, and effective governance.

This definition includes *what* government does and *how* government does it. Scholars who study what government does focus on government performance or policy outputs such as the economy (Citrin 1974; Hetherington 2005; Miller 1974), whereas scholars who study how government goes about its work focus on process, public perceptions of whether government is fair and effective (Hibbing and Theiss-Morse 2002). There has been a uniform decline among all social and demographic groups in government trust since the 1950s (Citrin and Luks 2001); however, its decline has not been a uniform freefall (Orren 1997), and it is influenced by political scandals (Chanley et al. 2000; Hetherington and Rudolph 2015), economic conditions (Chanley et al. 2000; Citrin 1974), and the salience of domestic versus foreign policy issues (Hetherington and Rudolph 2015).

Recently, Intawan and Nicholson (2018) focus on implicit trust, a type of gut-level, automatically expressed trust rooted in early political socialization. The interesting thing about implicit trust is that people may not even be aware of it since it is captured by a videogame-like task measuring reaction times to people rapidly matching the words "trust" or "distrust" to "government." If a person is faster at matching "trust" and "government" than they are at matching "distrust" and government, it means they are implicitly trustful of government. Using this measure, Intawan and Nicholson (2018) found that most respondents implicitly trust government and that implicit trust is largely unrelated to the type of trust as self-reported in surveys. Since implicit trust is a relatively new measure, scholars have no way of knowing whether it has increased or decreased since the 1950s, but since it is the product of early political socialization processes it is likely to have remained stable over the years. When we refer to "trust" in this chapter we are referring to the type that is self-reported in a survey and will use the term implicit trust to mean the reaction-time measure.

Since trust in government is low and has been generally in decline since the late 1950s, scholars have questioned its meaning. In other words, is low trust bad for a political system? Easton (1975) identified trust as a central ingredient for understanding system support, public acceptance of the government's authority and legitimacy. This type of deep-seated, generalized support is described by Easton as diffuse support. It is a long-term "reservoir of good will" that stems from socialization, political stability, and perceived government effectiveness. Whereas diffuse support involves underlying support for the regime, specific support is short-lived, focused on the current cast of political actors that inhabit political institutions and the policies they create.

Although Easton envisioned political trust as a type of diffuse support, empirical research has found political trust to be related to either diffuse (Miller 1974) or specific (Citrin 1974) support or both (Hetherington 1998). Intawan and Nicholson's (2018) measure of implicit trust, on the other hand, was only related to measures of diffuse support, suggesting that diffuse support is more a gut-level feeling than specific support. Regardless of the extent to which trust in government reflects diffuse or specific support, political trust is an important aspect of a functioning government and healthy democracy. It can impact whether citizens participate in the political process (Donovan and Bowler 2004), who they vote for (Hetherington 1999), and public support for government programs and policy (Hetherington 2005; Hetherington and Rudolph 2015).

2.3 Political Trust and Partisanship

We focus on partisanship and its growing influence as the partisan public becomes more affectively polarized. Regardless of the government's accomplishments, partisans discount the effectiveness of government if it is controlled by the out-party. Since political trust is in no small part a reflection of the performance of incumbent officeholders, party control of government feeds political trust (Citrin and Green 1986; Hetherington and Rudolph 2015; Morisi et al. 2019).[2] Simply put, Democrats are less trustful of government when Republicans run the government and Republicans are less trustful of government when Democrats are in charge. This pattern is consistent with the argument that the trust in government survey question captures specific support since it is temporary, sensitive to which party is in power. In contrast, implicit trust (the reaction time measure) is unrelated to party identification, further underscoring how it captures diffuse support, the generalized support underlying a regime.

American government, of course, is divided into three branches of government and it is the visibility of the branches of government, and the partisan makeup of its occupants, that the public responds to when evaluating government as whole. The presidency is the most visible branch of government so if evaluations of incumbent officeholders affect trust, a strong connection between presidential evaluations and political trust should exist. Citrin and Green (1986) find evidence of how Reagan's leadership had reversed the decline in political trust but despite being a broad-based shift, it was overwhelmingly concentrated among Republicans. Miller and Borelli (1991) also found that assessment of presidential character during the 1980s mattered in all but one of the years in their

---

2 It is important to note, however, that the relationship between trust and attitudes towards the branches of government and political trust are reciprocal; evaluations of Congress and the president affect trust in government, but political trust also affects evaluations of Congress and the president (Hetherington 1998).

study. Since partisanship is a strong predictor of presidential evaluations (e.g., Republican identifiers are much more likely to approve of Republican presidents than Democrats), it is not surprising that trust in government rises and falls depending on partisan control of the presidency. Similarly, Keele (2005) found a "president-in-power" effect, showing that partisan bias colors trust in government when the office of the presidency shifts from one party to another, with partisans trusting government more when their party is in power.

Scholars have also found that evaluations of Congress affect trust in government (Feldman 1983; Hetherington 1998; Williams 1985). Accounting for a variety of factors, including presidential approval, Feldman (1983) found that trust in Congress was the dominant factor affecting trust in government. He suggests that the strong relationship between Congress and political trust might be attributed to the way the questions are worded rather than the relative salience of the presidency and Congress. Hetherington (1998) found that increases in congressional approval consistently boosted political trust, but presidential approval had less consistent effects.

As found with the presidency, changes in party control of Congress are key to understanding partisan differences in congressional approval and, by association, political trust (Gershtenson et al. 2006; Keele 2005). Keele (2005) showed that changes in party control of the House and Senate affected the relative trust levels of Democrats and Republicans but that the effects of congressional approval were considerably smaller than the effects of presidential approval. In the aftermath of the 2002 congressional elections, Gershtenson et al. (2006) found that Republican identifiers became more, and Democratic identifiers less, trusting of government when party control of the Senate switched hands from the Democrats to the Republicans.

The ebb and flow of whether the presidency or Congress play a larger role in explaining trust in government is probably due to the relative visibility of each branch and public perceptions of how good (or bad) a job each is doing in their respective positions. The Supreme Court ought to have some influence on political trust as well but to our knowledge there is no research on the topic. One possible reason for this neglect is because the Court is not nearly as visible as the presidency and Congress. Although the Court decides about eighty cases a term, only a few of them garner much media attention. Furthermore, the Court does not allow television coverage of proceedings and justices seldom, if ever, give interviews. As Hibbing and Theiss-Morse (2003) observe, the inner workings of the Supreme Court are opaque. The Court is clearly different in how it functions and the public views it as less than fully political, at least compared to Congress (Hansford et al. 2018). That said, the Court has become increasingly politicized and as such the public has increasingly viewed it in a partisan light (Boddery and Yates 2014;

Clark and Kastellec 2015; Nicholson and Hansford 2014; Nicholson and Howard 2004).

Although we are not aware of any research that looks at the relationship between political trust and public evaluations of the Supreme Court, many studies look at attitudes towards the Court, including its legitimacy, a key ingredient in diffuse support. Legitimacy is the Court's currency, its ability to make authoritative, binding decisions. As recognized by Alexander Hamilton in Federalist #78, the Supreme Court is heavily reliant on legitimacy since it "has no influence over either the sword or the purse." Despite controversial rulings, the Court's legitimacy has largely remained intact since its decisions come wrapped in legal symbols (e.g., black robes) that invoke the Court's legitimacy (Gibson et al. 2014).

Until the early 2000s, there was scholarly disagreement about whether legitimacy perceptions of the Supreme Court had become partisan. Examining data from the mid-1980s through the mid-2000s, Gibson (2007) found no evidence that perceptions of the Court's legitimacy were connected to ideological or party identification. However, other studies have found that ideological or partisan agreement with the Court affected legitimacy perceptions (Bartels and Johnston 2013) and acceptance of its decisions (Nicholson and Hansford 2014). As discussed in Chapter 7 of this volume, the increasing conservatism of the Supreme Court provides fertile ground for polarized evaluations of its membership and decisions, providing more opportunities for partisan public responses to Court decisions and, under some circumstances, polarized public trust in government. For example, Chapter 14 discusses the Supreme Court's blockbuster ruling in *Dobbs v. Jackson* that ended the constitutional right to abortion and its polarizing effects on American politics, a decision which appears to have produced a sizeable dent in the Court's legitimacy (Gibson 2024). Given the high visibility of the decision, it is possible that the polarization of legitimacy perceptions of the Supreme Court will add more fuel to polarized trust in government, further deepening the partisan divide.

2.4 Political Trust and Affective Polarization

Although there is a strong relationship between partisanship and political trust, the connection has grown dramatically over the last twenty years with the increase in affective polarization. Figure 2.2 depicts the average of the trust in government measure from the American National Elections Studies and the average feeling thermometer ratings for the Democratic and Republican parties by the respondent's party identification. As discussed earlier, the feeling thermometer ranges from 1–100, with values over fifty representing warm feelings and values under fifty capturing cold feelings. The black lines represent a Democratic party identifier's feeling towards their own party (solid black line) and the out-party (dashed black line) whereas the dark gray lines represent a Republican party identifier's

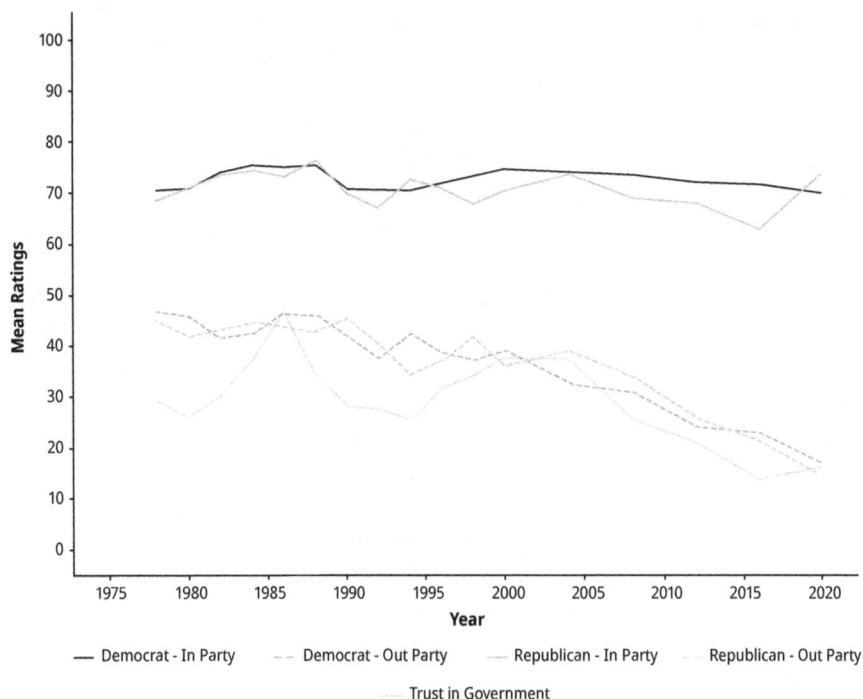

Figure 2.2: Affect towards political parties and trust in government, 1978–2020.
Source: American National Election Study Cumulative File, 2022.

feelings towards their own party (solid dark gray line) and the out-party (dashed dark gray line). The top portion of Figure 2.2 shows that partisans, both Democrats and Republicans, have warm feelings towards their own party but that those feelings have not changed much over time. The bottom lines of Figure 2.2 show that partisans' feelings toward their out-party (e.g., Democratic party identifier's feelings towards the Republican party) have declined over time, becoming colder. The light gray line depicting trust in government shows a decline in trust, moving in tandem with the colder feelings partisans express for the out-party.

In their book *Why Washington Won't Work*, Hetherington and Rudolph (2015) argue that negative feelings towards the out-party, especially among those whose party does not control the presidency, has polarized trust in government. Polarized trust, the near absence of trust among party identifiers opposite the president, contributes to government dysfunction since trust is essential to compromise and consensus. How does trust play this role? Since most people know very little about politics, Hetherington and Rudolph (2015) propose that trust in government serves as a "heuristic" or rule of thumb for ordinary people to arrive at an opinion about government policies or actions. A person may know few of the details of a new government policy, but they do know whether they trust or distrust government and can use that feeling as an information shortcut. Where this matters the most is when people are asked to make an ideological sacrifice, e.g., a conservative person supporting a liberal leader's policy. Now that trust among party identifiers opposite the president is nearly extinct, ideological sacrifice has largely dissolved, and government no longer functions properly (Hetherington and Rudolph 2015).

Using panel data from the American National Election Studies (ANES), Hetherington and Rudolph (2015) document the origins of polarized trust and show that it began in the early 2000s and stems from hyper-partisanship, including negative sentiment towards the out-party (a key ingredient of affective polarization) and biased perceptions and information processing. The bias is evident in perceiving political conditions in a way that advantage their own party and disadvantage the out-party (e.g., Democrats think the economy is strong when their party controls the presidency and Republicans think it is struggling) and weighting evaluative criteria differently to the benefit of their party and the detriment of the out-party. For instance, under a Democratic president, Democrats will pay more attention to favorable economic indicators such as low unemployment and Republicans will pay more attention to unfavorable economic news such as high inflation.

Democrats and Republicans, however, are not the same with respect to withholding trust from an out-party president. Hetherington and Rudolph (2015) find that trust in government is generally low no matter who is in office, but compared to Democrats, Republicans are more trusting of government when they are in power compared to Democrats when their party is in control. Morisi et al. (2019) suggest that the ideological asymmetry in political trust stems from the "pro-government" attitudes typically associated with the Democratic party and liberal values, providing intrinsic motivation to trust the out-party government even if that external motivation is lacking, reducing some of the effects of partisan bias and motivated reasoning (Morgeson et al. 2022).

2.5 Conclusion

As we conclude this chapter, the Biden administration is in its final days, winding down operations while Donald Trump's transition team is planning to take office. A great deal will change when the new president is sworn in since it means new people and different priorities in Washington. Although the lives of most Americans will not immediately change on January 20, 2025, their orientation towards government will shift dramatically. Republicans, who have been distrustful of government for the last four years, will feel a great deal more trust in government, hoping the new administration accomplishes great things. Democrats, on the other hand, will be much less trusting, hoping the new administration falls short in its efforts to alter the status quo. Put bluntly, nearly half the country will not trust government and thus will be unsupportive of the Trump administration's efforts to address the nation's problems. Sometimes those differences may be due to legitimate policy differences. Or, a partisan may often like a policy proposal on its face, but when they learn the opposing party's president is behind it, they are likely to oppose it (Nicholson 2012).

As partisans continue to see the three branches of government as an increasingly partisan vessel for political activism, cross-partisan trust in government will continue to plummet. All of this is made worse with affective polarization, where partisans seem very comfortable rejecting anything that the out-party does. As huge swaths of the public distrust government due to their partisan makeup, not only will American government continue to find it difficult to solve problems (Hetherington and Rudolph 2015), but this is likely to contribute to the erosion of democratic norms and democratic backsliding, the topic of Chapter 15 in this volume. Democratic norms are "the 'fundamental values' or 'rules of the game' considered essential for constitutional government" (McClosky 1964, 362). As democratic norms erode, the potential for democratic backsliding or complete democratic breakdown increases (Druckman 2024; Levitsky and Ziblatt 2018; Lieberman et al. 2019). There is evidence that partisans who are highly polarized are more likely to support investigations of corruption in the out-party (Westwood et al. 2019) and prefer in-party candidates regardless of whether they violate democratic norms like election integrity, checks and balances, or constitutional freedoms (Graham and Svolik 2020).

The motivation behind anti-democratic attitudes likely stems from perceived threats of the opposing party, as partisans believe the restriction of norms may be necessary as protection from the threats posed by the out-party.[3] Affective po-

---

3 Perceived threats by the out-party may stem from fear of policy-enactment or the perceived threat to racial status (Mutz 2018).

larization and increasingly partisan rhetoric shape the perceptions that the opposing party poses existential threats to the nation, leading to the breakdown of mutual trust among citizens (Lee 2022). These perceptions and behaviors create a self-reinforcing cycle of perceived fear, dislike, and distrust among partisans that further entrench anti-democratic attitudes, making social cohesion and the restoration of democratic principles increasingly difficult.

Discussion Questions

1 How does the concept of the "ideal citizen" differ from the current state of partisanship in the United States?
2 How do perceptions of a political party as an existential threat affect democratic norms and political behavior?
3 How does the decline of trust in government, especially among people whose party doesn't control Washington, affect the government's ability to solve problems?
4 How can the new administration address the issue of polarization and build trust among all Americans, regardless of partisanship?
5 What strategies could potentially be employed to reduce affective polarization and promote greater political trust and social cohesion in the United States?

References

Abramowitz, Alan I., and Steven Webster. 2016. "The Rise of Negative Partisanship and the Nationalization of U.S. Elections in the 21st Century." *Electoral Studies* 41 (March): 12–22.

Achen, Christopher H., and Larry M. Bartels. 2016. *Democracy for Realists: Why Elections Do Not Produce Responsive Government*. Princeton University Press.

Arceneaux, Kevin, and Rory Truex. 2023. "Donald Trump and the lie." *Perspectives on Politics* 21 (3): 863–79.

Bankert, Alexa. 2024. *When Politics Becomes Personal: The Effect of Partisan Identity on (Anti-) Democratic Behavior*. Cambridge University Press.

Bartels, Brandon L., and Christopher D Johnston. 2013. "On the Ideological Foundations of Supreme Court Legitimacy in the American Public." *American Journal of Political Science* 57 (1): 184–99.

Bartels, Larry M. 2002. "Beyond the Running Tally: Partisan Bias in Political Perceptions." *Political Behavior*.

Berelson, Bernard R., Paul F. Lazarsfeld, and William McPhee. 1954. *A Study of Opinion Formation on a Presidential Campaign*. University of Chicago Press.

Boddery, Scott S., and J. Jeff Yates. 2014. "Do Policy Messengers Matter? Majority Opinion Writers as Policy Cues in Public Agreement with Supreme Court Decisions." *Political Research Quarterly* 67 (4): 851–63.

Campbell, Angus, Philip E. Converse, Warren E. Miller, and Donald E. Stokes. 1960. *The American Voter*. University of Chicago Press.

Chanley, Virginia A., Thomas J. Rudolph, and Wendy M. Rahn. 2000. "The Origins and Consequences of Public Trust in Government: A Time Series Analysis." *Public Opinion Quarterly* 64 (3): 239–56.

Citrin, Jack. 1974. "Comment: The Political Relevance of Trust in Government." *American Political Science Review* 68 (3): 973–88.

Citrin, Jack, and Donald Philip Green. 1986. "Presidential Leadership and the Resurgence of Trust in Government." *British Journal of Political Science* 16 (4): 431–53.

Citrin, Jack, and Samantha Luks. 2001. "Political trust revisited: Déjà vu all over again?" In *What is it about government that Americans dislike?*, edited by John R. Hibbing and Elizabeth Theiss-Morse. Cambridge University Press.

Clark, Tom S. and Jonathan P. Kastellec. 2015. "Source Cues and Public Support for the Supreme Court." *American Politics Research* 43 (3): 504535.

Dahl, Robert A. 1992. "The Problem of Civic Competence." *Journal of Democracy* 3 (4): 45–59.

Donovan, Todd, and Shaun Bowler. 2004. *Reforming the Republic: Democratic Institutions for the New America*. Prentice Hall.

Donovan, Kathleen, Paul M. Kellstedt, Ellen M. Key, and Matthew J. Lebo. 2020. "Motivated Reasoning, Public Opinion, and Presidential Approval." *Political Behavior* 42 (4): 1201–21.

Druckman, Jamie N. 2024. "How to study democratic backsliding." *Advances in Political Psychology* 45 (Suppl. 1): 3–42.

Easton, David. 1975. "A Re-Assessment of the Concept of Political Support." *British Journal of Political Science* 5 (4): 435–57.

Evans, Geoffrey, and Robert Andersen. 2006. "The Political Conditioning of Economic Perceptions." *Journal of Politics* 68 (1): 194–207.

Feldman, Stanley. 1983. "The Measurement and Meaning of Trust in Government." *Political Methodology* 9 (3): 341–54.

Fiorina, Morris P. 1981. *Retrospective voting in American national elections*. Yale University.

Fiorina, Morris, Samuel J. Abrams, and Jeremy Pope. 2005. *Culture War? The Myth of a Polarized America*. Pearson-Longman.

Gershtenson, Joseph, Jeffrey Ladewig, and Dennis L. Plane. 2006. "Parties, Institutional Control, and Trust in Government." *Social Science Quarterly* 87: 882–902.

Gibson, James L. 2024. "Losing legitimacy: The challenges of the *Dobbs* ruling to conventional legitimacy theory." *American Journal of Political Science* 68: 1041–56.

Gibson, James L. 2007. "The Legitimacy of the US Supreme Court in a Polarized Polity." *Journal of Empirical Legal Studies* 4 (3): 507–38.

Gibson, James L., Milton Lodge, and Benjamin Woodson. 2014. "Losing, but Accepting: Legitimacy, Positivity Theory, and the Symbols of Judicial Authority." *Law & Society Review* 48 (4): 837–66.

Graham, Matthew H, and Milan W Svolik. 2020. "Democracy in America? Partisanship, Polarization, and the Robustness of Support for Democracy in the United States." *American Political Science Review* 114 (2): 392–409.

Green, Donald P., Bradley Palmquist, and Eric Schickler. 2002. *Partisan Hearts and Minds: Political Parties and the Social Identities of Voters*. Yale University Press.

Hansford, Thomas G., Chanita Intawan, and Stephen P. Nicholson. 2018. "Snap Judgment: Implicit Perceptions of a (Political) Court." *Political Behavior* 40: 127–47.

Heit, Evan, and Stephen P. Nicholson. 2010. "The Opposite of Republican: Polarization and Political Categorization." *Cognitive Science* 34: 1503–16.

Hetherington, Marc J. 1998. "The Political Relevance of Political Trust." *American Political Science Review* 92 (4): 791–808.

Hetherington, Marc J. 1999. "The Effect of Political Trust on the Presidential Vote, 1968–96." *The American Political Science Review* 93 (2): 311–26.

Hetherington, Marc J. 2001. "Resurgent mass partisanship: The role of elite polarization." *American political science review* 95 (3): 619–31.

Hetherington, Marc J. 2005. *Why Trust Matters: Declining Political Trust and the Demise of American Liberalism*. Princeton University Press.

Hetherington, Marc J., and Thomas J. Rudolph. 2015. *Why Washington Won't Work: Polarization, Political Trust, and the Governing Crisis*. University of Chicago Press.

Hibbing, John R., and Elizabeth A. Theiss-Morse. 2002. *Stealth Democracy: Americans' Beliefs about How Government Should Work*. Cambridge University Press.

Huber, Gregory A., and Neil Malhotra. 2017. "Political Homophily in Social Relationships: Evidence from Online Dating Behavior." *The Journal of Politics* 79 (1): 269–83.

Huddy, Leonie, Lilliana Mason, and Lene Aarøe. 2015. "Expressive Partisanship: Campaign Involvement, Political Emotion, and Partisan Identity." *American Political Science Review* 109 (1): 1–17.

Hui, Iris. 2013. "Who is your preferred neighbor? Partisan residential preferences and neighborhood satisfaction." *American Politics Research* 41 (6): 997–1021.

Intawan, Chanita, and Stephen P. Nicholson. 2018. "My Trust in Government Is Implicit: Automatic Trust in Government and System Support." *The Journal of Politics* 80 (2): 601–14.

Iyengar, Shanto, Gaurav Sood, and Yphtach Lelkes. 2012. "Affect, Not Ideology: A Social Identity Perspective on Polarization." *The Public Opinion Quarterly* 76: 405–31.

Iyengar, Shanto, and Sean J. Westwood. 2015. "Fear and Loathing across Party Lines: New Evidence on Group Polarization." *American Journal of Political Science* 59 (3): 690–707.

Iyengar, Shanto, and Masha Krupenkin. 2018. "Partisanship as Social Identity; Implications for the Study of Party Polarization." *The Forum* 16 (1): 23–45.

Keele, Luke. 2005. "The Authorities Really Do Matter: Party Control and Trust in Government." *The Journal of Politics* 67 (3): 873–86.

Key, V. O., Jr. 2013. *The Responsible Electorate: Rationality in Presidential Voting, 1936–1960*. Harvard University Press.

Lee, Amber Hye-Yon. 2022. "Social Trust in Polarized Times: How Perceptions of Political Polarization Affect Americans' Trust in Each Other." *Political Behavior* 44 (3): 1533–54.

Levendusky, Matthew. 2009. *The Partisan Sort: How Liberals Became Democrats and Conservatives Became Republicans*. University of Chicago Press.

Levitsky, Steven, and Daniel Ziblatt. 2018. "How Wobbly Is Our Democracy." *New York Times*. January 27, 2018. https://www.nytimes.com/2018/01/27/Opinion/Sunday/Democracy-Polarization.html.

Lieberman, Robert C., Suzanne Mettler, Thomas B. Pepinsky, Kenneth M. Roberts, and Richard Valelly. 2019. "The Trump Presidency and American Democracy: A Historical and Comparative Analysis." *Perspectives on Politics* 17 (2): 470–79.

Luskin, Robert C. 2002. "From Denial to Extenuation (and Finally Beyond): Political Sophistication and Citizen Performance." In *Thinking about Political Psychology*, edited by James H. Kuklinski, 281–305. Cambridge University Press.

MacKuen, Michael B., Robert S. Erikson, and James A. Stimson. 1992. "Peasants or Bankers? The American Electorate and the U.S. Economy." *American Political Science Review* 86 (3): 597–611.

Martherus, James L., Andres G. Martinez, Paul K. Piff, and Alexander G. Theodoridis. 2021. "Party Animals? Extreme Partisan Polarization and Dehumanization." *Political Behavior* 43: 517–40.

Mason, Lilliana. 2015. "'I Disrespectfully Agree': The Differential Effects of Partisan Sorting on Social and Issue Polarization." *American Journal of Political Science* 59 (1): 128–45.

Mason, Lilliana. 2018. "Ideologues without Issues: The Polarizing Consequences of Ideological Identities." *Public Opinion Quarterly* 82 (S1): 866–87.

McCarty, Nolan M., Keith T. Poole, Howard G. Rosenthal, and Howard Rosenthal. 2008. *Polarized America: The Dance of Ideology and Unequal Riches*. MIT Press.

McClosky, Herbert. 1964. "Consensus and Ideology in American Politics." *American Political Science Review* 58 (2): 361–82.

Miller, Arthur H. 1974. "Political Issues and Trust in Government: 1964–1970." *American Political Science Review* 68 (3): 951–72.

Miller, Arthur H., and Stephen A Borrelli. 1991. "Confidence in Government during the 1980s." *American Politics Quarterly* 19 (2): 147–73.

Morgeson III, Forrest V., Pratyush Nidhi Sharma, Udit Sharma, and G. Tomas M. Hult. 2022. "Partisan Bias and Citizen Satisfaction, Confidence, and Trust in the U.S. Federal Government." *Public Management Review* 24 (12): 1933–56.

Morisi, Davide, John T. Jost, and Vishal Singh. 2019. "An Asymmetrical 'President-in-Power' Effect." *American Political Science Review* 113 (2): 614–20.

Mutz, Diana C. 2018. "Status Threat, Not Economic Hardship, Explains the 2016 Presidential Vote." *Proceedings of the National Academy of Sciences* 115 (19). Proceedings of the National Academy of Sciences: E4330–39.

Nadeau, Richard, and Michael S. Lewis-Beck. 2001. "National Economic Voting in U.S. Presidential Elections." *The Journal of Politics* 63 (1): 159–81.

Nicholson, Stephen P. 2012. "Polarizing Cues." *American Journal of Political Science* 56: 52–66.

Nicholson, Stephen P., and Robert M. Howard. 2003. "Framing Support for the Supreme Court in the Aftermath of Bush v. Gore." *The Journal of Politics* 65 (3): 676–95.

Nicholson, Stephen P., and Thomas G. Hansford. 2014. "Partisans in Robes: Party Cues and Public Acceptance of Supreme Court Decisions." *American Journal of Political Science* 58 (3): 620–36.

Nicholson, Stephen P., Chelsea M. Coe, Jason Emory, and Ann V. Song. 2016. "The Politics of Beauty: The Effects of Partisan Bias on Physical Attractiveness." *Political Behavior* 38: 883–98.

Orren, Gary. 1997. "Fall from Grace: The Public's Loss of Faith in Government." In *Why People Don't Trust Government*, 77–107.

Sears, David O., and Carolyn L. Funk. 1999. "Evidence of the Long-Term Persistence of Adults' Political Predispositions." *The Journal of Politics* 61 (1): 1–28.

Shafranek, Richard M. 2021. "Political Considerations in Nonpolitical Decisions: A Conjoint Analysis of Roommate Choice." *Political Behavior* 43: 271–300.

Tajfel, Henri. 1978. *Differentiation between Social Groups: Studies in the Social Psychology of Intergroup Relations*. Academic Press.

Tajfel, Henri, and John C. Turner. 1986. "The Social Identity Theory of Intergroup Behavior." In *Psychology of Intergroup Relation*, edited by S Worchel and W.G. Austin, 7–24. Nelson Hall.

Westwood, Sean J., Erik Peterson, and Yphtach Lelkes. 2019. "Are There Still Limits on Partisan Prejudice?" *Public Opinion Quarterly* 83 (3): 584–97.

Williams, John T. 1985. "Systemic Influences on Political Trust: The Importance of Perceived Institutional Performance." *Political Methodology* 11 (1/2): 125–42.

Zhong, Chen-Bo, Katherine W. Phillips, Geoffrey J. Leonardelli, and Adam D. Galinsky. 2008. "Negational Categorization and Intergroup Behavior." *Personality and Social Psychology Bulletin* 34 (6): 793–806.

Stephanie Davis and Charles J. Finocchiaro

3 Compromise and Consequence: The Impact of Institutions on American Representation

"It's hard to exaggerate just how much damage Senate malapportionment has done to American democracy," wrote Ian Millhiser (2021), a senior political correspondent for *Vox*. He was covering the Build Back Better Act (BBBA), the most ambitious of three major bills driving President Biden's policy agenda. The $3.75 trillion measure included funding for electric vehicle (EV) incentives and other clean energy programs, grants for rural broadband access, initial funding for states to develop universal childcare programs for pre-K, and much more. After sailing through the House of Representatives, the bill stalled in the Senate because of a single senator—Democrat Joe Manchin, who represented West Virginia, a state that accounts for just 0.5 percent of the U.S. population. Millhiser's article expressed the same frustration of many Americans—that the BBBA is just the "latest victim of America's anti-democratic Senate." Once again, the Senate's structure of equal state representation appeared poised to allow small states to block a national policy priority favored by the nation's majority (Newport 2021).

To be fair, it certainly seemed like the Senate's small-state bias was to blame for the BBBA stalemate. Many Americans also appeared to support the Democrat's policy initiatives. In the 2020 election, President Joe Biden won the popular vote by a sizeable margin, while Democrats gained control of the Senate and maintained control in the House. Biden's policy proposals came during a time of unified government. Though House Democrats could easily pass the BBBA, they introduced it as a budget reconciliation bill to help clear Senate obstacles. Typically, the Senate's unlimited debate rule would require at least sixty senators (a supermajority in the 100-member body) to pass a bill, but a budget reconciliation bill needs only a simple majority (fifty-one votes) to pass in the Senate. When the BBBA moved to the Democrat-controlled Senate, most members expected it to zip through—straight to the president's desk for his signature.

Yet much to the Democratic Party's chagrin, Sen. Manchin announced he would vote against it, citing concerns about the bill's long-term fiscal impact and its effect on his West Virginia constituents. In a press release to his constituency, he stated, "If I can't go back home and explain it, I can't vote for it" (2021). Manchin's opposition meant that Senate Democrats fell one vote short of passing the BBBA. While portions of Biden's agenda were eventually enacted, including a scaled-down version of the original bill in the form of the Inflation Reduction Act

https://doi.org/10.1515/9783111591902-003

of 2022, Manchin's role and critical vote doomed the program as initially envisioned.

The situation surrounding the Build Back Better Act illustrates the core idea of this chapter: how compromises made at the Constitutional Convention more than two centuries ago continue to shape our political system. The Senate, a product of the Great Compromise, is a prime example. The compromise established a bicameral Congress: a House of Representatives, where power is determined by population, and a Senate, where all states, regardless of size, have equal representation. The Senate's structure ensures smaller states have a say in national policy-making to help balance power between large and small states, but it also grants outsized power to senators representing only a fraction of the population. The twenty-five smallest states have nearly 55 million residents, while the twenty-five largest states have more than 284 million (U.S. Census Bureau 2024). Put another way, half of the members of the Senate together represent just 16 percent of Americans. In the case of the BBBA, the Senate's equal representation empowered a single senator from a small state—representing just 0.5 percent of Americans—to block legislation backed by a majority of voters and lawmakers. Over time, the two bodies have evolved differently, in part because the Constitution gives each the power to determine their own rules of operation. While the House generally operates as a majority-rule body (no matter how narrow the majority), the Senate gives individual members much more sway.

Every institution outlined in the U.S. Constitution reflects trade-offs made at the Constitutional Convention. The fifty-five delegates who attended may have had similar ideas about democratic governance, but they were representing over 1 million citizens with a diverse set of preferences about how to achieve democratic governance. The blending of unique perspectives helps explain the creation of key constitutional features like the Electoral College, a fragmented legislature, a single executive with limited enumerated authority, an arduous process for amending the Constitution, and more. The Senate's structure of equal representation makes it a strong contender for the most contentious of the institutions. To demonstrate the lingering effects of compromise during the Constitutional Convention, in this chapter we will explore in more detail how the Senate's design, born of historical compromise, continues to shape and sometimes frustrate modern governance.

3.1 A Note on Institutions

Equal apportionment in the Senate is just one of many contentious features of American political institutions. Others, like the Electoral College, lifetime judicial appointments, and federalism, also face intense public scrutiny—at times even producing decisions that leave large portions of the public dissatisfied.[1] Modern examples include presidential election outcomes—such as in 2000 and 2016—that result in a victor who received fewer popular votes than his opponent. Lifetime judicial appointments allow justices to issue rulings that defy public sentiment, such as *Texas v. Johnson* (1989), which struck down flag-burning bans despite 60 percent opposition. Congress attempted to override it with a constitutional amendment, but despite 70 percent of the public supporting the amendment, it failed in the House by thirty-four votes (Roper Center for Public Opinion Research 1990). These structures were designed to balance competing interests, but they frequently raise questions about fairness and representation in modern governance. Because of institutional complexities like these, policymaking in any democracy is not straightforward. The results are a conglomeration of individual preferences culminating in one decision. Some policies enjoy broad public support but fail to become law, while others succeed despite significant opposition. A policy's success or failure is always impacted by the institutions involved, which can lead people to question whether the system is functioning as intended or requires reform.

To understand policy outcomes, we must first understand the institutional structures that govern them. A political institution is a set of pre-determined rules, norms, and procedures, often situated in an organization, that provides the framework for how we are governed. Agreeing on the rules ahead of time can create a predictable (if not always level) playing field for those involved. This idea of pre-determined rules is so intuitive to human beings that we do this all the time without thinking. James Harrington, a seventeenth-century English political theorist, famously illustrated the concept of institutions with a hypothetical example. In his scenario, two girls are given a cake to share, but neither trusts the other to make a fair cut without leaving the larger portion for herself. Harrington suggested that the girls, driven by their desire for fairness, will settle on a solution where one girl cuts the cake and the second girl will select first among the pieces (Harrington 1771).

---

1 For a recent example involving the judiciary, see https://www.pewresearch.org/politics/2022/07/06/majority-of-public-disapproves-of-supreme-courts-decision-to-overturn-roe-v-wade/

The fifty-five delegates at the Constitutional Convention in Philadelphia bargained in a similar way about the pre-determined rules and structures that would become the U.S. Constitution. They were faced with the task of creating an institution that would mediate and solve collective action problems so that governing officials could effectively go about the business of governing. Despite the delegates' unified support of democratic principles and desire for good policy output, coming to an agreement about how best to accomplish these goals while incorporating the varied policy preferences required tremendous compromise. In deciding on these governing institutions, the delegates essentially were trying to facilitate one big group project involving millions of people, all with different preferences, with the end goal of finding consensus on policy choices.

3.2 The Great Compromise

The U.S. Constitution established institutions designed to balance and include competing interests, with the legislative branch as the focus of this effort. The Virginia delegation proposed a two-chamber legislature with representation based on state population. Smaller, less populated, states feared the many senators of larger states would dominate the legislature, so the New Jersey delegates proposed an alternative: equal representation for each state, regardless of population. Neither plan was fully democratic in nature. The Virginia Plan marginalized small states, while the New Jersey Plan diminished the influence of large states. The deadlock was broken by the suggestion of a bicameral legislature that blended the two plans, with representation by population in the House and equal representation by state in the Senate, allowing the Convention to move forward.

Most delegates agreed that this arrangement had significant advantages. The U.S. Senate would serve as "an additional impediment . . . against improper acts of legislation" (Madison, *Federalist* 62) and help prevent the tyranny of the majority over the minority (*Federalist* 58). The delegates not only anticipated that small states would block legislation originating in the House, but they considered it to be a desirable check against hasty legislation from the majority. Madison wrote ". . . as the faculty and excess of law-making seem to be the diseases to which our governments are most liable . . . this part of the Constitution may be more convenient in practice than it appears . . ." (*Federalist* 62). The criticism that a small minority might use Senate apportionment to thwart the will of the nation's majority citizens is well-founded because that is what the founders intended. The Senate's malapportionment was intentional. Congress's design has downstream consequences for institutions like the Electoral College, as well, since the number of electors granted to each state is equal to the number of House members plus two (corresponding to the two senators).

3.3 Unequal Representation

There have always been more small (less populated) states than large states. During the First Congress, ten of the thirteen states contained less than 238,000 people, while the three largest states (Virginia, Massachusetts, and Pennsylvania) contained at least 360,000. In 1788, Delaware's population was a mere 37,000 compared to Virginia's 420,000. As the nation and its population grew, the number of less populated (small) states, like Montana, continued to outnumber the more populated (large) states, like New York. This imbalance frustrates citizens in large states, but Senate critics argue that there is more at stake with equal representation in the Senate than losing policy battles. They argue that equal apportionment in the Senate is not consistent with democratic principles. How can the U.S. political system embody democracy when votes are unequal? Democratic theorist Robert Dahl (1989) writes, "in a democratic vision, opportunities to exercise the power of the state . . . are, or at any rate ought to be, distributed equally among citizens" (325).

Many contend democratic representation should translate to "one-person, one-vote," and until the Senate meets this requirement, America does not meet the ideal democratic standard.[2] The comments below, appearing in *The Washington Post* and *The New York Times*, regard the Senate as an institutional antithesis to the "one-person, one vote" principle:

> There are 100 senators . . . This means that 51 senators – senators from 26 states – can block any law. The population of the smallest 26 states totals less than 57 million individuals . . . in a country with more than 325 million people. This means that the votes of those 57 million people would be more powerful than the votes of all the rest (Reiman 2016).

> This was always a betrayal of one-person-one-vote equality, in that a voter in rural Wyoming has more than three times the power of a voter in New Jersey, the country's most densely populated state (Johnson 2016).

---

2 The principle of "one person, one vote" is the idea that each person's vote should be weighted equally. Prior to a series of Supreme Court decisions in the mid-twentieth century, most state legislative districts and seats in the U.S. House of Representatives were unequally apportioned.

Those who advocate for proportional representation in the Senate often point to the "one-person, one-vote" principle espoused by the U.S. Supreme Court during the reapportionment revolution in the 1960s, when the Court undertook the task of overturning more than a century of redistricting practices that resulted in at times drastically unequal populations across state legislative and U.S. House districts. The majority opinions of *Baker v. Carr* (1962), *Wesberry v. Sanders* (1964), and *Reynolds v. Sims* (1964) assert the democratic necessity of *approximately* equal representation. Justice Black wrote the following in *Wesberry*'s majority opinion: "The conception of political equality from the Declaration of Independence, to Lincoln's Gettysburg Address, to the Fifteenth, Seventeenth, and Nineteenth Amendments can mean only one thing – one person, one vote."[3]

In 2014, California's state population was 38.8 million compared to Wyoming's population of 584,153. That makes it possible for senators who represent a small minority of U.S. citizens to alter or block legislation from the House, which, by its nature, requires the votes of representatives comprising a majority of U.S. citizens in order to pass legislation. While the Senate has always been structured this way, the disparity has increased over time. Prior to 1900, senators representing about 30 percent of the population could form a majority in the Senate. Since 1900, that number has dropped below 20 percent, meaning an even *smaller* portion of the population can now control Senate decisions (Lee and Oppenheimer 1999, 10–11). This trend could have major implications for democracy and governance, which is why political scientists continue to study its effects. In 2024, Archer et al. proposed a modified Connecticut Compromise to address the growing disparity by amending the Constitution to add 100 additional seats in the Senate. While each state would retain a minimum of two seats, the added seats would be apportioned by population, thereby remedying some of the imbalance between large and small states.

3.4 Malapportionment Definition

We use the term malapportionment to refer to "the discrepancy between the shares of legislative seats and the shares of population held by geographical units" (Samuels and Snyder 2001, 652). In the case of the U.S. Senate, the share of seats is equal (two seats per state, or 2 percent of the total 100 seats) across the geographical units (states which vary widely in population). Lee and Oppenheimer (1997, 1999) developed a measure of a state's "degree of malapportion-

---

3 *Wesberry v. Sanders*, 376 U.S. 1 (1964).

ment" to reflect how much a state is overrepresented or underrepresented in the Senate. The mathematical formula for the degree of malapportionment in each state (referenced using the subscript $_i$) is:

$$degree\ of\ malapportionment_i = \frac{population\ of\ state_i}{(national\ population/50)}.$$

Understanding the formula is easier when you see an example. Let's take Wyoming, which has a very low malapportionment score of 0.09 (severely overrepresented). We calculate that by taking the state population of 584,057 in 2023 and then dividing it by the ratio of one fiftieth of the national population, or 334,914,895 divided by 50. Table 1 shows that both Wyoming and Vermont have relatively similar degrees of malapportionment, although that is no guarantee that the states are similar politically. Vermont is a progressive (or liberal) state in the northeast, typically voting for Democrats for president, while Wyoming is quite conservative and Republican. At the other end of the spectrum are very large states that are highly malapportioned (severely underrepresented), such as Texas and California—the former more conservative and the latter more liberal. Yet they both suffer a significant degree of underrepresentation in the Senate. Each comprises about 10 percent of the national population, although that combined 20 percent of the nation has just a 4 percent share of voting power in the Senate.

Still, many perceive the small state bias in the Senate translates to a conservative bias. Johnson and Miller (2023) conducted a simulation to estimate how a more proportional Senate might have affected the outcome on ninety-four key votes between 1961 and 2019. Using a hypothetical apportionment scheme (one that still slightly favored small states—as the constitutional delegates intended), they found that a more proportional Senate would have resulted in more liberal outcomes—at least on the more salient votes. If small states remain predominantly red and larger states remain blue, then the Senate may continue to produce more conservative policies on some key votes. The BBBA example is worth returning to here, with West Virginia's Joe Manchin representing a state benefitting from malapportionment. Indeed, West Virginia is twelfth on the list in Table 3.1. It is also important to note that these differences in influence arising from Senate representation extend to the Electoral College as well.

These differences might, at first glance, seem to have much to do with geography. If you pay attention to presidential elections, you are probably familiar with the maps that show which party wins each state's electoral college votes (nearly all of which are awarded to the statewide winner, with nothing for second place). The maps are drawn at the state level, although geography does not correspond with population. Several of the more malapportioned states, particularly in the

Table 3.1: Degree of malapportionment among U.S. States in 2023.

State	Population	% of National Population	Population Density	Malapportionment Score
Wyoming	584,057	0.17	6	0.09
Vermont	647,464	0.19	70	0.10
Alaska	733,406	0.22	1	0.11
North Dakota	783,926	0.23	11	0.12
South Dakota	919,318	0.27	12	0.14
Delaware	1,031,890	0.31	529	0.15
Rhode Island	1,095,962	0.33	1,055	0.16
Montana	1,132,812	0.34	8	0.17
Hawaii	1,435,138	0.43	223	0.21
Maine	1,395,722	0.42	45	0.21
New Hampshire	1,402,054	0.42	157	0.21
West Virginia	1,770,071	0.53	73	0.26
Idaho	1,964,726	0.59	24	0.29
Nebraska	1,978,379	0.59	26	0.30
New Mexico	2,114,371	0.63	17	0.32
Kansas	2,940,546	0.88	36	0.44
Mississippi	2,939,690	0.88	62	0.44
Arkansas	3,067,732	0.92	59	0.46
Iowa	3,207,004	0.96	57	0.48
Nevada	3,194,176	0.95	29	0.48
Utah	3,417,734	1.02	42	0.51
Connecticut	3,617,176	1.08	749	0.54
Oklahoma	4,053,824	1.21	59	0.61
Oregon	4,233,358	1.26	44	0.63
Kentucky	4,526,154	1.35	114	0.68
Louisiana	4,573,749	1.37	105	0.68
Alabama	5,108,468	1.53	101	0.76
South Carolina	5,373,555	1.60	179	0.80
Minnesota	5,737,915	1.71	72	0.86
Colorado	5,877,610	1.75	57	0.88
Wisconsin	5,910,955	1.76	109	0.88
Maryland	6,180,253	1.85	634	0.92
Missouri	6,196,156	1.85	90	0.93
Indiana	6,862,199	2.05	191	1.02
Massachusetts	7,001,399	2.09	894	1.05
Tennessee	7,126,489	2.13	173	1.06
Arizona	7,431,344	2.22	66	1.11
Washington	7,812,880	2.33	118	1.17
Virginia	8,715,698	2.60	221	1.30
New Jersey	9,290,841	2.77	1,259	1.39
Michigan	10,037,261	3.00	177	1.50
North Carolina	10,835,491	3.24	223	1.62

Table 3.1 (continued)

State	Population	% of National Population	Population Density	Malapportionment Score
Georgia	11,029,227	3.29	192	1.65
Ohio	11,785,935	3.52	288	1.76
Illinois	12,549,689	3.75	225	1.87
Pennsylvania	12,961,683	3.87	289	1.94
New York	19,571,216	5.84	414	2.92
Florida	22,610,726	6.75	423	3.38
Texas	30,503,301	9.11	117	4.55
California	38,965,193	11.63	250	5.82

Note: State population data sourced from the U.S. Census Bureau. Population density (per square mile), percentage of the national population, and malapportionment scores are calculated using census data. Source: U.S. Census Bureau, "State Population Totals and Components of Change: 2020–2023," Vintage 2023, https://www.census.gov/data/tables/time-series/demo/popest/2020s-state-total.html, accessed on November 1, 2024.

American West, are fairly large in geographic terms but small in population (e.g., Wyoming, the Dakotas, Alaska, and Montana). And while these states are conservative, in the northeast and mid-Atlantic there are states small in land size (like Vermont, Delaware, and Rhode Island) that have similar populations but higher population density. This has led some political geographers and other observers to argue that population-adjusted maps like those in Figure 3.1 are a better way to represent how the country votes in presidential elections (Newman 2016). Recent presidential elections are quite similar in terms of state-level voting, with just a handful of swing states determining the outcome, but they look much more balanced between the parties in these figures—and better reflect the near 50/50 division of the country—when population is accounted for more accurately. These maps draw states in relation to their population rather than their geographic size.

3.5 Examining the Consequences of Malapportionment in the Senate

While the Framers had several principled, as well as pragmatic, reasons for apportioning seats in the Senate equally among the states, we want to highlight three important implications of this feature of the Constitution's design: variation in voter influence and representation, legislative and policy outcomes, and the preservation of state interests.

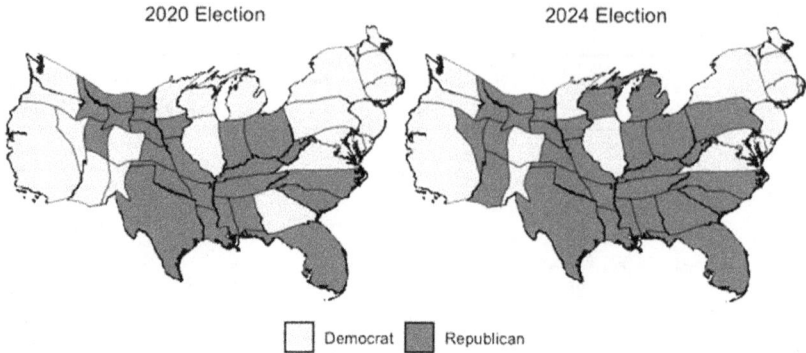

Figure 3.1: Cartographic representations of population-adjusted presidential vote.
Source: Data from https://www.fec.gov/introduction-campaign-finance/election-results-and-voting-in formation/

First, the simple fact that each state has two senators means that the representational experience of ordinary voters, and the constituents who are represented by them, varies widely across the country. At one extreme, a person living in Wyoming is one among nearly 600,000 people. Put another way, the ratio of senators to individuals is 300,000 to one. In contrast, there are about 39 million Californians, a ratio of 19.5 million to one. For the mathematically-inclined, that is a difference of two orders of magnitude. As the political scientists Frances Lee and Bruce Oppenheimer describe in their book *The Senate: The Unequal Consequences of Equal Representation*, those living in small states report both higher quality and higher quantity contact with their senators than their large-state counterparts.

When it comes to policymaking, there are also important differences that seem to result from the disparity between population and representation. Small states are "cheaper" partners for those seeking to build a legislative coalition, in that the distribution of federal funds can go farther among a number of small states who receive a disproportionate advantage—and this is precisely what you observe on some issues such as transportation funding (Lee 2000), which tend to favor small states (think about that as you travel federal highways on your next road trip). On a similar note, Lee and Oppenheimer (1999) argue that the policy focus of senators in large states tends to be different, as they concentrate more on salient national issues while small-state senators tend to prioritize parochial, local issues.

All of this, in turn, means that small states are especially guarded when it comes to preserving their own interests in the Senate. Since early in the history of the American republic, efforts to change the balance of power between large and small states has consistently been met with strong opposition from the comparatively large coalition of small states. This also makes the process of amending the Constitution particularly sensitive to small-state interests as all successful amendments to date have taken the path that requires a super-majority of two-thirds in *both* houses of Congress, followed by the approval of three-fourths of the states.

3.5.1 Case Study of Legislative Effectiveness

To further understand the policymaking consequences of Senate malapportionment, we examine how effectiveness in the legislative process tracks with state size. One might assume, based on prior work, that if small-state senators have an outsized influence due to the appeal of building coalitions made up of colleagues from the relatively more numerous smaller states that these legislators usually would be advantaged. An additional point in their favor is the fact that small-state senators often face less electoral competition, on average, since the politics of many of these states are quite homogeneous. This allows senators to establish the tenure in office and seniority on committees that it takes to wield added influence over legislation. For these reasons, we might expect small state senators to be outsized players on the legislative stage.

One way to assess effectiveness is with the use of "scores" developed by Volden and Wiseman (2014), which are based on the number of bills legislators write and how those bills fare in the legislative process—whether they receive further action of various sorts (e.g., in committee) and eventually become law. These legislative effectiveness scores (LES) are also calibrated to account for the significance of the bills, since some involve major changes to salient policy issues while other have significantly less reach, like commemorating a minor holiday. This allows Volden and Wiseman to capture what they define as effectiveness: "the proven ability to advance a member's agenda items through the legislative process and into law" (18).

While much of the early research on effectiveness focused on the House, Volden and Wiseman (2018) later conducted an analysis of the Senate in which they found factors that matter in the House—like being a member of the majority party or a committee or subcommittee chair—also matter in the Senate, although it is less hierarchical than the House, thus reflecting the common view of the upper chamber as a legislative body composed of "equals."

One thing that their analysis did not consider is state size. As such, we added a measure of malapportionment to determine whether some of the small-state advantages we described in the previous section translate into LES. We were sur-

prised to find that, at first glance, the effect was the opposite of what we anticipated, even when accounting for a range of other influences. While we do not
report the statistical results here, we uncovered a small but positive effect for
malapportionment, meaning that senators from those states systematically *disadvantaged* in Senate representation seemed to do *better* than their colleagues
when it came to legislative effectiveness. This pattern is reflected in Figure 3.2,
which smooths the relationship in the data between the level of LES on the (vertical) y-axis and the degree of malapportionment on the (horizontal) x-axis and
shows the highest levels of malapportionment are associated with higher legislative effectiveness.

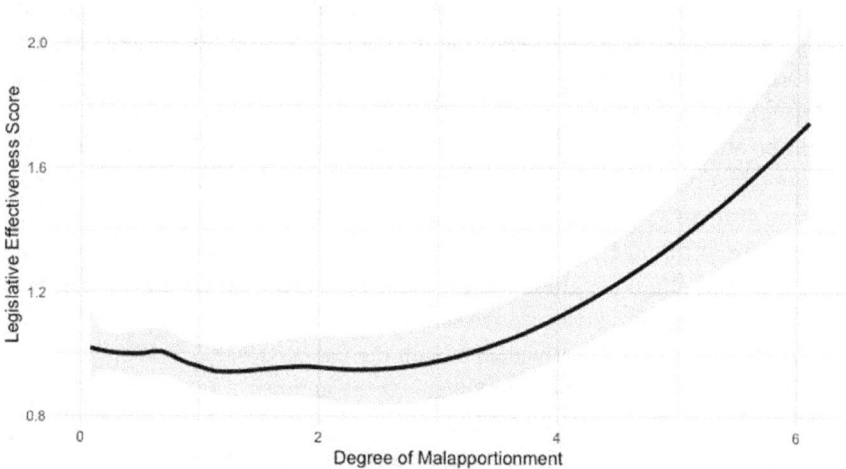

Figure 3.2: Smoothed trend of legislative effectiveness by malapportionment.

However, delving a bit deeper into the data, we found that this result was driven
by a handful of very influential cases, mostly from California. To demonstrate
this, Figure 3.3 zooms out and presents the actual distribution of effectiveness
scores on the (vertical) y-axis plotted against the degree of malapportionment on
the (horizontal) x-axis, with each dot representing a single senator. Consistent
with Table 3.1, there are many more small states with low malapportionment
scores compared to large states with high scores. That helps to explain the sizeable cluster of senators near the bottom left of the figure. Yet you can also see the
small number of highly effective senators from the most malapportioned end of
the scale on the right.

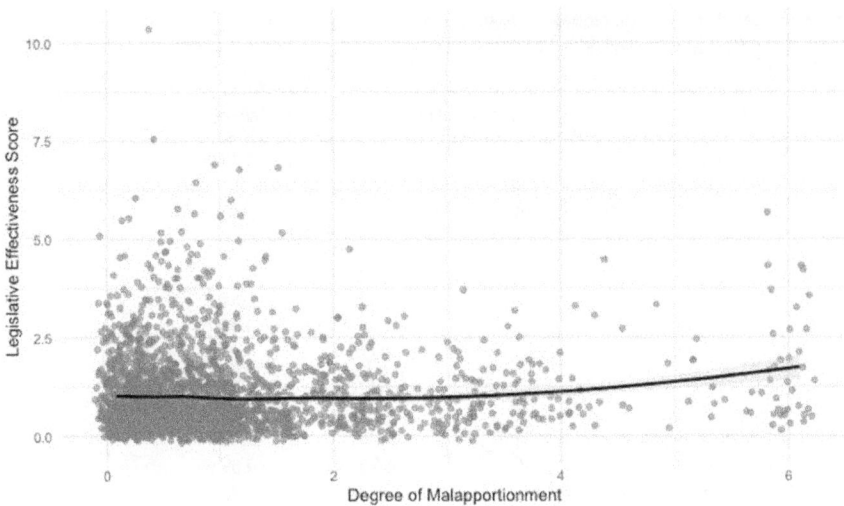

Figure 3.3: Scatterplot of legislative effectiveness by malapportionment.

In Table 3.2, we list the senators who had a score above 4.0 at least once in the period from 1973 to 2023 (the 93rd to 117th Congresses).[4] The list is arranged in ascending order by degree of malapportionment, with small states that are overrepresented appearing first and large states that are disadvantaged by malapportionment appearing last. In short, these are the most effective among the highly effective legislators, the cream of the legislative crop from that fifty-year period. Notably, of the approximately two dozen names on the list, just a handful come from the largest states—in recent years, Senators John Cornyn of Texas and Diane Feinstein of California are the most prominent among them. Less well known is Senator Gary Peters of Michigan, who nonetheless put one of the highest LES scores on the board for his home state of Michigan. In contrast, many more small states populate this list, with Vermont's Patrick Leahy, Orrin Hatch of Utah, and Chuck Grassley of Iowa among the more familiar recent names.

Of course, there are many more small-state senators compared to their large-state counterparts, as reflected in the large cluster in the bottom left of Figure 3.3 above. How should we make sense of this pattern? While the deck is stacked in favor of the small states institutionally, as Volden and Wiseman describe in their book, there are habits effective legislators tend to exhibit that go beyond gaining the seniority required for effectiveness or wielding a committee gavel that carries

---

4 A number of senators achieved this feat more than once. For those individuals, we list only the most recent congress in which they received that score.

Table 3.2: Senators with the highest legislative effectiveness scores by degree of malapportionment.

Cong.	Senator	State	LES Score	Mal. Score
112	Patrick Leahy	VT	5.60	0.10
104	Ted Stevens	AK	4.60	0.11
96	Howard Cannon	NV	10.19	0.18
96	Frank Church	ID	4.44	0.21
97	James McClure	ID	4.26	0.21
103	John Rockefeller	WV	5.13	0.35
108	Orrin Hatch	UT	4.44	0.41
104	Robert Dole	KS	4.87	0.49
109	Chuck Grassley	IA	4.45	0.50
98	Bob Packwood	OR	4.54	0.57
112	Joseph Lieberman	CT	4.06	0.57
98	Strom Thurmond	SC	4.78	0.69
102	Dennis DeConcini	AZ	4.33	0.77
108	Ben Campbell	CO	4.12	0.78
93	John Sparkman	AL	4.03	0.85
95	Warren Magnuson	WA	4.65	0.87
95	Henry Jackson	WA	5.69	0.87
107	Paul Sarbanes	MD	4.08	0.95
108	John McCain	AZ	4.21	0.97
110	Edward Kennedy	MA	5.97	1.06
111	John Kerry	MA	4.03	1.06
113	Robert Menendez	NJ	4.52	1.39
117	Gary Peters	MI	6.73	1.51
100	Howard Metzenbaum	OH	4.84	2.21
117	John Cornyn	TX	4.49	4.51
112	Dianne Feinstein	CA	4.42	6.05
102	Alan Cranston	CA	4.48	6.07

the influence to set the agenda in one's favor. While those tools are of great importance, Volden and Wiseman (2014) argue "that lawmakers can lead from anywhere. And their early successes pave the way to becoming great lawmaking leaders later in their careers" (161). The strategies that lead to greater effectiveness are developing a policy agenda that plays to a legislator's own strengths and is rooted in their state's unique needs, an entrepreneurial approach to the use of power, openness to compromise, and cultivation of allies within and beyond the chamber (193). As such, there is hope for even the most institutionally-relegated legislator. A look at the most and least successful legislators listed in Table 3.3 suggests that there are indeed some potential paths to solutions for the problems that ail the Senate, some of which are tied to the broader systemic problems noted in the introductory chapter.

Table 3.3: The most and least effective senator in each congress, 1973–2023.

Cong.	Most Effective Senator	LES Score	Mal. Score	Least Effective Senator	LES Score	Mal. Score
93	H. Jackson (WA, D)	7.05	0.83	W. Huddleston (KY, D)	0.01	0.80
94	H. Jackson (WA, D)	5.10	0.85	J. Culver (IA, D)	0.03	0.67
95	H. Jackson (WA, D)	5.69	0.87	H. Byrd (VA, R)	0.02	1.18
96	H. Cannon (NV, D)	10.20	0.18	G. Mitchell (ME, D)	0.01	0.25
97	S. Thurmond (SC, R)	5.72	0.69	P. Sarbanes (MD, D)	0.06	0.92
98	O. Hatch (UT, R)	6.16	0.34	D. Evans (WA, R)	0.01	0.92
99	O. Hatch (UT, R)	4.46	0.35	J. Stennis (MS, D)	0.01	0.54
100	A. Cranston (CA, D)	5.69	5.82	C. Bond (MO, R)	0.03	1.04
101	E. Kennedy (MA, D)	6.70	1.21	J. Kerrey (NE, D)	0.04	0.32
102	E. Kennedy (MA, D)	5.60	1.18	J. Kerrey (NE, D)	0.03	0.32
103	J. Rockefeller (WV, D)	5.13	0.35	H. Mathews (TN, D)	0.00	1.00
104	O. Hatch (UT, R)	7.73	0.39	C. Dodd (CT, D)	0.05	0.63
105	O. Hatch (UT, R)	4.51	0.40	J. Sessions (AL, R)	0.01	0.81
106	B. Campbell (CO, R)	4.73	0.76	Z. Miller (GA, D)	0.01	1.45
107	B. Campbell (CO, R)	4.65	0.78	B. Nelson (NE, D)	0.01	0.30
108	C. Grassley (IA, R)	5.16	0.50	T. Carper (DE, D)	0.03	0.14
109	C. Grassley (IA, R)	4.45	0.50	B. Mikulski (MD, D)	0.08	0.94
110	E. Kennedy (MA, D)	5.97	1.06	R. Shelby (AL, R)	0.01	0.78
111	P. Leahy (VT, D)	5.61	0.10	C. Goodwin (WV, D)	0.01	0.30
112	P. Leahy (VT, D)	5.60	0.10	R. Shelby (AL, R)	0.03	0.77
113	R. Menendez (NJ, D)	4.52	1.39	J. Sessions (AL, R)	0.00	0.76
114	O. Hatch (UT, R)	3.39	0.47	J. Sessions (AL, R)	0.06	0.75
115	C. Grassley (IA, R)	3.60	0.48	J. Kyl (AZ, R)	0.02	1.10
116	G. Peters (MI, D)	5.02	1.52	R. Shelby (AL, R)	0.10	0.76
117	G. Peters (MI, D)	6.73	1.51	C. Hyde-Smith (MS, R)	0.02	0.44

In short, while small states are advantaged, there is room for large states to "win" and make a difference in effective lawmaking. It may require more time and effort on the part of their senators (e.g., building up seniority, accruing positions of committee and party leadership, etc.), but it can happen. And, of course, a good deal of legislating occurs behind the scenes in ways that these metrics do not pick up. For example, a senator's name may not be attached as the sponsor of a bill, but they may have been able to insert a provision in the bill that allows them to provide meaningful representation for their home state.

3.6 Debates on Reform and Proposals for Change

Do people see Senate malapportionment as a problem? Certainly a common objection voiced about American politics is that Congress is often gridlocked, and that getting much of anything done requires compromise. The Senate's small-state advantage locks in a disproportionate voice for those who live in less populous states, meaning that policy outcomes are likely biased in their favor. As we noted at the outset, the smallest twenty-five states (together comprising 50 percent of the Senate) make up just 16 percent of the population. In that sense, less than one-fifth of the American public constitutes a majority of the upper house of Congress. Even if one were to add the wrinkle of the filibuster—the right of individual senators to extended debate (or "talking a bill to death"), which can only be prevented when sixty senators agree to invoke cloture and cut off debate—the smallest thirty states making up just over 25 percent of the nation's population could still cobble together a winning coalition. Put another way, a supermajority of 60 percent of the Senate can be built on a coalition excluding 75 percent of the U.S. population.

A range of proposals have been identified to address the malapportionment of the Senate. The simplest, but least likely, is to alter the Constitutional structure in order to put in place a different representational scheme. But this is extraordinarily unlikely since it would not be enough to simply amend the Constitution, since the Framers singled out the provision calling for equal representation in the Senate as non-amendable. Moreover, for the same structural reasons that small states oppose other reforms like altering the Electoral College, anything that might diminish their influence is likely a non-starter. A good deal of that hesitancy is partisan. The small-state coalition is more Republican today than it has been historically—at various times in American history, the Senate has benefitted different partisan and regional alliances.

One potential remedy to partisan imbalance that would not require changing the Constitution, but would nonetheless require legislative action, is granting statehood to the District of Columbia and/or one or more of the unincorporated U.S. territories in the hope of evening the playing field for both parties. Puerto Rico, with a population of nearly 3.3 million and similar in size to Utah, receives most of the attention on this front. Washington, D.C., has a population of just under 700,000, putting it above Wyoming and Vermont. Still, there is no guarantee that these would-be states will reliably lean Democratic or Republican once in the Union.

Any changes in Senate representation would have implications for the Electoral College, as well—the other key constitutional feature impacted by malapportionment that we mentioned earlier in this chapter. While the Electoral College could itself be formally changed via Constitutional amendment, there are other proposals to make it more reflective of the popular vote, thus effectively diminishing the disproportionate influence of small states.

One such proposal is the National Popular Vote Interstate Compact, in which participating states agree to cast their Electoral College votes for the presidential candidate who wins the most popular votes nationally once the critical mass of an electoral vote majority has agreed to the arrangement. To date, sixteen states plus the District of Columbia have signed on to the Compact. Together, those states hold 196 of the 270 electoral votes required to elect a president.[5]

Data from the Pew Research Center (2023) illuminates Americans' support for a range of reform proposals. For example, 65 percent of Americans favor changing presidential elections so that the candidate with the most votes wins; however, the split is quite stark by party, with Democrats favoring the change 82–16, while a small majority of Republicans would keep the current system (52–47 opposed to change). In the same survey, large majorities favored term limits for members of Congress and age limits for Supreme Court justices. Yet, about two-thirds *opposed* amending the Constitution to give larger states greater representation. While younger people were more supportive (45 percent), in no age group did a majority favor the change.

3.7 Conclusion: The Constitution's Legacy for Representation

The U.S. Constitution reflects a series of strategic compromises that the Framers saw as necessary to achieve ratification. Key to the compromise was the Senate's role as a check on the House. While the Senate has evolved considerably over its history, it retains key features and a unique character all its own. Its members were elected indirectly, via state legislatures, until the ratification of the 17th Amendment in 1913 gave the people the right to choose their senators by popular vote. As such, there is a precedent for fundamental changes to key aspects of Senate representation. Yet that was an era in which the Senate was seen as out of touch and under the control of moneyed interests. An important question for

---

5 The nonpartisan League of Women Voters has supported the Compact as part of its One Person One Vote campaign. Read more at: https://www.lwv.org/blog/what-national-popular-vote-interstate-compact

today is what it might take to convince a super-majority of Americans that the body requires further alteration.

For all the ills of malapportionment and the greater voice given to small states in the upper house, the Senate nonetheless plays a remarkable role in the American system of government. By virtue of the longer six-year terms served by its members and the less hierarchical nature of the body, senators enjoy a good deal of individual influence and independence, often acting to delay or force compromise on key issues facing the country. While the way the Senate operates is often a frustration to those who dislike gridlock, one by-product is that when the Senate does legislate it tends to produce more moderate legislation that is typically bipartisan, at least to some degree. Whether it is the costs or the benefits of the system that win out should be left to the individual observer to determine for himself or herself. But it would be difficult to argue that the Senate is operating out of line with a good deal of its history and what many would say the Framers intended.

Discussion Questions

1 What is the meaning of an institution as discussed in this chapter?
2 Describe the Great Compromise and discuss some of its implications.
3 What is malapportionment and how does it impact the U.S. Senate? How malapportioned is the U.S. state that you most closely identify with?
4 Describe the concept of legislative effectiveness. Why are some senators more effective than others?
5 Do you think the Senate should be reformed? Why or why not? And if so, how?

References

Archer, J. Clark, Stanley D. Brunn, Kenneth C. Martis, and Gerald R. Webster. 2024. "United States Senate Malapportionment: A Geographical Investigation." *Political Geography* 113 (August): 103129.

Baker v. Carr. 1962. 369 U.S. 186. Argued April 19–20, 1961, and reargued October 9, 1961. Decided March 26, 1962.

Build Back Better Act. H.R. 5376, 117th Congress. Introduced September 27, 2021. https://www.con gress.gov/bill/117th-congress/house-bill/5376.

Dahl, Robert A. 1989. *Democracy and Its Critics*. Yale University Press.

Engaging Data. 2024. "US County Electoral Map – Land Area vs Population." https://engaging-data. com/county-electoral-map-land-vs-population/.

Federal Election Commission. n.d. *Election Results and Voting Information*. Accessed February 4, 2025. https://www.fec.gov/introduction-campaign-finance/election-results-and-voting-information/.

Hamilton, Alexander, James Madison, and John Jay. *The Federalist Papers*. Edited by Clinton Rossiter. Signet Classics, 2003. https://guides.loc.gov/federalist-papers/full-text.

Harrington, James. 1771. *The Oceana and Other Works of James Harrington, with an Account of His Life by John Toland*. Becket and Cadell.

Johnson, Steven. 2016. "Why Blue States Are the Real 'Tea Party'." *New York Times*. December 3. https://www.nytimes.com/2016/12/03/opinion/sunday/why-blue-states-are-the-real-tea-party. html.

Lee, Frances E. 2000. "Senate Representation and Coalition Building in Distributive Politics." *American Political Science Review* 94 (1): 59–72.

Lee, Frances E., and Bruce I. Oppenheimer. 1997. "Senate Apportionment: Competitiveness and Partisan Advantage." *Legislative Studies Quarterly* 22 (1): 3–24.

Lee, Frances E., and Bruce I. Oppenheimer. 1999. *Sizing Up the Senate: The Unequal Consequences of Equal Representation*. University of Chicago Press.

Johnson, Richard, and Lisa L. Miller. 2023. "The Conservative Policy Bias of US Senate Malapportionment." *PS: Political Science & Politics* 56 (1): 10–17.

Manchin, Joe. 2021. "Manchin Statement On Build Back Better Act." Office of Senator Joe Manchin. December 19. https://www.manchin.senate.gov/newsroom/press-releases/manchin-statement-on-build-back-better-act.

Millhiser, Ian. 2021. "Build Back Better is the Latest Victim of America's Anti-democratic Senate." *Vox*. December 21. https://www.vox.com/2021/12/20/22846504/senate-joe-manchin-build-back-better-democrats-republicans-43-million.

Newman, Mark. 2016. "Maps of the 2016 US Presidential Election Results." https://public.websites. umich.edu/~mejn/election/2016/.

Newport, Frank. 2021. "Biden Approval, Legislation and the American Public." Gallup. November 19. https://news.gallup.com/opinion/polling-matters/357623/biden-approval-legislation-american-public.aspx.

Pew Research Center. 2023. "Americans' Dismal Views of the Nation's Politics." September 19. https://www.pewresearch.org/politics/2023/09/19/how-americans-view-proposals-to-change-the-political-system/.

Reiman, Jeffrey. 2016. "Letters to the Editor: Questioning the Electoral College and 'One Person, One Vote'." *The Washington Post*. November 28. https://www.washingtonpost.com/opinions/question ing-the-electoral-college-and-one-person-one-vote/2016/11/28/feb5b586-b355-11e6-bc2d -19b3d759cfe7_story.html.

Rodden, Jonathan. 2010. "The Geographic Distribution of Political Preferences." *Annual Review of Political Science* 13 (1): 321–40.

Roper Center for Public Opinion Research. 1990. "Public Opinion on the Flag." *The Public Perspective*. July/August.

Samuels, David, and Richard Snyder. 2001. "The Value of a Vote: Malapportionment in Comparative Perspective." *British Journal of Political Science* 31 (4): 651–71.

Texas v. Johnson, 491 U.S. 397 (1989).

U.S. Census Bureau, Population Division. 2024. Annual Estimates of the Resident Population for the United States, Regions, States, District of Columbia, and Puerto Rico: April 1, 2020 to July 1, 2024 (NST-EST2024-POP). December.

Volden, Craig, and Alan E. Wiseman. 2014. *Legislative Effectiveness in the United States Congress: The Lawmakers*. Cambridge University Press.

Volden, Craig, and Alan E. Wiseman. 2018. "Legislative Effectiveness in the United States Senate." *Journal of Politics* 80 (2): 731–35.

Wesberry v. Sanders. 1964. 376 U.S. 1. Argued November 18–19, 1963. Decided February 17, 1964.

Ryan D. Williamson and Jordan A. Windham

4 Is the Legislature Broken? The Evolving Dysfunction of Congress and Paths to Reform

The United States Congress, designated as the First Branch of government under the Constitution, holds a pivotal role as the legislative body responsible for representing the American people through the enactment of laws. Its primary responsibility is to pass bills and implement policy changes that address the evolving needs and demands of its constituents. This representative nature of Congress is foundational to the democratic process, as it ensures that the voices of diverse communities across the nation are heard and addressed through legislative action. Congress engages in debates, negotiations, and collaborations to craft legislation that reflects the public's interests, serving as a crucial mechanism for translating the will of the people into concrete policies.

In recent years, however, Congress has witnessed growing dysfunction and a decline in productivity, primarily attributed to increasing hyperpartisanship (Binder 2015). This has created an environment where political gridlock is common, and the legislative process becomes stalled (Lee 2015). Partisan divisions have deepened, leading to difficulties in reaching bipartisan agreements and passing meaningful legislation. Consequently, many critical issues remain unaddressed, causing frustration among citizens and eroding trust in the legislative process. The lack of productivity in Congress can be seen in the decreasing number of bills passed and the protracted negotiations that often yield only minimal legislative achievements.[1]

The stagnation in Congressional activity inadvertently opens avenues for unelected officials in the executive branch and powerful interest groups to exert greater influence over policy outcomes.[2] As Congress struggles to fulfill its legislative duties, these entities step in to fill the vacuum, often shaping policies through executive orders, regulatory changes, or lobbying efforts (Lowande 2024). This shift diminishes the role of elected representatives and potentially skews policy

---

1 https://washingtonstatestandard.com/2024/08/08/congress-limps-toward-the-end-of-a-disappointing-session-with-just-78-laws-to-show
2 https://www.washingtonpost.com/news/monkey-cage/wp/2015/08/20/if-congress-keeps-cutting-its-staff-who-is-writing-your-laws-you-wont-like-the-answer

---

Ryan D. Williamson, Jordan A. Windham, University of Wyoming

https://doi.org/10.1515/9783111591902-004

decisions towards narrower interests, rather than the broader public good. The increasing influence of these non-elected actors underscores the importance of a functional and proactive Congress to maintain a balance of power and ensure that legislative decisions remain aligned with the democratic principles set forth in the Constitution.

Given these challenges and dangers, there is a need for reform within Congress to restore its functionality and enhance its capacity to serve the public effectively. Ultimately, fostering a political culture that prioritizes the long-term interests of all Americans over immediate partisan gains is essential. By addressing these structural and cultural issues, Congress can better fulfill its foundational role as the First Branch, ensuring it remains a responsive and effective institution in the face of contemporary challenges. With this in mind, the remainder of this chapter will highlight the myriad problems within Congress, discuss the consequences of these problems, and identify potential solutions to improve the overall functioning of the institution.

4.1 What's Wrong with Congress?

Dysfunction characterized the 118th Congress from its first vote, notably through the fourteen additional rounds of balloting needed to elect Kevin McCarthy as Speaker of the House.[3] The slim Republican majority in the House, elected in 2022 and tied for the fifth-smallest ever, limited leadership's ability to act, as it took only four defectors to block any party-line actions, as McCarthy's speakership balloting demonstrated.[4] These intra-party divisions foreshadowed the challenges McCarthy faced in his record-breaking speakership. Despite securing his role after fourteen failed votes and concessions to Freedom Caucus holdouts, McCarthy served as Speaker for only 269 days—the shortest tenure in 147 years and the third shortest ever.[5] Over those nine months, McCarthy presided over a historically dysfunctional Congressional session, where polarization, a small majority, and his concessions undermined governance.[6]

After initially failing to pass a budget, McCarthy worked with Democrats to prevent a government shutdown by funding the government for forty-five days

---

3 https://www.nytimes.com/interactive/2023/01/04/us/politics/house-speaker-vote-tally.html
4 https://www.pewresearch.org/short-reads/2023/05/05/narrow-majorities-in-u-s-house-have-become-more-common-but-havent-always-led-to-gridlock
5 https://www.cnn.com/2023/10/03/politics/house-speaker-shortest-kevin-mccarthy-dg/index.html
6 https://gai.georgetown.edu/political-dynamics-of-the-second-session-of-the-118th-congress

despite opposition from fellow Republicans.[7] Amid Trump's urging for a shut-down rather than a bipartisan compromise, Representative Matt Gaetz (R-FL) led Republican defectors against McCarthy's continuing resolution meant to prevent a shutdown without passing a full budget.[8] McCarthy's previous collaboration with President Joe Biden to raise the debt limit, and thus prevent a default, fur-ther alienated McCarthy from his party.[9]

Choosing bipartisanship over catering to the Freedom Caucus ultimately led to McCarthy's downfall. Gaetz spearheaded McCarthy's ouster, leading seven other Republicans in invoking a concession that McCarthy had made to obtain the Speakership, allowing a single member to call a vote to "vacate" the Speaker.[10] This unprecedented "motion to vacate" ousted McCarthy and was the first suc-cessful vote of its kind.[11] Following his removal, McCarthy resigned from Con-gress, further tightening the Republican majority before the second session of the 118th Congress.[12]

After three weeks without a leader and multiple failed nominations, Rep. Mike Johnson (R-LA) assumed the speakership, inheriting McCarthy's challenges —his tenure marked by extreme partisanship and numerous failed votes.[13] House leadership typically relies on procedural votes, which are usually successful, but the 118th Congress set a modern record for failed procedural votes, with six by February 2024.[14] In January 2024, Johnson faced backlash for a budget deal with Democrats that prevented a shutdown, resulting in twelve Republicans and Democrats uniting to defeat a procedural vote for unrelated legislation.[15] John-son's struggles echoed his predecessor's issues after compromising with President Biden to raise the debt ceiling the previous year.[16]

---

7 https://www.cnn.com/2023/10/05/politics/house-speaker-chaos-what-matters/index.html
8 https://www.nytimes.com/2023/09/29/us/politics/trump-shutdown.html
9 https://apnews.com/article/joe-biden-debt-ceiling-budget-signing-f78a000d83cf85ffbaa2d08637844053
10 https://www.npr.org/2023/10/02/1203008202/mccarthy-speaker-gaetz
11 https://www.cnn.com/2023/10/04/politics/speaker-ousted-historical-comparison-what-matters/index.html
12 https://apnews.com/article/kevin-mccarthy-house-speaker-reelection-84fc76226de7d20e140325bbe87622c8
13 https://www.newsweek.com/full-list-mike-johnson-vote-losses-house-speaker-1867847
14 https://www.politico.com/newsletters/inside-congress/2024/02/15/house-gop-sets-rule-vote-failure-record-00141801
15 https://rollcall.com/2024/02/26/state-of-suspension-lawmakers-gripe-about-fast-tracked-bills-under-johnson/
16 https://www.washingtonpost.com/politics/2023/06/06/house-republicans-debt-ceiling-mccarthy-procedural-vote/

The Speaker of the House wields significant influence over the House Rules Committee, as the Speaker typically appoints the majority of its members, including the chair. This control allows the Speaker to manage the legislative agenda and strategically shape the rules for debate to align with their party's objectives. Consequently, rules proposed by the committee are generally expected to pass without much difficulty, as they reflect the priorities and strategies of the majority party leadership. The Freedom Caucus's refusal to support rule votes on insufficiently conservative deals underscores the new challenges faced by contemporary Congressmembers.[17] As renegade members oppose even the votes agreeing on how legislation is to be considered, House leadership has been forced to advance legislation by suspending its rules, effectively limiting the body's ability to debate and negotiate nuanced solutions to complex issues.[18] This has turned suspension, usually reserved for non-controversial bills, into the main vehicle for negotiating compromises on must-pass legislation.[19] Consequently, while Congress is expected to address increasingly intricate problems, its capacity to fulfill this role is flattened.

The 118th Congress highlights the dysfunction in contemporary politics. Speakers McCarthy and Johnson presided over a notably unproductive Congress.[20] The first session's first legislation passed in late March, rather than January or February, with only thirty-five bills passed, mostly minor measures or temporary extensions due to

---

17 In the U.S. House of Representatives, a rules vote typically involves setting the terms for how a specific piece of legislation will be debated or amended on the floor. When a member of the majority party in the U.S. House of Representatives does not support a rules vote, it can indicate several factors such as disagreement with party leadership, which suggests a rift within the majority, or tactical reasons where the member aims to negotiate changes or express concerns about legislation management. It may also reflect ideological differences, as the member's beliefs might not align with the party's stance, or serve as a political message to constituents about issues that matter to them. Ultimately, such opposition can highlight internal dissent and potentially impact the party's unity and effectiveness in the legislative process.

18 Suspension of the rules is a legislative procedure used in the U.S. House of Representatives to expedite the consideration of certain bills (typically non-controversial ones). When a bill is brought up under suspension of the rules, it requires a two-thirds majority for passage rather than a simple majority. This process allows for quicker debate and limits discussion, typically to 40 minutes, with no amendments allowed. Suspension of the rules is often used for bills deemed to have broad bipartisan support, making it an efficient way to move legislation through the House without the time-consuming procedures that usually accompany more contentious bills. The process is usually reserved for measures that are expected to pass easily, such as resolutions, commemorative bills, or legislation with widespread support.

19 https://rollcall.com/2024/02/26/state-of-suspension-lawmakers-gripe-about-fast-tracked-bills-under-johnson/

20 https://www.axios.com/2023/12/19/118-congress-bills-least-unproductive-chart

missed deadlines.[21] The 2023 session was the least productive since Nixon's era, with the second session following suit.[22] As of the time of writing (October 2024), only eighty-two measures have been signed into law, a significant drop from Congress's consistent baseline of 280 bills since the 82nd Congress in 1951.[23] Indeed, this represents the nadir of a trend where five of the six most unproductive first sessions in Congress have occurred since 2011.[24] During this period, few noteworthy policies were enacted, with the fiscal responsibility and defense authorization acts being the only two major bills passed.[25] Meanwhile, crucial issues like border security and foreign aid never made it to the floor despite being the priority of key legislators.[26] The legislative output primarily consisted of uncontroversial bills, such as renaming Veterans Affairs clinics and minting commemorative coins, revealing a Congress struggling to fulfill its legislative duties effectively.[27]

When it was suggested that his "inexperience" contributed to the dysfunction in Congress, Speaker Johnson stated, "I don't think this is a reflection on the leader; I think this is a reflection on the body itself."[28] This comment is not without merit. While uninspiring, the gridlock in the 118th Congress is not new in US politics, as demonstrated in Figure 1, which depicts the number of bills that ultimately became law every year between 1947 and 2023.[29] Though there is variation year-to-year, we nonetheless see a steady decline in productivity over time. Whereas Congress once saw several hundred public laws enacted each year, that figure has dwindled to such an extent that reaching 200 would be above average in recent years.

It is important to note that Congress's lack of productivity is not an artifact of having less to do. It is not as though there are no bills waiting to be advanced through the legislative process. In fact, the reality is quite the opposite. Figure 4.2 depicts the number of measures introduced in Congress during the same period as Figure 4.1 (1947–2023). Though the number of measures introduced is not as high as it was during the 1960s and 1970s, we nonetheless see a steady increase

---

21 https://gai.georgetown.edu/political-dynamics-of-the-second-session-of-the-118th-congress
22 https://www.axios.com/2023/12/19/118-congress-bills-least-unproductive-chart
23 https://washingtonstatestandard.com/2024/08/08/congress-limps-toward-the-end-of-a-disappointing-session-with-just-78-laws-to-show/
24 https://www.axios.com/2023/12/19/118-congress-bills-least-unproductive-chart
25 https://gai.georgetown.edu/political-dynamics-of-the-second-session-of-the-118th-congress/
26 https://washingtonstatestandard.com/2024/08/08/congress-limps-toward-the-end-of-a-disappointing-session-with-just-78-laws-to-show/
27 Although it is not uncommon for most of the legislation passed in a Congress to be highly consensual (see Carson, Finocchiaro, and Rohde 2010), the ratio of consensual to controversial legislation passed was significantly higher in the 118th Congress.
28 https://www.newsweek.com/full-list-mike-johnson-vote-losses-house-speaker-1867847
29 However, for an alternative measure of legislative productivity, see chapter 8.

over the last three decades. In short, members of Congress seem to be devoting considerable time and energy to introducing bills, but those pieces of legislation are not becoming actual policy. This is consistent with Lee (2016), who points out that members are engaging in a "perpetual campaign" and therefore engage in partisan "messaging" bills. The primary purpose of these bills is to stake out a position on an issue but not actively see that the position becomes policy.

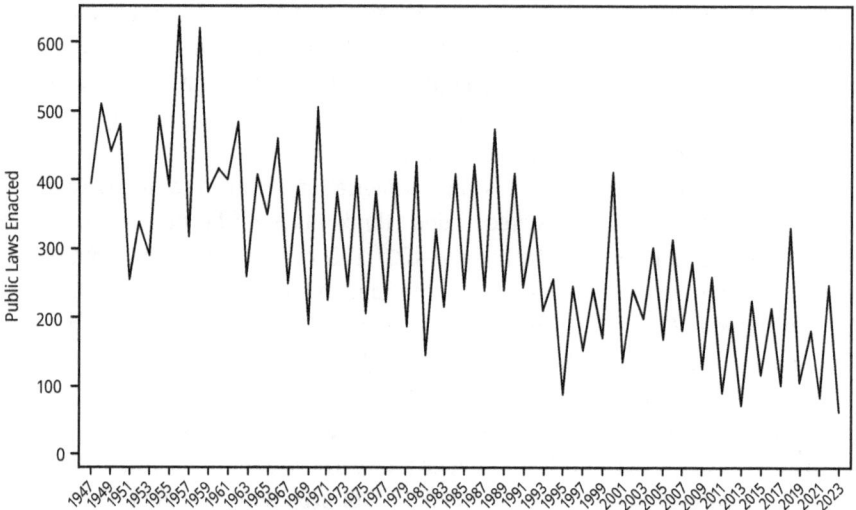

Figure 4.1: Number of public laws enacted, 1947–2023.
Source: https://www.senate.gov/legislative/ResumesofCongressionalActivity1947present.htm

These trends in increased partisanship have become significantly more common in Congress, particularly since the commencement of the Biden administration, and they are not limited to "messaging" bills. A notable example occurred during Biden's 2023 State of the Union address, where his remarks were met with loud protests, boos, and disruptive outbursts, including Representative Marjorie Taylor Greene (R-GA) yelling "liar."[30] Such confrontations signal a deterioration of civil discourse and mutual respect that were once expected in legislative proceedings. This aggressive atmosphere has permeated the House of Representatives, where intra-party partisanship has reached new heights.

This shift in dynamics manifested itself in attempts by members like Marjorie Taylor Greene and co-sponsor Thomas Massie (R-KY) to oust Speaker Johnson, ac-

30 https://thehill.com/homenews/administration/3848522-greene-yells-liar-after-biden-remark-on-medicare-social-security-during-state-of-the-union/

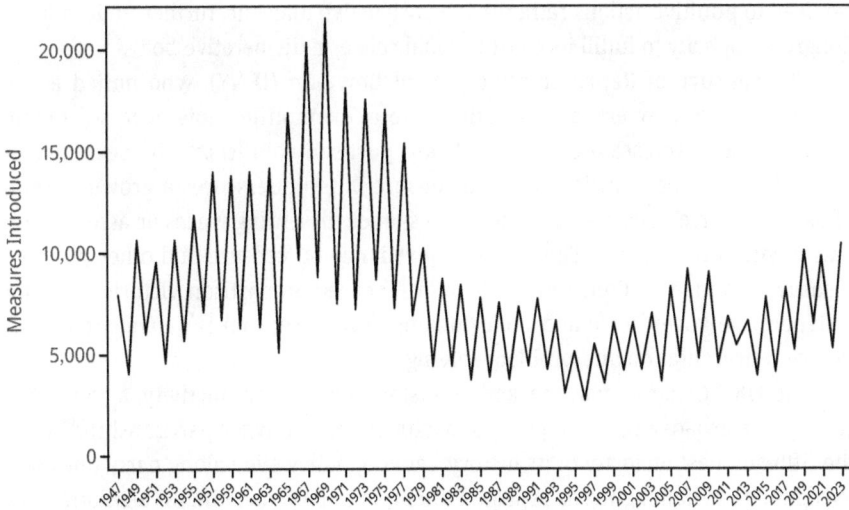

Figure 4.2: Number of measures introduced in Congress, 1947–2023.
Source: https://www.senate.gov/legislative/ResumesofCongressionalActivity1947present.htm

cusing him of "aiding and abetting the Democrats and Biden administration in destroying our country."[31] While this particular attempt was defeated by a bipartisan vote, it nonetheless garnered forty-three votes, including eleven from Republicans, underscoring a worrying trend where partisanship drives such efforts devoid of substantial grounds.[32] This environment has fostered a significant increase in sanctions among members, as shown by the fact that only twenty-six legislators have been censured in the history of the House,[33] with two occurring during the 118th Congress.[34] The House's decision to censure Representative Rashida Tlaib (D-MI) for her criticisms of Israel's post-Hamas attack highlights how polarized opinions

31 https://abcnews.go.com/Politics/marjorie-taylor-greene-triggers-vote-motion-oust-speaker/story?id=110043228

32 https://abcnews.go.com/Politics/marjorie-taylor-greene-triggers-vote-motion-oust-speaker/story?id=110043228

33 Historically, censures have involved egregious behaviors such as treasonous conduct, assault of another member, bribery, and sexual misconduct. https://www.everycrsreport.com/reports/RL31382.html#_Toc477184242

34 https://thehill.com/homenews/house/4346266-gop-advances-bowman-censure-resolution-teeing-up-final-vote/

can lead to punitive actions rather than constructive dialogue, further undermining Congress' capacity to fulfill its constitutional role as a deliberative body.[35]

The censure of Representative Jamaal Bowman (D-NY), who pulled a fire alarm to avoid a government shutdown vote, exemplifies how even seemingly trivial actions can escalate into significant partisan conflicts.[36] The Secretary of the GOP conference's insistence on a censure vote underscores a growing trend of using punitive measures as a means to silence dissenting voices or assert dominance within the party.[37] This increasing reliance on censure and other punitive measures points to a Congress that is more focused on partisan victories than on collaborative governance and policymaking, a mindset that is detrimental to effective representation and problem-solving.

The 118th Congress was marked by historically low productivity, a trend that reflects the broader issues of political dysfunction and hyper-partisanship.[38] With the fifth-smallest majority in its history, moving policy even along party lines was exceptionally challenging, as repeated attempts to pass meaningful legislation are faced with insurmountable obstacles, often from within one's own party.[39] The inability to find common ground creates a legislative environment where productivity is severely hampered, and reaching consensus is more elusive than ever.[40]

These developments reveal how obstructionist tactics and internal conflicts are spreading beyond traditional party lines. Moderate Republicans, frustrated by the leadership's inability to enforce discipline, began consulting the obstructive Freedom Caucus for tactics, even resorting to temporarily defeating special rules on unrelated legislation to protest policy exclusions, like the absence of SALT (State and Local Tax) provisions in proposed tax extender deals.[41] This intra-party turmoil reflects a faltering dissolution of party discipline, where prioritizing productivity takes a backseat to partisanship and political maneuvering.

Comments from lawmakers like Rep. Don Bacon (R-NE) illustrate the frustrations caused by such internal dysfunction. "When I came in, Pete Sessions was the chairman of Rules. He says: 'Vote against the rules, I'll kick your ass.' And

---

35 https://apnews.com/article/congress-house-censure-resolution-tlaib-8085189047a4c40f2d44ada4604aa076
36 https://www.npr.org/2023/12/08/1218095236/house-censure-rep-jamaal-bowman-fire-alarm
37 https://thehill.com/homenews/house/4346266-gop-advances-bowman-censure-resolution-teeing-up-final-vote/
38 https://washingtonstatestandard.com/2024/08/08/congress-limps-toward-the-end-of-a-disappointing-session-with-just-78-laws-to-show/
39 https://gai.georgetown.edu/political-dynamics-of-the-second-session-of-the-118th-congress/
40 https://www.politico.com/newsletters/inside-congress/2024/02/15/house-gop-sets-rule-vote-failure-record-00141801
41 https://thehill.com/homenews/house/4441163-moderates-freedom-caucus-tactics/

that's the way it should be. If you don't like the bill, vote no on the actual bill," said Rep. Bacon. "I wish there were consequences for that kind of behavior."[42] His lament underscores the desire for a more unified party structure that prioritizes legislative output over internal squabbles. Rep. Chip Roy (R-TX) echoed these frustrations on the House floor. "One thing. I want my Republican colleagues to give me one thing. One. That I can go campaign on and say we did," Roy said. "One!"[43] Roy's frustration with the lack of significant Republican accomplishments underscores the need for a renewed focus on policy rather than perpetual infighting.

This is not unique to the House, however. The Senate also exemplifies legislative stagnation, raising serious questions about its ability to fulfill its constitutional duties.[44] While activity is higher in the Senate, that is in no small part a result of the inability to curtail individual behavior the same way House leadership can (Wolfensberger 2018; Madonna and Williamson 2023). A mere fifty-one bills were passed by the 118th Congress in the Senate, which is an alarmingly low number that highlights the institution's diminished capacity for meaningful legislative action.[45] Many of these bills focused on mundane matters, such as naming post offices and other ceremonial accolades, demonstrating a lack of engagement with pressing national issues that require decisive action.[46]

In a particularly telling episode, Senate Republicans faced significant political pressure from influential figures such as Republicana Donald Trump and Mike Johnson, which resulted in the collapse of a bipartisan border security deal crafted by some of their own Republican colleagues.[47] This failure not only showcases the challenges of bipartisan negotiation but also underscores the growing influence of external political forces in shaping legislative outcomes, often at the expense of substantive policy advancements. The dynamics at play indicate a system that prioritizes political survival over effective governance, and this trend could have long-lasting repercussions on legislative efficacy.

GOP Senator Lisa Murkowski's (R-AK) comments regarding the failed border security deal underscore the long-term consequences of such failures on future

---

42 https://www.politico.com/newsletters/inside-congress/2024/02/15/house-gop-sets-rule-vote-failure-record-00141801

43 https://thehill.com/homenews/house/4311429-chip-roy-gets-heated-over-spending-strategy-were-pissing-it-all-away/

44 https://presidentialtransition.org/reports-publications/unconfirmed-reducing-number-senate-confirmed-positions/

45 https://www.senate.gov/legislative/ResumesofCongressionalActivity1947present.htm

46 https://www.axios.com/2023/12/19/118-congress-bills-least-unproductive-chart

47 https://www.cnn.com/2024/02/06/politics/republican-opposition-senate-border-bill/index.html

bipartisan efforts. "I have a difficult time understanding again how anyone else in the future is going to want to be on that negotiating team – on anything," said Murkowski.[48] If potential negotiators believe their efforts will routinely face opposition from within their own party or be derailed by external influences, their willingness to engage in collaborative policymaking will likely diminish. As a result, the current climate fosters an environment of increased reluctance to pursue bipartisan solutions, further entrenching legislative gridlock. Furthermore, statements from Senate leaders like John Barrasso (R-WY) suggest that major policy issues, such as border security, may be better addressed through upcoming elections rather than through effective legislative dialogue.[49] This orientation shifts the focus from shaping viable legislative solutions to a reliance on electoral cycles as the primary means of resolving complex issues, thereby emphasizing political theater over practical governance (Bergquist 2020). Such an approach risks embedding the perception that Congress is unable to act decisively when action is most needed, ultimately eroding public support in legislative institutions (Flynn and Harbridge 2015).

The Senate's political theater extends to other critical policy areas as well, further complicating efforts to enact substantive legislation. A prime example of this phenomenon is the blocking of an In-Vitro Fertilization (IVF) bill, which underscores how urgent policy debates become entangled with electoral strategy and partisan brinkmanship.[50] Despite garnering endorsements from influential figures like Trump, who supports IVF, strategic maneuvering within the Senate led to its blockage.[51] This reflects the deep-seated partisan divisions that often overshadow constructive dialogue and compromise. As lawmakers focus on maintaining political postures and scoring points ahead of elections, essential policy initiatives are sidelined, leaving pressing societal needs unaddressed.[52] The deliberate choice to prioritize political theater over legislative action perpetuates a cycle of unproductivity that can frustrate both constituents and advocates for reform. Overall, these tactics further detract from Congress's ability to effectively

---

48 https://www.cnn.com/2024/02/07/politics/republicans-congress-leadership-fights/index.html
49 https://www.politico.com/live-updates/2024/02/06/congress/barrasso-a-no-00139785
50 https://www.theguardian.com/us-news/2024/sep/17/senate-vote-ivf-bill-democrats-republicans-election
51 https://www.theguardian.com/us-news/2024/sep/17/senate-vote-ivf-bill-democrats-republicans-election
52 https://presidentialtransition.org/reports-publications/unconfirmed-reducing-number-senate-confirmed-positions/

legislate, creating an environment in which ideals such as cooperation and governance are overshadowed by the relentless pursuit of political advantage.[53]

In summary, the 118th Congress, marked by a historically low legislative output, reveals the detrimental effects of persistent partisanship and intra-party conflict.[54] At a time when addressing critical national issues like immigration reform, railway safety, and children's online protection is imperative, Congress's inability to enact major legislation signals a pressing need for reform.[55] Without a shift towards collaborative, effective governance that transcends party lines and focuses on policy over politics, Congress risks further diminishing its role as a critical governing body.

4.2 Why Does this Matter?

The current state of dysfunction and hyperpartisanship in Congress significantly impacts public perception of the institution. Overall public approval of Congress remains alarmingly low, particularly when contrasted with the approval ratings that individual representatives often receive within their own districts (Carson and Jacobson 2024). This discrepancy highlights a broader dissatisfaction with Congress as a body, even if constituents feel positively about their specific representatives. The perceived ineffectiveness and partisan gridlock contribute to the negative view that many Americans hold, raising concerns about the ability of Congress to address national issues competently.

This relationship is illustrated in Figure 4.3. Gallup has asked citizens, "Do you approve or disapprove of the way Congress is handling its job?" for several decades. Figure 3 shows the percentage responding with "approve" or "disapprove" around October of each year dating back to 1994. From this, we see that Congress witnessed a dramatic increase in approval following the September 11 terrorist attacks of 2001, but that support quickly dissipated and has remained quite low ever since. Indeed, between 2014 and 2024, approval averaged only 17 percent and reached as low as 9 percent in 2013. This is not a function of respondents not having an opinion, however. As demonstrated by the dashed grey line, many citizens actively disapprove of the job Congress is doing. Between 2014

---

53 https://washingtonstatestandard.com/2024/08/08/congress-limps-toward-the-end-of-a-disappointing-session-with-just-78-laws-to-show/
54 https://washingtonstatestandard.com/2024/08/08/congress-limps-toward-the-end-of-a-disappointing-session-with-just-78-laws-to-show/
55 https://gai.georgetown.edu/political-dynamics-of-the-second-session-of-the-118th-congress/

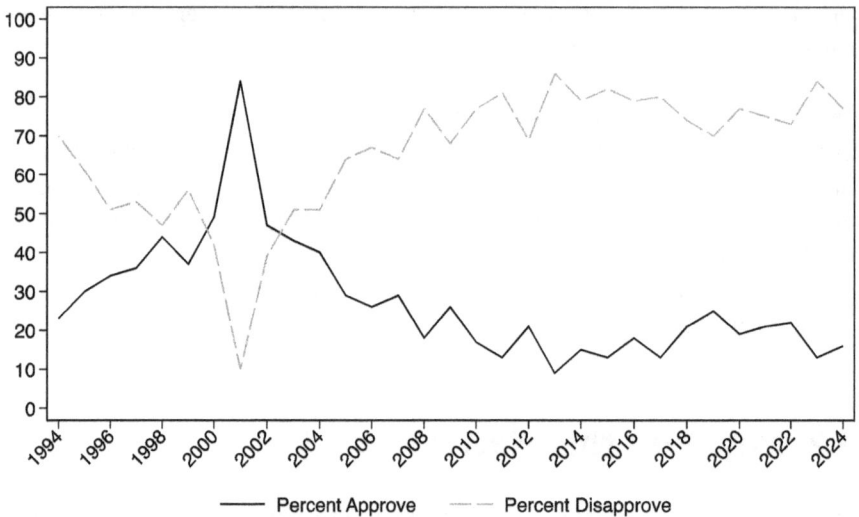

Figure 4.3: Congressional job approval over time.
Source: https://news.gallup.com/poll/1600/congress-public.aspx

and 2024, nearly four out of every five respondents expressed a negative view of Congress.

One critical consequence of this fraught environment is the loss of legislative experience due to retirements and resignations. Figure 4.4 depicts the number of voluntary retirements from the House of Representatives between 1994 and 2024.[56] Between 1994 and 2014, an average of thirty-four members decided to not seek reelection to the House. Since then, that average has increased to almost forty-five members—more than one-tenth of the entire chamber. When seasoned lawmakers exit, often prematurely, it leads to a depletion of institutional knowledge and expertise that is crucial for effective governance.[57] Such departures can exacerbate the challenges already faced by Congress, further diminishing its capacity to function seamlessly.

Former Speaker of the House Kevin McCarthy's decision to retire in December 2023 exemplifies this trend. McCarthy's departure, following his unprecedented re-

---

[56] This data comes from *Vital Statistics on Congress* and does not include members who were defeated in primary elections.
[57] https://www.npr.org/2023/10/29/1207593168/congressional-term-limits-explainer

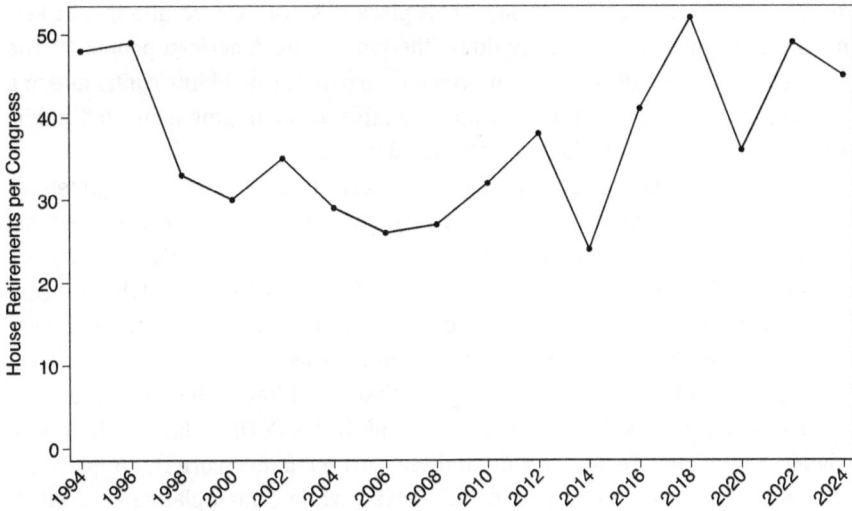

Figure 4.4: Number of retirements from the house of representatives over time.
Source: https://www.brookings.edu/wp-content/uploads/2024/11/2-7-Full.pdf

moval from the Speaker position, ended a seventeen-year tenure in the House.[58] His departure not only marked the loss of a key leader but also underscored the instability and volatility in congressional leadership. McCarthy's experience and strategic acumen, honed over nearly two decades, are difficult to replace. The ascension of Mike Johnson, McCarthy's successor, illustrates the challenge of filling such a void effectively. Johnson, serving only his fourth term and having never chaired a House standing committee, lacks the traditional experience expected of a Speaker.[59] This specific situation highlights how the current political climate necessitates rapid ascension, sometimes at the expense of seasoned leadership. It raises further concerns about the preparedness of new leaders to navigate the complexities and demands of high-level congressional roles.

Other notable resignations further illustrate the trend. Ken Buck (R-CO), a five-term representative, stepped down before completing his last term, expressing deep dissatisfaction with the state of Congress. Buck lamented, "It is the worst year of the nine years and three months that I've been in Congress, and having talked to former members it's the worst year in 40 or 50 years to be in

---

58 https://abcnews.go.com/Politics/kevin-mccarthy-retiring-congress-after-ousted-house-speaker/story?id=105425178.
59 https://www.texastribune.org/2023/10/25/mike-johnson-house-speaker-texans

Congress."[60] He would go on to say, "This place has just evolved into this bicker-ing and nonsense and not really doing the job for the American people."[61] The heightened sense of dysfunction and constant partisan squabbling contribute to a working environment that many find untenable, discouraging dedicated public servants from continuing their congressional careers.

The loss of experienced representatives also disrupts leadership pipelines that are vital for supplying seasoned leaders who can legislate effectively. Among recent departures are three Republican committee chairmen—Cathy McMorris Rodgers (R-WA), Mike Gallagher (R-WI), and Mark Green (R-TN)—whose retire-ments were unexpected, as they had not yet reached party-imposed term limits.[62] Their exits, coupled with those of other leaders poised to step down due to term limits, suggest a broader attrition of talent that could have otherwise guided fu-ture legislative efforts. The comments of Frank Lucas (R-OK), Chair of the House Science, Space, and Technology Committee, further underscore the precarious-ness facing congressional Republicans.[63] Lucas, while contemplating re-election, voiced concerns about the potential shift to minority status, which makes the prospect of continuing a congressional career less appealing for many.[64] This sen-timent indicates an underlying fear among lawmakers of operating from a weak-ened position, which can accelerate decisions to retire rather than endure legisla-tive stagnation.

Moreover, the trend of experienced representatives retiring raises questions about the changing composition of Congress. As veteran lawmakers exit, there is a risk that their seats will be filled by individuals more focused on partisan bat-tles than on substantive governance. These new entrants may prioritize ideologi-cal purity over pragmatic problem-solving, potentially perpetuating gridlock and reducing Congress's effectiveness even further. The voluntary exit of knowledge-able lawmakers in favor of partisan newcomers can exacerbate the challenges facing Congress. As frustration with the current political landscape grows, attract-ing candidates committed to effective governance becomes increasingly difficult.

60 https://www.cnn.com/2024/03/12/politics/ken-buck-leaving-congress-early/index.html
61 https://rollcall.com/2024/03/12/colorados-ken-buck-to-make-early-exit-from-the-house-next-week/
62 https://www.nbcnews.com/politics/congress/republican-dysfunction-drives-wave-house-retire ments-rcna139642
63 https://www.nbcnews.com/politics/congress/republican-dysfunction-drives-wave-house-retire ments-rcna139642
64 https://www.nbcnews.com/politics/congress/republican-dysfunction-drives-wave-house-retire ments-rcna139642

This shift in focus from collaborative policymaking to partisan posturing threatens not only the quality of legislation but also the integrity of the institution itself.

The need for policymaking does not disappear simply because Congress does want to do it. Congress' abdication of its Constitutional responsibility to lead the legislative process creates an opportunity for unelected actors to step in. Interest groups can therefore play a pivotal role in shaping the legislative landscape by developing and promoting proposed legislation that aligns with their specific agendas. These entities often craft "model bills," which are designed to address issues that resonate with their members' interests. Once a bill is formulated, interest groups engage in strategic outreach to lawmakers, lobbying for the introduction and support of their proposals in Congress. This process involves a variety of tactics, such as providing legislators with detailed research, offering expert testimonies at hearings, and mobilizing grassroots campaigns to demonstrate public support. Through these efforts, interest groups aim to influence the policies and priorities of elected officials, often providing the necessary resources and information that lawmakers may not have readily available.

However, the influence of interest groups raises important questions about representation in the democratic process. These groups are typically composed of unelected individuals who unite around particularized interests, which can vary widely from environmental sustainability to business interests, labor rights, or healthcare reforms. As a result, their priorities and perspectives may not reflect the diverse needs and opinions of the broader constituency that Congress is expected to represent. This disconnect can result in a legislative environment where policies favor a narrow set of interests over the general public's welfare, leading to potential inequities in how laws are crafted and implemented.

Additionally, Congress has increasingly forfeited significant portions of its policymaking responsibilities, leading to a marked rise in the reliance on executive orders issued by the president. This trend can be attributed to a variety of factors, including partisan gridlock, the complexity of contemporary issues, and a growing tendency for lawmakers to avoid politically contentious debates. As a result, important policies that traditionally would have undergone extensive legislative scrutiny and public discourse are now often enacted through executive action (Howell 2003; Lowande 2024). This shift undermines the foundational principles of the legislative process, which emphasize thorough discussion, compromise, and representation of diverse constituencies. By circumventing Congress, executive orders can be issued swiftly but often lack the depth and comprehensive nature that comes from a rigorous legislative process, limiting their ability to address the multifaceted challenges facing the nation.

Moreover, the increasing reliance on executive orders not only results in policies that may be more reactive and narrowly focused but also raises concerns regarding their longevity and permanence. Unlike legislation passed by Congress, which requires a more involved process for repeal, executive orders are inherently easier to overturn or modify by subsequent administrations (Byers et al. 2020; Rudalevige 2021). This vulnerability contributes to a lack of stability in important policy areas, creating an environment where initiatives may change dramatically with each new presidential term. This cyclical nature of policymaking driven by executive action fosters uncertainty for both agencies tasked with implementation and a public reliant on consistent governance. Ultimately, this trend towards diminished legislative engagement is detrimental, as it undermines the checks and balances vital to a healthy democracy and leads to fragmented policies that fail to serve the enduring interests and needs of the populace.

The dual issues of congressional dysfunction and hyperpartisanship erode both the legislative effectiveness and public trust essential to democracy. The loss of experienced lawmakers and the influx of partisans uninterested in governance only compound these issues, suggesting an urgent need for reform.

4.3 What Can be Done about This?

Good policy is the bedrock of responsible governance, and it is the primary responsibility of Congress to construct and implement those policies. When Congress is mired in dysfunction, there is a risk that lawmakers may rely too heavily on unelected bureaucrats or interest group lobbyists to influence or outright dictate the agenda. This reliance can weaken the accountability legislators owe to their constituents, as decisions may be swayed by those who do not directly represent the public's interests. Ideally, elected officials should lead the policymaking process, ensuring transparency, accountability, and responsiveness to the needs of their electorate.

Trust in institutions, particularly legislative bodies like Congress, is a foundational aspect of a functioning democracy (Bianco 1994). When citizens lose faith in these institutions due to perceived ineffectiveness or corruption, the very fabric of democratic governance is strained. Trust is built when institutions are seen as capable, fair, and attentive to public needs. Dysfunction and hyperpartisanship erode this trust, as they lead to the perception that Congress is more focused on political gamesmanship than on serving the common good.

Rebuilding this trust requires Congress to exhibit a commitment to functional governance, characterized by compromise and collaboration. Lawmakers must demonstrate that they can rise above partisan divides to deliver solutions that benefit the nation. By doing so, they not only address the immediate policy needs but also solidify the public's confidence in their capacity to lead. This trust is essential for ensuring public support and cooperation, which are vital for the successful implementation of policies.

There are several avenues for potential change within Congress. First is a consideration of reforming the institution itself. The Select Committee on the Modernization of Congress, known as the House Modernization Committee, laid a foundation for transforming the U.S. House of Representatives into a more effective, efficient, and responsive institution. Created with a bipartisan mandate, the committee tackled longstanding structural and operational challenges. Although the committee has been dissolved, its vision for a modern Congress continues to influence reform efforts across the legislative landscape.

One recommendation from the House Modernization Committee is to embrace remote functionality within Congress. By institutionalizing tools that allow for remote participation in committee meetings and votes, Congress ensures that legislative processes continue seamlessly, even amidst unforeseen circumstances like emergencies or health crises like the COVID-19 pandemic. This capability not only preserves the continuity of governance but also mitigates the risks associated with physical gatherings, thereby safeguarding the health and safety of lawmakers and staff. Moreover, it enables members who may face travel restrictions or personal obligations to engage fully in the legislative process, ensuring that no representative's voice is lost. This adaptability contributes to a more resilient and efficient Congress, capable of maintaining its functions without compromising on deliberation or decision-making.

The inclusion of remote tools also significantly enhances the inclusivity and representativeness of Congressional activities. By lowering physical barriers to participation, Congress can better accommodate diverse voices and perspectives, fostering a legislative environment where all members have equal opportunities to contribute. This inclusivity is crucial for representing the varied interests and needs of the American populace accurately. Furthermore, the ability to participate remotely allows Congress to leverage expertise from various geographical and demographic backgrounds, enriching debates and enhancing the quality of policy outcomes. As a result, Congress becomes more effective in crafting legislation that addresses the complexities of national and global challenges, streamlining its operations to focus on delivering impactful, well-rounded solutions efficiently. Hearing from new and varied perspectives should help counter the narrative that certain interest groups and lobbyists have captured Congress's attention and are biasing legislative outcomes in their favor.

In a reimagined Congress, transparency serves as a foundational pillar, reflecting a commitment to openness, accountability, and the restoration of public trust in legislative activities. By live-streaming every committee meeting and legislative session, Congress invites citizens to witness the democratic process first-hand, demystifying the intricacies of policymaking and debates. This real-time access allows constituents to stay informed and engaged, fostering a stronger connection between elected officials and the electorate, and rebuilding trust through visibility. Furthermore, archiving all proceedings in a publicly accessible database extends this transparency beyond mere observation, allowing the public to review and analyze legislative actions at their convenience. This comprehensive availability of information empowers citizens to hold their representatives accountable, facilitating an informed electorate that can engage meaningfully in civic discourse. When citizens see that their leaders are operating openly and transparently, it enhances credibility and establishes a trust-driven relationship between the government and the public. Ideally, fostering greater trust should enable legislators to deviate from partisan narratives in the pursuit of good policy without being punished electorally for doing so.

Refining legislative processes offers a transformative opportunity for Congress to become not only more effective and efficient but also less polarized. By revising existing rules surrounding debates and filibusters, Congress can introduce "fast-track" procedures specifically designed for non-controversial or high-priority legislation, such as infrastructure development or national security measures. This approach allows these essential bills, which typically enjoy broad support, to move more swiftly through the legislative pipeline without being bogged down by procedural inertia or partisan standoffs. Such streamlining ensures that significant, time-sensitive issues are addressed promptly, reflecting a Congress that prioritizes decisive action alongside thorough deliberation. Moreover, by reducing the time spent on contentious debate for universally beneficial measures, lawmakers can focus their energies on more complex issues, thereby allocating resources more efficiently and fostering an environment where cooperation is valued over conflict. This would ostensibly increase both the quantity and the quality of legislation that makes it out of Congress.

Furthermore, collaboration across party lines is not just beneficial but essential for a Congress that truly represents and serves the diverse needs of its constituents. Establishing permanent bipartisan working groups in critical areas such as healthcare, education, and defense could significantly enhance legislative effectiveness. By acting as dedicated incubators for cross-party policy development, these groups would foster an environment where dialogue and problem-solving are prioritized over political rivalry. This continuous engagement across party lines would encourage lawmakers to move beyond entrenched positions, paving the way for policies that are balanced and holistic. As a result, Congress would be better equipped to address complex national issues, leading to legislative outcomes that more accurately reflect the wide-ranging priorities and aspirations of the American populace. Legislators and constituents alike would likely experience increased satisfaction, as this cooperative approach would demonstrate a commitment to working in the nation's best interest rather than adhering strictly to partisan agendas.

Another recommendation involves investing in the professional development of those who support Congress—both staff and legislators. This is a strategic move that can significantly enhance legislative productivity and the quality of policymaking. Comprehensive training programs focused on essential skills such as negotiation, conflict resolution, and policy analysis can equip the congressional workforce with the tools necessary to navigate the complexities of modern governance. By fostering a more competent and versatile team, Congress can streamline the legislative process, making it more efficient in crafting, debating, and enacting laws. This professional growth translates directly into more sophisticated and well-informed policy initiatives, as staff and legislators are better prepared to tackle the multifaceted challenges that policies address. As a result, the legislative body becomes more adept at developing nuanced solutions that address the intricate needs of the nation, leading to policies that are not only innovative but also practical and impactful.

There are reforms outside of Congress that should be considered as well. Electoral reforms aimed at ensuring fair representation are pivotal in shaping a more diverse and representative Congress. Implementing systems such as ranked-choice voting allows voters to rank candidates in order of preference, which can lead to more nuanced electoral outcomes that better reflect the electorate's diverse views (John, Smith, and Zack 2018). This approach mitigates the often-polarizing effects of traditional voting systems by ensuring that elected representatives have broader support among constituents, as they must appeal to a wider base to secure not only first-choice votes but also second and third choices. The result is a Congress composed of individuals who are more attuned to the varied perspectives within their districts, enhancing the body's overall diversity and capability to address a broad spectrum of issues comprehensively.

Moreover, independent redistricting commissions aim to eliminate gerrymandering, a practice that manipulates electoral district boundaries to favor specific political parties. By establishing unbiased entities to draw district lines, electoral maps can more accurately reflect the demographic and political makeup of the population, thereby ensuring that each vote carries equal weight. This move toward fairness and equity in representation means that elections are more competitive and outcomes more reflective of genuine public opinion, rather than engineered majorities (Carson et al. 2014; Edwards et al. 2017; Williamson 2019; Williamson and King 2022). As a result, elected legislators are more likely to focus on consensus-building and policies that benefit a broader constituency, fostering a legislative environment less driven by partisan interests and more conducive to policymaking.

The concept of open primaries further enhances this framework by allowing voters, regardless of party affiliation, to participate in selecting candidates. This system incentivizes candidates to appeal to a broader audience, including independents and moderates, thereby encouraging more centrist and pragmatic approaches (Gerber and Morton 1998; Grose 2020). By reducing the emphasis on appealing solely to the party base, open primaries can diminish the influence of partisan extremism, leading to the election of legislators who are committed to serving the wider needs of their constituents. This method fosters a political culture where policy proposals are evaluated on their merits rather than partisan alignment, promoting an atmosphere of cooperation and reducing the obstacles to legislative progress.

While it is easy to blame members of Congress for this dysfunction, it is important to recognize that voters play a pivotal role as well. Increasingly, voters view cooperation and compromise as negative aspects of legislating that should be avoided. Therefore, members of Congress who wish to keep their seats are also going to view cooperation and compromise negatively. Even if legislators do see working with the other party as a positive opportunity, they may avoid following through with the idea out of fear of being punished electorally for it. When the electorate values these traits, candidates who emphasize bipartisan cooperation and ethical governance are more likely to succeed. This shift in voter priorities supports a culture of governance rooted in thoughtful policymaking, where the focus is on solving real issues through dialogue and compromise. Legislators elected under such expectations are incentivized to work across party lines and prioritize policy outcomes over partisan victories. This cultural evolution within the electorate can reduce the polarization that often stymies legislative progress, as lawmakers become more committed to the shared goal of advancing the nation's interests rather than nurturing divisive political loyalties.

Ultimately, the impact of these reforms is far-reaching, leading to a Congress better equipped to tackle the diverse and complex challenges facing the nation. As the legislative body becomes more representative of the electorate's true composition, it can cultivate an atmosphere where diverse voices are heard and integrated into policymaking. This inclusivity fosters innovation and adaptability, essential traits for effective governance in a rapidly changing world. A Congress that embodies the characteristics of fair representation, integrity, and collaboration is not only more productive but also more resilient, capable of sustaining democratic principles and fulfilling its role as a true representative of the people's will.

Discussion Questions

1 How has hyperpartisanship contributed to the dysfunction and lack of productivity in Congress in recent years?
2 In what ways does the decline in Congressional productivity impact the balance of power between elected representatives and non-elected officials in the executive branch?
3 How has the trend of "messaging" bills and a "perpetual campaign" mindset affected the legislative process in Congress?
4 What factors contribute to the public's low approval ratings of Congress, and how do these ratings differ from the approval of individual representatives?
5 What steps can be taken to rebuild public trust in Congress and enhance its role as a functional and representative governing body?

References

Bergquist, Parrish. 2020. "Congress as Theatre: How Advocates Use Ambiguity for Political Advantage." *Journal of Public Policy* 40 (1): 51–71.

Bianco, William T. 1994. *Trust: Representatives and Constituents.* University of Michigan Press.

Binder, Sarah. 2015. "The Dysfunctional Congress." *Annual Review of Political Science* 18: 85–101.

Byers, Jason, Jamie Carson, and Ryan Williamson. 2020. "Policymaking by the Executive: Examining the Fate of Presidential Agenda Items." *Congress & the Presidency* 47 (1): 1–31.

Carson, Jamie, Charles Finocchiaro, and David Rohde. 2010. "Consensus, Conflict, and Partisanship in House Decision Making: A Bill-Level Examination of Committee and Floor Behavior." *Congress and the Presidency* 37 (3): 231–53.

Carson, Jamie L., Michael H. Crespin, and Ryan D. Williamson. 2014. "Reevaluating the Effects of Redistricting on Electoral Competition, 1972–2012." *State Politics & Policy Quarterly* 14 (2): 165–77.

Carson, Jamie, and Gary C. Jacobson. 2024. *The Politics of Congressional Elections,* 11th edition. Rowman & Littlefield.

Edwards, Barry, Michael Crespin, Ryan D. Williamson, and Maxwell Palmer. 2017. "Institutional Control of Redistricting and the Geography of Representation." *The Journal of Politics* 79 (2): 722–26.

Flynn, D.J., and Laurel Harbridge. 2016. "How Partisan Conflict in Congress Affects Public Opinion: Strategies, Outcomes, and Issue Differences." *American Politics Research* 44 (5): 875–902.

Gerber, Elisabeth R., and Rebecca B. Morton. 1998. "Primary Election Systems and Representation." *Journal of Law, Economics, & Organization* 14 (2): 304–24.

Grose, Christian R. 2020. "Reducing Legislative Polarization: Top-Two and Open Primaries Are Associated with More Moderate Legislators." *Journal of Political Institutions and Political Economy* 1 (2): 267–87.

Howell, William. 2003. *Power Without Persuasion: The Politics of Direct Presidential Action.* Princeton University Press.

John, Sarah, Haley Smith, and Elizabeth Zack. 2018. "The alternative vote: Do changes in single-member voting systems affect descriptive representation of women and minorities?" *Electoral Studies* 54: 90–102.

Lee, Frances E. 2015. "How Party Polarization Affects Governance." *Annual Review of Political Science* 18: 261–282.

Lowande, Kenneth. 2024. *False Front: The Failed Promise of Presidential Power in a Polarized Age.* University of Chicago Press.

Madonna, Anthony J., and Ryan D. Williamson. 2023. "Interbranch Warfare: Senate Amending Process and Restrictive House Rules." *Political Research Quarterly* 76 (1): 279–91.

Rudalevige, Andrew. 2021. *By Executive Order: Bureaucratic Management and the Limits of Presidential Power*. Princeton University Press.

Williamson, Ryan D. 2019. "Examining the Effects of Partisan Redistricting on Candidate Entry Decisions." *Election Law Journal: Rules, Politics, & Policy* 18 (3): 214–26.

Williamson, Ryan D., and Bridgett A. King. 2022. "Redistricting and incarceration: Examining the electoral consequences of New York's prohibition on prison gerrymandering." *State Politics & Policy Quarterly* 22 (4): 418–37.

Wolfensberger, Donald R. 2018. *Changing cultures in Congress: From fair play to power plays*. Columbia University Press.

Jamie Carson and Stewart Ulrich

5 Disrupting the Norm: Redefining Presidential Nominations in Modern Politics

5.1 Introduction

The U.S. presidential nomination process has undergone significant transformations since the 1960s, shifting from a party-controlled system to a more voter-driven one. Prior to the 1970s reforms, party elites wielded substantial influence in selecting nominees through conventions and caucuses, often prioritizing candidates who aligned with party leadership rather than grassroots preferences. However, the Democratic Party's post-1968 reforms—spurred by the contentious 1968 convention and growing demands for transparency—introduced a greater reliance on state primaries and caucuses to allocate delegates based on voter preferences (Aldrich 1980; Cohen et al. 2008). This shift democratized the process, allowing rank-and-file voters to play a decisive role in candidate selection. These changes were adopted by the Republican Party as well, leading to the modern system where candidates compete in a sequence of state contests. This evolution has increased the importance of campaign strategy, media coverage, and fundraising, while also reducing the ability of party elites to broker nominations, fundamentally altering the balance of power in presidential politics.

In the past two decades, the presidential nomination process has undergone additional and noteworthy changes, influenced by shifts in technology, party dynamics, voter behavior, and campaign finance (Jewitt 2019; Mazo and Dimino 2020; Schatzinger and Martin 2020). This has fundamentally reshaped how presidential candidates are selected, how they campaign and raise money, and how the electorate engages with the presidential nomination process. Understanding these developments provides invaluable insight into the evolving nature of American democracy and the forces that shape it.

One of the most notable changes in the nomination process has been the rise of social media and digital campaigning. Over the past twenty years, the internet and platforms like Twitter, Facebook, YouTube, and TikTok have become central to how candidates communicate with voters. These tools allow candidates to bypass traditional media channels, directly engaging with their base and mobilizing

Jamie Carson, University of Georgia
Stewart Ulrich, Sam Houston State University

https://doi.org/10.1515/9783111591902-005

support (Norrander 2019; Sides et al. 2019). The use of data analytics and micro-targeting has also become prevalent, enabling campaigns to tailor messages to specific demographics with unprecedented precision (Panagopoulos 2016). This digital transformation has democratized the nomination process to some extent, allowing lesser-known candidates to gain visibility and compete with established figures (Azari 2016).

The role of political parties in the nomination process has also evolved. While parties once had considerable control over the selection of candidates (Aldrich 1980; Cohen et al. 2008; Jewitt 2019), this influence has waned due to the rise of primaries and caucuses as the primary means of determining nominees. In recent years, the power of party elites, often referred to as "superdelegates," has diminished, particularly within the Democratic Party, which reduced the number of superdelegates after the contentious primary seasons in 2008 and 2016, when Hillary Clinton battled Barack Obama and Bernie Sanders respectively (Sides et al. 2019). This shift has contributed to a more grassroots-driven selection process, where the preferences of rank-and-file voters hold more sway than the endorsements of party leaders.

Campaign finance has been another area of significant change in the nomination process. The Supreme Court's 2010 decision in *Citizens United v. FEC* profoundly altered the landscape by allowing unlimited spending by corporations, unions, and individuals through Super PACs.[1] This ruling has led to an influx of money into the nomination process, giving wealthy donors and interest groups greater influence over which candidates can sustain their campaigns (Mutch 2014; Schatzinger and Martin 2020). The increasing reliance on Super PACs has also contributed to a more prolonged and competitive primary season, as candidates with substantial financial backing can remain in the race longer, even without broad voter support (Norrander 2019). At the same time, the shift to online fundraising has made it far easier for citizens to donate money to candidates and freed up time that candidates once had to use to devote to this task (Stromer-Galley 2019).

Finally, voter participation and engagement in the nomination process have seen both positive and negative shifts. On one hand, the expansion of early voting and mail-in ballots has made it easier for more people to participate in primaries and caucuses (Herrnson et al. 2019). But concerns about voter suppression and the impact of disinformation have raised questions about the fairness and accessibility of the process (Daniels 2020; Hajnal et al. 2017). Additionally, the polarization of the electorate has led to more ideologically extreme candidates emerging

---

1 558 U.S. 310 (2010).

from the nomination process, as candidates increasingly cater to the more activist and partisan voters who dominate primaries.

We focus on several case studies in this chapter that illustrate how the presidential nomination process has evolved during the past 20 years. Along the way, we examine candidate-specific factors shaping individual elections, along with changes in party dynamics, shifts in campaign finance, and evolving voter behavior. These changes have made the process more accessible in some ways while also introducing new challenges and complexities. As the United States continues to grapple with these developments, the future of the nomination process will likely see further transformations, reflecting the ongoing tensions between democracy, money, and power in American politics.

5.2 Hillary Clinton vs. Barack Obama in the 2008 Democratic Primary

The 2008 Democratic nomination process was one of the most notable and contentious in modern U.S. political history, culminating in Barack Obama's eventual selection as the party's presidential nominee. Hillary Clinton entered the race as the presumed frontrunner, with deep institutional support, widespread name recognition, and the backing of powerful Democratic leaders. However, Obama, a relatively unknown senator from Illinois, captured the imagination of voters with his message of hope, change, and unity, drawing large crowds and mobilizing a broad coalition. His campaign's superior grassroots organizing, innovative use of technology, and focus on smaller donor contributions gave him an edge that was initially underestimated by political elites (Abramson et al. 2009).

Behind the scenes, the 2008 primary season was fraught with controversy. As Clinton and Obama competed in a drawn-out battle for delegates, tensions between their campaigns escalated. Clinton's team, confident in her experience and early lead, was slow to grasp the depth of Obama's appeal and the efficiency of his delegate strategy (Abramson et al. 2009). A key factor was the proportional delegate system in the Democratic primaries, which allowed Obama to consistently win delegates in states where he narrowly lost the popular vote as reflected in Figure 5.1. This technical mastery of the delegate game, engineered by his campaign manager David Plouffe, gave him a significant advantage, even in states where Clinton's support was strong (Arbour 2009).

Superdelegates became a point of major contention during the 2008 nomination process. These unelected party insiders, free to support any presidential candidate, were initially expected to overwhelmingly back Clinton, given her ties to the Democratic establishment. However, as Obama's momentum grew, many superdelegates faced intense pressure to support the candidate who was winning the most pledged delegates and states. This shift in superdelegate support, combined with Obama's ability to secure endorsements from influential party figures, was critical in tilting the balance of power toward his nomination, despite Clinton's continued success in the later primaries (Southwell 2012).

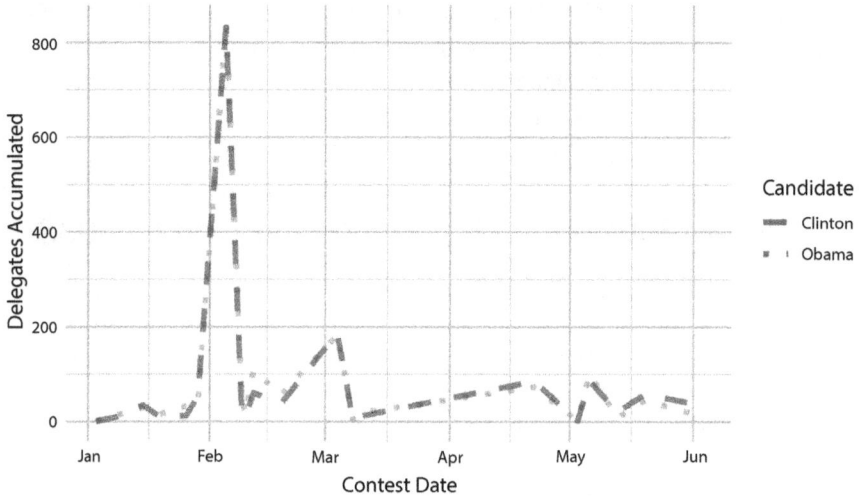

Figure 5.1: Delegate accumulation during the 2008 Democratic Primary Contest.
Source: https://www.thegreenpapers.com/P08/D-PU.phtml

Race and gender also played significant roles in the dynamics of the primary. Clinton's supporters felt she was unfairly treated by the media, often encountering sexist commentary for instance. Meanwhile, Obama faced racist undertones in attacks on his background and identity. The tension between the historic nature of both candidacies heightened divisions within the Democratic electorate. Clinton's campaign expressed frustration over what they saw as bias in the press toward Obama, while Obama's supporters felt they were challenging an entrenched political dynasty. These divisions raised significant concerns about whether the party could unite after such a bruising contest (Huddy and Carey 2009).

The Democratic National Convention in Denver marked the culmination of Obama's rise but not without some initial controversy. Clinton supporters pushed for a full roll call vote at the convention, despite Obama having secured the majority of delegates. A symbolic moment of unity came when Clinton released her delegates and cut short the convention roll call, calling for the convention to approve Obama as the Democratic nominee by acclamation, ending months of bitter rivalry.[2]

Obama's nomination as the first African American candidate for a major political party was historic, but it also reflected a broader shift in Democratic politics, as grassroots energy and outsider campaigns gained newfound power in shaping the party's future (Abramson et al. 2009). Both of Obama's presidential campaigns harnessed the use of new technology, mainly social media and Facebook, as a way to connect with voters and bypass some of the traditional communication methods (Borah 2016). This marked a shift in presidential politics that would change the way presidential candidates campaigned for votes moving forward.

5.3 Mitt Romney and the 2012 Republican Nomination

After the decisive victory in 2008 for the Democratic candidate, Republicans shifted their attention to trying to make Obama a one-term president. The 2012 Republican presidential race highlighted deep divisions within the party. Mitt Romney, a former Massachusetts governor and businessman, faced challenges winning support from the conservative base. Having previously run for the nomination in 2008, Romney was seen as the establishment favorite because of his political experience, financial backing, and moderate stances on issues like health care and the economy. However, many within the Republican Party were skeptical of his conservative credentials, particularly regarding his role in creating Massachusetts' healthcare law, which was seen as a precursor to Obamacare.[3] Despite these concerns, Romney's well-funded and well-organized campaign made him a strong contender from the start (Abramson et al. 2014; Sides and Vavreck 2014).

Throughout the primary season, Romney faced strong competition from a series of more conservative candidates who briefly surged in popularity. Candidates like Rick Perry, Michele Bachmann, Newt Gingrich, and Rick Santorum each posed significant challenges to Romney's frontrunner status. The conservative base, eager for an alternative to what they viewed as Romney's moderate stances on key issues, rallied behind these candidates at different points in the race. How-

---

2 David Rogers and Amie Parnes, "Democrats Nominate Obama by Acclamation," *Politico*, August 28, 2008, https://www.politico.com/story/2008/08/democrats-nominate-obama-by-acclamation-012895

3 Kenneth P. Vogel, "Pawlenty Pans 'Obamneycare'," *Politico*, June 12, 2011, https://www.politico.com/blogs/politico-now/2011/06/pawlenty-pans-obamneycare-036599

ever, each of Romney's challengers faced difficulties sustaining momentum due to gaffes, lack of funding, or organizational weaknesses. This "anyone but Romney" dynamic prolonged the primary battle but ultimately failed to produce a viable alternative to the front-runner (Abramson et al. 2014; Norrander 2013).

One of the key issues that led to Romney's eventual selection was his superior delegate strategy and campaign infrastructure. While his rivals frequently shifted in the polls, Romney's team focused on winning delegates, particularly in states that awarded delegates proportionally, much like Obama did four years earlier. His ability to steadily accumulate delegates, even in states where he did not win the popular vote, kept him in the lead throughout the primary season. Romney's financial advantage also allowed him to far outspend his rivals in key battlegrounds, helping to solidify his standing in the race. This methodical approach, combined with his discipline on the campaign trail, set him apart from his more erratic competitors (Johnson 2014; Sides and Vavreck 2014).

Despite his growing delegate count, Romney struggled to connect with the party's conservative wing, particularly evangelical voters and the Tea Party movement, both of whom viewed him as too moderate. His Mormon faith also became an issue for some evangelical Christians, adding another layer of complexity to his candidacy. As a result, Romney's path to the nomination was filled with skepticism and resistance from a significant portion of the GOP base. This dissatisfaction fueled the rise of Rick Santorum, who emerged as Romney's main competitor after early primary and caucus victories in more conservative-leaning states like Iowa and South Carolina. However, Santorum's campaign ultimately faltered due to a lack of resources and Romney's dominant organization (Abramson et al. 2014; Sides and Vavreck 2014).

The Republican National Convention in Tampa not only marked Romney's official nomination but also underscored divisions within the party. While most of the party's leadership and prominent figures rallied around Romney, some conservative activists remained lukewarm, still harboring doubts about his commitment to their values. In an effort to unite the party, Romney selected Congressman Paul Ryan, a fiscal conservative and Tea Party favorite, as his running mate. This move was seen as an attempt to solidify support among the conservative base, particularly on issues like the budget and entitlement reform (Krumel and Enami 2017).

Romney's eventual nomination represented the triumph of the party's establishment wing while highlighting tensions between moderate and conservative factions that would continue to shape the GOP in the years to come (Abramson et al. 2014; Sides and Vavreck 2014). Romney was able to keep the grassroots wing of the party at bay, and his nomination was a win for the establishment party leaders. But his 2012 nomination opened a rift that ultimately would be exploited by Donald Trump.

5.4 Hillary Clinton vs. Bernie Sanders in 2016

After winning the White House for two consecutive elections with Obama, Democrats wondered who could carry Obama's legacy into another term. Vice President Joe Biden was seen as one possibility, as he had already run for president two times previously, but the death of his son Beau to cancer in 2015 put a stop to his plans. Hillary Clinton stepped up and was seen as the likely candidate. Her victory over Bernie Sanders in the 2016 Democratic nomination for president marked another significant moment in the evolution of the presidential nomination system. This contest highlighted the tension between the party establishment and grassroots movements, as well as the changing dynamics of voter engagement, fundraising, and the role of superdelegates within the Democratic Party. Clinton's win underscored the challenges and complexities of navigating a nomination process increasingly influenced by both traditional party mechanisms and insurgent populist movements (Aldrich et al. 2019; Sides et al. 2019).

One of the most notable aspects of Clinton's victory was the stark contrast between her campaign and Sanders' grassroots movement. Sanders energized a broad base of younger, more progressive voters with his message of economic equality and social justice, challenging the party establishment's preference for a more moderate candidate like Clinton. This represented a significant shift in the Democratic nomination process, as it revealed deep divisions within the party between its progressive and centrist wings. Clinton's ability to secure the nomination despite this insurgency not only highlighted the enduring influence of the party establishment but also exposed the growing power of grassroots movements in shaping the party's future (Sides et al. 2019).

Clinton's victory also demonstrated the changing nature of campaign finance within the nomination process. While Sanders relied heavily on small-dollar donations from a large number of individual supporters, Clinton benefited from more traditional fundraising methods, including contributions from wealthy donors and political action committees (PACs). This dichotomy highlighted the evolving strategies candidates must employ to succeed in the nomination process. Sanders' fundraising success with small donors challenged the conventional wisdom that large-scale fundraising was essential for securing a nomination, signaling a potential shift in how future campaigns might be financed and managed (Aldrich et al. 2018).

Another significant factor in Clinton's win was the role of superdelegates— party officials and leaders who are free to support any candidate regardless of primary or caucus results—which had been a factor eight years earlier in the primary race against Obama. Throughout the 2016 primary season, Clinton secured the overwhelming majority of superdelegates, which bolstered her position as the frontrunner and ultimately helped her secure the nomination. This reliance on superdelegates sparked controversy and debate within the party, as many Sanders supporters viewed the system as undemocratic and favoring the establishment candidate. The controversy surrounding superdelegates in 2016 led to reforms within the Democratic Party, reducing their influence in future nomination processes, representing a significant change in how the party selects its candidates (Sides et al. 2019).

Ultimately, Clinton's win over Bernie Sanders in the 2016 Democratic nomination for president represented a change in the nomination system by highlighting the growing influence of grassroots movements, the evolving landscape of campaign finance, and the controversial role of superdelegates. While Clinton's victory reaffirmed the power of the party establishment, it also exposed deep divisions within the Democratic Party and set the stage for future reforms in the nomination process. The 2016 contest served as a turning point in how the Democratic Party navigated the competing interests of its diverse electorate and managed the challenges of modern campaigning.

5.5 Donald Trump in 2016: An Unlikely Republican Nominee

In 2016, Republicans saw an opportunity to reclaim the presidency after Obama's two terms, hoping the trend of party turnover in the White House would hold. The nomination of Donald Trump that year was one of the most surprising and divisive moments in the party's history. A real estate mogul and television personality with no political experience, Trump entered the race as a long-shot candidate in a crowded field of established Republican politicians. Although initially dismissed as a fringe contender, his unconventional campaign style quickly resonated with the GOP base, tapping into a growing wave of populist sentiment. His bold rhetoric on immigration, trade, and national security, along with his brash, anti-establishment persona, resonated with many disillusioned voters. This early surge caught party elites off guard, as they underestimated Trump's ability to tap into the frustration felt by large segments of the Republican electorate (Jewitt 2016; Sides et al. 2019).

Throughout the primary season, Donald Trump's rise created deep divisions within the Republican Party. Many party leaders, including influential figures like Jeb Bush and Mitt Romney, openly opposed his candidacy, viewing him as a threat to the GOP's traditional values and long-term viability. Despite this opposition, Trump's appeal to white working-class voters, his ability to dominate media coverage, and his outsider status made him increasingly difficult to stop. His opponents failed to coalesce around a single alternative, with candidates like Ted Cruz, Marco Rubio, and John Kasich each vying to be the primary anti-Trump candidate. This fragmentation, reflected in Figure 5.2, allowed Trump to rack up primary wins despite consistently polling below 50 percent in many states (Byers and Carson 2017).

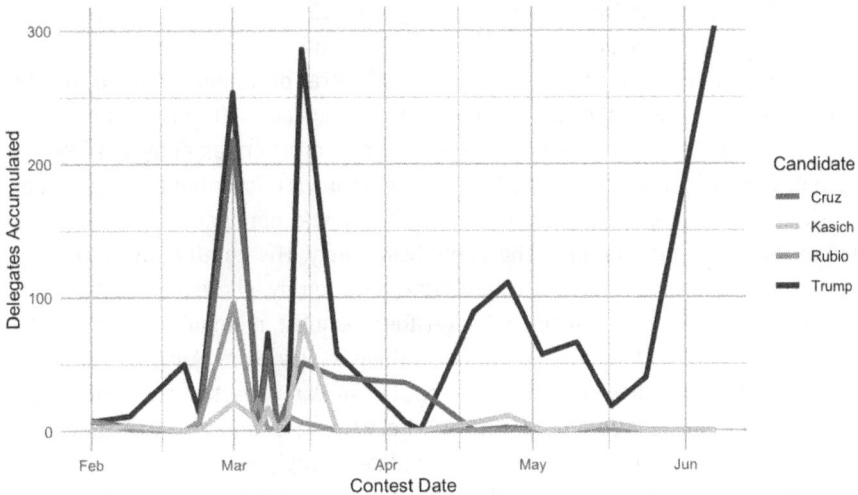

Figure 5.2: Delegate accumulation during the 2016 Republican Primary Contest.
Source: https://www.thegreenpapers.com/P16/

The Republican National Committee (RNC) faced mounting challenges as Trump's momentum grew. Party leaders were initially reluctant to embrace his candidacy, concerned about his lack of conservative credentials, controversial statements, and unpredictable behavior. There were discussions among anti-Trump Republicans of a contested convention, where delegates could potentially block his nomination. However, as Trump continued to win primaries and accumulate delegates, the possibility of such a scenario diminished. The "Never Trump" movement, composed of conservatives deeply opposed to his nomination, gained media attention but ultimately failed to stop his rise. By the time Trump secured enough delegates for the nomination, the RNC had little choice but to begin uniting behind him (Aldrich et al. 2019).

A key factor in Trump's success was his ability to reshape the political landscape through his media dominance. Unlike traditional candidates who relied on paid advertising and careful messaging, Trump's bombastic style and provocative statements consistently generated free media coverage.[4] His use of social media, especially Twitter, allowed him to bypass traditional gatekeepers and speak directly to voters. This relentless media presence made it difficult for his rivals to compete, as they struggled to capture attention and counter his populist message. Trump's ability to dominate the news cycle, coupled with his sharp attacks on opponents, helped him secure the Republican nomination despite lacking widespread support within the party's leadership (Azari 2016).

The Republican National Convention in Cleveland cemented Trump's takeover of the GOP, though not without controversy. Several prominent Republicans, including past nominees like Mitt Romney and John McCain, refused to attend or endorse Trump. There were also public displays of division, as delegates loyal to Trump's primary rivals attempted to force a floor vote to unbind delegates and block his nomination. Despite these efforts, Trump was nominated, marking a dramatic shift in the direction of the Republican Party. His nomination reflected a broader revolt against the party establishment, driven by a base increasingly skeptical of traditional conservatism and eager for a populist, nationalist platform. This shift would continue to define the GOP over the next few years (Aldrich et al. 2019).

Trump's rise to power within the Republican Party marked the culmination of a shift that began years before the 2016 election. He demonstrated that party leaders had limited ability to block a candidate strongly favored by the base. By leveraging social media, particularly Twitter, Trump communicated directly with his supporters, strengthening his connection with them and paving the way to his nomination (Stolee and Caton 2018).

5.6 Joe Biden Wins the 2020 Democratic Nomination

Trump's 2016 win shocked Democrats, who were assured of Clinton's lead in the polls and ability to beat the unconventional Republican candidate. The party vowed to beat Trump at the next election and embarked on a lengthy primary process that produced a large field of candidates. Joe Biden's victory in the 2020 Democratic nomination for president represented a significant shift in the presidential nomination process, particularly in how the party navigated its internal

---

4 Nicholas Confessore and Karen Yourish, "$2 Billion Worth of Free Media for Donald Trump," *The New York Times*, March 16, 2016, https://www.nytimes.com/2016/03/16/upshot/measuring-donald-trumps-mammoth-advantage-in-free-media.html

divisions, responded to an evolving electorate, and adapted to exceptional circumstances. Biden's success highlighted the party's move towards unity in the face of polarization, the strategic importance of coalition-building, and the critical role of endorsements and electability in securing the nomination (Trish and Menner 2021).

One of the most notable changes exemplified by Biden's win was the Democratic Party's response to its divisions. Following the contentious 2016 primary between Hillary Clinton and Bernie Sanders, the party faced a potential repeat of deep ideological rifts. However, there was a concerted effort among Democratic leaders and voters in 2020 to rally early around a candidate who could unify the party and appeal to a broad spectrum of the electorate. Biden emerged as the consensus candidate, seen as a moderate choice who could bridge the gap between the party's progressive and centrist wings. His nomination reflected a strategic shift toward prioritizing party unity over ideological purity, signaling a new approach in the face of rising polarization (Best and Ladewig 2024).

Biden's nomination also underscored the importance of coalition-building within the Democratic Party. Unlike previous candidates who relied heavily on a single demographic or ideological base, Biden's campaign successfully garnered support from a diverse coalition of voters, including African Americans, suburban voters, and older Democrats. His decisive victory in South Carolina, powered by overwhelming support from Black voters, proved pivotal in securing the nomination and underscored the critical role that key constituencies play in the nomination process. Biden's ability to build and maintain this broad coalition highlighted a shift in how candidates appeal to the party's increasingly diverse electorate (Aldrich et al. 2022).

Endorsements and perceptions of electability played a particularly crucial role in Biden's nomination, marking another significant change in the process. In the lead-up to Super Tuesday, Biden received a wave of high-profile endorsements from former rivals and party leaders, which helped consolidate support and create a sense of momentum. This strategic rallying around Biden was driven by the belief that he was the candidate most likely to defeat Trump in the general election. The emphasis on electability, rather than ideological alignment or policies, signaled a shift in the party's priorities, reflecting a pragmatic approach to the nomination process in an era of intense partisan competition (Hitefield and Hood 2021).

In sum, Joe Biden's win in the 2020 Democratic nomination for president represented a significant change in nomination politics by highlighting the importance of party unity, coalition-building, and the strategic use of endorsements and electability. His nomination demonstrated how the Democratic Party could adapt to internal divisions and the demands of an evolving electorate, emphasizing a pragmatic approach in a highly polarized environment. Biden's success in navigating these dynamics reshaped the nomination process, setting a new precedent for how future candidates may seek to secure their party's nomination (Aldrich et al. 2022).

5.7 Three Successive Elections with Donald Trump as the Republican Nominee

Donald Trump's selection as the Republican nominee for president in 2016 and again in 2024 profoundly challenged the traditional system of selecting presidential candidates in the United States (whereas his nomination in 2020 represented the norm of renomination of a sitting president). His candidacy defied conventional political norms, reshaping the Republican Party and altering the broader landscape of American politics. Trump's rise highlighted shifts in voter behavior, the role of media, the weakening of party elites' influence, and the growing appeal of populism within the Republican electorate (Carson et al. 2026).

Trump's renomination by his party in 2024 is notable considering his remarkable political comeback. For a sitting president to lose reelection and go on to be renominated by the party in the next election cycle is unprecedented in the modern era. The two previous presidents who lost reelection, Jimmy Carter and George H.W. Bush, quickly and quietly exited the political arena when they left office. Gerald Ford briefly flirted with the idea of a comeback in 1980 but did not go through with it. Trump's third nomination shows his hold on, and support among, the party faithful was strong despite multiple candidates running in the 2024 primary. The subsequent 2024 general election win was also historic as it makes Trump the first president since Grover Cleveland in 1892 to win two nonconsecutive presidential terms.

One of the most significant ways Trump's candidacy challenged the existing system was through his rejection of traditional political qualifications, which had generally been seen as an important predictor of presidential performance in office (Simon and Uscinski 2012). His success demonstrated a shift in the electorate's priorities, where voters were increasingly drawn to outsiders who positioned themselves as disruptors of the status quo. This break from tradition signaled a weakening of the conventional criteria for presidential candidates and opened the door for non-traditional figures to seek the highest office (Aldrich et al. 2019).

Trump's use of social media, particularly Twitter and Truth Social, also disrupted the traditional nomination process. This strategy not only allowed him to dominate the news cycle but also to mobilize a large and highly engaged voter base. His unfiltered and often controversial messages resonated with many voters who felt alienated by the mainstream media and political establishment. This shift in how candidates engage with the public upended the conventional media strategies of presidential campaigns and underscored the growing importance of digital platforms in modern politics (Merry 2022).

The weakening of the influence of party elites and traditional gatekeepers was another key aspect of Trump's challenge to the nomination process. Historically, party leaders and key donors played a crucial role in vetting and supporting candidates who aligned with their vision for the party. However, Trump's candidacy in 2016 caught many party elites off guard, as he was able to win the nomination despite a lack of initial support from the Republican establishment. His ability to rally a broad base of voters without relying on elite endorsements demonstrated a shift toward a more populist and grassroots-driven process, where the power of party leaders was significantly diminished (Sides et al. 2019).

Trump's embrace of populism and his appeal to a disaffected segment of the electorate further challenged the existing system. His rhetoric, which often centered on themes of nationalism, anti-immigration, and skepticism of globalism, resonated with voters who felt left behind by economic and cultural changes (Howell and Moe 2020). This populist appeal allowed Trump to build a loyal and fervent base that propelled him to the nomination in 2016 and 2024, even in the face of significant opposition from within his own party. This shift toward populism marked a departure from the more ideologically driven campaigns of previous Republican candidates and reshaped the party's platform and priorities.

In short, Donald Trump's selection as the Republican nominee for president in 2016 and again in 2024 challenged the existing system of selecting presidential candidates by breaking away from traditional qualifications, transforming media engagement strategies, weakening the influence of party elites, and embracing a populist message. His candidacies have had a lasting impact on the Republican Party and American politics, especially following his decisive win in 2024, redefining what it means to be a viable presidential candidate and signaling a shift toward a more populist and outsider-driven political landscape. As politics continues to evolve, Trump's legacy in the nomination process will likely influence how future candidates approach their campaigns and how parties select their leaders (Carson et al. 2026).

5.8 Joe Biden, Kamala Harris, and the 2024 Democratic Nomination

Joe Biden began 2024 committed to running for reelection, despite increasing concerns about his ability to wage a presidential campaign. In mid-July, President Joe Biden made the historic decision to withdraw from the 2024 presidential race following his disastrous debate performance against Donald Trump three weeks earlier. His announcement came amidst growing concerns about his age and ability to continue serving effectively, especially following a series of public missteps.[5] Despite previous efforts to reinforce his candidacy with rallies and interviews over the ensuing weeks, a large portion of Democratic voters, along with a significant majority of independents, expressed doubts about his viability as the nominee. This pressure was further intensified by key Democratic donors and party leaders such as former President Barack Obama and former Speaker of the House Nancy Pelosi pressing for a change at the top of the ticket (Carson et al. 2026).

Biden's eventual decision was rooted in a recognition that continuing his candidacy might harm the Democratic Party's chances of defeating Donald Trump in the general election. Polls revealed increasing dissatisfaction among Democrats, and Biden faced mounting calls to step aside. In his formal announcement, Biden emphasized his pride in the achievements of his administration but noted that stepping down was in the best interest of the nation and the party. Shortly after his withdrawal, Biden fully endorsed Vice President Kamala Harris to succeed him as the Democratic nominee. He highlighted her as an extraordinary partner in his administration and reaffirmed that selecting her as his running mate in 2020 had been one of his best decisions. Biden urged the party to unite behind Harris, framing her candidacy as essential to defeating Donald Trump and continuing their shared policy goals.[6]

Harris, already serving as vice president, became the presumptive Democratic nominee following Biden's endorsement, and the party quickly pivoted to build momentum around her candidacy. This move sought to consolidate Democratic support, stave off potential challenges within the party, and project a unified front heading into the general election. Kamala Harris' selection as the Dem-

5 Toluse Olorunnipa and Patrick Svitek, "Biden Makes Stunning Decision to Pull Out of 2024 Race," *The Washington Post*, July 21, 2024, https://www.washingtonpost.com/politics/2024/07/21/joe-biden-drops-out/

6 Bill Barrow, "Joe Biden Wants to Pass the Baton to Kamala Harris. Here's How that Might Work," *AP News*, July 21, 2024, https://apnews.com/article/biden-harris-election-2024-democrats-withdrawal-trump-c8b82fa105953e8f485c769580f7da49

ocratic nominee in 2024 marked a significant departure from traditional methods of selecting presidential candidates, challenging established norms and reshaping the political landscape. Her nomination was influenced by factors such as her historic candidacy, evolving party dynamics, and the role of decision-making within the Democratic Party. These elements combined to create a candidacy that defied conventional expectations and highlighted the changing nature of the American political system (Carson et al. 2026).

One of the most notable ways Harris' selection challenged the existing system was through the emphasis on identity politics and the representation of diverse communities. As the first woman of color, and the first person of both South Asian and African American descent to be nominated for president by a major party, Harris' candidacy underscored the growing importance of demographic representation in the Democratic Party. Her nomination reflected a broader shift within the party toward embracing candidates who can appeal to and represent its increasingly diverse electorate. This focus on identity and representation challenged the traditional model, which often favored candidates with more conventional backgrounds and appeal to a broader, but less diverse, base (Aldrich et al. 2022).

Harris' path to the nomination also highlighted the evolving role of party elites and the influence of high-level endorsements in the selection process. Unlike previous candidates who emerged from competitive primary battles, Harris benefited significantly from the support of party leaders and key endorsements early in the process. This demonstrated a shift away from the more grassroots-driven, voter-centered approach that has characterized recent Democratic primaries. Instead, her nomination underscored the power of elite decision-making within the party, where influential figures can rally around a candidate they believe best represents the party's future and has the best chance of winning the general election.[7]

Finally, Harris' nomination challenged the traditional metrics of electability that have historically dominated the selection process. Despite facing criticism over her past role as a prosecutor and questions about her ability to win over certain voter demographics, Harris' selection indicated a broader reevaluation of what constitutes a "viable" candidate. The Democratic Party's decision to nominate her suggested a willingness to prioritize issues of representation, identity, and progressive values over conventional wisdom about electability, signaling a new direction for the party in an increasingly polarized political environment.

---

7 Melissa Quinn et al., "Kamala Harris Wins Enough Delegate Support for Democratic Presidential Nomination After Biden Drops Out," *CBS News*, July 23, 2024, https://www.cbsnews.com/live-updates/biden-drops-out-2024-presidential-race/

With her eventual defeat in the 2024 election, Democratic elites will likely be revisiting these same issues as they prepare for the 2028 presidential cycle.[8]

In sum, Kamala Harris' eventual selection as the Democratic nominee for president in 2024 challenged the existing system of selecting presidential candidates by emphasizing identity politics, shifting the balance of power toward party elites, and redefining traditional notions of electability. Her candidacy represented a significant moment in American politics, reflecting the ongoing evolution of the Democratic Party and the changing dynamics of the nomination process. As the political landscape continues to evolve, especially considering her defeat to Donald Trump in the 2024 election, Harris' nomination may serve as a bellwether for future candidates and the strategies they employ to secure their party's nomination.

One notable change during the 2024 Democratic primaries that did not have much effect due to the lack of credible challengers to President Biden was the DNC voting to change the primary calendar. After the disastrous 2020 Iowa caucuses, which due to a malfunction with a smartphone app led to a significant delay in results being released, and the Black Lives Matter protests in the wake of George Floyd's murder in 2020, it was determined that more diverse states should be first in the primary calendar. South Carolina was moved to the front, followed by Nevada, New Hampshire, Georgia, and then Michigan.[9] While this did not have much bearing on the 2024 race, it is likely to be a major factor in the 2028 Democratic primary.

5.9 The Modern Nomination Process

The presidential nomination contests discussed in this chapter share a common theme: the diminishing influence of parties and the rise of grassroots power. Barack Obama, a relatively unknown state senator just four years before his presidential run, defied party expectations by securing the Democratic nomination in 2008, despite early predictions favoring Hillary Clinton. Similarly, Mitt Romney's struggles in 2012 to prove his conservative credentials highlighted the growing difficulty establishment figures face in winning over skeptical party bases. Donald

---

8 Emily Rose Bennett and Angelina Katsanis, "11 Democratic Thinkers on What the Party Needs Right Now," *Politico*, November 7, 2024, https://www.politico.com/news/magazine/2024/11/07/10-democratic-thinkers-on-what-the-party-needs-right-now-00187993

9 Brittany Shepherd, "Democrats Approve New Primary Calendar for 2024," *ABC News*, February 4, 2023, https://abcnews.go.com/US/democrats-approve-new-primary-calendar-2024/story?id=96894345

Trump's victory in 2016 marked the peak of this trend, demonstrating how an outsider could capitalize on these shifting dynamics. On the Democratic side, Bernie Sanders' strong performance in 2016 revealed a significant faction of the party resistant to Clinton's establishment candidacy, further emphasizing the growing influence of outsiders.

One major factor driving this evolution is the changing nature of campaign fundraising. The rise of the internet and social media has empowered candidates to rely on small-dollar donations from grassroots supporters rather than traditional big-money donors. In the past, candidates who lacked establishment support often struggled to sustain their campaigns due to funding shortages. Now, grassroots funding enables these candidates to remain competitive much longer, even when party elites oppose them. This shift has opened the door for unconventional candidates to emerge and secure major party nominations. Candidates advocating policies outside the preferences of party elites are no longer immediately sidelined, and their campaigns can gain traction in ways that would have been nearly impossible two decades ago.

As a result of these changes, the political landscape has become more unpredictable, with outsiders frequently breaking through and reshaping party dynamics. Predicting future party nominees has become increasingly difficult in this new era of decentralized power. The rise of grassroots influence and outsider candidates signals a departure from the more predictable patterns of the past, ensuring that the paths to leadership will remain dynamic and potentially surprising.

5.10 Conclusion

Over the past 20 years, the politics underlying the presidential nomination process has shifted significantly, reflecting deeper changes in American political culture and party dynamics. One of the most notable transformations is the growing influence of primary voters and grassroots activists, which has fundamentally altered how candidates position themselves and campaign during the primaries (Steger 2016). Prior to the early 2000s, party elites and influential donors had a much stronger hand in shaping the outcome of the primaries through endorsements and fundraising. However, in more recent election cycles, particularly since the rise of social media, candidates have been able to appeal directly to voters, bypassing traditional party gatekeepers. This shift has democratized the process, empowering a broader range of voices, but has also contributed to increased polarization within both parties, as candidates must now cater to more ideologically motivated voters in the primaries.

Another major change is the rise of outsider candidates, who have been able to challenge and often defeat establishment figures in both major parties. The 2016 election stands as a clear example, with Donald Trump winning the Republican nomination despite lacking traditional political experience and support from party elites. On the Democratic side, Bernie Sanders mounted unexpectedly strong challenges in 2016 and 2020 by tapping into discontent among progressive voters. These developments indicate that the traditional model of working through party institutions, building consensus, and securing key endorsements is no longer the sole pathway to securing a nomination.

Furthermore, the calendar and rules surrounding the nomination process have evolved in ways that have impacted the strategies of candidates. The front-loading of primaries—where key states like Iowa, New Hampshire, South Carolina, and Nevada used to have disproportionate influence early in the race—forces candidates to build momentum quickly or risk losing viability. With the changes Democrats made to the primary calendar in 2024, it is yet unclear how this will affect future nominations for president. At the same time, changes in delegate allocation rules, such as the increased use of proportional representation, have prolonged the primary process and made it more difficult for any one candidate to lock up the nomination early. These developments have introduced new strategic complexities, requiring candidates to build broader coalitions across different states and regions to secure victory.

In conclusion, the politics of the presidential nomination process over the past two decades has been shaped by a combination of technological advancements, the erosion of elite control, and shifts in the rules governing the primaries. While these changes have made the process more open and accessible to a wider range of candidates, they have also contributed to deeper polarization and unpredictability in both major parties. As American politics continues to evolve, the nomination process is likely to face further changes, reflecting the ongoing tension between democratic participation and party cohesion.

Discussion Questions

1 How has the diminishing influence of party elites affected the type of candidates who can successfully secure presidential nominations?
2 What role has social media played in empowering grassroots movements and small-dollar donors in the nomination process?
3 In what ways has the rise of outsider candidates like Donald Trump and Bernie Sanders reshaped the dynamics of the modern nomination process?

4 How might recent changes to the Democratic primary calendar, such as adjustments in 2024, influence the future of presidential nominations in both parties?
5 How does the unpredictability of the modern nomination process challenge traditional methods of predicting political outcomes and party cohesion?

References

Abramson, Paul R., John H. Aldrich, and David W. Rohde. 2009. *Change and Continuity in the 2008 Elections*. CQ Press.

Abramson, Paul R., John H. Aldrich, Brad T. Gomez, and David W. Rohde. 2014. *Change and Continuity in the 2012 Elections*. CQ Press.

Abramson, Paul R., John H. Aldrich, Brad T. Gomez, and David W. Rohde. 2016. *Change and Continuity in the 2012 and 2014 Elections*. CQ Press.

Aldrich, John H. 1980. *Before the Convention: Strategies and Choices in Presidential Nomination Campaigns*. University of Chicago Press.

Aldrich, John H., Jamie L. Carson, Brad T. Gomez, and David W. Rohde. 2019. *Change and Continuity in the 2016 Elections*. CQ Press/Sage.

Aldrich, John H., Jamie L. Carson, Brad T. Gomez, and Jennifer L. Merolla. 2022. *Change and Continuity in the 2020 Elections*. Rowman & Littlefield.

Arbour, Brian. 2009. "Even Closer, Even Longer: What if the 2008 Democratic Primary Used Republican Rules?" *The Forum* 7 (2). https://doi.org/10.2202/1540-8884.1301.

Azari, Julia R. 2016. "How the News Media Helped to Nominate Trump." *Political Communication* 33 (4): 677–80. https://doi.org/10.1080/10584609.2016.1224417.

Best, Samuel J., and Jeffrey W. Ladewig. 2024. *Toppling Trump: How Party Elites Steered Joe Biden to the Democratic Nomination and Victory in the 2020 Presidential Election*. Springer.

Borah, Porismita. 2016. "Political Facebook Use: Campaign Strategies Used in 2008 and 2012 Presidential Elections." *Journal of Information Technology & Politics* 13 (4): 326–38.

Byers, Jason, and Jamie Carson. 2017. "What's Rules Got to Do with It? Parties, Reform, and Selection in the Presidential Nomination Process." In *Changing How America Votes*, edited by Todd Donavan, 142–55. Rowman & Littlefield.

Carson, Jamie L., Brad T. Gomez, and Jennifer L. Merolla. 2026. *Change and Continuity in American Elections: 2024 Edition*. Bloomsbury, Forthcoming.

Cohen, Marty, David Karol, Hans Noel, and John Zaller. 2008. *The Party Decides: Presidential Nominations Before and After Reform*. University of Chicago Press.

Daniels, Gilda R. 2020. *Uncounted: The Crisis of Voter Suppression in the United States*. New York University Press.

Hajnal, Zoltan, Nazita Lajevardi, and Lindsay Nielson. 2017. "Voter Identification Laws and the Suppression of Minority Votes." *Journal of Politics* 79 (2): 363–79.

Herrnson, Paul S., Michael J. Hanmer, and Ho Youn Koh. 2019. "Mobilization Around New Convenience Voting Methods: A Field Experiment to Encourage Voting by Mail with a Downloadable Ballot and Early Voting." *Political Behavior* 41 (4): 871–95.

Hitefield, Aaron A., and M.V. Hood, III. 2021. "The 2020 Presidential Nomination Process." In *The 2020 Presidential Election in the South*, edited by Scott E. Buchanan and Branwell Dubose Kapeluck, Lexington Books.

Howell, William G., and Terry M. Moe. 2020. *Presidents, Populism, and the Crisis of Democracy*. University of Chicago Press.

Huddy, Leonie, and Tony E. Carey J. 2009. "Group Politics Redux: Race and Gender in the 2008 Democratic Presidential Primaries." *Politics & Gender* 5 (1): 81–96.

Jewitt, Caitlin E. 2019. *The Primary Rules: Parties, Voters, and Presidential Nominations*. AUniversity of Michigan Press.

Johnson, Dennis W. 2014. *Campaigning for President 2012: Strategy and Tactics*. Routledge.

Krumel, Thomas P. Jr., and Ali Enami. 2017. "Balancing the Ticket While Appealing to the Base: The Game Theory Behind Mitt Romney's Selection of Paul Ryan as His Presidential Running Mate." *Party Politics* 23 (5): 498–506.

Mazo, Eugene D., and Michael R. Dimino. 2020. *The Best Candidate: Presidential Nomination in Polarized Times*. Cambridge University Press.

Merry, Melissa K. 2022. "Trump's Tweets as Policy Narratives: Constructing the Immigration Issue via Social Media." *Politics & Policy* 50 (4): 752–72.

Mutch, Robert E. 2014. *Buying the Vote: A History of Campaign Finance Reform*. Oxford University Press.

Norrander, Barbara. 2013. *Fighting Off Challengers: The 2012 Nomination of Mitt Romney*. Routledge.

Norrander, Barbara. 2019. *The Imperfect Primary: Oddities, Biases, and Strengths of U.S. Presidential Nomination Politics*. Routledge.

Panagopoulos, Costas. 2016. "All About That Base: Changing Campaign Strategies in U.S. Presidential Elections." *Party Politics* 22 (2): 179–90.

Schatzinger, Henrik M., and Steven E. Martin. 2020. *Game Changers: How Dark Money and Super PACs are Transforming U.S. Campaigns*. Rowman & Littlefield.

Sides, John, and Lynn Vavreck. 2014. *The Gamble: Choice and Chance in the 2012 Presidential Elections*. Princeton University Press.

Sides, John, Michael Tesler, and Lynn Vavreck. 2019. *Identity Crisis: The 2016 Campaign and the Battle for the Meaning of America*. Princeton University Press.

Simon, Arthur M., and Joseph E. Uscinski. 2012. "Prior Experience Predicts Presidential Performance." *Presidential Studies Quarterly* 42 (3): 514–48.

Southwell, Priscilla L. 2012. "A Backroom Without the Smoke? Superdelegates and the 2008 Democratic Nomination Process." *Party Politics* 18 (2): 267–83.

Steger, Wayne P. 2016. "Conditional Arbiters: The Limits of Political Party Influence in Presidential Nominations." *PS* 49 (4): 709–15.

Stolee, Galen, and Steve Caton. 2018. "Twitter, Trump, and the Base: A Shift to a New Form of Presidential Talk?" *Signs and Society* 6 (1): 147–65.

Stromer-Galley, Jennifer. 2019. *Presidential Campaigning in the Internet Age*. Oxford University Press.

Trish, Barbara, and William Menner. 2021. *Inside the Bubble: Campaigns, Caucuses, and the Future of the Presidential Nomination Process*. Routledge.

Gbemende Johnson, Yao Yao and Hannah Lee

6 Peeking Behind the Curtain: The Federal Bureaucracy, Transparency, and Judicial Oversight

6.1 Introduction

6.1.1 The Trump Administration and Transparency

From refusing to voluntarily release White House visitor logs (Kennedy 2017) to alleged overuse of the Freedom of Information Act (FOIA) document redactions process (Evers 2020), the first Trump Administration faced repeated criticism over its implementation and facilitation of transparency. Members of the administration apparently requested government officials curtail FOIA requests by refraining from email communications (Leopold 2018) and purposefully labeled communications and documentation as "Congressional Records" to exempt documents from FOIA (Georgantopoulos 2017). Early in Trump's first term, CBS News reported "People who asked for records under the Freedom of Information Act received censored files or nothing in 78 percent of 823,222 requests, a record over the past decade" (CBS News 2018). In that same report, CBS News found that in nearly one-third of cases, the government reversed its decision to withhold records when requesters appealed (CBS News 2018).

Similarly, various media groups and transparency organizations were critical of the Trump Administration's employment of redactions in response to records requests. For example, The Center for Public Integrity argued that it received nearly "completely redacted" documents concerning President Trump's order to halt aid to Ukraine from the Department of Defense (Smith 2019). The Center for Public Integrity argued that despite agency claims that the documents fell under "deliberative process" exemptions, much of the material was potentially "simply factual" (Smith 2019), which would not be protected by the deliberative process privilege—a form of executive privilege (Johnson 2019).

Additionally, actors in the Trump Administration were accused of improper preservation (or in some instances purposeful destruction) of presidential and agency records (Karni 2018; Johnson and George 2023). For example, White House aides were accused of using encrypted apps that would delete messages once read (Gerstein 2018). Furthermore, multiple Freedom of Information Act requests

Gbemende Johnson, Yao Yao, Hannah Lee, University of Georgia

https://doi.org/10.1515/9783111591902-006

by transparency advocacy group American Oversight revealed that several senior government officials wiped their cell phone records around the end of their tenures, potentially in violation of retention requirements established by the Federal Records Act (Wild et al. 2022). After these reports were made public, the Department of Homeland Security (DHS) and the Department of Defense (DOD) released a memo ". . . reminding [senior leaders] to retain [a] federal record, including text messages" (Wild et al. 2022, n.p.).

6.1.2 The Biden and Obama Administrations' Transparency Missteps

While there was a bright spotlight on transparency during the Trump Presidency, presidential administrations of both parties have faced tough criticism regarding their implementation of federal transparency policy and direct actions taken by high-profile officials. For example, the National Institutes of Health (NIH) faced congressional scrutiny in response to reports that officials attempted to purposely evade potential FOIA requests. Specifically, the House Select Subcommittee on the Coronavirus Pandemic subpoenaed emails of NIH officials including Dr. David Morens, NIH scientist and previous aid to Dr. Anthony Fauci (former White House Chief Medical Advisor to the President). In email correspondence occurring during the Biden Administration, Dr. Morens apparently stated: "I learned from our FOIA lady here how to make emails disappears after I am foia'd [sic] but before the search starts, so I think we are all safe" (Mueller 2024, n.p.). Another email from Morens noted, "The best way to avoid FOIA hassles is to delete all emails when you learn a subject is getting sensitive" (Finley 2024, n.p.). The scandal regarding Morens' communication became ammunition for Republicans critical of the NIH and its handling of the COVID-19 government response.

Additionally, the Obama Administration's Department of Homeland Security, Department of Justice, and Department of State each faced high-profile scandals over records preservation practices (Lee and Jalonick 2019; Wagner 2018) and agency willingness to share requested documents with Congress (Johnson 2019). Specifically, then-Attorney General Eric Holder's refusal to share documents related to an Alcohol, Tobacco, and Firearm (ATF) operation resulted in his being held in contempt by Congress (Peralta 2012).

While most would note that these incidents across administrations are harmful for achieving effective government transparency, it is important to acknowledge that attacks on executive branch transparency are often wielded as a partisan tool by Republicans and Democrats alike. Specifically, out-party congressional representatives and allies will loudly criticize the incumbent administration for a lack of forthrightness with the public (and other branches of government). However, these critics often become much less vocal when concerns are raised about the transparency practices of party-congruent presidential administrations.

6.1.3 Transparency Troubles

This chapter discusses the federal bureaucracy with a focus on transparency. Federal agencies play a central role in American government. The size of the federal administrative state has grown substantially since the Great Depression, arguably in line with the expectations of the public. Currently, the federal bureaucracy is comprised of hundreds of agencies and departments, and millions of civilian employees. Agencies make rules managing workplace safety and environmental standards, and adjudicate disputes involving election processes, immigration decisions, and social security benefits. These responsibilities are important in their own right; however, the public's awareness of these activities facilitated by transparency laws is essential in terms of promoting proper implementation of congressional policy, fiscal responsibilities in the disbursement of government funds, and accountability in the case of violations of legal and ethical standards. Despite these benefits of greater transparency, there is also understandably a desire among executive branch officials to maintain greater autonomy over executive branch information (Johnson 2019), which can lead to disputes between the executive branch and Congress (Selin and Milazzo 2021), the public, and the courts.

6.2 What is Government Transparency?

Most would agree that government transparency is an objectively important value and central component of effective and representative governance. However, the concept of government transparency is complex and entails various dimensions (Adeoye and Ran 2024; Ball 2009; Hollyer et al. 2014). According to Finel and Lord (1999, 316), "Transparency comprises the legal, political, and institutional structures that make information about the internal characteristics of a government and society available to actors both inside and outside the domestic political system."

Building from this definition, we divide government transparency *practices* into three broad categories: "government-proactive" transparency; "public-proactive" transparency;[1] and "participatory" transparency.[2] Government pro-active transparency entails the government practice of readily disclosing and sharing internal information, such as policy-specific information or performance/economic indicators (Islam 2006; Porumbescu et al. 2017), with the public at large, without a prior and direct request from the public (GAO 2021). For example, the Department of Veterans Affairs (VA) routinely publishes statistics on the rate of VA claims filed, the number of claims processed, and the agency's claim backlog.[3] Similarly, the Administrative Procedure Act (APA) requires agencies (in most instances) to notify the public in advance of proposed agency rulemaking to allow for affected and interested parties to provide feedback (Potter 2019). Importantly, pro-active government disclosure sometimes requires the prior government collection of information of external and private actors. The publishing of campaign contribution donor information by the Federal Election Commission (FEC) requires that political committees and campaign donors report their contributions from the public (Wood 2024).

"Public-proactive" transparency entails the availability and disclosure of internal government information upon specific *request* from the public (Cuillier and Davis 2019; Islam 2006; Johnson 2023; Roberts 2008; Wasike 2020). Specifically, since 2019 at least 125 countries have passed Freedom of Information (FOI) laws (UNESCO 2019), and a key component of these policies is the requirement that government entities release requested information to public requesters (Banisar 2002; Michener 2011). Information requested could entail records related to government policy, records submitted by commercial entities, or requests for information about the requester (e.g. immigration records, investigatory files) (Kwoka 2016; Wood and Lewis 2017). For example, during Fiscal Year 2023, over 1 million separate requests were made for government information through the U.S. Freedom of Information Act (DOJ 2023). Importantly, these laws usually entail exceptions for personal privacy and/or national security concerns, making such information exempt from disclosure.

In this context, "participatory transparency" refers to the ability to attend, observe meetings, and participate in formal meetings of government officials and organizations (Adams 2004; Kirkland and Harden 2022; Piotrowski and Borry 2010; Kim and Lee 2017). These meetings could include local school board meet-

---

1 This is also referred to as "passive" transparency (Grimmelikhuijsen et al. 2019; Mabillard and Keuffer 2022).
2 Importantly, the boundaries of these categories are not completely opaque. For example, government-proactive transparency such as the advance publication of proposed rules can entail participatory elements such as allowing the public to comment on proposed regulations.
3 "Veterans Benefits Administration Reports." U.S. Department of Veterans Affairs. https://www.benefits.va.gov/reports/detailed_claims_data.asp

ings, meetings between regulators and interested stakeholders,[4] and meetings of federal level committees. Open meeting laws, or "sunshine laws," require that government bodies/committees allow members of the public to attend and/or participate in meeting proceedings (Kirkland and Harden 2022). For example, Kirkland and Harden (2022, 52) note that all 50 U.S. states have open meeting laws that include requirements for various degrees of openness in state legislative proceedings. These meetings also facilitate the direct sharing of information with interested stakeholders, a forum for direct and immediate feedback (Einstein et al. 2018), and, in some instances, the ability for the public to shape the agenda of the proceedings (Kim and the Lee 2017). Features of open meetings laws, such as advanced meeting notices and agendas, public comment availability, and space access can contribute to the extent that such meetings align with values of transparency (Piotrowski and Borry 2010).

6.2.1 Benefits of Transparency

Scholars, transparency advocates, and government officials point to many benefits of government transparency. Awareness of government activity, performance, and the motivations underlying the actions of government officials can promote the presence of an informed public (Lupia 2015) and *potentially* allow for more informed decision-making (Fenster 2006). Transparency can also bring about greater policy compliance, contingent on the type of policy and one's understanding of government policy (Porumbescu et al. 2017). Scholars also find evidence that government transparency can enhance public trust (Grimmelikhuijsen et al. 2024, Ripamonti 2024). For example, Ripamonti (2024) shows that the act of government disclosure of financial and economic information is associated with increased level of trust among survey respondents. And the feedback from the public because of an awareness of proposed government activity can aid the improvement and performance of public policy and services (Islam 2006; Kosack and Fung 2014; Fenster 2006). If information about the underperformance of a given policy is made widely available, it could spur collective action among citizens to push for needed policy adjustments (Fung et al. 2007).

Transparency is arguably a necessary component of holding those engaged in illegal and unethical practices accountable (Ackerman and Sandoval-Ballesteros 2006; Ball 2009; Cordis and Warren 2014). Specifically, the presence of strong state

---

4 Regulators also hold "closed-door" meetings with lobbyists, stakeholders, and the subjects/targets of regulation (Yackee 2015).

Freedom of Information laws is associated with higher conviction rates for state and local officials for corruption, and an eventual decrease in corruption rates given the increase in the probability of detection (Cordis and Warren 2014).[5]

On a practical dimension, the ability to access individualized requester-specific internal government information can aid members of the public in addressing their own needs when attempting to utilize government services, or when seeking redress from adverse government action. This could include accessing necessary information when an individual attempts to appeal a denial of access to social welfare provisions, or the attempt by a government employee to gather evidence to redress misconduct concerns from a government employer.

6.2.2 Transparency Tensions

The benefits of transparency also co-exist with transparency complications and tensions (Adeoye and Ran 2024; Fenter 2006). Specifically, the implementation of transparency is not costless. Staff resources, funding, and technical infrastructure are important components of policy effectiveness across issue areas. However, for most agencies, transparency implementation is not the primary mission of the organization (Wilson 1989). Adhering to the legal requirements of transparency laws could be seen as drawing resources from core organizational goals. Halachimi and Greiling (2013, 579) note that the additional information required to be produced by transparency requirements can reduce a "government's capacity to function, as the resources available to it are finite."

Also, while some analyses find increased levels of trust towards government with increased transparency, scholars have also found that greater transparency either has a negligible or *negative* effect on public trust. Trust as a concept entails dimensions of perceived benevolence, competence, and honesty of the government organization in question (Grimmelikhuijsen 2012). Negative assessments and reduced trust could accompany greater awareness of government scandal or "disenchantment" with heightened visibility of internal government operations (Bovens 2003; Grimmelikhuijsen 2012, 8). Additionally, as transparency can lead to the exposure of greater government corruption (which is essential for account-

---

5 One characteristic of a strong state FOIA law is the presence of harsher penalties for violating FOIA requirements (Cordis and Warren 2014).

ability), it can also lead to greater perceptions of corruption in government (Costas-Pèrez 2014).[6]

Lastly, some caution that increased transparency in certain contexts could either increase conflict, or, at the very least, make bargaining between political actors more difficult as the statements/positions of either side are open to public scrutiny (Finel and Lord 1996). In their analysis of international conflict, Finel and Lord (1996, 316) argue that the increased information that accompanies enhanced transparency "can undermine behind-the-scenes efforts at conflict resolution." Specifically, it can become difficult for the actors involved to distinguish "signals" from "noise" (320).

6.3 Federal Transparency Architecture

6.3.1 "Participatory" Transparency and the Federal Advisory Committee Act (FACA)

Importantly, these concerns do not necessarily lead to calls for reduced transparency but rather reflect the need for extensive consideration of necessary resources and potential consequences when lawmakers craft transparency policy. A flurry of legislative activity followed the Nixon Administration and Watergate scandal, including a series of bills known as "Good Government"[7] legislation aimed at restoring public confidence and trust in government operation, in part by bringing about greater transparency (Bradley 1996; Croley and Funk 1997). The Federal Advisory Committee Act (FACA) was passed by a bipartisan majority in Congress and enacted in 1972 to enhance the transparency and accountability of federal advisory committees, which are committees, working groups, and task forces convened to examine a variety of policy issues and provide information and recommendations to federal government actors. FACA emerged from concerns that the number and work of advisory groups were in some cases "inefficient" and "redundant" (Beierle and Long 1999; CRS 2016), operating without sufficient openness and public oversight, yet still wielding significant influence within government (Beierle and Long 1999). There were also concerns regarding the in-

---

6 Costas-Pèrez (2014) also notes the importance of a free press in the exposure of corruption, in conjunction with increased perceived government corruption.

7 Additional components of the "Good Government" legislative initiative included the 1976 Government in Sunshine Act, which mandated that meetings of federal agencies be open to the public and be announced in advance with recorded written minutes. 5 U.S.C. § 552b (1976).

fluence of political or special interest influence on advisory committee deliberations and outcomes (Croley and Funk 1997).

FACA creates guidelines for the establishment, operation, and termination of federal advisory committees (created by Congress, the President, and federal agencies).[8] Key provisions require that these committees operate transparently by holding public meetings, keeping accessible records, and publishing meeting notices in the Federal Register (CRS 2024).[9] Presidents are also required to report to Congress on the activities and composition of federal advisory committees.

Since its initial enactment, FACA has been subject to executive action and amended multiple times to enhance oversight of advisory committees. In 2024, the FACA Final Rule issued by the General Services Administration (GSA) introduced further updates, particularly around public accessibility of records. Approximately 1,000 federal advisory committees were in operation during Fiscal Year 2023 (CRS 2024).

6.3.2 "Government-Proactive Transparency and Federal Spending"

One persistent matter of contention among political parties is over the allocation of federal spending. However, the issue of making federal spending more visible to the public has often found bipartisan congressional support (Williamson 2007). In 2006, Congress unanimously passed the Federal Funding Accountability and Transparency Act (FFATA) to enhance transparency in federal spending and to address the demand for accessible information on the amounts and recipients of government spending.[10] The legislation's sponsors included then-Senator Barack Obama (D-IL) and Tom Coburn (R-OK). Supporters included media organizations, unions, and interest groups such as the Gun Owners of America and People for the Ethical Treatment of Animals (CRS 2009).

The FFATA required the Office of Management and Budget (OMB) to create a publicly accessible online database, USAspending.gov, to track all federal awards,

---

8 Some advisory committees are exempt from FACA requirements such as committees operating within the CIA and the Federal Reserve (CRS 2016).

9 Committees under FACA are allowed to close certain meetings in accordance with the open-meeting exemptions under the Government in Sunshine Act. For example, Committees are allowed to close meetings to the public when deliberations could involve discussion of classified information, propriety data, and information raising personal privacy concerns. 5 U.S.C. § 552b (c) (1976).

10 31 U.S.C. §§ 6101–6106 (2006).

including grants, contracts, loans, and other financial assistance.[11] Key provisions mandate that all federal agencies report detailed information about the recipients of federal funds, the purpose and amount of each award, and the location of the receiving entities.[12] Amendments to FFATA, such as the 2008 Government Funding Transparency Act, further expanded reporting requirements, and mandated that agencies provide information on the identity and compensation of top officials if their organizations received significant federal awards, if such information is not otherwise available.[13] Despite these efforts, concerns emerged about the implementation of these transparency initiatives. Specifically, the U.S. Government Accountability Office noted that some agencies were reporting incomplete data or claiming exemptions from reporting federal award spending data. For example, the GAO reported that $619 billion in federal awards (assistance programs) were underreported in Fiscal Year 2012. The 2014 Digital Accountability and Transparency Act (DATA Act)[14] broadened the FFATA's scope by requiring the standardization of data formats across agencies to improve accuracy, accessibility, and cross-agency comparisons (GAO 2019a; GAO 2019b). The passage of the DATA Act is notable as it was approved by the often-gridlocked, low-productivity 114th Congress with strong bipartisan support (Prokop 2014).

While the passage of FFATA and the DATA Act are admirable instances of bipartisan governance, their implementation illustrates the infrastructure, effort, and complexity that coincides with the *maintenance* of "government-proactive" transparency.

6.4 "Public-Proactive" Transparency and The Freedom of Information Act

6.4.1 The Push for Access

The hallmark of federal government transparency between the federal bureaucracy and public is the Freedom of Information Act, first signed by President Lyndon B. Johnson in 1966 (Halstuk and Chamberlin 2006). Prior to FOIA, Section 3 of

---

11 A federal award is "any expenditure of Federal Funds through grants, subgrants, contracts, subcontracts, loans, awards, cooperative agreements, purchase orders, task orders, delivery orders, or other forms of financial assistance." Ibid.
12 31 U.S.C. §§ 6101–6106 (2006).
13 Ibid.
14 31 U.S.C. §§ 6101 note (2014).

the 1946 Administrative Procedure Act was technically a transparency provision to facilitate public disclosure of government records. However, there were vocal complaints from transparency activists, legal scholars, and journalists that the provision was woefully inadequate in facilitating public access to government information (Johnson and George 2023; Pozen 2005). Members of Congress were also highly critical of what they saw as an executive branch unwillingness to share important information with its co-equal institutional partner (Baron 2022). While under consideration by Congress, the law was met with stiff and nearly universal resistance from executive branch officials who raised concerns about the willingness of government and economic entities to provide information to the federal government that could subsequently be disclosed to the public (Lebovic 2018). There were also agency concerns regarding confidentiality and quality of agency deliberations with the possibility of public disclosure, and the resources required to implement the extensive transparency policy (Lebovic 2018).[15,16]

While stressing the importance of government transparency, Congress also included multiple exemptions with the FOIA that reflected legitimate agency concerns regarding public disclosure and allowed federal executive branch agencies to withhold requested records in certain circumstances. These exemptions include situations where the personal privacy of an individual (or individuals) would be compromised, records with national security implications, and records concerning law enforcement investigations.[17]

The current implementation of the Freedom of Information Act has been shaped by multiple amendments, executive orders/directives, guidance from the U.S. Attorneys General, and judicial intervention in suits filed by requesters. For example, after a series of early Supreme Court decisions that were arguably highly deferential to the executive branch's preference to withhold requested records, Congress amended the Freedom of Information Act to clarify its exemptions and reinforce the judiciary's ability to scrutinize executive branch reasoning for withholding records.[18] The most recent amendment to the Freedom of Infor-

---

15 According to Lebovic (2018), the Civil Service Commission was the only agency out of twenty-seven departments to speak in favor of the bill.

16 From its inception, the Freedom of Information has contained aspects of pro-active transparency. Specifically, the FOIA required agencies to publish authorized rules and their amendments in the Federal Register.

17 5 U.S.C. § 552 (b).

18 For example, in *EPA v. Mink*, 410 U.S. 73 (1973), the Supreme Court ruled that the federal courts did not have the authority to review *in-camera* records withheld under Exemption 1 (Johnson 2023). The subsequent 1974 FOIA amendments provided explicit authorization for federal courts to review *in-camera* disputed records.

mation Act was the 2016 FOIA Improvement Act, which codified a presumption of disclosure for withheld records, noting that agencies should only withhold information if the release of information would cause foreseeable harm to an "interest protected by an exemption."[19] The Act also stressed greater proactive transparency on the part of the executive branch by requiring that records that were requested at least three times be made available online.[20]

Public use of the Freedom of Information Act has increased substantially over time and reached a record number of requests per fiscal year during the first Trump and Biden Administrations (see Figure 6.1). Records received through FOIA have been used by journalists in high-profile news stories, academic researchers, individuals engaged in litigation with the government, and for genealogical research purposes. Research also shows that a substantial portion of requester are "commercial" requesters (Kwoka 2016), who seek information "that furthers the commercial, trade or profit interest of the requesters."[21]

Importantly, like the transparency measures discussed earlier, the increase in the use of FOIA is also accompanied by challenges—with one key challenge being agency resources. Specifically, agency staff, time, and effort are required to retrieve, review, and release requested records to the public. In a 2023 survey of information access professionalism, a majority of respondents noted that additional staff resources were the greatest need.[22] And with the growth of digital technology, the potential search parameters for retrieving potential requested records can become increasingly expansive and time-intensive. Some have also directed criticism at so-called "vexatious" requesters (Markus 2024), whose repeated and/or voluminous requests have been characterized as abusive or burdensome to the transparency process given the extensive agency resources that are sometimes required to fulfill the request(s).[23]

---

19 5 U.S.C. § 552 (a) (2) (II)(E).

20 5 U.S.C. § 552 (a) (2) (D)(ii)(II).

21 For example, in her analysis of FOIA users, Kwoka (2016) finds that commercial requesters were the largest category of FOIA users during FY 2013 for the Securities and Exchange Commission (SEC), Food and Drug Administration (FDA), and the Environmental Protection Agency (EPA). Some commercial requesters will submit requests for information regarding other commercial entities and resell the information received through FOIA (Kwoka 2016). Some scholars argue that the abundance of commercial requesters seeking information for subsequent proprietary gain potentially distorts the initial goals of FOIA that were advocated by media outlets (Kwoka 2016).

22 Freedom of Information Act Advisory Committee 2022–2024 Term. *Resources Subcommittee Final Report and Recommendations.* 2024. https://www.archives.gov/files/resources-subcommittee-report-5-23-2024-1.pdf

23 Ruotolo v. Department of Justice, Tax Div., 53 F. 3d 4 - Court of Appeals, 2nd Circuit 1995.

Number of Requests Received, FY 2012–2023

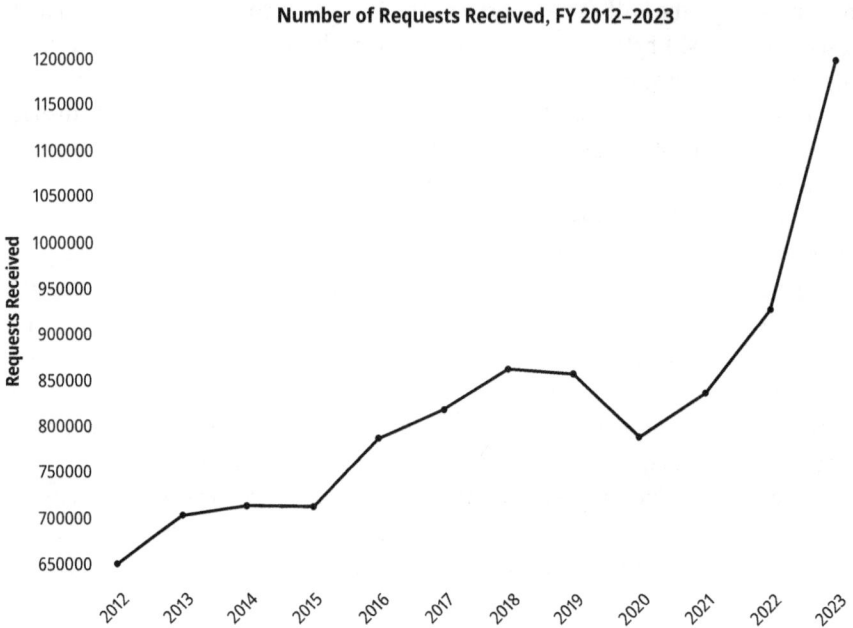

Figure 6.1: FOIA requests received, FY 2012–2023.

6.4.2 Transparency in Federal Court

When responding to a FOIA request, an agency can release all the requested information, or release some of the information and explain that other responsive records are being withheld because the information is protected from release under a given exemption(s). An agency can also withhold all the requested information under one or more exemptions. Depending on the nature of the request, an agency may note that none of the requested records could be located. Figure 6.2 illustrates aggregate FOIA dispositions to record requests since 2012, showing that the percentage of FOIA requests that result in a "full grant," or the release of all requested records, has trended downward over time. If a requester is unsatisfied with an agency's response (or lack of response), a requester has the right to sue the agency in federal court after exhausting the opportunities to challenge the response directly with the agency. Importantly, the vast majority of FOIA requests do not result in litigation; however, the number of district court case filings involving FOIA requests has steadily increased over time (as seen in Figure 6.3).[24] In addition to suing an agency for withholding requested records, requesters can also sue because the agency allegedly did not conduct an adequate search for the requested records, or if the requester believes they were improperly charged fees to have their request processed.

Disposition of Requests, FY 2012–2023

Disposition type • full_denial ▲ full_grant ◼ no_records + others ⊠ partial_grant

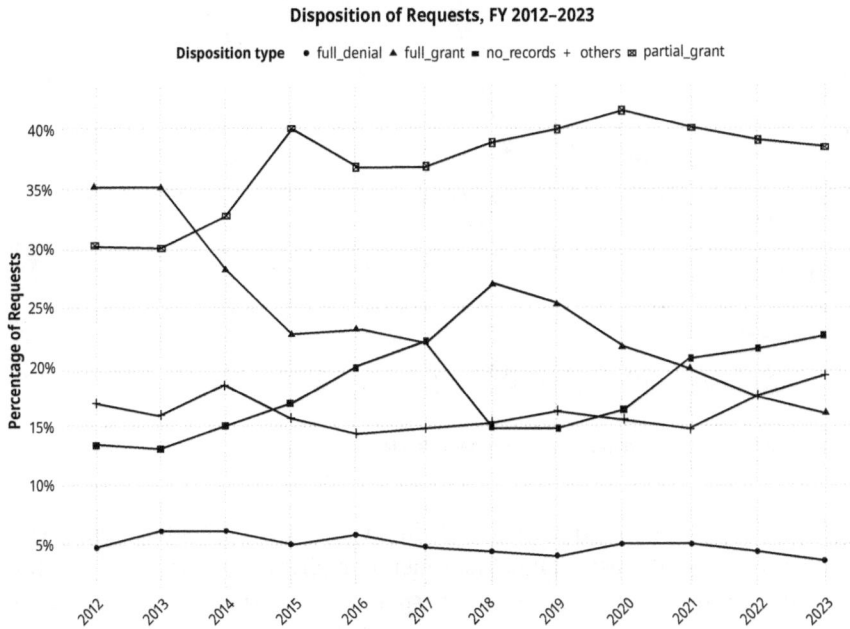

Figure 6.2: Disposition of FOIA requests, FY 2013–2023.

Analyses of FOIA litigation show that agencies have a very high likelihood of success (Mart and Ginsburg 2014; Johnson 2019; Johnson and George 2023; Verkuil 2002), which is often the case for government litigants (Galanter 1974). Verkuil (2002) finds agency win rates as high as 90 percent in his descriptive analysis of FOIA litigation outcomes, and in their analysis of disputes involving direct challenges to an agency's decision to withhold requested records, federal district and

---

24 The majority of FOIA cases per year are usually filed in the D.C. District, which regularly hears cases involving federal administrative agency litigants. The dip in cases filed in calendar year 2020 and 2021 corresponds with the emergence of COVID-19, which substantially affected the administration of FOIA and the ability to process FOIA requesters. There was a decline in FOIA requests received and FOIA requesters processed in fiscal year 2020 (GAO 2022).

Number of FOIA Cases, 2012–2023

Case Type — DC — total

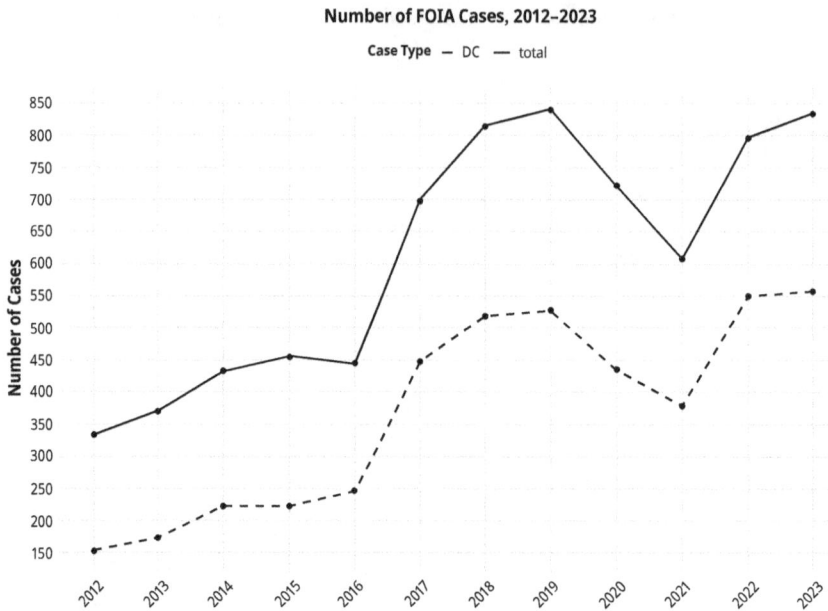

Figure 6.3: FOIA Cases filed in District Court per calendar year 2012–2023.

appellate courts were more likely to rule in favor of the withholding agency versus the requester (Johnson 2019). The general empirical consensus is that a litigant attempting to force executive transparency through litigation will leave court dissatisfied,[25] and this finding seems to hold across administrations. Even with the transparency controversies noted in the introduction involving the Trump Administration, federal courts generally continued to defer to the decision of the executive branch to withhold requested records, particularly in disputes involving records withheld by the Department of Justice, the agency also responsible for defending agencies when their FOIA decisions are challenged in court (Johnson and George 2023). Importantly, each dispute is unique in the nature of the records requested and the identity of the requester; however, in their analysis, Johnson and George (2023) find that federal judges ruled in favor of the Department of Justice in approximately 85 percent of rulings. To understand some of the considerations involved in disputes over highly salient records, below we

---

25 Importantly, there can be substantial discussion and negotiation between a requester and the agency under the guidance of a federal judge to reach an agreement (or understanding) over which the disputed documents can potentially be released to the requester before requesting the judge issue a ruling.

provide a detailed examination of a Freedom of Information Act dispute involving records prepared at the request of the White House—a FBI report on then-Supreme Court nominee Brett Kavanaugh.

6.4.3 Presidential Communications, the FBI, and the Kavanaugh Nomination:

6.4.3.1 Buzzfeed Inc, v. Federal Bureau of Investigation (2020)

After the retirement of Justice Anthony Kennedy from the Supreme Court in 2018, President Trump announced his nomination of Court of Appeals Judge Brett Kavanaugh to ascend to the vacant Supreme Court seat (Horsley 2018). Then-Judge Kavanaugh had many of the traditional qualifications expected for a Supreme Court nominee. At the time of his nomination, he served as a Court of Appeals Judge for the District of Columbia Circuit (appointed by President George W. Bush and confirmed by the Senate in 2006). Kavanaugh also had previous experience working in the George W. Bush White House Administration (Lewis 2004). The American Bar Association, which provides qualification ratings for federal judicial nominees, rated Kavanaugh as "well qualified" for the Supreme Court, their highest rating (Selk 2018). However, what seemed to be a traditional nomination process came under fire when Kavanaugh was accused of assaulting former high school classmate Christine Blasey Ford. Once news of the allegation emerged, some opposed to Kavanaugh's nomination demanded that President Trump withdraw Kavanaugh from contention, and the ABA called for an FBI investigation into the allegations (Selk 2018).

Supreme Court nominees undergo extensive investigation into their background (education, employment, financial, criminal history), in part to determine if there is any information that suggests a conflict of interest, unsuitability for federal office, and/or legal improprieties (Lederman 2016). Kavanaugh had the traditional background investigation performed by the Federal Bureau of Investigation (FBI). However, in the midst of the controversy surrounding his nomination, President Trump's White House counsel requested that the FBI conduct a supplementary background investigation (SBI) of Kavanaugh with a specific focus on the allegations raised by Ford.[26] The reported results of the background investigation noted that no evidence surfaced to corroborate the allegations of Ford; however, criticism of the extent and scope of the FBI's supplementary investiga-

---

26 *Buzzfeed, Inc. v. Federal Bureau of Investigation*, 613 F. Supp.3d 453 (2020).

tion emerged (McQuade 2019), and in late 2018 *Buzzfeed News* reporter Jason Leopold submitted multiple FOIA requests to gain access to FBI documents connected to Kavanaugh's nomination including FBI communications involving the allegations against Kavanaugh, FBI interview notes, and a copy of the SBI report that was sent to the White House and the Senate Judiciary Committee. The FBI released some of the requested records to the plaintiffs and made redacted records available online. However, the SBI report was withheld based upon the Freedom of Information Act's Exemption 5 under the umbrella of the "presidential communication privilege."[27] The FBI explained that the "presidential communication privilege" protected the SBI File on Kavanaugh given that[28]

> . . . the SBI File . . . was solicited by the White House Counsel's Office in the service of a core, nondelegable presidential function, namely, the appointment of a Supreme Court Justice, and, further, the privilege remains intact, without the need for personal invocation by the President and despite the furnishing of the file to the Senate Judiciary Committee.

The "presidential communications privilege" is a constitutionally "implied" privilege that protects from disclosure to outside parties (Rozell 1999) and communications between the president and their advisors and/or subordinates involving presidential responsibilities, policy development, and decision-making.[29] Importantly, in *U.S. v. Nixon* (1974),[30] the Supreme Court explained that this privilege is "qualified," meaning that disclosure can be ordered depending upon the nature of the need for the information (for example, evidence needed in a criminal proceeding).[31]

While *U.S. v. Nixon* (1974) involved an institutional battle over information between the president and Congress, interestingly, it would be subsequent Freedom of Information Act disputes between the executive branch and *public* that would define the contours of the presidential communications privilege (CRS 2012), in a manner pertinent to the 2020 *Buzzfeed* FOIA dispute. Specifically, *Judicial Watch v. Department of Justice* (2004)[32] involved a FOIA request for pardon petitions received by the Department of Justice for consideration by the President. The DOJ withheld the records in part under the presidential communications privilege; however, the Court of Appeals for the D.C. Circuit ruled that the presi-

---

27 The language of Exemption 5 has been interpreted to encompass a number of privileges that allow the executive branch to withhold records such as the "attorney-client" privilege and "deliberative process privilege" (Johnson 2019).

28 *Buzzfeed, Inc. v. Federal Bureau of Investigation*, 613 F. Supp.3d 453 (2020).

29 *U.S. v. Nixon (I) 418 U.S. 683* (1974).

30 Ibid.

31 Ibid.

32 365 F. 3d 1108 (D.C. Cir. 2004).

dential communications privilege did not apply because the pardon applications were "internal agency documents" that were not solicited *directly* by the Office of the President; rather solicitation and review of the pardon applications were delegated to the Deputy Attorney General's Office. Subsequently, in the FOIA case of *Loving v. Department of Defense* (2008),[33] the Court of Appeals for the D.C. Circuit ruled that the presidential communications privilege applied to documents *viewed* by the President, as this would involve "communications that directly involve the President,"[34] even if they were not solicited by the president directly.[35]

In the *Buzzfeed* dispute, District Judge Beryl A. Howell (appointed by President Barack Obama), cited both *Judicial Watch* and *Loving* and explained that the SBI for Kavanaugh "was 'solicited and received' by 'immediate White House advisers' with 'broad and significant responsibility for investigation and formulating . . . advice to be given to the president.'" *Buzzfeed*/Leopold countered, however, that the presidential communication should not apply to the Kavanaugh SBI file in part because the file did not *aid* the president in the decision-making process related to the Kavanaugh nomination given that the president expressed his intention to move ahead with the nomination prior to the release of the background report. Judge Howell remained unpersuaded by this argument, remarking that a judicial investigation of the White House's reasoning for ordering the SBI would "turn the whole point of the presidential communications privilege on its head by undermining the President's ability to 'make decisions confidentially.'" Judge Howell concluded that the SBI was fully protected from disclosure by the presidential communications privilege.

Judges are not legally required to consider the public interest and salience of the information in question when an agency raises Exemption 5 to withhold records. However, this case involved a request for uniquely salient records involving an investigation of criminal allegations against a potential Supreme Court justice, which undoubtedly would be of significance to substantial portions of the public. Although the public's right to know and access internal government information is a key value that motivated the passage of FOIA, federal judges are also very sensitive to a president's needs for discretion and confidentiality with their closest advisors and subordinates, as illustrated in Judge Howell's ruling. While this case involved a request for uniquely salient records, the outcome here reflects the outcome in the vast majority of FOIA disputes that reach federal court, which is judicial support for the agency's decision to withhold requested information.

---

33 550 F. 3d 32 (D.C. Cir 2008).

34 *In re Sealed Case*, 121 F.3d at 751–52 (D.C. Cir 1997).

35 Ibid.

6.5 Looking Ahead: Transparency and The Second Trump Administration

Project 2025 (formally titled *Mandate for Leadership. The Conservative Promise*) is an extensive and detailed proposal developed by The Heritage Foundation and other conservative organizations to provide a blueprint for administrative governance and to "reform the failings of big government and an undemocratic administrative state."[36] President Trump distanced his 2024 campaign from the project once media reporting on specific proposals of Project 2025 increased (Giles 2024); however, since his re-election in November 2024, he has selected several Project 2025 contributors for positions in his second administration (Barrow 2024). Throughout the proposal, Project 2025 highlights the need for greater transparency in the operation of federal agencies and policy implementation throughout the government (Dans and Groves 2024). Some key areas highlighted for greater transparency involve policies previously favored by the Biden Administration.

For example, after the U.S. Supreme Court overturned *Roe v. Wade* (1973), which provided constitutional protections for abortion access, President Biden issued multiple executive orders to facilitate access to reproductive services.[37] Additionally, the Biden Administration reversed Trump-era restrictions on Title X funding, reinstating support for organizations like Planned Parenthood that provide or refer abortion services (Nittle 2021).

Project 2025 advocates for increased transparency in the regulation of abortion pills and their manufacturers, such as Danco and GenBioPro, with the goal of enhancing oversight and challenging current regulatory practices (Severino 2023, 459). By emphasizing the disclosure of inspection records, compliance reports, and post-marketing safety data, the initiative seeks to ensure that manufacturers are held accountable and that their products meet established safety standards. However, transparency in these areas could provide a foundation for implementing more stringent regulations on abortion pills, which would align with objectives of some conservative advocates to limit access to abortion services.

Project 2025 also stressed the increased need for transparency towards the implementation of diversity, equity, and inclusion (DEI) policies (Burke 2023, 358),

---

36 "About Advisory Board." *Project 2025 Presidential Transition Project*, https://www.project2025.org/about/advisory-board/ (accessed November 29, 2024).

37 Joseph R. Biden Jr., *Executive Order on Strengthening Access to Affordable, High-Quality Contraception and Family Planning Services* (Washington, D.C.: The White House, June 23, 2023), https://www.whitehouse.gov/briefing-room/presidential-actions/2023/06/23/executive-order-on-strengthening-access-to-affordable-high-quality-contraception-and-family-planning-services/ (accessed November 20, 2024).

which were strongly supported by the Biden Administration. During the first week of the Trump's second term as president, federal agencies were ordered to report information on employees whose work incorporated DEI policies to the Office and Management and Budget (Lebowitz 2025), and also report efforts to "disguise" DEI programs and policies (Beitsch 2025). Also noted in the report is the need for greater transparency around union financial practices (Berry 2023, 599), potentially highlighting areas where opponents of unionization perceive inefficiencies or misuse of funds by union organizations.

This raises an important question of whether transparency administered in this manner could be viewed as "politicized" and/or "weaponized" transparency (Robinson 2019), in its focus on policy priorities of the political opposition. Importantly, research shows that transparency laws are more likely to emerge in areas with greater political competition, as this aids the ability of political parties/ groups to gain access to information of their opposition (Berline 2014). So perhaps what appears as targeted or politicized transparency is another component of democratic governance, which entails battles over political office, public opinion, and *information*. As mentioned previously, FOIA requests spiked during the first Trump Administration, so a situation could emerge where political opponents use existing transparency policy to "monitor the monitoring" of Trump Administration officials as the new 2025 Administration unfolds.

6.5 Conclusion

Transparency is an oft celebrated goal, and there are many federal policies in place that require federal agencies to ensure the availability of internal government information, whether through advance availability or direct public request. Despite various degrees of resistance from executive actors, federal transparency initiatives often receive high levels of bipartisan support in Congress. However, executive branch actors and transparency advocates often note that the financial and infrastructure support required to fully adhere to the provisions of legislated transparency is sometimes lacking. And as seen in the introduction, effective transparency implementation can also be stifled by attempts by political officials to avoid transparency requirements.

This chapter has provided an overview into the complexity of government transparency as it relates to the federal executive branch, including the risks and benefits that accompany transparency policy implementation. We also examined the various ways Congress has attempted to legislate transparency for the federal administrative state with a particular focus on the Freedom of Information Act, which mandates disclosure of records requested by the public. The high-profile FOIA dispute involving records related to Justice Brett Kavanaugh illustrates the central role of courts in settling transparency disputes, whereas key goals of Project 2025 raise questions on the permissible "boundaries" of transparency.

Discussion Questions

1 What are some potential benefits and tensions of government transparency that were **not** discussed in the chapter? How should governments address some of the tensions that you noted?
2 Because of agency's expertise and first-hand knowledge of government operations, judges sometimes take the posture of deferring to an agency's legal argument and perspective in various policy areas including questions of transparency. Do you think this deference is warranted? Why or why not?
3 Given the examples of high-ranking officials apparently attempting to avoid adherence to transparency policy, how should policymakers and/or courts respond to ensure FOIA remains an effective tool for transparency?
4 Do you agree with the suggestion that transparency can be "weaponized," or used in a way to purposely harm political opponents or policies? In terms of democratic governance where political competition is a central feature, is such use of *legal* transparency mechanisms problematic? Why or why not?
5 All fifty states have laws similar to the federal Freedom of Information Act. Review the provisions of the Freedom of Information law in your state. How is the law similar to the federal Freedom of Information Act? How is it different?

References

Ackerman, John M., and Irma E. Sandoval-Ballesteros. 2006. "The global explosion of freedom of information laws." *Admin. L. Rev.* 58 (2006): 85.

Adams, Brian. 2004. "Public meetings and the democratic process." *Public administration review* 64, no. 1 (2004): 43–54.

Adeoye, Olumide, and Bing Ran. "Government transparency: paradoxes and dilemmas." *Public Management Review* 26, no. 8 (2024): 2194–2217.

Ball, Carolyn. 2009. "What is transparency?" *Public Integrity* 11, no. 4 (2009): 293–308.

Banisar, David. 2002. "Freedom of information and access to government records around the world." *Privacy International* 4, no. 2 (2002).

Barber, C. R. 2022. "More Secret Trump and Pence Staffing Records Revealed Following Insider Lawsuit." *Business Insider*. April 1, 2022. https://www.businessinsider.com/secret-donald-trump-pence-transition-records-lawsuit-save-america-pac-2022-4 (accessed November 19, 2024).

Baron, Kevin M. "Informal and Private: Bargaining and Veto Threats over the Freedom of Information Act." *Congress & the Presidency*, vol. 49, no. 2 (2022): 165–99.

Barrow, Bill. 2024. "After Trump's Project 2025 denials, he is tapping its authors and influencers for key roles." *AP*. November 23, 2024. https://apnews.com/article/trump-project-2025-administration-nominees-843f5ff20131ccba5f056e7ccc5baf23 (accessed November 29, 2024).

Beierle, Thomas C., and Rebecca J. Long. 1999. "Chilling collaboration: The Federal Advisory Committee Act and stakeholder involvement in environmental decisionmaking." *Envtl. L. Rep. News & Analysis* 29: 10399.

Beitsch, Rebecca 2025. "Federal workers ordered to report efforts to 'disguise' DEI programs or face 'consequences." *The Hill*. January 23.https://thehill.com/homenews/administration/5102561-trump-dei-omb/ (accessed January 26, 2025).

Berliner, Daniel. "The political origins of transparency." *The Journal of Politics* 76, no. 2 (2014): 479–91.

Berry, Jonathan. 2023. "Department of Labor and Related Agencies." In *Mandate for Leadership. The Conservative Promise. Project 2025 Presidential Transition Project,* edited by Paul Dans and Steven Groves, 581–617. The Heritage Foundation. https://static.project2025.org/2025_MandateForLeadership_FULL.pdf (accessed December 1, 2024).

Bradley, Kathy. "Do You Feel the Sunshine–Government in the Sunshine Act: Its Objectives, Goals, and Effect on the FCC and You." *Fed. Comm. LJ* 49 (1996): 473.

Bridis, T. 2018. "US sets new record for censoring, withholding gov't files." *AP News*. March 12. https://apnews.com/article/business-arts-and-entertainment-personal-taxes-only-on-ap-united-states-government-714791d91d7944e49a284a51fab65b85 (accessed November 19, 2024).

Brown, Mark B. 2008. "Fairly balanced: The politics of representation on government advisory committees." *Political research quarterly* 61, no. 4 (2008): 547–60.

Bovens, Mark A.P. 2003. *De Digitale Republiek: Democratie en rechtsstaat in de informatiemaatschappij.* Amsterdam University Press.

Bur, Jessie. 2017. "Agencies struggle with accuracy in DATA Act reporting." *Federal Times*. November 8. https://www.federaltimes.com/federal-oversight/2017/11/08/agencies-struggle-with-accuracy-in-data-act-reporting/ (accessed November 19, 2024).

Burke, Lindsey M. 2023. "Department of Education." In *Mandate for Leadership. The Conservative Promise. Project 2025 Presidential Transition Project*, edited by Paul Dans and Steven Groves, 319–416. The Heritage Foundation. https://static.project2025.org/2025_MandateForLeadership_FULL.pdf (accessed December 1, 2024).

Bybee, Jay S. "Advising the president: Separation of powers and the Federal Advisory Committee Act." *Yale LJ* 104 (1994): 51.

Congressional Research Service (CRS). 2009. *The Federal Advisory Committee Act: Analysis of Operations and Costs*. Report No. R40520. Congressional Research Service. https://crsreports.congress.gov/product/pdf/R/R40520.

Congressional Research Service (CRS). 2012. *Presidential Claims of Executive Privilege: History, Law, Practice, and Recent Developments*. CRS Report RL30319, by Morton Rosenberg. Congressional Research Service. https://crsreports.congress.gov/product/pdf/RL/RL30319.

Congressional Research Service. 2024. *The Federal Advisory Committee Act: Overview and Selected Issues*. CRS Report R44253. Updated January 4, 2024. Library of Congress. https://crsreports.congress.gov/product/pdf/R/R44253

Cordis, Adriana S., and Patrick L. Warren. 2014. "Sunshine as disinfectant: The effect of state Freedom of Information Act laws on public corruption." *Journal of public economics* 115 (2014): 18–36.

Costas-Pérez, Elena. 2014. "Political Corruption and Voter Turnout: Mobilization or Disaffection?" *IEB Working Paper 2014/27*. Institut d'Economia de Barcelona.

Croley, Steven P., and William F. Funk. 1997. "The federal advisory committee act and good government." *Yale J. on Reg.* 14 (1997): 451.

Dans, Paul, and Steven Groves, eds. 2023. *Mandate for Leadership. The Conservative Promise. Project 2025 Presidential Transition Project*. The Heritage Foundation: https://static.project2025.org/2025_MandateForLeadership_FULL.pdf (accessed December 1, 2024).

Delkic, M. 2018. "How Times Journalists Uncovered the Original Source of the President's Wealth." *The New York Times*. October 2. https://www.nytimes.com/2018/10/02/insider/donald-trump-fred-tax-schemes-wealth.html (accessed November 19, 2024).

Department of Justice. 2023. *Summary of Annual FOIA Reports for Fiscal Year 2023: Highlights of Key Government-wide FOIA Data*. https://www.justice.gov/oip/media/1354721/dl?inline (accessed November 19, 2024).

Einstein, Katherine Levine, Maxwell Palmer, and David M. Glick. 2019. "Who participates in local government? Evidence from meeting minutes." *Perspectives on politics* 17, no. 1 (2019): 28–46.

Evers, A. 2020. "Did the Trump Administration Abuse the Redactions Process?" *American Oversight*. January 7. https://www.justsecurity.org/67943/did-the-trump-administration-abuse-the-redactions-process/ (accessed November 19, 2024).

Finel, Bernard I., and Kristin M. Lord. 1999 "The surprising logic of transparency." *International studies quarterly* 43, no. 2 (1999): 315–39.

Finley, Allysia. 2024. "What was Anthony Fauci's Top Aide Hiding? *Wall Street Journal*. May 26, 2024. https://www.wsj.com/articles/what-was-anthony-faucis-top-aide-hiding-investigation-0d890911 (accessed November 19, 2024).

Fung, Archon, Mary Graham, and David Weil. 2007. *Full disclosure: The perils and promise of transparency*. Cambridge University Press.

Galanter, Marc. 1974. "Why the Haves Come out Ahead: Speculations on the Limits of Legal Change." *Law and Society Review* 9 (1): 95–160.

Georgantopoulos, M. A. 2017. "These Federal Agencies Agreed To Conceal Some Of Their Communications From The Public." *BuzzFeed News*. May 8. https://www.buzzfeednews.com/article/maryanngeorgantopoulos/federal-agencies-conceal-communications#.cb5KkV3G7 (accessed November 19, 2024).

Gerstein, Josh. 2018. "Judge hears suit on Trump White House use of encrypted apps." *Politico*. January 17. https://www.politico.com/story/2018/01/17/white-house-encrypted-apps-hearing-343774 (accessed November 19, 2024).

Giles, Ben. 2024. "Trump again distances himself from Project 2025." *NPR*. August 22. https://www.npr.org/2024/08/22/g-s1-19202/trump-project-2025-border-immigration (accessed November 30, 2024).

Grimmelikhuijsen, Stephan, Femke de Vries, and Robin Bouwman. "Regulators as guardians of trust? The contingent and modest positive effect of targeted transparency on citizen trust in regulated sectors." *Journal of Public Administration Research and Theory* 34, no. 1 (2024): 136–49.

Grimmelikhuijsen, Stephan, Peter John, Albert Meijer, and Ben Worthy. "Do freedom of information laws increase transparency of government? A replication of a field experiment." *Journal of Behavioral Public Administration* 2, no. 1 (2019).

Halachmi, Arie, and Dorothea Greiling. 2013. "Transparency, e-government, and accountability: Some issues and considerations." *Public Performance & Management Review* 36, no. 4 (2013): 562–84.

Halstuk, M. E., and B. F. Chamberlin. "The freedom of information act 1966–2006: A retrospective on the rise of privacy protection over the public interest in knowing what the government's up to." *Communication law and policy* 11, no. 4 (2006): 511–64.

Hollyer, James R., B. Peter Rosendorff, and James Raymond Vreeland. 2014. "Measuring transparency." *Political analysis* 22, no. 4 (2014): 413–34.

Horsley, Scott. 2018. "Trump Taps Brett Kavanaugh As His 2nd Supreme Court Pick." *NPR*. July 9. https://www.npr.org/2018/07/09/624727227/trump-to-name-his-second-supreme-court-pick (accessed November 19, 2024).

Islam, Roumeen. "Does more transparency go along with better governance?" *Economics & Politics* 18, no. 2 (2006): 121–67.

Johnson, Gbemende E. "Adjudicating executive privilege: Federal administrative agencies and deliberative process privilege claims in US District courts." *Law & Society Review* 53, no. 3 (2019): 823–50.

Johnson, Gbemende E., and Tracey E. George. "To preserve, release, and litigate: Dimensions of executive branch transparency." *Presidential Studies Quarterly* 53, no. 2 (2023): 209–33.

Karni, Annie. 2018. "Meet the guys who tape Trump's paper back together." *Politico*. June 10. https://www.politico.com/story/2018/06/10/trump-papers-filing-system-635164 (accessed November 19, 2024).

Kennedy, Merrit. 2017. "White House Says It Will No Longer Release Visitor Logs To The Public." NPR. April 14. https://www.npr.org/sections/thetwo-way/2017/04/14/523968950/white-house-says-it-will-no-longer-release-visitor-logs-to-the-public (accessed November 19, 2024).

Kim, Soonhee, and Jooho Lee. "Citizen participation, process, and transparency in local government: An exploratory study." *Policy Studies Journal* 47, no. 4 (2019): 1026–47.

Kirkland, Justin H., and Jeffrey J. Harden. 2022. *The Illusion of Accountability: Transparency and Representation in American Legislatures*. Cambridge University Press

Kroll, Andy and *ProPublica*, Nick Surgery, and *Documented*. 2024. Inside Project 2025's Secret Training Videos. *ProPublica*. August 10. https://www.propublica.org/article/inside-project-2025-secret-training-videos-trump-election (accessed November 30, 2024).

Kosack, Stephen, and Archon Fung. "Does transparency improve governance?" *Annual Review of Political Science* 17, no. 1 (2014): 65–87.

Kwoka, Margaret B. "Foia, Inc." *Duke LJ* 65 (2016): 1361.

Lauderdale, Derace. 2024. "A bill with the potential to improve federal spending transparency." *Federal News Network*. September 9. https://federalnewsnetwork.com/workforce/2024/09/a-bill-with-the-potential-to-improve-federal-spending-transparency/ (accessed November 19, 2024).

Lebovic, Sam. 2018. "How administrative opposition shaped the Freedom of Information Act." In *Troubling transparency: The history and future of freedom of information*, 13–33. Columbia University Press.

Lebowitz, 2025. "Federal employees are told to name colleagues who work in DEI roles or risk 'adverse consequences'." *NBCNews*. January 25. https://www.nbcnews.com/politics/white-house/federal-workers-told-name-dei-colleagues-risk-adverse-consequences-rcna188871 (accessed January 25, 2025).

Lederman, Josh. 2016. "The intrusive investigation behind Supreme Court Nominations." *PBSNews*. February 16. https://www.pbs.org/newshour/nation/the-intrusive-investigation-behind-supreme-court-nominations.

Lee, Matthew, and Mary Clare Jalonick. 2019. "38 people cited for violations in Clinton email probe." *Associated Press*. October 19. https://apnews.com/article/14b14afc5d8647858489a2cf5385c28d (accessed November 19, 2024).

Leopold, J. 2018. "John Kelly Instructed A DHS Official Not To Email Staff To Avoid Public Scrutiny." *BuzzFeed News*. June 8. https://www.buzzfeednews.com/article/jasonleopold/john-kelly-dhs-official-email-foia-public-scrutiny (accessed November 19, 2024).

Leopold, J., and A. Cormier. 2021. "These Emails Reveal The Drama When GSA Blocked Biden." *BuzzFeed News*. January 9. https://www.buzzfeednews.com/article/jasonleopold/trump-biden-transition-delayed-gsa (accessed November 19, 2024).

Leopold, J., K. Nocera, S. Mimms, A. Cormier, E., Hall and E. Loop. 2019. "Robert Mueller Report Secret Trump Investigation Memos Revealed After BuzzFeed FOIA Lawsuit." *BuzzFeed News*. December 2. https://www.buzzfeednews.com/article/jasonleopold/mueller-report-secret-memos-2 (accessed November 19, 2024).

Lewis, Neil. 2004. "Bush Aide on Court Nominees Faces Fire as Nominee Himself." *The New York Times*. April 28. https://www.nytimes.com/2004/04/28/us/bush-aide-on-court-nominees-faces-fire-as-nominee-himself.html (accessed November 19, 2024).

Light, Paul C. 2009. *A government ill executed: The decline of the federal service and how to reverse it*. Harvard University Press.

Mabillard, Vincent, and Nicolas Keuffer. "Does freedom of information contribute to more open administrations? An empirical analysis of the link between active and passive forms of transparency." *International Review of Public Administration* 27, no. 1 (2022): 55-72.

Markus, Ben. 2024. "Public records in Colorado could become not-so-public under bill." *CPR News*. February 15. https://www.cpr.org/2024/02/15/proposed-bill-new-restrictions-for-colorado-public-records-access/ (accessed January 20, 2025).

McQuade, Barbara. 2019. "New allegations against Brett Kavanaugh mean Congress must finish what the FBI started." September 17. *NBC News*. https://www.nbcnews.com/think/opinion/new-allegations-against-brett-kavanaugh-mean-congress-must-finish-what-ncna1055526.

Michener, Greg. "FOI laws around the world." *Journal of Democracy* 22, no. 2 (2011): 145–59.

Mueller, Benjamin. 2024. "Health Officials Tried to Evade Public Records Laws." *The New York Times*. May 28. https://www.nytimes.com/2024/05/28/health/nih-officials-foia-hidden-emails-covid.html (accessed November 14, 2024).

Nittle, Nadra. 2021. "Biden Administration Expands Access to Title X Funding for Family Planning and Contraception." *The 19th*. October 7. https://19thnews.org/2021/10/title-x-contraception-family-planning/ (accessed November 21, 2024).

Peck, Michael. 2017. "Audit says federal transparency website isn't accessible enough." *Federal Times*. October 3. https://www.federaltimes.com/it-networks/2017/10/03/audit-says-federal-transparency-website-isnt-accessible-enough/ (accessed November 19, 2024).

Peralta, Eyder. 2012. "Holder Found in Contempt of Congress." *National Public Radio*. June 28. https://www.npr.org/sections/thetwo-way/2012/06/28/155928783/house-set-for-vote-on-holding-attorney-general-holder-in-contempt (accessed November 19, 2024).

Peterson, Andrea. 2014. "Is the White House trying to blow up an open data bill?" *The Washington Post*. January 29. https://www.washingtonpost.com/news/the-switch/wp/2014/01/29/is-the-white-house-trying-to-blow-up-an-open-data-bill/ (accessed November 19, 2024).

Piotrowski, Suzanne J., and Erin Borry. 2010. "An analytic framework for open meetings and transparency." *Public Administration and Management* 15, no. 1 (2010): 138.

Porumbescu, Gregory, Albert Meijer, and Stephan Grimmelikhuijsen. 2022. *Government transparency: State of the art and new perspectives*. Cambridge University Press.

Porumbescu, Gregory A., Meghan IH Lindeman, Erica Ceka, and Maria Cucciniello. 2017. "Can transparency foster more understanding and compliant citizens?" *Public Administration Review* 77, no. 6 (2017): 840–50.

Pozen, David E. "The mosaic theory, national security, and the freedom of information act." *Yale LJ* 115 (2005): 628.

Pozen, David E. "Transparency's ideological drift." *Yale LJ* 128 (2018): 100.

Prokop, Andrew. 2014. "Beating the odds: Why one bill made it through a gridlocked Congress-and so many don't." *Vox*. May 22. https://www.vox.com/2014/5/22/5723878/how-a-bill-becomes-a-law-in-2014 (accessed November 19, 2024).

Ripamonti, Juan Pablo. "Does being informed about government transparency boost trust? Exploring an overlooked mechanism." *Government Information Quarterly* 41, no. 3 (2024).

Roberts, A. 2006. *Blacked out: Government secrecy in the information age.* Cambridge University Press.

Robinson, Nick. "Foreign Agents in an Interconnected World: FARA and the Weaponization of Transparency." *Duke LJ* 69 (2019): 1075.

Romm, T., J. Bogage, and L. H. Sun. 2020. "Newly revealed USPS documents show an agency struggling to manage Trump, Amazon and the pandemic" September 17. https://www.washingtonpost.com/us-policy/2020/09/17/usps-trump-coronavirus-amazon-foia/ (accessed November 19, 2024).

Rozell, Mark J. 1999. "The Law: Executive Privilege: Definition and Standards of Application." *Presidential Studies Quarterly* 29 (4): 918–30.

Selin, Jennifer L., and Caylie Milazzo. 2021. "The Law: "If Men Were Angels": The Legal Dynamics of Overseeing the Executive Branch." *Presidential Studies Quarterly* 51 (2): 426–49.

Selk, Avi. 2018. "The American Bar Association had concerns about Kavanaugh 12 years ago. Republicans dismissed those, too." *The Washington Post*. September 28. https://www.washingtonpost.com/politics/2018/09/28/american-bar-association-had-kavanaugh-concerns-years-ago-republicans-dismissed-those-too/.

Severino, Roger. 2023. "Department of Health and Human Services" in *Mandate for Leadership. The Conservative Promise. Project 2025 Presidential Transition Project*, edited by Paul Dans and Steven Groves, 449–502. The Heritage Foundation. https://static.project2025.org/2025_MandateForLeadership_FULL.pdf (accessed December 1, 2024).

Smith, R. J. 2019. *Trump administration resists Ukraine disclosures ordered by court.* Center for Public Integrity. December 12. https://publicintegrity.org/national-security/ukraine-documents-dod-omb-foia/ (accessed November 30, 2019).

United Nations Educational, Scientific, and Cultural Organization. *Powering sustainable development with access to information: highlights from the 2019 UNESCO monitoring and reporting of SDG indicator 16.10.2.* https://unesdoc.unesco.org/ark:/48223/pf0000369160 (accessed November 19, 2024).

U.S. Government Accountability Office, *DATA TRANSPARENCY: Oversight Needed to Address Underreporting and Inconsistencies on Federal Award Website*, GAO-14–476 (Washington, DC, 2014)

U.S. Government Accountability Office (GAO). 2019a. DATAACT: Quality of DATA Submissions Has Improved but Further Action is Needed to Disclose Known Data Limitations, GAO-20–75. Washington, DC.

U.S. Government Accountability Office (GAO). 2019b. *DATA Act: OMB, Treasury, and Agencies Need to Improve Completeness and Accuracy of Spending Data and Disclose Limitations.* GAO-19–286. Government Accountability Office. https://www.gao.gov/assets/gao-19-286.pdf.

U.S. Government Accountability Office. 2021. *Freedom of Information Act: Actions Needed to Improve Agency Compliance with Proactive Disclosure Requirements*, GAO-21–254.

U.S. Government Accountability Office. 2022. Freedom of Information Act: Selected Agencies Adapted to COVID-19 Challenges but Actions Needed to Reduce Backlogs, GAO-22–105845.

U.S. Library of Congress. 2024a. Congressional Research Services. *The Federal Advisory Committee Act (FACA): Overview and Considerations for Congress*, by Meghan Stuessey and Kathleen E. Marchsteiner. R47984.

U.S. Library of Congress. 2024b. Congressional Research Services. *The Freedom of Information Act (FOIA): A Legal Overview*, by Benjamin M. Barczewski. R46238.

U.S. Library of Congress. 2016. Congressional Research Services. *Federal Advisory Committees: An Introduction and Overview*, by Meghan Stuessy. R44253.

U.S. Library of Congress. 2012. Congressional Research Services. Presidential Claims of Executive Privilege: History, Law, Practice, and Recent Developments, by Todd Garvey and Alissa M. Dolan. R42670.

U.S. Library of Congress. 2009. Congressional Research Services. *The Federal Funding Accountability and Transparency Act: Implementation and Proposed Amendments*, by Garrett Hatch. RL34718.

Verkuil, Paul R. 2002. "An Outcomes Analysis of Scope of Review Standards." *Wm. & Mary L. Rev.* 44: 679.

Wagner, A. Jay. "Longstanding, Systemic Weaknesses: Hillary Clinton's Emails, FOIA's Defects and Affirmative Disclosure." *U. Fla. JL & Pub. Pol'y* 29 (2018): 359.

Wasike, Ben. "FOI in transition: a comparative analysis of the Freedom of Information Act performance between the Obama and Trump administrations." *Government Information Quarterly* 37, no. 2 (2020): 101443.

Wild, W., E. Kaufman, and B. Starr. 2022. "DHS to stop wiping phones without backups | CNN Politics." August 4. https://www.cnn.com/2022/08/04/politics/homeland-security-secret-service-phones/index.html (accessed November 19, 2024).

Wilson, James Q. 1989. *Bureaucracy: What government agencies do and why they do it.*

Williamson, Elizabeth. 2007. "OMB Offers an Easy Way to Follow the Money." *Washington Post.* December 13. https://www.washingtonpost.com/wp-dyn/content/article/2007/12/12/AR2007121202701.html?nav=rss_politics/fedpage (accessed November 19, 2024).

Wood, Abby K., and David E. Lewis. "Agency performance challenges and agency politicization." *Journal of Public Administration Research and Theory* 27, no. 4 (2017): 581–95.

Wood, Abby K. "Disclosing Campaign Financing." *Oxford Handbook of American Election*, forthcoming, USC CLASS Research Paper No. 24–1. Available at SSRN: https://ssrn.com/abstract=4690456 (accessed November 19, 2024).

Yackee, Susan Webb. "Invisible (and visible) lobbying: The case of state regulatory policymaking." *State Politics & Policy Quarterly* 15, no. 3 (2015): 322–344.

Kirk A. Randazzo, Abigail Hassett and Anna Puente

7 The Judicial Balancing Act: Ideology, Law, and Legitimacy in Supreme Court Decisions

At the end of the Supreme Court's 2023–2024 term, a 6–3 majority delivered its decision in the case *Trump v. United States*.[1] Writing on behalf of an ideologically split majority, Chief Justice Roberts stated that presidents (and former presidents) are entitled to immunity from federal prosecution for "official acts" taken while in office. Essentially, this ruling indicated that the rule of law in the United States does not apply to everyone. The case involved actions taken by President Donald Trump following the election in 2020 that culminated in the violent insurrection on January 6, 2021. Facing indictment and trial on four counts of criminal activity by special counsel Jack Smith, Trump appealed to the Supreme Court following defeat in the U.S. Court of Appeals for the District of Columbia. The justices' decision examined presidential authority across three broad categories: a) official acts that reflect the core constitutional powers of the executive for which presidents possess absolute immunity; b) other official acts that exist outside these core constitutional powers, for which presidents possess presumptive immunity; and c) unofficial acts for which no immunity exists. By rendering such a decision and creating these new categories of presidential authority, the Supreme Court inserted itself into a highly contentious political situation and ensured that future cases would require judicial scrutiny to determine precise distinctions across the categories.

This case serves as a poignant reminder about how the Supreme Court can affect the political landscape across the United States. Additionally, it illustrates how ideological biases among the justices can become enshrined in the law when decisions are rendered by the Court. This means that the ideological preferences of the justices—their personal beliefs and partisan feelings about how things should work—are becoming part of the fabric of law in the United States. These aspects therefore beg the question to what extent has the Court become ideologically biased? Relatedly, what are the potential ramifications for legislative actions, public perception, and the institutional legitimacy of the Supreme Court?

---

1 603 U.S. 593 (2024).

Kirk A. Randazzo, Abigail Hassett, Anna Puente, University of South Carolina

https://doi.org/10.1515/9783111591902-007

This chapter examines these questions by focusing initially on public perceptions of the Court in response to the increasingly polarized voting behavior of the justices.

7.1 Public Opinion and the Court

In *Planned Parenthood v. Casey* (1992),[2] Justices O'Connor, Kennedy, and Souter noted that the Supreme Court's legitimacy, "depends on making legally principled decisions under circumstances in which their principled character is sufficiently plausible to be accepted by the Nation." For decades scholars have debated whether the Supreme Court relies on its legitimacy to render decisions that represent the rights of the minority (Bickel 1965) or the will of the majority (Hall and Ura 2015). Regardless of which assessment is more accurate, there is no question that the Court currently faces an erosion of this legitimacy. For much of recent history, the institution experienced a tremendous amount of public support, with opinion ratings hovering around 60–70 percent approval (Jones 2024). Compared to Congress, whose approval ratings hovered closer to 40 percent, the Court's approval was staggering (Gallup 2024). Yet, recent public opinion surveys (see Figure 7.1 from Gallup) demonstrate the Supreme Court's approval among the public has dropped below 50 percent for the first time ever (Jones 2024). The question remains as to why.

Part of the answer involves how average people evaluate the Supreme Court, and this is often through two different lenses: specific support and diffuse support. The former captures the immediate reaction a person has toward a specific decision. For example, does the individual like (or agree with) the Court's decision we mentioned earlier, *Trump v. United States* (2024)? This kind of support is temporary and tends to become less important (or less salient) over time. Diffuse support is more complex and tends to capture what scholars refer to as institutional legitimacy. For the Supreme Court, this involves a perception that the institution makes decisions in a fair and legally principled manner, over long periods of time. This allows the Court to develop a "reservoir of goodwill" (Bartels and Johnston 2013, 2020) through which the public places its trust in the institution, even when there is widespread disagreement with a single decision. Because diffuse support is more complex, scholars often try to learn more about it by asking broader questions focused on democratic values or whether individuals would support significant changes to the institution. For example, questions may arise about whether a respondent believes the Court is too mixed up in politics, if the

---

2 505 U.S. 833 (1992).

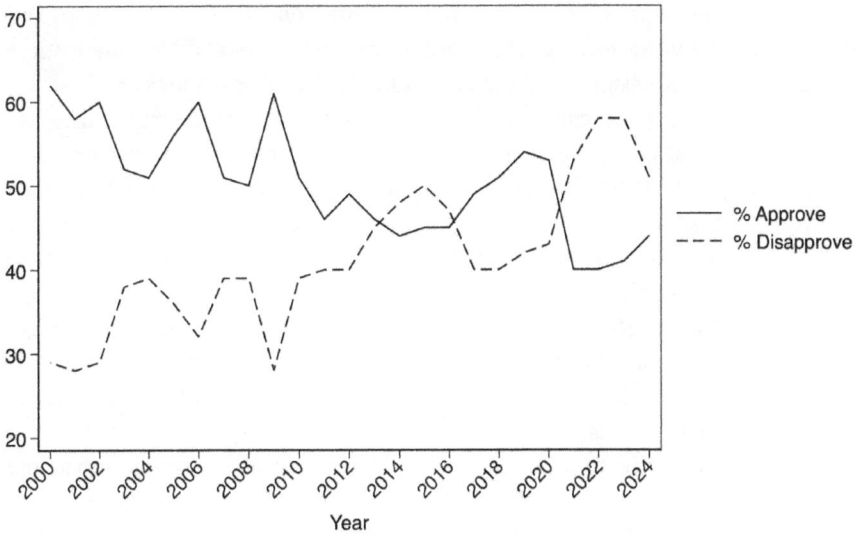

Figure 7.1: Public approval of the Supreme Court.[3]

Court favors certain groups (Gibson et al. 2003), or a respondent's willingness to sanction the Court under certain circumstances (Badas 2019; Gibson et al. 2003).

Historically, these kinds of questions revealed broad support for the Supreme Court as an institution. However, in recent years, this broad support faces potential erosion that largely falls along partisan and ideological lines. Individuals who tend to vote for Republican candidates respond with significantly higher approval ratings for the Court than individuals who vote for Democratic candidates. Additionally, people's views of the Supreme Court are shaped by the politicians they like or dislike (Armaly 2018), which reinforces this partisan divide.

7.2 Supreme Court Voting

Another part of the answer to eroding public support for the Supreme Court involves lack of information related to how the justices appointed to that institution operate on a daily basis. Quite simply, how do they vote? Generally speaking, the public has little to no knowledge about how the Court makes decisions. The vast

---

3 Reported July 30, 2024. See Gallup website: https://news.gallup.com/poll/647834/approval-su preme-court-stalled-near-historical-low.aspx

majority of Court operations happen behind closed doors. This is by design and the justices enjoy the secrecy. Therefore, to better understand how the justices vote requires a discussion about the Court's fundamental operations.

In an average year, the Court formally resolves between sixty and eighty cases. The process begins when a litigant (who lost a case at a lower court) petitions the Supreme Court for a writ of *certiorari*. Approximately 8000 petitions per year get filed and the justices have discretion to determine which cases they will review and which they will deny. It takes at least four (out of nine) justices to grant *certiorari*, at which point the case is accepted and scheduled for oral argument. Each litigant receives approximately thirty minutes to present their argument before the Court, during which time the justices ask a series of questions to the attorneys seeking to clarify areas of law. Following oral argument, the justices go into conference; this is a closed-door meeting where only the nine members of the Supreme Court are allowed in the room. Here the justices take an initial vote about whether they wish to affirm or reverse the decision of the lower court, based solely on the initial briefs and the oral argument of the attorneys. Once this vote occurs, the Chief Justice (if he is in the majority) determines who will write the official opinion, whether that involves assigning this to himself or another member of the majority coalition.[4] Following this conference, the justices begin writing drafts of their opinions (including any concurrences or dissents) and circulating these drafts to their colleagues. This process can take several months after which the justices go into conference again and take the official vote for the case. This vote not only decides whether the Court affirms or reverses the lower court's decision but also establishes the majority opinion (along with any concurrences and dissents) that get reported to the public.

So, what influences a justice to vote in a particular way on a specific case? It is important to recognize that they make these decisions based on several different considerations. The first aspect is the law. Justices care about the law and are often constrained both by statutes passed by Congress (Randazzo and Waterman 2014) and by previous Court precedent (Bailey and Maltzman 2008). Second, they are also influenced by the institutional rules of the Court and by each other (Epstein and Knight 1998). Third, we need to remember that they are people, with thoughts, feelings, and personal concerns. This means they care about having a good working environment, vacation time, and liking their job (Collins 2008; Black et al. 2019). Finally, they rely on their own ideological preferences when in-

---

4 If the Chief Justice is not in the majority at this conference, the senior Associate Justice in the majority determines the opinion writer.

terpreting laws that are not entirely clear (Segal and Spaeth 1993). This is why conservative justices tend to vote differently than their more liberal brethren.

Though John Roberts famously stated during his confirmation hearing that, "Judges and justices are servants of the law, not the other way around. Judges are like umpires. Umpires don't make the rules, they apply them" (Roberts 2005, n.p.), this notion of the apolitical judge making decisions based on the law is fading. Rather, scholars of the judiciary have demonstrated repeatedly that judges are political actors who rely on their personal policy preferences when making decisions (Segal and Cover 1989; Martin and Quinn 2002; Bailey 2017). Scholars have also demonstrated that the justices occasionally consider public opinion, particularly when there are strong shifts toward previously non-salient topics (Casillas et al. 2011). This leads us to ask whether the current downward trends in public approval of the Supreme Court will influence the justices to change behavior. Given that these trends are increasingly partisan in nature, it seems as if the justices may simply ignore responses that do not align with the ideological preferences of the current Court majority.

7.3 Contentious Nominations

Another aspect contributing to the potential ideological biasness of the Court is the increasing partisanship surrounding judicial nominations. Historically, nominations to the Supreme Court were not seen as partisan issues. For example, Justice Antonin Scalia was confirmed on a unanimous vote (98–0). Justices Stephen Breyer and Ruth Bader Ginsburg received overwhelming support from both parties in their confirmations as well. Breyer was confirmed by a vote of 87–9 and Ginsburg received confirmation by a vote of 96–3.

In contrast, the current political environment is significantly more divided along partisan lines, and this has affected nominations and confirmation to the Supreme Court. Since 2016, four nominations in particular bear discussion. The first involves Merrick Garland. Following the death of Justice Antonin Scalia in early 2016, the Supreme Court was left with four conservative and four liberal justices, which made the question of Scalia's replacement critically important for the ideological future of the institution. The Republican-controlled Senate, led by Majority Leader Mitch McConnell, maintained that the vacancy should not be filled until after the 2016 presidential election, so that the people could be given a say in the direction of the Court. Democrats, on the other hand, argued that President Barack Obama had the Constitutional right to fill the vacancy, especially given that the election was not set to take place until more than seven months later (Elving 2018). In March of 2016, President Obama nominated Merrick Garland, but Democrats in the Senate needed at least *some* support from their Republican colleagues if Garland's appointment was to move forward. With virtually no bipartisan support, the Senate never took a formal vote on Garland's confirmation, despite his nearly twenty years of experience as a federal judge on the U.S. Court of Appeals for the District of Columbia Circuit. After President Donald Trump won the 2016 election and took office, he nominated Neil Gorsuch to fill the vacancy, who was confirmed by a narrow vote that fell nearly entirely along party lines.[5]

Less than a year and a half later, President Trump had the opportunity to make another Supreme Court appointment when Justice Anthony Kennedy retired from the bench. Trump's nominee, Brett Kavanaugh, prompted four full days of Senate confirmation hearings that captured the attention of the public and clearly illustrated just how deep the partisan divide had become. Marked by high emotions as Democrats questioned Kavanaugh on issues such as the role of ideology on the bench and the possibility of overturning *Roe v. Wade* (1973) (Fram et al. 2018), the hearings took a scandalous turn when Dr. Christine Blasey Ford's allegations of sexual assault took center stage (Fram et al. 2018; Gresko 2018; NPR 2018). Kavanaugh denied all allegations against him, though that proved to do little in terms of garnering Democratic support. When it came time for the final vote, Kavanaugh was confirmed with exactly fifty votes (the bare minimum required) including one sole Democratic vote.[6]

Two years later, Trump was yet again positioned to appoint another conservative justice to the Court after Justice Ruth Bader Ginsburg, a liberal giant and a trailblazer for women's rights and racial equality, died in mid-September 2020 of pancreatic cancer. There was already a 5–4 conservative majority on the Court prior to Ginsburg's death, which meant that Trump's nomination would only further solidify and fortify the Court's conservative slant (Mascaro 2020). The circumstances surrounding Trump's nomination of Amy Coney Barrett seemed rather familiar as it was once again a presidential election year, though this time with a Republican president in office and only two months until election day. However, in stark contrast to 2016, Senate Republicans did not seem to have any concerns about the proximity of a new Court appointment to the upcoming presidential election. Meanwhile, Democrats now took the position that the Court vacancy should not be filled until after the election (Jalonick and Mascaro 2020; Mascaro 2020). Ultimately, Democratic efforts to delay Barrett's appointment proceedings

---

5 https://www.senate.gov
6 https://www.senate.gov

were futile. The Republican-controlled Senate was able to confirm Barrett about one week prior to the election without a single vote from the Democratic party.[7]

Finally, in early 2022 Joe Biden nominated Ketanji Brown Jackson to the Court shortly after Justice Stephen Breyer announced his retirement. Democrats applauded the nomination, but Senate Republicans, now in the minority, voiced concern that Jackson had been too lenient during her tenure as a federal appellate judge (Mascaro 2022; Sprunt 2022). Despite a general lack of Republican support, Ketanji Brown Jackson was confirmed as the first Black woman to ever serve on the Supreme Court, with a 53–47 vote that largely fell along party lines (Sherman and Jalonick 2022).

These nominations to the Supreme Court, marked by intense confirmation hearings and party-line votes, all serve to highlight the growing role that partisan ideology has played in the appointment process over the last decade. Looking ahead, one long-term concern is that appointments to the Supreme Court will not be determined by merit or experience but will instead become a function of which party has a majority in the Senate. Another concern is that final votes in the Supreme Court will increasingly fall along party lines, which could lead to further questions about the legitimacy of the Court and its rulings. For now, the Court has a distinct conservative tilt because, as the first president since Ronald Reagan to appoint more than two Justices to the Supreme Court, Trump was able to cement his influence on the court for decades to come. Only time will tell if the trend of confirming Justices almost entirely along party lines will continue or if we will eventually see more bipartisan support for Court nominees.

7.4 Court Ethics

Ethical concerns, specifically related to Supreme Court Justices' financial transparency, have recently come to the forefront of the public eye. In 2023, a groundbreaking report published by ProPublica revealed that Justice Clarence Thomas had accepted, and failed to report, lavish trips and gifts paid for by Dallas-based businessman and GOP donor, Harlan Crow, for over two decades (Kaplan et al. 2023). Subsequent reports brought to light further unreported vacations, gifts, and financial benefits that various members of the Court had received (Jones 2023; Schwartz 2023; Sherman 2023; Przybyla 2023), including, notably, a fishing trip taken by Justice Samual Alito paid for by billionaire Paul Singer (Elliott et al. 2023). That some members of the Supreme Court had failed to report such finan-

---

7 https://www.senate.gov

cial gains raised serious ethical concerns regarding transparency, recusals, and undue influences on the court. The fact that there was no binding official code of conduct only made matters worse as the news elicited public outcry condemning the Justices for their actions.

Until recently, members of the Court have been solely responsible for deciding what to include (and what to omit) on their annual financial reports, and, as statements from Thomas and Alito highlight, these decisions have often been based on semantics or technicalities. In his 2022 annual filing, Justice Thomas claimed that he was "not aware of anything in the Judicial Conference regulation" that had previously required members of the Court to report private trips paid for by personal friends (Totenberg 2023). In an article he wrote for the *Wall Street Journal*, Alito similarly defended his actions, citing the instructions he was given that stated, "personal hospitality need not be reported" (Alito 2023, n.p.).

However, claims that members of the Court had been unduly influenced by unreported financial gains from private interests could not be so easily dismissed. Once the allegations of impropriety came to light, it was noted that Alito and Thomas had not recused themselves from past cases in which their benefactors had a vested interest (Elliott et al. 2023). For example, concerns have been raised that Justice Alito did not recuse himself from cases involving Paul Singer's hedge fund, even after going on a fishing trip funded by Singer. Alito denied that he had any conflicts of interest, because as he claimed, he was unaware of Singer's association with such cases (Alito 2023; Elliot et al. 2023).

Despite the judges' efforts to exonerate themselves from allegations of malfeasance, public pressure for the Supreme Court to adopt an officially binding ethics code became impossible to ignore. In November of 2023, more than 230 years after its first assembly, the Supreme Court adopted its very first official code of conduct. It is worth noting, however, that the code begins with a statement asserting that the members of the Court had long adhered to very similar guidelines, and that the official adoption of a code of conduct was a mere formality to placate the public and dispel criticism arising from the absence of an official code.[8] However, the Supreme Court Code of Conduct does not contain any stated mechanisms for enforcement, and short of impeachment procedures, all disciplinary action against justices will be handled in-house (Lampe 2023; Waldman 2023).

---

8 https://www.supremecourt.gov/opinions/slipopinion/23

7.5 Recent Court Decisions

In addition to the case, *Trump v. United States* (2024) that we mentioned earlier, the Supreme Court recently handed down decisions in two additional cases that suggest the conservative justices (with their significant majority) are willing to increasingly wade into politically charged areas. The first case, *Loper Bright Enterprises v. Raimondo* (2024),[9] garnered less attention than the *Trump* presidential immunity decision, but is no less important. The case started when a group of commercial fishermen sued the National Marine Fisheries Service after it implemented a rule requiring companies to fund various 'at-sea monitoring' programs (the estimated cost of which was $710 per day). The primary legal issue in contention involved the 1984 precedent articulated by the Court in *Chevron USA v. Natural Resources Defense Council*,[10] which stated that courts must defer to interpretations of law reached by government agencies. Writing on behalf of a 6–2 majority, Chief Justice John Roberts rejected the *Chevron* principle. Instead, he stated that the Administrative Procedure Act of 1946 required courts to "decide all relevant questions of law." Therefore, the *Chevron* ruling was based on a faulty premise. The practical implication of the *Loper Bright* decision is that Congress can no longer rely on administrative agencies to craft rules and regulations based on the experts working in those agencies. Rather, Congress itself must pass legislation whenever a change is needed. Given how difficult it has become for Congress to pass new laws, many legislative scholars (including the authors of this chapter) believe that the *Loper Bright* decision will significantly erode the modern administrative state that has developed since the New Deal in the 1930s.

The second case recently handed down by the Supreme Court is *Dobbs v. Jackson Women's Health Organization* (2022).[11] This case developed after Mississippi passed the Gestational Age Act in 2018, which prohibited all abortions (with few exceptions) after fifteen weeks. The Jackson Women's Health Organization, which at the time was the only licensed abortion facility in the state, sued. It claimed that Mississippi's new law violated the constitutional right to an abortion as articulated by the Supreme Court in the cases *Roe v. Wade* (1973)[12] and *Planned Parenthood of Pennsylvania v. Casey* (1992).[13] However, when the Supreme Court heard the appeal, Justice Alito disagreed. Writing on behalf of a 6–3 majority, he

---

9 603 U.S. 369 (2024). Justice Brown Jackson recused herself because she had not yet been appointed when the Court heard oral arguments.
10 467 U.S. 837 (1984).
11 597 U.S. 215 (2022).
12 410 U.S. 113 (1973).
13 505 U.S. 833 (1992).

issued an opinion that overturned *Roe* and *Casey*. As Alito argued, the Constitution makes no reference to abortion explicitly and no such right is implicitly protected by any constitutional provision. Additionally, Alito stated that rights not explicitly mentioned must be "deeply rooted in this Nation's history and traditions" and "implicit in the concept of ordered liberty." The overturning of *Roe* and *Casey* marked the first time that the Supreme Court has revoked constitutional rights previously accepted by the justices. Given that every justice acknowledged the importance of the *Roe* precedent, the decision in *Dobbs* catapulted the country into a new legal framework in which states were allowed to craft their own laws about reproductive rights. Some chose to further enshrine abortion protections and others moved to limit access or abolish abortions outright (see Chapter 14 for more details).

Regardless of whether one agrees with the Court's decisions in *Loper Bright* and *Dobbs* or not, what these two cases demonstrate (along with the decision in *Trump v. United States*) is that the conservative justices on the Supreme Court are increasingly willing to use their ideological majority to address politically controversial issues. This, combined with the ethical issues and the contentious nominations, is one of the primary reasons that public opinion of the Court has dropped to its lowest level ever. Additionally, it begs the question of whether the public will demand institutional reforms in the future.

7.6 What Comes Next?

A relatively simple question—what comes next?—unfortunately does not have a relatively simple answer. Previously, whenever questions about institutional reforms to the Supreme Court arose, its legitimacy (i.e., its diffuse support) was sufficient to prevent lawmakers from making significant changes. Now that public approval of the Court has dropped so low, several proposals have been introduced. The first is a code of ethics. Though the justices adopted an ethics code in 2023, the rules are incredibly weak, as alluded to earlier. Essentially, the justices get to monitor and police themselves; they are the ones to determine whether a fellow justice has an ethical violation. As Michael Waldman (2023) of the Brennan Center acknowledged soon after the adoption, "nobody is wise enough to be the judge in their own case. Yet the justices will still judge themselves. There is no mechanism to enforce the code – no arbiter to enforce, apply, or even interpret these rules" (n.p.). To address these issues, the Senate most recently introduced the Supreme Court Ethics Act (2023). It would require the Court to appoint an ethics investigation counsel who would investigate complaints and adopt rules to enforce the code. The individual would also issue a public report every year to describe the steps taken to address ethics complaints. However, with the Senate moving from Democratic to Republican control after the 2024 election, it is likely that this proposal will not move forward nor become law any time soon.

The second proposed institutional change would increase the number of justices. This proposal, introduced by Representative Adam Schiff (D-CA) and Senator Edward Markey (D-MA), would add four new justices to the Court; thereby increasing its number from the current nine to thirteen. As Schiff stated in July 2024, "Republicans have transformed the Supreme Court into a partisan vehicle for their conservative policies, endangering our democracy, reproductive rights, and environmental standards. It's time to pass the Judiciary Act to ensure the Court serves justice, not political interests." Since the number of justices is not determined by the Constitution, Congress only needs to pass a statute specifying the number. Over the history of the United States, there have been as few as five and as many as ten justices. Congress set the current number at nine following the U.S. Civil War and it allowed for one justice per judicial circuit. Given that there are now thirteen judicial circuits, Schiff and Markey argue that the Court should expand to match this growth. However, as with the first proposed institutional reform, it is unlikely that this will move forward given the composition of Congress following the 2024 election.

The final institutional reform would create term limits for the justices. Such a suggestion is widely popular with Americans, many of whom also like the idea of term limits for members of Congress (Smart and Sturm 2013). Unlike the previous reform, which can adjust the number of justices by congressional statute, Article III of the Constitution provides all federal judges with life tenure. Therefore, most people initially thought that enacting term limits would require a constitutional amendment. However, in 2021, President Biden formed a commission on Supreme Court reforms. One of the ideas generated by this commission offers a novel proposal. As former federal appellate judge, Diane Wood (2024) explains, in this new proposal, "justices would continue to have life tenure and salary protection, but they would participate in the apex appellate work of the Supreme Court for *only* 18 years. After that, they would continue to serve as senior Article III justices (assuming they wish to do so rather than simply retire), but they would be assigned to the lower federal courts" (n.p.). With staggered terms across the nine justices, this means that a vacancy would occur every two years; giving presidents two nominations per four-year term. Similar to the previous proposed reforms, it is extremely unlikely that this proposal will become reality even if it enjoys broad public support. Since both chambers of Congress, the White House, and the Supreme Court are dominated by conservatives there is little probability that they will mandate these kinds of structural changes because they currently enjoy disproportionate influence and obviously would not want to give this up (and Democrats would likely feel the same way if the situation were reversed).

7.7 Conclusion

As the introduction to this book indicates, "in recent decades American politics has been characterized by growing dysfunction and polarization, posing significant threats to the democratic process . . . One significant consequence of these political trends is the erosion of public trust in political institutions, a fundamental pillar of democracy." The recent actions of the Supreme Court—from contentious nominations to ethical concerns to decisions that wade into politically controversial areas—contribute to the growing polarization in the United States. As a consequence, public approval of the Court as an institution is at an all-time low. Since the probability of any institutional reforms within the Supreme Court are low, the erosion of public trust in the Supreme Court will likely continue. If the Court's conservative majority continues to exercise its ideological muscle by revoking additional rights, the public's sense of frustration and disillusionment will only increase.

Discussion Questions

1 To what extent is the Supreme Court able to transform society and under what conditions should the Court exercise its authority?
2 Should the justices of the Supreme Court adjust their decisions and/or behavior based on public opinion? Why or why not?
3 According to extensive research on Supreme Court voting, the two most dominant influences on the justices' decisions are: a) their individual ideological preferences; and b) the law. If these two influences point to different outcomes, which should prevail and why?
4 What steps are needed to decrease the political and partisan divides within the nomination and confirmation process of Supreme Court justices?
5 Should the Supreme Court be reformed? If so, what reforms are necessary to address concerns? If not, how should concerns be handled?

References

Alito, S. 2023. "Justice Samuel Alito: ProPublica Misleads Its Readers." *The Wall Street Journal*. June 20. https://www.wsj.com/articles/propublica-misleads-its-readers-alito-gifts-disclosure-alaska-singer-23b51eda.

Armaly, Miles T. 2018. "Extra-Judicial Actor Induced Change in Supreme Court Legitimacy." *Political Research Quarterly* 71 (3): 600–13.

Associated Press. 2023. "Justice Alito accepted Alaska resort vacation from GOP donors, report says." *AP News*. June 21. https://apnews.com/article/alito-supreme-court-ethics-fishing-trip-thomas -924606543d555cdfc87595428fd7619c.

Badas, Alex. 2019. "The Applied Legitimacy Index: A New Approach to Measuring Judicial Legitimacy." *Social Science Quarterly* 100 (5): 1848–61.

Bailey, Michael A. 2017. "Measuring Ideology on the Courts." In *Routledge Handbook of Judicial Behavior*. Routledge.

Bailey, Michael A., and Forrest Maltzman. 2008. "Does Legal Doctrine Matter? Unpacking Law and Policy Preferences on the U.S. Supreme Court." *American Political Science Review* 102 (3): 369–84.

Bartels, Brandon L., and Christopher D. Johnston. 2013. "On the Ideological Foundations of Supreme Court Legitimacy in the American Public." *American Journal of Political Science* 57 (1): 184–99.

Bartels, Brandon L., and Christopher D. Johnston. 2020. *Curbing the Court: Why the Public Constrains Judicial Independence*. Cambridge University Press.

Bickel, Alexander M. 1965. *Politics and the Warren Court*. Harper & Row.

Black, Ryan C., Ryan J. Owens, Justin Wedeking, and Patrick C. Wohlfarth. 2019. *The Conscientious Justice How Supreme Court Justices' Personalities Influence the Law, the High Court, and the Constitution*. Cambridge University Press.

Bush, D. 2018. "Analysis: What we learned from more than 39 hours of Kavanaugh confirmation hearings." *PBS News*. September 7. https://www.pbs.org/newshour/nation/analysis-what-we-learned-from-more-than-39-hours-of-kavanaugh-confirmation-hearings.

Casillas, Christopher J., Peter K. Enns, and Patrick C. Wohlfarth. 2011. "How Public Opinion Constrains the US Supreme Court." *American Journal of Political Science* 55 (1): 74–88.

Collins, Paul M. 2008. "The Consistency of Judicial Choice." *The Journal of Politics* 70 (3): 861–73.

Congressional Research Service. 2023. *The Supreme Court Adopts a Code of Conduct*. https://crsreports. congress.gov/product/pdf/LSB/LSB11078.

Durkee, A. 2024. "Supreme court ethics controversies: All the scandals that led Biden to endorse code of conduct." *Forbes*. July 29. https://www.forbes.com/sites/alisondurkee/2024/07/29/su preme-court-ethics-controversies-all-the-scandals-that-led-biden-to-endorse-code-of-conduct/.

Elliott, J., J. Kaplan, and A. Mierjeski. 2023. "Justice Samuel alito took luxury fishing vacation with GOP billionaire who later had cases before the court." *ProPublica*. June 20. https://www.propublica. org/article/samuel-alito-luxury-fishing-trip-paul-singer-scotus-supreme-court.

Elving, R. 2018. "What happened with Merrick garland in 2016 and why it matters now." *NPR*. June 29. https://www.npr.org/2018/06/29/624467256/what-happened-with-merrick-garland-in-2016-and-why-it-matters-now.

Epstein, Lee, and Jack Knight. 1998. *The Choices Justices Make*. Congressional Quarterly Inc.

Fram, A., L. Mascaro, and M. Daly. 2018. "Kavanaugh sworn to high court after rancorous confirmation." *AP News*. October 7. https://apnews.com/article/north-america-ap-top-news-sexual-misconduct-supreme-courts-courts-8234f0b8a6194d8b89ff79f9b0c94f35.

Gallup. 2024. "Congress and the Public." Gallup. December 31. https://news.gallup.com/poll/1600/congress-public.aspx.

Gibson, James L. 1978. "Judges' Role Orientations, Attitudes, and Decisions: An Interactive Model." *American Political Science Review* 72 (3): 911–24.

Gibson, James L, Gregora A. Caldeira, and Vanessa A. Baird. 1998. "On the Legitimacy of National High Courts." *American Political Science Review* 92 (2): 343–58.

Gibson, J.L., G.A. Caldeira, and L.K. Spence. 2003. "Measuring Attitudes toward the United States Supreme Court." *American Journal of Political Science* 47 (2): 354–67.

Gou, Angie. 2022. "As Unanimity Declines, Conservative Majority's Power Runs Deeper than the Blockbuster Cases." *Scotusblog*. https://www.scotusblog.com/2022/07/as-unanimity-declines-conservative-majoritys-power-runs-deeper-than-the-blockbuster-cases/.

Gresko, J. 2018. "5 takeaways: Kavanaugh's Supreme Court confirmation hearing." *AP News*. September 7. https://apnews.com/supreme-court-of-the-united-states-c8ed878e1f5a4345bdc8c82d0b4ec484.

Hall, Matthew E. K., and Joseph Daniel Ura. 2015. "Judicial Majoritarianism." *American Political Science Review* 109 (4): 673–89.

Ho, Daniel E., and Kevin M. Quinn. 2010. "How Not to Lie with Judicial Votes: Misconceptions, Measurement, and Models." *California Law Review* 98 (3): 813–76.

Jalonick, M. C., and L. Mascaro. 2020. "Trump chose Barrett days after Ginsburg's death, papers show." *AP News*. September 30. https://apnews.com/article/election-2020-virus-outbreak-donald-trump-ruth-bader-ginsburg-amy-coney-barrett-4b50c5a95588ab80d88dbe0803a3a729.

Jones, D. 2023. "What to know about the Supreme Court and ethical concerns." *NPR*. May 5. https://www.npr.org/2023/05/05/1174057179/supreme-court-congress-ethical-hearing.

Jones, Jeffrey M. 2024. "Party Divisions in Views of Supreme Court Keep Ratings Low." *Gallup*. https://news.gallup.com/poll/651527/party-divisions-views-supreme-court-keep-ratings-low.aspx.

Kaplan, J., J. Elliott, and A. Mierjeski. 2023. "Clarence Thomas secretly accepted luxury trips from GOP donor." *ProPublica*. April 6. https://www.propublica.org/article/clarence-thomas-scotus-undisclosed-luxury-travel-gifts-crow.

Lampe, Joanna R. 2023. "The Supreme Court Adopts a Code of Conduct." *Congressional Research Service*: *Legal Sidebar*. https://crsreports.congress.gov/product/pdf/LSB/LSB11078.

Martin, Andrew D., and Kevin M. Quinn. 2002. "Dynamic Ideal Point Estimation via Markov Chain Monte Carlo for the U.S. Supreme Court, 1953–1999." *Political Analysis* 10 (2): 134–53.

Mascaro, L. 2020. "Barrett confirmed as Supreme Court justice in partisan vote." *AP News*. October 27. https://apnews.com/article/election-2020-donald-trump-virus-outbreak-ruth-bader-ginsburg-amy-coney-barrett-82a02a618343c98b80ca2b6bf9eafe07.

Mascaro, L. 2022. "Takeaways: Joy, tears, culture wars dominate Jackson hearing." *AP News*. March 24. https://apnews.com/article/ketanji-brown-jackson-hearing-day-3-highlights-95aea2b41a957788f3dd072fb1e396f2.

Naylor, B. 2018. "Brett Kavanaugh offers fiery defense in hearing that was A national cultural moment." *NPR*. September 28. https://www.npr.org/2018/09/28/652239571/brett-kavanaugh-offers-fiery-defense-in-hearing-that-was-a-national-cultural-mom.

NPR Staff. 2018 "READ: Christine Blasey Ford's opening statement for senate hearing." *NPR*. September 26. https://www.npr.org/2018/09/26/651941113/read-christine-blasey-fords-opening-statement-for-senate-hearing.

Przybyla, H. 2023. "Law firm head bought Gorsuch-owned property." *Politico*. April 25. https://www.politico.com/news/2023/04/25/neil-gorsuch-colorado-property-sale-00093579.

Randazzo, Kirk A., and Richard W. Waterman. 2014. *Checking the Courts: Law, Ideology, and Contingent Discretion*. SUNY Press.

Roberts, John G., Jr. 2005. "Chief Justice Roberts Statement – Nomination Process." https://www.uscourts.gov/educational-resources/educational-activities/chief-justice-roberts-statement-nomination-process.

Schiff, Adam, and Edward Markey. 2024. "The Judiciary Act." https://schiff.house.gov/news/press-releases/schiff-markey-colleagues-push-to-expand-supreme-court-amidst-crisis-of-confidence.

Segal, Jeffrey A., and Albert D. Cover. 1989. "Ideological Values and the Votes of U.S. Supreme Court Justices." *American Political Science Review* 83 (2): 557–65.

Segal, Jeffrey A., and Harold J. Spaeth. 1993. *The Supreme Court and the Attitudinal Model*. Cambridge University Press.

Schwartz, M. 2023, April 28). "Jane Roberts, who is married to Chief Justice John Roberts, made $10.3 million in commissions from elite law firms, whistleblower documents show." *Business Insider*. April 28. https://www.businessinsider.com/jane-roberts-chief-justice-wife-10-million-commissions-2023-4.

Sherman, M. 2023. "Justice Clarence Thomas reports he took 3 trips on Republican donor's plane last year." *AP News*. August 31. https://apnews.com/article/supreme-court-ethics-finances-justices-thomas-alito-08ec6e88a7c29c55c9d3991903ca0db7.

Sherman, M., and M. C. Jalonick. 2022. "Jackson confirmed as first Black female high court justice." *AP News*. April 7. https://apnews.com/article/ketanji-brown-jackson-supreme-court-confirmation-f39263cdbb0c59c8a20a48edf9b6786e

Smart, Michael, and Daniel M. Sturm. 2013. "Term Limits and Electoral Accountability." *Journal of Public Economics* 107: 93–102.

Solman, P. 2023. "Read the Supreme Court's first-ever ethics code." *PBS News*. November 13. https://www.pbs.org/newshour/politics/read-the-supreme-courts-first-ever-ethics-code.

Sprunt, B. 2022. "Judge Ketanji Brown Jackson confirmation hearings: What happened Tuesday." *NPR*. March 22. https://www.npr.org/2022/03/22/1087967982/judge-ketanji-brown-jackson-confirmation-hearings-what-happened-on-tuesday.

Supreme Court. n.d. *Code of Conduct for Justices of the Supreme Court of the United States*. Accessed October 31, 2024. https://www.supremecourt.gov/about/Code-of-Conduct-for-Justices_November_13_2023.pdf.

Supreme Court. n.d. "History and Traditions." Accessed October 31, 2024. https://www.supremecourt.gov/about/historyandtraditions.aspx.

Totenberg, N. 2023. "Now-released forms reveal more trips gifted to Justice Clarence Thomas by Harlan Crow." *NPR*. August 31. https://www.npr.org/2023/08/31/1196993118/justices-thomas-alito-financial-disclosures.

The White House. President Barack Obama. n.d. "President Obama's Supreme Court Nomination." Accessed October 23, 2024. https://obamawhitehouse.archives.gov/scotus.

U.S. States Senate. 2024. "Supreme Court Nominations (1789-Present)." October 2. https://www.senate.gov/legislative/nominations/SupremeCourtNominations1789present.htm

U.S. Senate. 2023. "Supreme Court Ethics Act (S. 325)." https://www.congress.gov/bill/118th-congress/senate-bill/325.

U.S. Senate. 2023. "U.S. senate roll call votes 115th congress – 1st session." August 11. https://www.senate.gov/legislative/LIS/roll_call_votes/vote1151/vote_115_1_00111.htm?congress=115&session=1&vote=00111.

U.S. Senate. 2023. "U.S. senate roll call votes 115th congress – 2nd session." August 11. https://www.senate.gov/legislative/LIS/roll_call_votes/vote1152/vote_115_2_00223.htm.

U.S. Senate. 2023. "U.S. senate roll call votes 116th congress – 2nd session." August 11. https://www.senate.gov/legislative/LIS/roll_call_votes/vote1162/vote_116_2_00224.htm?congress=116&session=2&vote=00224.

U.S. Senate. 2023. "U.S. senate roll call votes 117th congress – 2nd session." August 10. https://www.senate.gov/legislative/LIS/roll_call_votes/vote1172/vote_117_2_00134.htm.

Waldman, Michael. 2023. "New Supreme Court Ethics Code is Designed to Fail." Brennan Center. November 14. https://www.brennancenter.org/our-work/analysis-opinion/new-supreme-court-ethics-code-designed-fail.

Walsh, D. 2020. "Takeaways from Amy Coney Barrett's judiciary confirmation hearings." *NPR*. October 15. https://www.npr.org/2020/10/15/923637375/takeaways-from-amy-coney-barretts-judiciary-confirmation-hearings.

Wood, Diane P. 2024. "Why Term Limits for Supreme Court Justices Make Sense." Brennan Center. August 19. https://www.brennancenter.org/our-work/analysis-opinion/why-term-limits-supreme-court-justices-make-sense.

James M. Curry

8 Capitol Gains and Losses: Navigating Leadership in Today's Polarized Congress

> "I don't think the Lord Jesus himself could manage this group."
> Representative Troy Nehls (R-TX) about leading the House
> Republican Conference[1]

> "Organize, don't agonize."
> Mantra of former-Speaker of the House, Nancy Pelosi (D-CA)[2]

On October 2, 2023, Representative Matt Gaetz (R-FL) kicked off a process that had not been seriously attempted in the House of Representatives in over 100 years: he filed a motion to vacate the Speaker's chair. This motion, which can be offered by any member of the House at any time, forces a vote to remove or keep the current Speaker of the House in their position. "Bring it on," was the only response from Speaker Kevin McCarthy (R-CA).[3] The next day, Gaetz and his allies brought the smoke. Eight Republicans voted alongside every House Democrat, and for the first time in congressional history a sitting speaker was forced from the office.[4]

Congressional leaders today face a brave new world. The story of Kevin McCarthy's downfall reflects our modern political dynamics (see Chapter 4 for a more extended discussion of these events). Politics today is more contentious and fraught, with unprecedented polarization between the parties (McCarty 2019), intense two-party electoral competition (Lee 2016), disenchantment and distrust in American governing institutions (McGrath 2017), and rising public animosity (Mason 2018; Webster 2020). These changes have bled into Congress, with a greater focus than ever on manufacturing conflict, party messaging (Gelman 2020), and doing things that can gain attention on social media (Russell 2025).

At first glance, these changes sound like bad news for congressional leaders. They are dealing with intra-party factions at each other's throats, an opposing party that is happy to watch them squirm, and an American public that mostly

---

1 Sahil Kapur et al., "'We're ungovernable': House Republicans nix votes on two funding bills as shutdown deadline nears," NBC News, November 9, 2023.
2 Kathy Spillar, "Speaker Nancy Pelosi's Fearless Feminist Legacy," Ms., November 11, 2022.
3 Haley Talbot et al., "Matt Gaetz moves to oust Kevin McCarthy as House speaker," CNN.com, October 2, 2023.
4 See, Roll Call #519, 118th Congress, 1st Session.

James M. Curry, University of Utah

https://doi.org/10.1515/9783111591902-008

treats leaders on Capitol Hill with disdain. For Kevin McCarthy, leading the House Republican Conference often was agony. And McCarthy is not alone; Nancy Pelosi, Paul Ryan, Mitch McConnell, and John Boehner all experienced trials of leadership that were unheard of for much of the previous century. Each saw their leadership challenged or threatened by factions within their own parties, and each earned themselves the disdain of people on both sides of the aisle. Modern congressional leadership is no bed of roses.

However, students of American politics and Congress should be cautious in concluding that changes to our politics have only made congressional leadership harder. Taking stock of the current situation, we should understand our current political context as providing both challenges and opportunities. In some ways, congressional leadership has rarely been more difficult. The current political climate presents new problems for leaders as they attempt to organize and lead their parties. At the same time, and because of the same changes in our politics, congressional leaders are now empowered on Capitol Hill in ways that their predecessors could have only dreamed up. This duality has come to define the world of congressional party leadership.

8.1 The Role of Context in Understanding Congressional Leadership

Political scientists have long presented the political context faced by congressional party leaders as a central force explaining their power. Simply, party leaders —here understood as the top leaders of each party in each chamber, such as the Speaker of the House, the Senate Majority Leader, and the Minority Leaders in each chamber—are thought to be able to exercise more power when the context enables it. This perspective is most apparent in scholarship that adopts a principal-agent framework to understanding congressional leadership, whereby leaders are selected as agents of their rank-and-file and are delegated power as a division of labor to reduce the inefficiencies inherent in collective action (see Krehbiel 1991; Kiewiet and McCubbins 1991). Party leaders exist to grease the skids for successful legislating, however, they are expected to be tightly monitored by their followers. The political context can both restrict and augment their power.

In this telling, leaders can only exercise significant power when there is broad agreement among their rank-and-file to do so. Party leaders, in other words, are not more or less powerful because of their skill, style, or force of will, but because they inhabit a context in which their followers enable them to be more powerful. Cooper and Brady (1981) made a case for this perspective by examining the different approaches adopted by House Speakers Joseph Cannon (R-IL) and Sam Rayburn (D-TX). Cannon's leadership (1903–1911) was more aggressive and hierarchical because he led a unified House Republican Party that was willing to delegate significant power to his office. Rayburn, on the other hand, led a deeply fractured Democratic Party (from 1940–1961) that allotted him fewer formal powers. He had no choice but to adopt a less aggressive style that was more focused on bargaining and maintaining relationships.

Some of the most prominent theories of party power are imbued with this logic. It is central to Aldrich and Rohde's (2000) theory of *conditional party government*, by which party members in Congress delegate more powers to their leaders and expect them to act more aggressively to use those powers under a certain *condition*—when the party is more cohesive in its priorities and preferences and the other party is more unified in its opposition. The political context is also a central point in prominent agenda setting theories of congressional power (e.g., Cox and McCubbins 2005) in which majority party leaders are delegated complete control over the congressional agenda but are only expected to advance legislation that their party's members are unified behind. The implication is clear; party leaders are more empowered and can more easily lead when their party is unified and cohesive but can do very little otherwise.

Not all scholarship expects leaders to only be empowered under these conditions. Rubin (2025), for example, argues that under the right conditions a *divided* party can result in powerful leadership. If a party is split into two or more relatively balanced and competing factions, leaders are placed in the central role of mediating among competing power centers, giving them great opportunities to lead. It is only when the factions are imbalanced that leaders may find themselves in a weakened position. In this sense, party cohesion *or* in-cohesion could create a better or worse context for strong leadership, depending on the specifics. Strahan (2007) also challenged the standard contextual paradigm. Examining the leadership of Henry Clay, Thomas Reed, and Newt Gingrich, Strahan showed that while each was affected by the context of their time in power, each was also able to lead in ways that were independent of that context. Context is not fate. There remains a role for leaders' individual traits, skills, and decisions to shape their successes and failures.

Ultimately, then, understanding how the current moment affects congressional leadership requires close consideration, and an openness to the possibility that the context of the times may cut both ways—helping and hindering leaders. Taking stock of the current situation, this is what we see. In some ways, congressional leadership has never been more challenging. In other ways, leaders have never been more empowered.

8.2 Capitol Losses: How Leadership has Become More Challenging

Several of the recent changes to our politics have made congressional party leadership more challenging. Rising conflict between the parties has made building the necessary bipartisan support for legislative action more difficult. Meanwhile, changes to the political environment that have elevated the importance of intraparty divisions and factionalism have created new difficulties for congressional leaders as they try to organize and unify their membership.

Let's start with the rise in party conflict. In many ways, Democrats and Republicans have never been more divided. But for Congress and congressional leaders, the biggest change is that the parties have greater incentive to fight with each other than in the past. For most of American history, party politics was such that one side was ascendant, holding large and durable majorities in the House and the Senate, while the other party was an almost permanent minority. Among these uncompetitive eras was a long period of Democratic Party dominance. From 1932 until 1994 Democrats controlled the House for all but four years, and the Senate for just a few less.

Today, however, we live in an era of insecure majorities, as Lee (2016) labels it. Majorities on Capitol Hill since 1995 have been tenuous and small. Since then, party control of the House of Representatives has changed hands four times—in 2006, 2010, 2018, and 2022. The Senate has changed hands six times—in 2001,[5] 2002, 2006, 2014, 2020, and 2024. The sizes of majorities in our modern era have been historically small, as well. See Figure 8.1 for reference, which shows the size of party majorities in the House and Senate since 1901. Prior to the 1980s, majorities in the House and Senate were typically large. For the first ninety-five years of the twentieth century (1901–1994), majority parties in the House and Senate held, on average, 59 percent of the seats in each chamber, and it was common for a party to sweep elections and take control of 65 percent or even 70 percent of the seats. Since 1995, what stands out is the smallness of margins in both chambers, as the majority parties in the House and Senate have controlled, on average, just 53 percent of the seats in each chamber, and the margins are often even smaller than that.

Small and tenuous majorities make for different political calculations. In less competitive eras there was greater incentive for cooperation between the parties.

---

5 Control of the U.S. Senate switched in the middle of the 107th Congress (2001–02) as Senator Jim Jeffords of Vermont left the Republican Party and joined the Democrats, causing the GOP to lose control of the chamber.

(a) House of Representatives

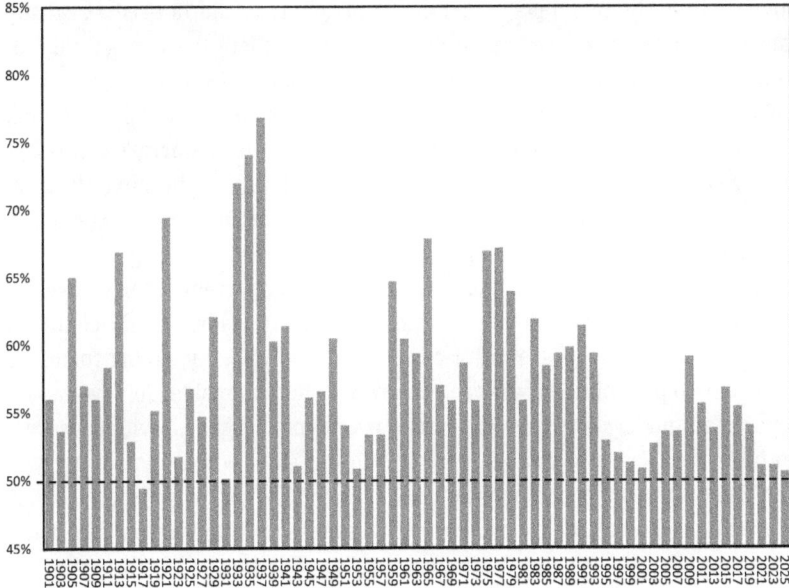

(b) Senate

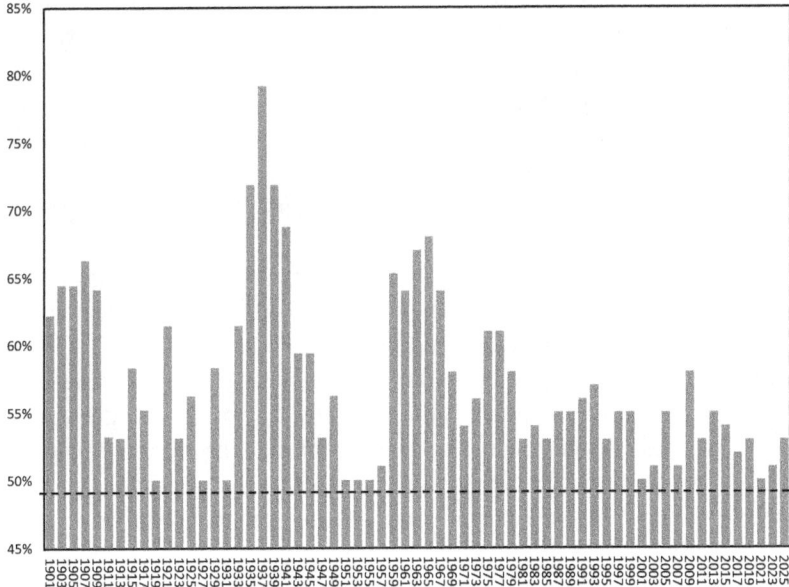

Figure 8.1: Size of party majorities, 1901–2025.
Source: Data collected by the author from https://history.house.gov/Institution/Party-Divisions/Party-Divisions/ and https://www.senate.gov/history/partydiv.htm.

Members of long-term majority parties did not see the minority as a threat to their power. Similarly, members of the minority generally did not see a realistic path back to taking control. The result was a dynamic where there was little reason to pick fights. Today, with the party in power's control tenuous, both sides are highly attentive to the electoral implications of every decision, bill, and vote. The minority sees electoral opportunity in opposing the majority's efforts at every turn. The majority, seeing the minority as a threat in the next election, wants to make as few concessions as possible while advancing its agenda as quickly as it can before it loses power (see Lee 2016).

This new environment means building bipartisan support for a party's agenda is much harder than before. In the past, majority party leaders could count on being able to cut deals with groups of centrists in the minority, giving them the votes necessary to pass bills. For years, Democratic congressional leaders bargained with Republican moderates while Republican presidents bargained with conservative southern Democrats to build suitable coalitions. Now, the minority party is more likely to hold together in opposition to the majority's legislative efforts. Bipartisanship requires leaders of the majority to negotiate with the leadership of the other party and forge agreements that can bring all or most of both parties together. This is no simple task in an era of high party polarization.

In addition to increased two-party conflict, the political context has changed in other ways that have often made it more difficult for congressional party leaders to organize and unify the members of their party. For one, while the memberships of both parties are generally more ideologically cohesive than in the past, the size of majorities in the House and Senate has meant than even a small amount of intra-party disagreement can result in disaster. Today, it takes *extremely* high levels of unity for House and Senate majority parties to put together enough votes on their side of the aisle to win on votes.

Consider Figure 8.2, which shows the average party unity scores among members of the majority party in the House and Senate,[6] alongside the party unity necessary to construct a chamber majority on a vote. This latter measure, in other words, is the percentage of majority party members that would need to vote 'yea' to get to a majority in the House (typically 218 votes) or in the Senate (either 50 or 51 votes). When the latter value is higher than the former, it suggests that the majority's typical unity in that year was generally not going to be enough to carry the day. In recent years, however, we see that even though levels of unity

---

6 Each member's party unity score is the percent of the party dividing roll call votes (those on which a majority of one party votes in opposition to a majority of the other) in a given year on which they voted with a majority of their party's members. The average party unity scores are simply the average for all members of the majority party in the House or Senate each year.

(a) House of Representatives

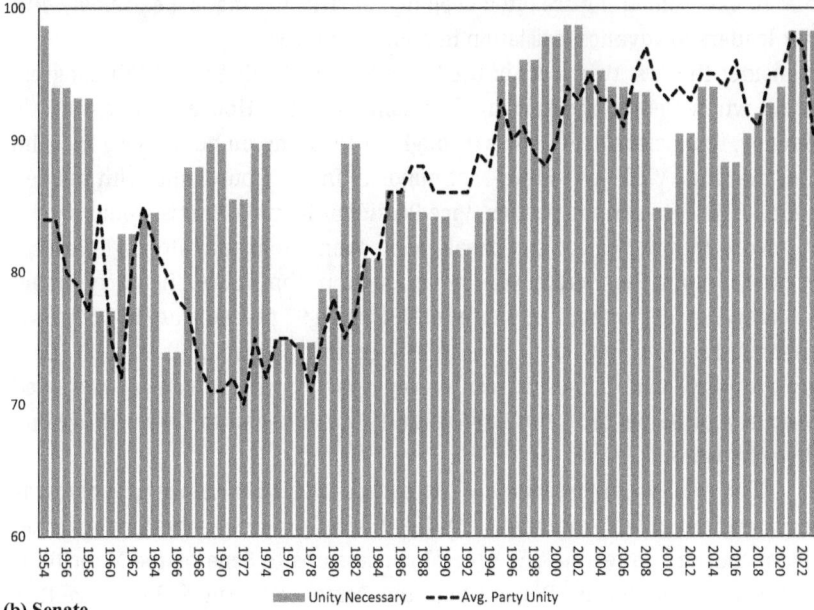

Unity Necessary — ==Avg. Party Unity

(b) Senate

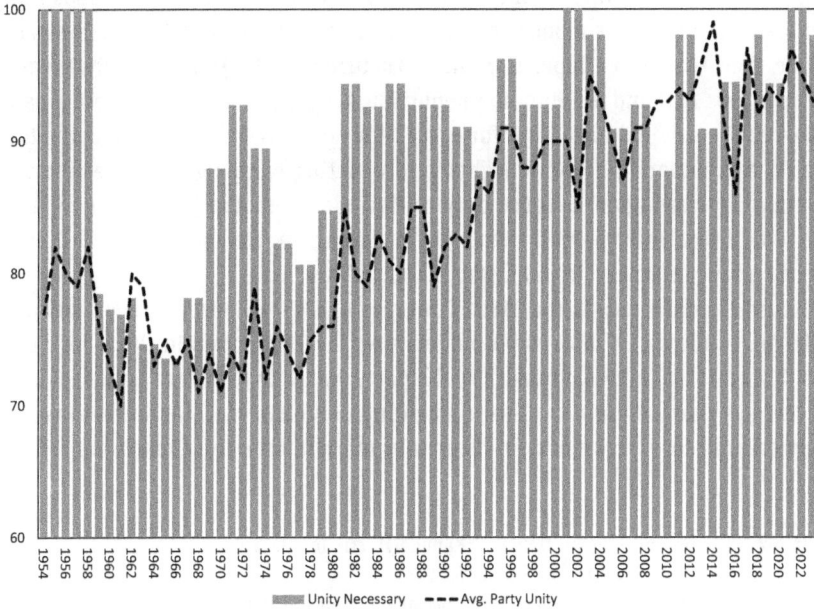

Unity Necessary — ==Avg. Party Unity

Figure 8.2: Majority party unity on Capitol Hill, 1954–2023.
Source: Congressional Quarterly, various editions. Compiled by author.

in the majority party are high, the levels necessary to obtain a chamber majority of votes to pass something are often even higher. This has made it extremely difficult for leaders to advance legislation in many instances.

Consider the first two years of the Biden administration (the 117th Congress, 2021–22), when Democrats held unified control of the House, Senate, and the presidency. Democrats held power throughout Washington but only by the slimmest of margins. With just a four-seat majority in the House, and with the Senate split 50–50 between the parties (Vice President Kamala Harris would need to cast a record number of votes to break ties),[7] even the historically high levels of party unity among Democrats were not enough. In the House, the party's members averaged a 98 percent unity rate in 2021 and a 97 percent rate in 2022, but a 98.2 percent rate was needed to consistently get to 218 votes. In the Senate, Democrats compiled two of the highest average party unity rates ever recorded: 97 percent and 95 percent. But perfect unity was needed to do anything on a single-party basis.

This reality stymied many of the party's legislative priorities. Democrats passed President Biden's ambitious COVID-19 relief proposal—the American Rescue Plan—but only after making several concessions to Senator Joe Manchin (I-WV)[8] to get him on board.[9] Beyond that, the Democrats struggled to move their agenda. Biden's $3.5 trillion Build Back Better plan collapsed due to opposition from Manchin and other moderate Democrats in the House and Senate. Pieces of it found their way into a bipartisan infrastructure bill (the Infrastructure Investment and Jobs Act) and the Inflation Reduction Act (in 2022), but both were a pale shadow of the original vision put forward. Other priorities, including passing the Equality Act, expanding voting rights, and enacting campaign finance reform, were muscled through the House only to find that Democratic senators by and large would not unify behind them. Again and again, Democrats found that it took just a few defections to put a stop to their plans.

House Republicans in the 118th Congress (2023–24) faced an even steeper challenge. Holding the same small majority as the Democrats in the prior Congress (222 seats—a four-seat majority), the party was able to only muster a 90 percent average party unity rate. This, though high by historical standards, was not nearly enough to overcome their razor thin margin. Like the Democrats before

---

7 Anthony Adragna and Eugene Daniels, "Kamala Harris breaks record for most tie-breaking votes cast in the Senate," Politico, December 5, 2023.

8 Manchin is listed here as an Independent because he left the Democratic Party in May 2024. However, throughout the 117th Congress he was still a Democrat.

9 Burgess Everett and Marianne LeVine, "'I have no idea what he's doing': Manchin perplexes with Covid aid power play," Politico, March 3, 2021.

them, the GOP would need to hold together more than 98 percent of its members on every vote to win the day. This proved nearly impossible. Indeed, House Republicans posted the lowest "win rate" on party dividing votes in more than forty years.[10] On their biggest priority—reducing federal spending—the party could never get on the same page. It took Speaker Kevin McCarthy (R-CA) and his leadership team months to put together a deficit-reduction proposal because the defection of even just a few members of his party conference repeatedly sent them back to the drawing board. Dissatisfaction with McCarthy's performance contributed to his removal from the office that fall, but the new Speaker, Mike Johnson (R-LA), was unable to do any better because there simply was not enough agreement among House Republicans about what spending to cut, or how to cut it. The final spending deal that Johnson negotiated with the White House had little impact on federal deficits. Domestic spending did not go down, and the federal budget deficit in fiscal year 2024 would be the third largest of the twenty-first century.[11]

Small majorities are not the only new challenge facing congressional leaders as they try to organize and unify their parties. The rise of the internet has also been a destabilizing force in party unity and leadership on Capitol Hill. At one point in time, the media environment was a benefit to congressional leaders. For most of the twentieth century, the media environment was what Prior (2007) refers to as "low choice." There were a small number of broadcast news networks and major national newspapers, and those media companies covered Congress under a "beat" model, whereby reporters covered the institution on day-to-day basis, and focused on building relationships with congressional leaders to gain insider access to the institution. This gave leaders a lot of control over the messages emerging from Capitol Hill. Leaders were better positioned to act as gatekeepers, deciding which of their members would be given opportunities to get in front of cameras and deliver the party message. Indeed, in the last few decades of the twentieth century and the first decade of the twenty-first, party leadership offices on Capitol Hill greatly expanded their communications efforts and influence (see Lee 2016; Gaynor 2024). Simply, the media environment helped congressional leaders keep their members in line.

The new media environment, in contrast, incentivizes public party infighting. Over the last fifteen or so years the media environment has become "high choice" (Prior 2007). News media has proliferated, first with cable news, then with the

---

10 Niels Lesniewski and Ryan Kelly, "House GOP had lowest win rate on 'party unity' votes since 1982," Roll Call, February 8, 2024.
11 William McBride, "Another Huge Federal Deficit in Fiscal Year 2024 Despite Surging Corporate and Other Tax Collections," Tax Foundation, October 10, 2024.

blogosphere, and now with social media. Members of Congress do not need the help or support of party leaders to get national coverage. In fact, the most efficient and effective way to get the media's attention is to do something that is combative or critical, or that can go viral on the internet (Ballard et al 2023; Costa 2025; Kosmidis and Theocharis 2020). Members of Congress recognize the power of the internet for their own political brand and influence. Social media is now a standard tool of choice for every lawmaker (Russell 2021; 2025).

The freedom and independence this provides members is a new challenge for party leaders as they try to keep their members in line and project unity on and beyond the Hill. Today, some of the most well-recognized members of Congress are not institutional power-players but relatively new members who initially made their names by going viral on social media: Matt Gaetz, Marjorie Taylor Greene, Alexandria Ocasio-Cortez, and so on. Not only do members of Congress not need the help of their leaders to get media attention, but a willingness to oppose, attack, or embarrass your own leaders is an effective strategy in getting the attention of the media. In January 2023, political news junkies were introduced to a new crop of Capitol Hill celebrities who gained fame by opposing Kevin McCarthy's speakership bid.

The rise of the internet has also made members of Congress less reliant on their party for campaign funds, robbing leaders of another tool that was once helpful in building party unity. As the costs of campaigns rose precipitously in the 1990s and early 2000s, congressional leaders used their abilities to raise large sums of money and transfer them to their colleagues as a way to earn their support (Cann 2008). Today, however, a single viral social media post can net a member of Congress millions of dollars in campaign donations (Kowal 2023). Indeed, taking steps to embarrass your own party or acting the part of a Capitol Hill renegade can be a fundraising boon. Representative Matt Gaetz saw his fundraising explode in the aftermath of his effort to depose Speaker McCarthy in October 2023.[12] Representative Marjorie Taylor Greene (R-GA) similarly raised millions of dollars after some of her remarks led House Democrats to strip her of her committee assignments in 2021.[13]

These challenges are only worsened by eroding public trust and support in governmental institutions. Public trust in the federal government has been at an all-time low in recent decades. Since 2010, fewer than one in five Americans say

---

12 See, Zach Montellaro, "Matt Gaetz deposed Kevin McCarthy and the donations came pouring in," Politico, February 1, 2024.
13 See, Olivia Beavers and Melanie Zanona, "MTG's eye-popping fundraising haul," Politico, April 7, 2021.

they trust the government to do the right thing.[14] The public's job approval of the U.S. Congress has been below 25 percent for most of the last two decades.[15] Support for governmental leaders also continues to erode. Congressional party leaders are among the least popular public officials in the United States. As of this writing, none of the four congressional party leaders has a favorability rating above 30 percent.[16]

This context makes it more appealing than ever for members of Congress to run for Congress by running against Congress. One of the most popular things a member of Congress or candidate can do is attack Congress and oppose its leaders. This is not an environment that makes it easy for leaders to get their members to go along with them. Most party members are in a better position with voters by standing against their own party's leaders in Washington. This dynamic has manifested itself in frequent challenges to party leaders at the start of every recent Congress. When Democrats took back control of the House of Representatives following the 2018 midterm elections, sixteen new and returning Democratic House members signed a letter vowing to oppose Nancy Pelosi's (D-CA), their leader's, election as Speaker.[17] A similar dynamic occurred with Kevin McCarthy (R-CA) when Republicans took control four years later. In both cases, the unpopularity of these leaders with many voters, including among their own partisans, encourages challenges to their positions in the Congress.

Altogether, congressional leadership today is no pleasure cruise. Conflict between the parties has raised new barriers to building the necessary bipartisanship for legislative success. Small majorities, a new media environment, and public distrust in Congress and U.S. government has made it harder for leaders to hold their party members together. This is not for the faint of heart. But, even so, it is not all bad news for leaders on Capitol Hill.

14 See, "Public Trust in Government: 1958–2024," Pew Research Center. https://www.pewre search.org/politics/2024/06/24/public-trust-in-government-1958-2024/
15 See, "Congress and the Public," GALLUP. https://news.gallup.com/poll/1600/congress-public. aspx
16 You can track the favorability ratings of U.S. political leaders here: https://www.realclearpol ling.com/polls/favorability/political-leaders
17 Clare Foran and Manu Raju, "Anti-Pelosi Democrats publicly vow opposition in House speaker race: 'The time has come for new leadership'," CNN.com, November 20, 2018.

8.3 Capitol Gains: New Opportunities for Congressional Leaders

Congressional leadership has undoubtedly become more challenging. But today's leaders also have powers and tools and their disposal that their predecessors could have only dreamed of. The combination of more cohesive party member-ships, and the new tools leaders have been provided as a result, puts them in the driver's seat and makes them the central players in negotiating and shaping policy outcomes on Capitol Hill.

For most of the twentieth century, Congress was characterized by adherence to a seniority system (Goodwin 1959; Polsby et al. 1969) and "regular order" processes (Smith 1989). Combined, this manner of doing business empowered committees and committee chairs over party leaders. Under "regular order," bills are considered in a sequential step-by-step process. Bills are introduced and referred to a single committee. That committee and its chair are empowered to consider the legislation (or not)—holding hearings and amending bills in mark-up meetings. Only if a bill is approved and reported by a committee is it considered on the floor, where it is open for debate and further amendment by the whole House or Senate. If it passes on the floor in one chamber, it is sent to the other chamber where the process repeats itself.

This manner of doing things greatly empowered committees to set the agenda and shape legislative outcomes. Committees had the power to either block legislation or send it to the floor after amending it to their liking (Denzau and Mackay 1983, Maltzman 1998; Snyder 1992). On the floor, there was a deference to each committee, as members of the other committees expected reciprocity when their bills came up, resulting in an institution-wide logroll (Fenno 1966, 1973). Committee membership itself was even controlled by the committees. The most senior member of each committee automatically took the chair's gavel. In the House, members were assigned to each committee not by their party but by the Ways and Means Committee. In the Senate, self-selection and seniority determined each senator's assignments. Each committee was a little fiefdom, and each chair was a feudal baron, out of the control of the institution, its members, or the parties (see, Burns 1963; Polsby 2004; Wilson 1885; Zelizer 2004).

Under these dynamics, party leaders had little power to control much of anything. It, ". . . fragmented and diffused power in the House, thereby crippling effective leadership and making it impossible to present or pursue a coherent legislative program" (DSG Staff 1970, 5171). Party leaders by and large took a secondary role to powerful committee chairs. As Speaker John W. McCormack (D-MA, 1962–1971) advised new members of Congress at the time, "Whenever you pass a committee chairman in the House, you bow from the waist. I do."[18] Speaker Sam Rayburn rarely even bothered to convene meetings of the House Democratic Caucus because it seemed of little use.

Things, however, have changed. In the 1970s, House Democrats began enacting changes aimed at making committees and entrenched committee chairs more responsive to the party (Rohde 1991; Deering and Smith 1997, 35–39). Republicans adopted similar party reforms in the 1990s, and in some cases went further (Aldrich and Rohde 1997; Deering and Wahlbeck 2006). Today, committee assignments and chairmanships are determined by a party committee led by the party's leadership. Committee-led "regular order" processes are mostly a thing of the past, replaced with centralized, party leadership-driven processes (Sinclair 2016; Wolfensberger 2018). Contemporary processes often involve bypassing the committee stages of the legislative process (Bendix 2016; Howard et al. 2020), and entail direct party leadership involvement in policymaking, including in the negotiation of policy (Curry 2015; Hanson 2014), setting the agenda (Harbridge 2015), and taking control of the consideration of legislation on the floor (Curry and Lee 2020a; Wallner 2013).

These changes were aided and abetted by rising party cohesion in the House and Senate (see Figure 8.1). More cohesive majority parties have been more willing to empower their leaders to lead, in order to overcome efforts and opposition and obstruction (Aldrich and Rohde 2000). In today's political environment, striking deals and moving legislation is hard because there is so much incentive for conflict. But centralized processes are well-suited to succeed under these dynamics (Curry and Lee 2020a). Moving most deliberations behind the scenes enables congressional leaders to avoid leaks and give negotiators more breathing room to explore potential agreements. Moving decision-making out of committees enables leaders to work around recalcitrant committee chairs or avoid involving members who would be otherwise problematic. Avoiding open processes, like committee markups or open floor amending opportunities, enables leaders to restrict conflict-minded legislators in both parties from offering poison-pill amendments or dilatory motions aimed solely at sewing discord or throwing a wrench in the gears.

The combination of these new centralized powers and high levels of party unity puts party leaders in the driver's seat as major policies are negotiated. Because more of each party's members are in relative agreement about what they want to do on policy, it becomes the job of the leadership to represent their interests in negotiations with the other party, the other chamber, or the White House. The leaders negotiate toward an agreement, expecting that they will be able to

---

18 Quoted in the *Wall Street Journal*, May 3, 1979, 1.

bring along most of their party's members to support the deal. This makes leaders the central players in policymaking these days.

This manner of doing business has helped Congress remain productive in developing and passing major bipartisan legislation, even today. Contrary to common belief, most laws continue to be enacted with broad, bipartisan support (see Curry and Lee 2020b). Laws passed in recent years have the same amount of support that they did in the 1970s or 1980s. The most common approach for a majority party to pass a law is to back down from the most controversial aspects of their proposal in order to win over votes from the other side of the aisle. This was true forty years ago, and it remains true today.

These centralized processes have helped Congress remain productive, as well. As Figure 8.3 shows, it is easy to miss the magnitude of new laws being produced by recent congresses. The first trend in the figure is a count of the number of new laws passed by Congress every two years starting in the 80th Congress (19487–48) and ending in the 117th Congress (2021–22). The second is a count of the number of *pages* of new law enacted by each of these congresses during this same period. While Congress is passing fewer laws, it is passing much bigger laws, accounting for more pages of new statutes than in the past. By this metric,

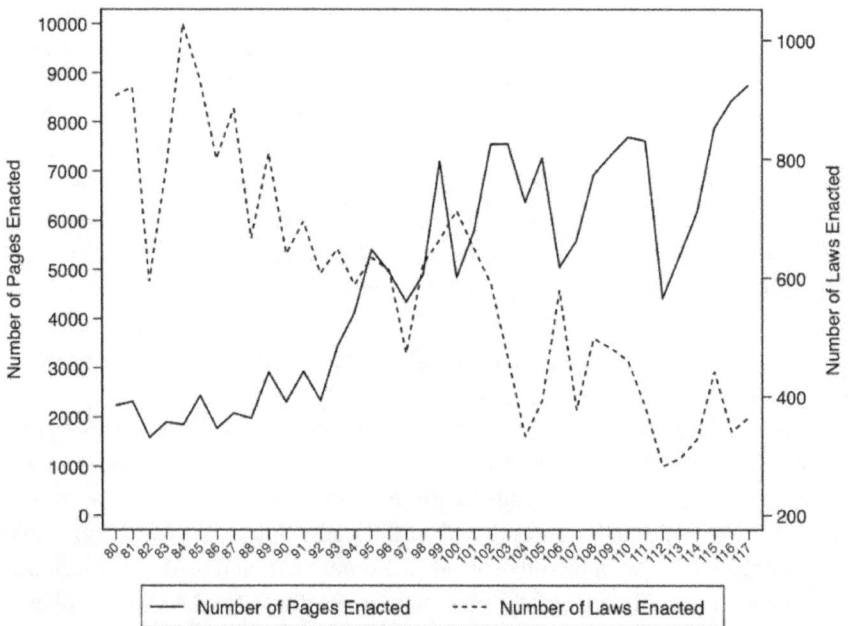

Figure 8.3: Congressional Productivity, 1947–2022.

two recent congresses—the 116th (2019–20) and the 117th (2021–22)—were the most productive in modern congressional history. Centralized authority empowers party leaders to cut big deals and put together legislative packages called "omnibus" bills. These bills often include dozens of different laws, which are combined into a single legislative vehicle for a vote (see Krutz 2001). The old way of doing things—passing individual bills one by one under open and decentralized processes—simply does not work in today's environment. What does work, and what has enabled Congress to keep being productive, has been an empowering of congressional leaders to cut big deals, assemble big legislative packages, and aggressively move them through the legislative process.

In this way, even though party leaders face arguably bigger challenges than in the past, they have been empowered by the members of their parties to take the reins and lead in a way that they were not allowed to previously. These powers provide greater opportunities for leaders. However, they still need to take steps to survive in a cutthroat political environment rife with conflict and acrimony.

8.4 The Duality of Modern Congressional Leadership

You can either die as speaker and worry about them taking you out, or live every day as your last. Get something out of it. If you lead and get big things done, your reputation enhances. Your ability to get the next deal done is enhanced. The view from the public, while not perfect, is better if you take action than if you sit and dither. Former Representative Patrick McHenry (R-NC)[19]

In the aftermath of Kevin McCarthy's removal from the Speakership, Representative Patrick McHenry (R-NC) found himself in a position he had likely never envisioned because it had never happened before. McHenry had been named Speaker Pro Tempore of the House of Representatives, charged with overseeing the proceedings of the chamber in the absence of an elected speaker. For the next three weeks, the House was paralyzed. Without a speaker the chamber is not permitted to do business, and Republicans could not agree on any member of their conference as suitable for the role. Trapped and helpless, presiding over a chamber that day-to-day could not conduct legislative business, and without a clear path

---

19 Major Garrett, "House is heading toward "nuclear" war over Ukraine funding, one top House GOP leader says," CBS News, February 22, 2024.

forward, McHenry presumably had a lot of time to think about what it is to be a leader.

His words nicely encapsulate the duality of modern congressional leadership. You can either "die as Speaker" or "live every day as your last," McHenry explains. Put in other words, you can survive by operating in fear of your own followers. You can capitulate to the most irascible elements of your party's membership, give in to obstinate factions, and seek to offend no one at every turn. You can take no risks, and presumably make no gains, except for surviving in the position until you retire or expire. You can, in other words, be a leader by dithering and choosing not to lead. Or you can "live every day as your last," using the powers instilled in contemporary leadership offices to act, negotiate, and "get big things done."

Today's congressional leaders face these competing choices every day. They operate in a political environment that is more challenging than that of their twentieth century predecessors. The parties have rarely been in greater conflict, their majorities on Capitol Hill have rarely been this small, and intra-party infighting has rarely been so consequential. The risks for a leader's power are fraught, as Kevin McCarthy found out. But the opportunities for leaders to manage the legislative process, develop and negotiate policy agreements, and shape the future of American public policy have also rarely been greater. There are few major policymaking accomplishments in the twenty-first century that did not involve party leaders at some level. Some only made it across the finish line because of the efforts of leaders in one or both parties.

As we observe congressional leadership in the coming years we should keep this duality in mind. Successful leadership is not a given, but neither is it a failure. In an era of deep political strife, we will see both outcomes occur in spades.

Discussion Questions
1   What are three reasons that congressional leadership has become more challenging in recent decades?
2   How do political scientists understand the role that political context plays in the power and influence of congressional leaders?
3   In what ways have party leaders become more empowered in Congress in recent decades?
4   Would you say that party leaders today are in a better position than those from 50 or 60 years ago? Despite the more difficult political environment, do they seem better able to lead, or not?
5   What is the duality of modern party leadership?

References

Aldrich, John H., and David W. Rohde. 1997. "The Transition to Republican Rule in the House: Implications for Theories of Congressional Politics." *Political Science Quarterly* 112 (4): 541–67.

Aldrich, John H., and David W. Rohde. 2000. "The Consequences of Party Organization in the House: The Role of the Majority and Minority Parties in Conditional Party Government." In *Polarized Politics: Congress and the President in a Partisan Era*, edited by Jon R. Bond and Richard Fleisher. CQ Press.

Ballard Andrew O., Ryan DeTamble, Spencer Dorsey, Michael Heseltine, and Marcus Johnson. 2023. "Dynamics of Polarizing Rhetoric in Congressional Tweets." *Legislative Studies Quarterly* 48 (1): 105–44.

Bendix, William. 2016. "Bypassing Congressional Committees: Parties, Panel Rosters, and Deliberative Processes." *Legislative Studies Quarterly* 41 (3): 687–714.

Burns, James MacGregor. 1963. *The Deadlock of Democracy*. Prentice-Hall.

Cann, Damon M. 2008. *Sharing the Wealth: Member Contributions and the Exchange Theory of Party Influence in the U.S. House of Representatives*. State University of New York Press.

Cooper, Joseph, and David W. Brady. 1981. "Institutional Context and Leadership Style: The House from Cannon to Rayburn." *American Political Science Review* 75 (2): 411–25.

Costa, Mia. 2025. *How Politicians Polarize: Political Representation in an Age of Negative Partisanship*. University of Chicago Press.

Cox, Gary W., and Mathew D. McCubbins. 2005. *Setting the Agenda: Responsible Party Government in the U.S. House of Representatives*. Cambridge University Press.

Curry, James M. 2015. *Legislating in the Dark: Information and Power in the House of Representatives*. University of Chicago Press.

Curry, James M., and Frances E. Lee. 2020a. "What is Regular Order Worth? Partisan Lawmaking and Congressional Processes." *Journal of Politics* 82 (2): 627–41.

Curry, James M., and Frances E. Lee. 2020b. *The Limits of Party: Congress and Lawmaking in a Polarized Era*. University of Chicago Press.

Denzau, Arthur T., and Robert J. Mackay. 1983. "Gatekeeping and Monopoly Power of Committees: An Analysis of Sincere and Sophisticated Behavior." *American Journal of Political Science* 27 (4): 740–61.

DSG Staff. 1970. "The Seniority System in the U.S. House of Representatives." *Congressional Record*, February 25: H5169–72.

Gaynor, Sorelle Wyckoff. 2024. "Following the leaders: Asymmetric party messaging in the U.S. Congress," *Legislative Studies Quarterly*, early view. https://doi.org/10.1111/lsq.12479

Gelman, Jeremy. 2020. *Losing to Win: Why Congressional Majorities Play Politics Instead of Make Laws*. University of Michigan Press.

Deering, Christopher J., and Steven S. Smith. 1997. *Committees in Congress*. CQ Press.

Deering, Christopher J., and Paul J. Wahlbeck. 2006. "U.S. House Committee Chair Selection: Republicans Play Musical Chairs in the 107th Congress." *American Politics Research* 34 (2): 223–42.

Fenno, Richard F. 1966. *The Power of the Purse: Appropriations Politics in Congress*. Little, Brown.

Fenno, Richard F. 1973. *Congressmen in Committees*. Little, Brown.

Goodwin, George. 1959. "The Seniority System in Congress." *American Political Science Review* 53 (2): 412–36.

Hanson, Peter. 2014. *Too Weak to Govern: Majority Party Power and Appropriations in the U.S. Senate*. Cambridge University Press.

Harbridge, Laurel. 2015. *Is Bipartisanship Dead? Policy Agreement and Agenda-Setting in the House of Representatives*. Cambridge University Press.

Howard, Nicholas O., and Mark E. Owens. 2020. "Circumventing Legislative Committees: The US Senate." *Legislative Studies Quarterly* 45 (3): 495–526.

Kiewiet, D. Roderick, and Mathew D. McCubbins. 1991. *The Logic of Delegation:Congressional Parties and the Appropriations Process*. University of Chicago Press.

Krehbiel, Keith. 1998. *Pivotal Politics: A Theory of U.S. Lawmaking*. University of Chicago Press.

Kosmidis, Spyros, and Yannis Theocharis. 2020. "Can Social Media Incivility Induce Enthusiasm? Evidence from Survey Experiments." *Public Opinion Quarterly* 84 (S1): 284–308.

Kowal, Michael. 2023. "The Value of a Like: Facebook, Viral Posts, and Campaign Finance in US Congressional Elections." *Media and Communication* 11 (3).

Lee, Frances E. 2016. *Insecure Majorities: Congress and the Perpetual Campaign*. University of Chicago Press.

Maltzman, Forrest. 1998. *Competing Principals: Committees, Parties, and the Organization of Congress*. University of Michigan Press.

Mason, Lilliana. 2018. *Uncivil Agreement: How Politics Became Our Identity*. University of Chicago Press.

McCarty, Nolan. 2019. *Polarization: What Everyone Needs to Know*. Oxford University Press.

McGrath, Michael. 2017. "Beyond Distrust: When the Public Loses Faith in American Institutions." *National Civic Review* (Summer): 46–51.

Polsby, Nelson W. 2004. *How Congress Evolves: Social Bases of Institutional Change*. Oxford University Press.

Polsby, Nelson W., Miriam Gallaher, and Barry Spencer Rundquist. 1969. "The Growth of the Seniority System in the U. S. House of Representatives." *American Political Science Review* 63 (3): 787–807.

Prior, Markus. 2007. *Post-Broadcast Democracy: How Media Choice Increases Inequality in Political Involvement and Polarizes Elections*. Cambridge University Press.

Rohde, David W. 1991. *Parties and Leaders in the Postreform House*. University of Chicago Press.

Rubin, Ruth Bloch. 2025. *Divided Parties, Strong Leaders*. University of Chicago Press.

Russell, Annelise. 2021. *Tweeting is Leading: How Senators Communicate and Represent in the Age of Social Media*. Oxford University Press.

Russell, Annelise. 2025. *Tweeting Scared: Congressional Crisis Communication and Constrained Capacity*. Oxford University Press.

Sinclair, Barbara. 2016. *Unorthodox lawmaking: New legislative Processes in the US Congress*. 5th ed. CQ Press.

Smith, Steven S. 1989. *Call to Order: Floor Politics in the House and Senate*. Roman & Littlefield Publishers.

Snyder, James M. 1992. "Committee Power, Structure-induced Equilibria, and Roll Call Votes." *American Journal of Political Science* 36 (1): 1–30.

Strahan, Randall. 2007. *Leading Representatives: The Agency of Leaders in the Politics of the U.S. House*. Johns Hopkins University Press.

Wallner, James I. 2013. *The Death of Deliberation: Partisanship and Polarization in the United States Senate*. Lexington Books.

Webster, Steven W. 2020. *American Rage: How Anger Shapes our Politics*. Cambridge University Press.

Wilson, Woodrow. 1885. *Congressional Government: A Study in American Politics*. Houghton Mifflin Co.

Wolfensberger, Donald R. 2018. *Changing Cultures in Congress: From Fair Play to Power Plays*. Columbia University Press.

Zelizer, Julian E. 2004. *On Capitol Hill: The Struggle to Reform Congress and Its Consequences, 1948–2000*. Cambridge University Press.

Lindsey Cormack
9 Voices of Influence: Outside Interests and Surrogate Representation

9.1 Introduction

Representation in Congress comes in many forms, and scholars have identified different ways of conceptualizing representation for groups, media, and ideas. This chapter focuses on three ways people and ideas are elevated in official legislator communications: surrogate representation for specific groups; the influence and promotion of outside media; and how certain terms or phrases emerge and spread in congressional communications.

Understanding congressional communications through these lenses reveals not only how legislators serve their constituents but also how they may influence broader political dynamics. Congressional communications function as a bridge between lawmakers and the public, reflecting both the priorities of elected officials and the ways external influences show up in activities of representation. By examining these communications, we can better understand the strategies legislators use to address group-specific needs, amplify media narratives, and shape public discourse through language and messaging.

9.2 Methodology

To analyze these phenomena, I examine the DCinbox database, a comprehensive archive of all official legislator-to-constituent e-newsletters from 2010 through the current day (Cormack 2017). This database is a good way to understand and track efforts at surrogate representation, the promotion of different news outlets, and the diffusion of different terms because of its long timeframe and universality as it encompasses every member of the Congress who sends official e-newsletters. It's also well suited to the questions at hand, because the database contains the official efforts of individual legislators, rather than their campaign or personal activities. This distinction allows for an examination of the actual work members of Congress perform while in office, separate from their actions when seeking office or engaging in personal self-promotion.

Lindsey Cormack, Stevens Institute of Technology

https://doi.org/10.1515/9783111591902-009

Something to note about official e-newsletters is that members of the Republican Party tend to send them far more frequently than members of the Democratic Party. This differential cannot be attributed to different seat shares in Congress, as congressional control has been relatively close over the past fifteen years (see Table 9.1 for the share of seats held by Democrats and Republicans and Figure 9.1 for the overall number of official e-newsletters sent by party). The only time legislators from both parties used official e-communications in similar amounts was at the start of the COVID-19 pandemic when nearly all efforts to communicate and connect with other people shifted online for most of the US.[1]

Table 9.1: Share of seats held by Democrats and Republicans in Congress (111th–118th Congresses).

Congress	Share of Democrats	Share of Republicans
118th Congress (2023–2024)	49.44%	50.56%
117th Congress (2021–2022)	50.75%	49.25%
116th Congress (2019–2020)	52.80%	47.20%
115th Congress (2017–2018)	45.37%	54.63%
114th Congress (2015–2016)	43.74%	56.26%
113th Congress (2013–2014)	47.85%	52.15%
112th Congress (2011–2012)	45.98%	54.02%
111th Congress (2009–2010)*	59.07%	40.93%

*DCinbox data starts in 2010.

This first insight reveals a fundamental disparity in how members of each party leverage the free incumbent perk of official communications. Republicans, who consistently send more newsletters, appear more willing to utilize these taxpayer-funded tools to amplify their messages, promote their legislative actions, and influence public discourse. This discrepancy not only shapes the volume of information reaching constituents but also reflects a broader dynamic in political strategy, where Republicans are more likely to view official e-newsletters as a proactive instrument of political engagement and agenda-setting.

A benefit of this database is that it is easy to track and visualize the prevalence of terms used over time by party. In the past, the database has been used to understand the prevalence of gendered topics in communications during the COVID-19 pandemic, where women legislators were more likely to write to constituents about families and children (Hellwedge and Cormack 2022), the environ-

---

1 In January 2021, a sizable chunk of DCinbox suffered a crash in inputs, which is regrettable, but luckily happened to legislators from both parties.

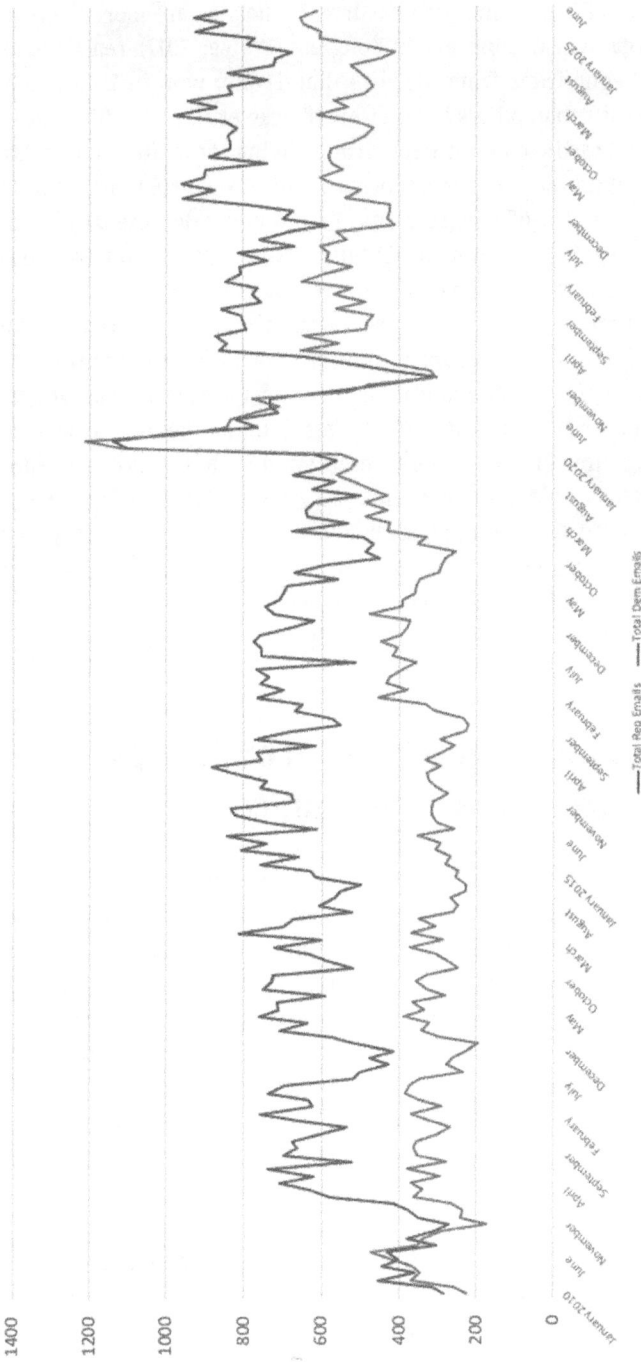

Figure 9.1: Volume of official Congress to Constituent e-newsletters by party, 2010–2024.

mental priorities of legislators, such has how Democrats are more likely to mention solar energy than Republicans in Congress (Walker 2017), reactions to trade policy where Republicans from districts that Trump won in 2016 make more references to tariffs than others in Congress (Clarke et al. 2020), differential focus on Medicare and Medicaid with Republicans giving more attention to issues of alleged fraud within those systems (Cormack and Brown 2021), and more. There are also related styles of congressional communication research on Twitter (Russell 2018; Russell 2021), but important distinctions between different mediums of communication remain (Blum et al. 2023; Green et al. 2024).

For the notion of surrogate representation, the searches are for individual terms designating different groups of interest. For looking at the prevalence of outside media groups in communications, and for terms signifying bigger ideas, the same term search approach is used. This is undoubtedly a departure from some other measures of surrogate representation such as surrogate representation through monetary donations connecting legislators with people who do not live in their districts (Gimpel et al. 2008; Keena 2024). But the strategy stays true to the idea that representation does not always happen in a direct way, and that there are different types of approaches members of congress may use to do work on behalf of constituencies that are not strictly linked by geography.

9.3 Surrogate Representation of Groups in Congressional Communications

Surrogate representation refers to how a legislator represents a set of people or interests that may be broader than their actual constituency (Mansbridge 2003). This style of representation has also been referred to as collective representation (Weissberg 1978) or institutional representation (Jackson and King 1989), but the basis remains the same. Surrogate representation occurs when legislators make overtures or actions on behalf of a group that may, or may not, occupy a large portion of their constituents. Legislators, therefore, may not have realizable electoral benefits from recognizing a specific group, but they choose to do so regardless.

Legislators engage in surrogate representation for a variety of reasons and for a number of groups. Sometimes their reasons are personal and not necessarily observable to researchers. Other times legislators have relationships with interest groups that facilitate broader representation goals, and sometimes situations make the focus on a certain type of group more salient. There are several professions that are idealized and mentioned in congressional communications that allow us to glimpse surrogate representation at work.

For instance, during the COVID-19 pandemic, regardless of the amount of attention typically paid to a group like nurses or doctors, there was an increase across the board in how much legislators of all types paid attention to individuals in those professions owing to the unfolding national health crisis. See Figure 9.2 below, which depicts the count of the total number of official e-newsletters sent by members of Congress to their constituents that mention "nurse" or "doctor."

Count of official congressional e-newsletters mentioning "nurse" and "doctor" over time, by party

Data: DCinbox

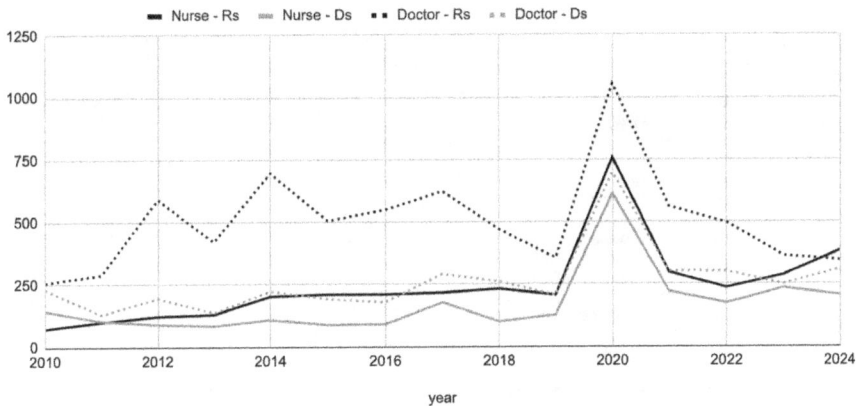

Figure 9.2: Mentions of nurse and doctor.

To better understand how different professions and societal roles are represented in communications by Congress, I present the total references to these roles by party, from 2010 to 2024 in Figure 9.3. It is immediately apparent that Republican legislators tend to mention all of these roles and positions more than Democrats, which is consistent with the overall use patterns of the medium. The most recognized group are veterans. In the fourteen years observed here, Republicans sent over 34,764 official e-newsletters that mention veterans, which means that 29 percent of all e-newsletters authored by Republicans talk about veterans in some way. All the other positions, save for sanitation workers and housekeepers, are mentioned in similar amounts within each party.

Veteran status differs from an occupation because it represents an identity based on a voluntary choice to serve, rather than a specific job or career, and veterans may pursue a wide range of occupations during or after their service. In the US, there are an estimated 16.8 million veterans, which is about 6.2 percent of the population of the United States over the age of eighteen (US Census 2022

American Community Survey 1-year estimates). As a contrast, looking at the terms mom or mother and dad or father—which are also identities that overlap with multiple different occupations and account for a greater share of the US population as nearly 158 million people in the US are either mothers or fathers (US Census 2016 Measuring America's People, Places, and Economy)—shows that veterans continue to stand out as the most mentioned group in the examination of surrogate representation.

Number of mentions of different occupations in official congressional e-newsletters, by party from 01/01/2010 - 11/22/2024

Data: DCinbox

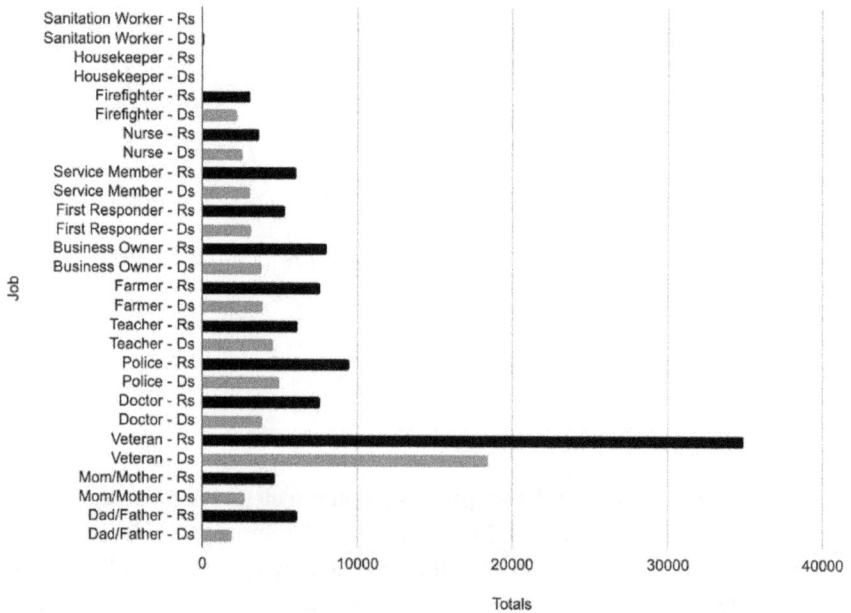

Figure 9.3: Mentions of various occupations.

Unlike many other parts of politics, legislator communication styles tend to be similar with respect to surrogate representation for the positions and roles analyzed. Both Democrats and Republicans tend to mention different sorts of constituents in positive ways, saying things like, "I'm proud to fight for our farmers," "we recognize our country's teachers for their outstanding service and dedication," and "I enjoyed meeting and praying for the first responders who keep the thousands of people safe," regardless of their party affiliation.

Surrogate representation in congressional communications provides a way to understand how legislators engage with and amplify the identities, roles, and professions of Americans. By highlighting groups like veterans, teachers, nurses, and first responders, legislators demonstrate a commitment to representing societal values and roles that resonate beyond their immediate constituencies. While patterns of surrogate representation reveal partisan differences in frequency, with Republicans utilizing this medium more generally, the underlying approach to valuing and affirming these groups remains largely similar across parties. This practice underscores the broader, symbolic role of Congress in shaping and sustaining the national narrative through inclusive communication efforts.

9.4 Outside Media Influence on Congressional Communications

Members of Congress oftentimes use their official communication to push constituents to watch or consume other types of media. They do this when talking about channels that they have been on for TV interviews about certain policy updates or stances, when pushing readers to check out an op-ed or other article they have penned in a paper on online outlet, or they will sometimes encourage readers to review articles, videos, or other media that comments on a policy or political issue that they agree with. Pushing readers to different media outlets include both older media like cable news and long-established papers and newer, primarily online, outlets.

Unlike the similarities observed in the previous section, in the analyses to come it is clear that Republicans and Democrats tend to prefer and talk about different sorts of media outlets, and that some media outlets have emerged over the past fifteen years while others have waned. The communication actions of members of Congress occur within the greater media environment, and to contextualize these choices it is helpful to have a better understanding of what that media environment looks like.

To assess the sorts of media referenced in official congressional e-newsletters, we examine the most communicated outlets across television, newspapers, and online platforms (with the understanding that sometimes these lines are blurred as everything increasingly moves to an online, on-demand style of delivery).

When considering traditional television media, one media outlet stands clearly above the rest in terms of mentions in official congressional e-newsletters: FOX news. Compared to CNN and MSNBC, FOX news is referenced five to ten times as much in official communications, on average, per year than any of the other traditional television channels, and the overwhelming majority of the mentions come from Republican legislators. The trends between 2010 and 2024 are presented in Figure 9.4.

References to traditional television media in official congressional e-newsletters over time, by party

Data: DCinbox

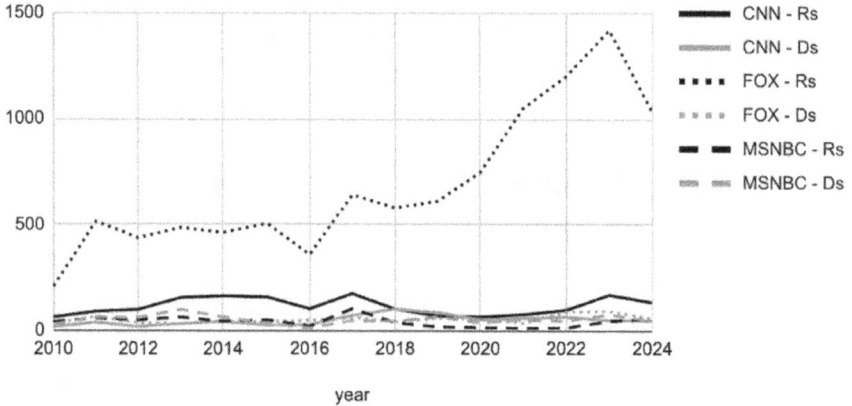

Figure 9.4: Number of references to television media.

The patterns in congressional references to media outlets reveal not only the preferences of legislators but also the larger political and ideological divides shaping American politics. The overwhelming mention of FOX News by Republican legislators, compared to the less frequent mentions of CNN and MSNBC, reflects the entrenched alignment of political factions with specific media platforms. This dynamic amplifies the role of partisan media in shaping public discourse and highlights the importance of understanding how members of Congress use their official communications to validate and promote these outlets.

In analyses of newspapers, we include the most widely circulated papers in the US, *The New York Times*, *The Wall Street Journal*, *The Washington Post*, and *USA Today*. These papers span general cultural interests, politics, and business. Interestingly, none of the paper outlets have nearly as much focus as FOX news, reaching a high point of 1,420 references from Republicans in 2023. Conversely, the most references to a newspaper came in 2017 when Democrats sent 340 official e-newsletters with a mention of *The New York Times*.

When assessing traditional newspaper outlets compared to traditional television media, Republicans in Congress tend to push their constituents to television and online versions of FOX news far more than Democrats do, and Democrats are far more apt to make references to each of the listed newspapers (save for *USA Today*), which neither party tends to write about all that often. The shift towards more promotion of traditional newspaper outlets by Democrats coincides with the time that Donald Trump, a Republican, was in office. In the years when Obama, a Democrat, was in office, Republican legislators sent more e-newsletters to constituents from these outlets. During the Biden administration things were mixed between the parties.

There are, of course, many other news outlets that tend to have smaller, more niche, and sometimes more partisan audiences that members of Congress will link to in their communications. Some of these are traditional television or newspaper outlets, but in recent years many take the form of online platforms that disseminate information through both video formats and written pieces. Each of these platforms tends to be referenced in lower volumes in official e-newsletters than bigger, more traditional outlets, but there are still interesting things to glean from the different rates of mentions by members of different parties.

First, let us consider the smaller operations that tend to the middle of the political spectrum according to the Ad Fontes bias chart:[2] *Forbes*, the *Associated Press* (AP), *The Guardian*, *Reuters*, and *Bloomberg News*. Of these outlets, only *Forbes* really stands out for use in Republican e-newsletters, and even then, most of these references occurred during the Obama administration and then subsided when co-partisan Trump took office.

For smaller media that tend to have either a clear left- or right-wing bias, partisans mostly make references to outlets that share their political leanings. Looking at some of the most referenced platforms of this sort in these communications in Figure 9.5 (*Newsmax, National Public Radio* (NPR), *Vox*, and *Breitbart*), there are a few partisan patterns that stand out. Interestingly, when compared to the low bias sources, these outlets tend to appear two to three times as much in congressional e-newsletters. It is important to note that two of these digital media operations started in 2014: *Newsmax* on the right and *Vox* on the left. *Newsmax* is both a digital and TV outlet that mostly hosts political, opinion-based talk shows. This is the most mentioned of the more biased outlets, with an overwhelming uptick in mentions after 2020 when Democrat Joe Biden took office. It was also during the Biden administration when mentions to pieces and clips on *Breitbart*,

---

2 The Ad Fontes Media Bias Chart, created by Ad Fontes Media, is a tool to evaluate media outlets along two dimensions: political bias and reliability. It categorizes sources based on a methodology that combines the evaluations of analysts with diverse political perspectives. Bias is measured on a spectrum ranging from extreme left to extreme right, while reliability spans from original fact reporting to opinion, propaganda, and even fabricated content.

which former chairman Steve Bannon described as a "platform for the alt-right," trended upwards. The more left-leaning outlets of *NPR* and *Vox* had their highest mentions between 2016 and 2020 when Republican Donald Trump was in office.

Smaller Media, High Bias Media References in Official Congressional E-newsletters, by party, over time

Data: DCinbox

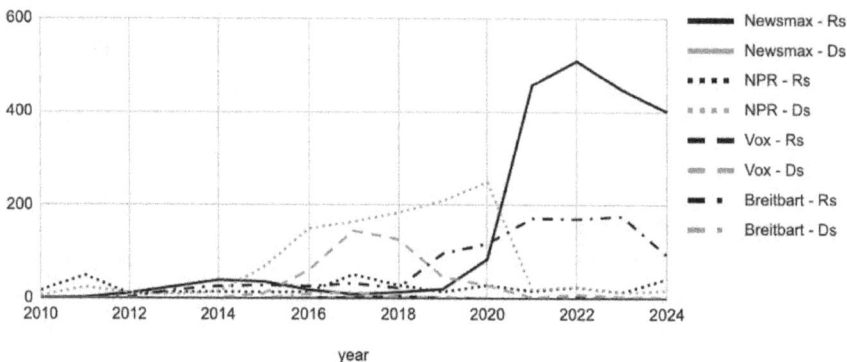

Figure 9.5: References to High-Bias Media.

When a legislator decides to push a news story or segment to his or her constituents, that is an act creating, or at least contributing to, the phenomena of "echo chambers." Media echo chambers occur when certain media are amplified and circulated among a population of consumers who likely already agree with part of the media's perspective due to prior exposure or related beliefs (Sunstein 2001). Meanwhile, other media that might present challenging information are often excluded, ignored, or even actively discredited. Echo chambers are a characteristic of modern communications and media across various domains, not just politics. However, in areas where decision-making depends on information, such as for legislators and voters, the risks posed by echo chambers are more significant than in spaces primarily focused on entertainment. Recent research indicates that routine exposure to partisan echo chambers conditions people to be less attuned to spot misinformation (Rhodes 2022).

In recent years, there has been a surge in online platforms catering to hyper-specific interests. However, for most members of Congress, communications continue to focus primarily on legacy media, such as traditional television and print, when deciding what to share with constituents. While traditional television and print outlets are the primary references used by members of Congress, the clear differences in how Republicans and Democrats amplify specific media sources highlight the role of partisanship in shaping communication choices. Republicans consistently lean toward promoting right-leaning television outlets like FOX News and digital platforms like *Newsmax* and *Breitbart,* while Democrats show a preference for more traditional newspapers such as *The New York Times* and left-leaning platforms like *NPR* and *Vox,* particularly during periods of opposing presidential administrations. These trends underscore the role of congressional communications in creating and reinforcing media echo chambers, amplifying partisan narratives, and shaping how constituents engage with news and political information.

9.5 Terminology Diffusion and External Interests

In congressional e-newsletters, specific phrases and terms are sometimes used by large numbers of legislators and in turn communicate a larger set of ideas to constituents through the shorthand of these terms. For instance, the phrase "Green New Deal" does not typically conjure a detailed list of policy options proposed by Democrats in the minds of individuals, but rather signal a nebulous set of environmentally aimed ideas. The same is true for phrases like "critical race theory," which does not bring to mind the scholarship of Derrick Albert Bell Jr. for most. Rather, seven out of ten Americans are unable to identify a specific meaning, but indicate that it has something to do with how race can be taught in school settings (Safarpour et al. 2021).

The use and diffusion of these shorthand terms for broader ideas can shape public opinion and work to change the political agenda for or against certain outcomes associated with specific terms. However, it is important to consider that meanings can shift over time. Take, for instance, the term "Obamacare." The first uses in official congressional e-newsletters from 2010 tend to be from Republicans to disparage the synonymous Affordable Care Act. President Obama himself eventually embraced the Obamacare moniker to recast the law as a signature achievement (Hopper 2015). And in later years, Democrats would come to embrace the term and champion the outcomes of the law—though Republicans still used it more frequently in a negative way in constituent communications (see Figure 9.6).

In recent years, nearly all buzzword, shorthand terms that catch on in congressional communications do so through the efforts of the Republican Party. This is true even if the words or phrases originated in Democratic or leftist politics. To illustrate this point in the most recent congresses, we can consider the following list of words and terms: Green New Deal, defund the police, woke, and Critical Race Theory, visualized in Figure 9.7.

Count of official congressional e-newsletters mentioning "Obamacare" over time, by party

Data: DCinbox

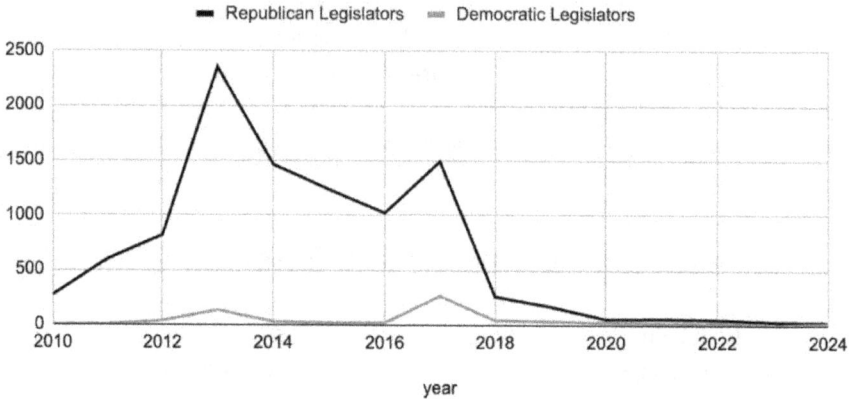

Figure 9.6: References of "Obamacare".

Counts of term and phrase use in official congressional e-newsletters over time, by party

Data: DCinbox

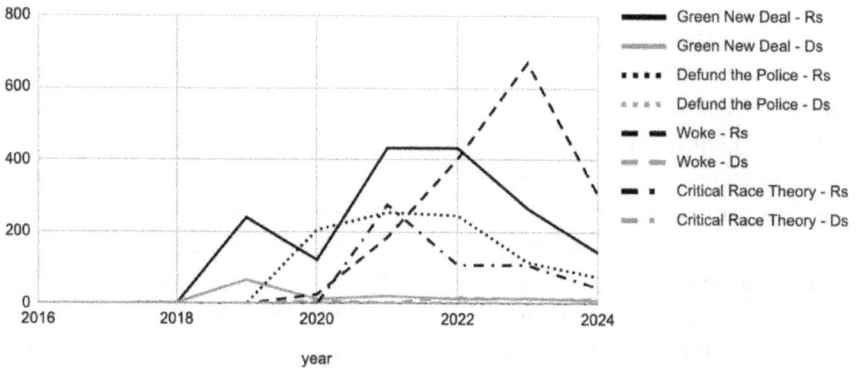

Figure 9.7: References to phrases associated with liberal ideologies.

In US politics, Jill Stein, the multiple-time Green Party candidate for president, called for a "Green New Deal" in 2012 laying out a set of policies and goals in a piece for *The Guardian* (Stein 2012). But it was not until 2018 that the term was used on official congressional e-newsletters when, on November 30, 2018, Ro Khanna (D-CA) wrote, "Following the recent release of the federal government's alarming climate change report, I support establishing a congressional select committee on a Green New Deal."[3] A month later, fellow Democrat Earl Blumenauer (D-OR) echoed this call, saying, "I'm focused on rebuilding and renewing America's crumbling infrastructure, advancing Medicare-for-all, and developing a Green New Deal to address the climate crisis." But within one year, the references to the Green New Deal took off in the Republican party as a way to disparage the goals of Democrats. In each successive year, Republican messages referenced the Green New Deal far more than Democrat ones and did so in a way to mock and decry the goals of the program idea.

A year later, the term "defund the police" made its way into congressional communication in a way that echoed the patterns of the Green New Deal. Originating through leftist activists after the 2020 murder of George Floyd by Minneapolis police officer Derek Chauvin, those fed up with historic and repeated police brutality argued that governments overspend on policing and that abolishing or defunding police agencies ought to be a governing priority. Importantly in the context of congressional communication, no federal legislator ever took to their official communications to call for defunding the police. Instead, of the six e-newsletters to ever mention "defund the police" sent by Democrats, four attempted to clarify that this narrative offered by many Republicans in power did not reflect the reality of efforts by Democratic legislators, while the other two reported on the calls of activists but did not endorse the idea.

In June 2020, as the Congress considered The Justice in Policing Act, Representative Susie Lee (D-NV) wrote, "Let me be clear: The Justice in Policing Act does not defund the police, but rather holds law enforcement accountable while improving community services and programs that have been neglected for decades."[4] In September 2020, Representative Jackie Speier (D-CA) sent an article about how "House Minority Whip Steve Scalise (R-LA) used Twitter to share a video that was misleadingly edited to distort Democratic presidential nominee Joe Biden's views on defunding the police."[5] Also in September 2020, Representative Steve Cohen (D-TN) sent a similar message indicating Biden and most prominent Democrats did not support defunding the police. Later, Andre Carson (D-IN) in November 2022 wrote, "Unfortunately, one narrative that is rampant is that Democrats support defunding the police. As a former law enforcement officer, I

---

3 https://www.dcinbox.com/email/?id=136926
4 https://www.dcinbox.com/email/?id=166038
5 https://www.dcinbox.com/email/?id=161930

have never supported defunding the police, and instead have served as a leader in Congress to reform policing."[6]

Yet in the content of the sheer volume of messages (895 in total) mentioning "defund the police," many tried to tie the activist slogan to federal Democrats. In December 2020, Representative Brian Babin (R-TX) wrote, "We must keep rejecting Democrat attempts to defund the police, grab our guns, and take away our rights to protect ourselves."[7] Kevin McCarthy (R-CA), a year later, told constituents, "While Democrats plotted ways to defund America's police forces, Republicans found new ways to celebrate those who keep us safe."[8] Just days before the 2022 midterm elections, Representative Tom Tiffany (R-WI) sent an e-newsletter saying, "While Joe Biden puts our national security at risk with his wide-open southern border, Democrats have simultaneously supported defunding the police, soft-on-crime policies, and reckless bail reform efforts, leaving Americans with an unprecedented crime wave."[9] And in October 2023, Senator John Cornyn (R-TX) wrote, "Democrats' soft-on-crime and defund-the-police agenda has led too many Americans to fall victim to violent criminals."[10]

Looking at the patterns and content on this topic in official communications shows the ability, or at least the effort expended, to transform a phrase originated as an activist slogan into a caricature of Democratic policies, despite clear efforts by Democratic members of Congress to distance themselves from the term.

Next on the scene were the terms "woke" and "critical race theory." Woke is a harder term to assess because it is used on occasion in official communications where it is meant by its simple definition as the act of arising from sleep in the morning, like when Representative Chris Pappas (D-NH) in 2019 wrote, "Yet again this week we woke up to the horrific news that 31 fellow Americans fell victim to another act of senseless violence because our government refuses to implement commonsense gun laws"[11] or when Senator Cory Gardner (R-CO) in 2019 sent, "Americans woke up 18 years ago in 2001 to realize nearly 3,000 people lost their lives in an attack against the United States by terrorists who struck at the very heart of our country."[12] But in more recent years, the word

---

6 https://www.dcinbox.com/email/?id=213459
7 https://www.dcinbox.com/email/?id=38908
8 https://www.dcinbox.com/email/?id=200008
9 https://www.dcinbox.com/email/?id=213616
10 https://www.dcinbox.com/email/?id=228233
11 https://www.dcinbox.com/email/?id=153168
12 https://www.dcinbox.com/email/?id=213616

has come to take on a shorthand meaning for a broader awareness of social inequalities in leftist circles, and a derision of that concept on the right.

The first "woke" reference in the stylistic meaning of the term in official e-
newsletters came on December 30, 2019, when Representative Barbara Lee (D-CA)
told constituents, "As we prepare to bring in the New Year, I want to thank you
for your support and for "staying woke" during what proved to be a very
challenging year for our country."[13] The first derisive mention came a few months
later on February 15, 2020, from Representative Matt Gaetz (R-FL) sending out a
hyperlink to the piece "School Choice and Greater Transparency Can Save Us
from Woke Classrooms" in the National Review. After this point, references to
"woke" took up a sharp uptick in Republican communications.

From 2020 to 2023, Republicans continued to write to constituents with their
negative thoughts on the concept of wokeness while Democrats did not offer up a
defense of the term but rather sought to argue the meaning was being misapplied
or continued to use it on occasion to refer to waking up in the morning. Republicans on the other hand nearly exclusively used the term in its non-literal meaning, saying things like "wasteful, woke spending," "Biden Administration's woke
executive orders," and "woke agenda."

Looking at the term "critical race theory" offers a similar lesson. The first reference to critical race theory or CRT in official congressional e-newsletters was
in November 2020 when Yvette Clarke (D-NY) wrote to constituents about how
the White House canceled an upcoming training session at the Centers for Disease
Control and Prevention about CRT after the Office of Management and Budget
under the Trump administration ordered "all federal agencies to 'cease and de-
sist' any government training programs that include any reference to 'critical
race theory' or 'white privilege'" (Wegmann 2020, n.p.). In the following year,
references to critical race theory skyrocketed to 275 from Republicans with just
two Democrats sending anything at all on the subject—neither defending nor promoting the term but rather passing along news stories about how conservative
activists were using the term to do battle with school boards across the country.

Here again, Republicans in Congress tended to use the newly emerging term
in ways to implicate Democrats. In December 2021, Representative Matt Gaetz
wrote, "The Left is seizing unconstitutional power through mandates, driving people from their jobs, destroying the American dollar, shattering our economy,
stealing elections, and embracing the bigoted doctrine of critical race theory, but
this WILL NOT be ignored."[14] In 2022 Representative Elise Stefanik (R-NY) told

---

13 https://www.dcinbox.com/email/?id=147982
14 https://www.dcinbox.com/email/?id=199923

constituents, "Additionally, parents in Upstate New York and the North Country are the primary stakeholder in their child's education and deserve a say in their child's education, but Far Left Democrats have pushed harmful COVID-19 mandates and Critical Race Theory throughout New York State, and shamefully used federal COVID-19 funds to implement this radical, woke agenda in New York classrooms."[15]

While initially a niche academic framework for analyzing systemic racism in legal systems, CRT has become a lightning rod in public discourse, with a good deal of this action likely driven by messaging from members of Congress. As soon as the phrase came onto the political scene, Republican legislators transformed CRT into a symbol of broader cultural grievances, framing it as a threat to American values and education. This reframing allowed them to associate CRT with broader critiques of Democratic policies, even when Democratic legislators themselves rarely engaged with the term in their communications.

In examining the use of shorthand terms in congressional communications, it becomes evident how such language can shape public discourse and influence political narratives. Any politically interested person consuming media in recent years was likely introduced to these short phrases and terms through the efforts of federal Republican legislators and the sustained and consistent communications efforts of their offices and the extended party network. As our collective media consumption patterns become increasingly bifurcated into hyper-specified algorithmically delivered content, the ability to push out a consistently used set of terms and phrases to signal a greater ideological concept is a very valuable political tactic. Terms like "Green New Deal," "defund the police," "woke," and "Critical Race Theory" serve as powerful tools for signaling broader ideological battles. While these terms often originate from activists, niche academic discussions, or media outlets, their adoption and framing by members of Congress reveal how external interests and societal debates are channeled into official legislative messaging. By co-opting and reframing these terms, legislators create a shorthand that resonates with their target audiences, often simplifying complex ideas into emotionally charged symbols. These patterns underscore the strategic role of legislative messaging in amplifying or even shaping external influences, molding the political agenda and mobilizing public opinion. Understanding this dynamic by studying the mechanics of political communication offers insights into its influence on democratic engagement.

---

15 https://www.dcinbox.com/email/?id=213583

9.6 Conclusion

Communicative surrogate representation is a way to enhance focus on a specific group. As seen in the analyses here, some groups tend to get far more attention in congressional communications than others, and oftentimes in ways that do not match up with their share in the population. We know from other research that legislators who share a background or characteristic such as occupation, sex, or race tend to introduce more legislation on behalf of or in ways that benefits others who share those characteristics (Barnes et al. 2021; Angevine 2017; Bratton and Haynie 1999). The connection between holding an identity, talking about that identity, and legislating on behalf of that identity is an area that is ripe for future research.

Media outlets and the narratives they tend to produce for audiences contribute to the framing and public opinion across multiple political issues. When members of Congress promote specific media outlets to their constituents, they amplify the influence of those outlets in at least two ways. First, by using their official communication channels to direct readers and viewers to these outlets, they lend them legitimacy and credibility. Second, they increase the likelihood that constituents will visit these media outlets. In this way, congressional communications act as both a reflection and a reinforcement of the external media landscape, shaping the broader political discourse.

As for terminology diffusion, recent years have been illustrative of specific party differences. Legislators from the Republican Party tend to write about the same sorts of themes and topics to constituents in ways that Democrats do not. They also tend to take terms or phrases that originate on the left and transform them into an abstract way for public opinion to understand an issue through shorthand rhetorical triggers.

Political representation and communication are made of a dynamic interplay of choices by legislators. By examining how a few different communication strategies play out in the most recent congresses, there are interesting insights to take from who members talk about, what media they tend to prioritize, and how terms are taken up and used by members of different political parties in contemporary US politics.

Discussion Questions

1 Can you identify examples of surrogate representation in your local community or state? Is there any reason to think we would see more or less of this on the federal level?

2   How might partisan preferences for certain media outlets shape public perception of news and policy issues? Do you think this would affect the credibility of different sources?
3   Are shorthand terms like "woke" or "green new deal" helpful or harmful in terms of conversations about politics?
4   Why might Republican legislators be more likely than Democrats to utilize the free incumbent perk of e-newsletters?
5   How do congressional communications contribute to the creation of echo chambers and the polarization of public opinion?

References

Ad Fontes Media. *Media Bias Chart*. Accessed January 8, 2025. https://www.adfontesmedia.com.

Angevine, Sara. "Representing all women: An analysis of congress, foreign policy, and the boundaries of women's surrogate representation." Political Research Quarterly 70, no. 1 (2017): 98–110.

Barnes, Tiffany D., Victoria D. Beall, and Mirya R. Holman. "Pink-collar representation and budgetary outcomes in US states." Legislative Studies Quarterly 46, no. 1 (2021): 119–154.

Blum, Rachel, Lindsey Cormack, and Kelsey Shoub. "Conditional Congressional communication: how elite speech varies across medium." *Political Science Research and Methods* 11, no. 2 (2023): 394–401.

Bratton, Kathleen A., and Kerry L. Haynie. "Agenda setting and legislative success in state legislatures: The effects of gender and race." *The Journal of Politics* 61, no. 3 (1999): 658–79.

Clarke, Andrew J., Jeffery A. Jenkins, and Nathan K. Micatka. "How Have Members of Congress Reacted to President Trump's Trade Policy?" *The Forum* 17, no. 4 (2020): 631–45.

Cormack, Lindsey. "DCinbox—Capturing every congressional constituent e-newsletter from 2009 onwards." *The Legislative Scholar* 2, no. 1 (2017): 27–34.

Cormack, Lindsey, and Heath Brown. "A decade of congressional efforts to conduct and communicate oversight of Medicare and Medicaid." *Public Policy & Aging Report* 31, no. 2 (2021): 47–52.

Gimpel, James G., Frances E. Lee, and Shanna Pearson-Merkowitz. "The check is in the mail: Interdistrict funding flows in congressional elections." *American Journal of Political Science* 52, no. 2 (2008): 373–94.

Green, Jon, Kelsey Shoub, Rachel Blum, and Lindsey Cormack. "Cross-Platform Partisan Positioning in Congressional Speech." *Political Research Quarterly* (2024): 10659129241236685.

Hellwege, Julia Marin, and Lindsey Cormack. "Writing "Home" in a Pandemic: The Prevalence of Gendered Topics in Congressional COVID-19 Communications." *The Forum* 20, no. 2 (2022): 293–310.

Hopper, Jennifer. "Obamacare, the news media, and the politics of 21st-century presidential communication." *International Journal of Communication* 9 (2015): 25.

Jackson, John E., and David C. King. "Public goods, private interests, and representation." *American Political Science Review* 83, no. 4 (1989): 1143–64.

Keena, Alex. "Out-Of-State Donors and Legislative Surrogacy in the US Senate." *Political Research Quarterly* (2024): 10659129241249171.

Mansbridge, Jane. "Rethinking representation." *American Political Science Review* 97, no. 4 (2003): 515–28.

Rhodes, Samuel C. "Filter bubbles, echo chambers, and fake news: How social media conditions individuals to be less critical of political misinformation." *Political Communication* 39, no. 1 (2022): 1–22.

Russell, Annelise. "US senators on Twitter: Asymmetric party rhetoric in 140 characters." *American Politics Research* 46, no. 4 (2018): 695–723.

Russell, Annelise. *Tweeting is leading: how senators communicate and represent in the age of Twitter*. Oxford University Press, 2021.

Safarpour, Alauna, David Lazer, Jennifer Lin, Caroline H. Pippert, James Druckman, Matthew Baum, Katherine Ognyanova et al. "The COVID States Project# 73: American attitudes toward critical race theory." 2021.

Stein, Jill. "Give Us a Mandate for What America Needs: a Green New Deal." *The Guardian*. October 14, 2012. https://www.theguardian.com/commentisfree/2012/oct/14/mandate-america-green-new-deal.

Sunstein, Cass R. *Echo chambers: Bush v. Gore, impeachment, and beyond*. Princeton University Press, 2001.

Walker, Teri J. *Today's environmental issues: Democrats and Republicans*. Bloomsbury Publishing USA, 2017.

Wegmann, Phillip. "Trump to Feds: Stop 'Anti-American' Training on 'Critical Race Theory'". *Real Clear Politics*. September 4, 2020. https://www.realclearpolitics.com/articles/2020/09/04/trump_to_feds_stop_anti-american_training_on_white_privilege_144145.html

Weissberg, Robert. "Collective vs. dyadic representation in Congress." *American Political Science Review* 72, no. 2 (1978): 535–47.

Bridgett A. King

10 The Politics of Running Free and Fair Elections

The federalist government structure in the United States creates a unique environment for elections and election administration. While many countries have national electoral management bodies responsible for establishing election calendars and rules, policies, and procedures, federalism creates an environment where, outside of a few limited federal statutes, states have the autonomy and the sovereignty to structure their elections in various ways. Variations include the voter registration deadline, the type of equipment and ballots used, rules about who is and is not allowed to become a poll worker, and the process for how the public servants who administer our elections at the local level are selected. This chapter discusses the structure of elections in the United States, its historical origins and evolution, and controversies, challenges, and opportunities.

In the early United States, as the colonies evolved into eventual states, rules for participation and administration varied greatly. This created a system that was not coherent, where colonies, counties, cities, and eventually states adopted different values in their charters and constitutions to determine what was or was not important regarding the qualifications to participate in a democracy and processes to ensure that eligible voters could cast ballots. From here, we see that the law shapes democracy and democratic participation differently for different people.

While we often understand the right to vote in the colonial United States as limited to property-owning white men aged twenty-one years and up, these were not the qualifying factors in all colonies. Religious exclusions were also used; in Massachusetts, for example, only members of the Congregational church could vote in the seventeenth century. In the eighteenth century, Catholics were disenfranchised in five states and Jews in four (Keyssar 2000). The exclusion of Catholics was often rooted in a fear that the Pope controlled Catholics and they would seek to undermine protestant society and thwart American values and institutions. Additionally, in larger cities, those granted political citizenship often had commercial affairs rather than residence within the city limits. Because city dwellers had different property types, they sought to outline property requirements in terms other than acreage or land (Keyssar 2000). As the American Revolution approached, some colonies became more lenient while others became

Bridgett A. King, University of Kentucky

https://doi.org/10.1515/9783111591902-010

more restrictive. Religious restrictions were lifted during the late seventeenth and early eighteenth centuries, and cities began to allow landowners to vote rather than just those with commercial enterprises.

Following the American Revolution, class differences drove discussions to expand or restrict the franchise. While wealthy Americans wanted to restrict the franchise to maintain economic and social advantages, poor Americans wanted to expand it to ensure they had a say in what happened in the newly formed nation. From these debates, two narratives arise regarding what the vote is. Some argued that the ballot or franchise is a privilege that the state could grant or take away based on its interest to justify restrictions.[1] Others who supported expansion argued that suffrage was a right.[2] In many colonies, these debates resulted in property ownership requirements replacing taxpaying requirements. Although no states that entered the union after 1790 had provisions that included property requirements as a requirement to vote, the taxpaying requirement (the requirement that voters be tax-paying citizens) remained and was adopted by states newly admitted to the union.[3] Where voting restrictions were loosened—such as dropping property restrictions or reduced/tax-paying requirements—the franchise opened up to a whole host of "undesirables": women, free Blacks, recent immigrants, poor whites, day laborers, factory workers, and other individuals who became a prominent fixture as the country moved toward industrialization. Many states responded to these population shifts by arguing that these groups of individuals were more likely to engage in fraud, did not have the moral character to participate, or were dependent on others and, therefore, unable to exercise free will in the voting booth. Consequently, states amended their constitutions to include policies that worked to limit voting access to the franchise for specific groups. For example, states added the word white to their constitutions (e.g., Indiana, New York, Ohio, and Wisconsin) or the word men to exclude non-white voters and women (Keyssar, 2000).

Poll taxes also emerged during this time (the late 1800s, early 1900s, after the Civil War) as a qualification for voting.[4] Many states required payment of the poll tax at a time separate from the election, requiring voters to bring receipts with

---

1 Franchise refers to the right to vote. —Also termed *elective franchise* (Black's Law Dictionary, 2024).

2 Suffrage refers to the right or privilege of participating in a public election by casting a vote—this was also termed *right* to vote (Black's Law Dictionary, 2024).

3 By the 1850s, there were only two property requirements remaining; they pertained to foreign-born residents of Rhode Island and African Americans in New York (Keyssar, 2000).

4 See Keyssar (2000), Appendix A.10 States with Taxpaying Requirements for Suffrage: 1870–1921.

them to the polls. If they could not locate such receipts, they could not vote. Although primarily associated with states of the former Confederacy, poll taxes were also in place in some northern and western states. For instance, California had a poll tax until 1914, when it was abolished through a popular referendum. In addition to poll taxes and grandfather clauses, states began to specify who was and was not a resident by instituting specific residency requirements. Residency requirements extended in some states to eliminate the ability of migrant and transient populations to participate. As cities and immigrant populations grew, so did fraud in elections. In 1800, Massachusetts adopted a voter registration policy designed to eliminate illegal voting and violence at the polls (Harris 1934). Other New England states shortly followed, but it was not until after the Civil War that registration laws were adopted in other regions of the country to respond to rampant fraud. Between 1860 and 1890 the majority of states adopted some form of voter registration (Harris 1934). Because early voter registration laws were easily circumvented, and repeating and colonization occurred frequently, registration laws became increasingly strict, and special registration commissions were established in large cities (Harris 1934).[5] As party members began to occupy these offices, partisan assessors used registration to ensure that only desirable voters who supported their candidates or party were registered and eligible to participate in elections (Keyssar 2000).

Political parties also formed positions regarding voting and elections, not based on what was right, honorable, and moral but on which populations were perceived more likely to support them. Political parties also sought not only to change election policy but also policies connected to the processes that would allow individuals to become citizens and subsequently vote. For example, Know Nothings supported requiring a twenty-one-year waiting period for immigrants before citizenship or the permanent denial of citizenship (Keyssar 2000, 67). They also advocated changes in state voting laws, including registration systems, literacy tests, and a fourteen-to-twenty-one-year post-naturalization period before a foreign-born male could vote.

In some states, foreign-born men who the federal government had not naturalized but who met property, taxpaying, and residency requirements could participate in elections. Many states changed their constitutions to limit voting to citizens to protect themselves from the potential influx of undesirable foreign-born voters. However, in the latter half of the 1800s, states in the upper Midwest (Wis-

---

5 Repeaters were people who voted repeatedly by changing their appearance. Colonizers were people brought into a precinct a few days before the election to vote. Floaters, repeaters who went from precinct to precinct and voted multiple times in each, were also used to commit fraud.

consin, Michigan, Indiana, and the territories of Oregon and Minnesota) opened the franchise back up to noncitizens who had lived in the United States for two years and who had filed their paperwork intending to become citizens. After the Civil War, a dozen more states in the South followed suit. Currently, in the United States, federal and state laws require citizenship as a requirement to vote in state and federal elections.[6] However, non-citizen voting was commonplace in the early United States, particularly outside the Northeast.

In the 1700s and 1800s, arguments for a more inclusive or exclusive franchise, state autonomy, and individual discretion were used to establish qualifications for participation and policies and procedures for voting and registration. The decisions that stemmed from these arguments laid the groundwork for our current system of fragmented and disjointed rules governing elections.

10.1 The Administration of Elections

Although there is an extensive record of the evolution of voting in the United States pertaining to eligibility and qualifications for participation, as well as federal interventions by Congress and the Supreme Court that have both expanded and limited access to the franchise, there is a scarcity of information about the evolution of election administration practices in the United States. Much of what we know about the calling of elections, polling locations, voting processes and equipment, and the state policy response to a rapidly changing national and political environment comes from *Election Administration in the United States* by Joseph P. Harris, published in 1934. According to Harris, the administrative approaches to elections in the early United States often followed English tradition.

The calling of elections occurred using two methods. In the New England colonies, election dates were fixed by statute, typically annually and in the early spring. In other colonies, the elections were called by a special writ, following the process used in England at the time.

> Detailed provisions were made for the publication of the writ by posting notices, reading the proclamation, and in some colonies by requiring notice to be read at the religious services. The hours for voting were not always provided by law, but, in comparison with the present practice, they were usually short. It was not unusual for the polling to start at nine

---

6 Currently, while no state's constitution explicitly allows noncitizens to vote in state or local elections and fifteen states explicitly prohibit it, the District of Columbia and municipalities in three states (California, Maryland, and Vermont) permit noncitizens to vote only in local elections.

o'clock in the morning, and the polls to be closed by two or three o'clock in the afternoon. However, there were elections which lasted for several days, contrary to the fixed custom which has since arisen for the election to be completed within a single day (Harris 1934, 13).

In New England, elections were typically held at the colony's capital, but as the population spread away from the capital, it was necessary to create a system where citizens could vote without having to travel there. Because of this, a system of voting was established where voters cast ballots at local meetings, and the ballots were sent to the capital by a deputy sheriff. Generally, local officials conducted elections, including the sheriff, coroner, or mayor (Harris 1934, 14). In Pennsylvania and other colonies, election judges and inspectors assisted the sheriff or deputy.

To cast ballots, states and local jurisdictions used a voice vote (*viva voce*), as was the practice in England, or some form of a paper ballot. In the voice vote system, the voter would state the name of the candidate or candidates they were supporting publicly. The name would then be recorded on paper.[7] The lack of secrecy often led to imitation and bribery.[8] In a paper vote system, voters would write their name under the name of the candidate that were supporting or write the name of the candidate(s) they were supporting by hand on a ballot. Eventually, handwritten ballots were replaced by printed ballots. In many instances, political parties began to prepare ballots, which were then placed in envelopes. The political parties often printed their ballots on paper of different colors or printed ballots with elaborate designs. Both approaches made it easy to see which party or candidate(s) a voter selected during a given election.

When some states required that all ballots be printed on white paper, parties used various shades and weights of paper that continued to make it easy to determine who the voter was supporting. The lack of secrecy created an environment where bribery ran rampant. Although the party ballots were unofficial, where they were accepted, a bribed voter could be handed a party ballot and watched until it was submitted to ensure the vote was cast. Over time, party-printed ballots were replaced with government-printed secret or Australian ballots. "Australian ballots are official ballots containing the names of all candidates, printed by public officers at public expense, upon uniform paper, and distributed only at the polls, where it was marked in secret" (Harris 1934, 17).

As the Australian ballot was adopted across the United States following 1890, new requirements, including nominating candidates so that their names would

---

7 Votes may also have been cast by a show of hands (Harris 1934).
8 Shoulder hitters, big guys who hit your shoulders to remind you how to vote, were used to intimidate voters in polling locations.

be printed on the official government-printed ballot, were written into local and state statutes. Toward the end of the nineteenth century, voting machines emerged, and statutes that allowed their use were adopted in many states. To address election fraud and violence, election boards were created in many states with the express purpose of promoting election reform. However, like voter registration, the boards eventually fell under the control of party organization members and provided little to no improvements (Harris 1934, 19).

The Acme Voting Machine was invented in the late 1880s. It allowed poll workers to count the exact number of ballots cast compared to the number of registered voters. The machine had a tabulator activated by a lever mechanism that released the ballot into the box. Before the Acme Voting Machine and systematic voter registration, there was no way to ensure that each voter cast only one ballot. Although the Acme Machine could provide an accurate total of the number of ballots cast, it did not guarantee the integrity of the vote count. Election officials could "tear" or "mark" a ballot to make it invalid or stuff the ballot box with additional votes. A decade later, the Lever Voting Machine was first used in Lockport, New York. Using the Lever Machine, which was designed to make voting private and accurate:

> Voters would pull a large handle to close the machine's curtains, ensuring a secret ballot. Then, a voter would see a board with candidate names, offices, and parties. Each candidate's name, office and party were arranged in a row with small levers directly above them for voters to choose from. Once a voter pushed down a lever, the machine would lock to prevent a duplicate vote. (Thomas 2023, n.p.)

Voting machine technology continued to advance, addressing accessibility for voters with disabilities, readability and usability, the production of documentation necessary for independent audits, and ease of use and maintenance for election administrators.

By the close of the nineteenth century, population growth, technological advances, regularly scheduled elections, and frequent changes to election law transformed US elections into an increasingly time-consuming and complicated process. Into the twentieth century, as technology continued to advance, the federal government took a more active role in elections and voting in the US, reshaping administrative processes and structures, and political parties began to establish and solidify ideologically diverse preferences for election policies and administrative processes.

10.2 Federal Intervention

Although there has been considerable federal intervention regarding the qualifications and rules for participation, limited federal legislation has expressly focused on administering elections. Although the 1965 Voting Rights Act (VRA) is perhaps most frequently cited as the piece of federal legislation that provided redress for *some* discriminatory laws and procedures by reducing state autonomy in election administration, before the 1965 VRA, the Civil Rights Acts of 1960 and 1964 aimed to remedy discriminatory election policies and practices.[9] The 1960 Act strengthened the federal government's role by allowing federal referees to investigate complaints of voter discrimination and register qualified voters, required voting records to be preserved for twenty-two months, and allowed federal judges to issue registration orders and replace state registrars with federal officials. The 1964 Act, while addressing multiple issues related to segregation and discrimination, also required the equal application of election standards, allowed for the appointment of temporary voter registrars, required the compilation of voter registration data as specified by the Act, and established a presumption of literacy for all who had completed sixth grade in an accredited, English language instruction school (Civil Rights Act of 1964).

The 1965 Voting Rights Act prohibited states and political subdivisions from imposing or applying qualifications, standards, practices, or procedures to deny or abridge the right to vote on account of race or color (Section 2); established a coverage formula under which federal intervention in the electoral process was permitted (Section 4(b));[10] authorized the appointment of federal voting examiners (Section 3) by the Civil Service Commission (Section 6) to determine the qualifications, and require the enrollment, of individuals by state and local officials to vote in all federal, state, and local elections (Section 7); suspended the use of literacy tests (Section 4); required that new voting laws in covered states and local jurisdictions be approved, before taking effect (Section 5); abolished the poll tax in federal elections (Section 10); and prohibited any person, acting under

---

9 Before the 1960 and 1964 Acts, the 1957 Civil Rights Act established the Civil Rights Division of the Department of Justice. It empowered federal officials to prosecute individuals who conspired to deny or abridge a citizen's right to vote. It also created a Civil Rights Commission that could investigate allegations of voter infringement (Civil Rights Act 1957).

10 In states and political subdivisions in which any test or device was used as a condition of voter registration in the November 1, 1964, election and either less than 50 percent of persons of voting age were registered on that date or less than 50 percent of persons of voting age voted in the election of November 1964. Section 4(b) was ruled unconstitutional in *Shelby v. Holder* (2013).

color of law or otherwise, from intimidating, threatening, or coercing any person for attempting to vote or voting (Section 11).[11,12]

Although the federal interventions of the 1950s and 1960s reduced many administrative barriers to participation in the US, gaps in participation persisted—namely for racial and ethnic minorities, the poor, less educated, and the young. The decision to vote is often described as the result of a cost-benefit calculus. An individual will vote when the benefits received from voting exceed the costs (Key 1949; Downs 1957; Bauer 1990). Subsequent federal interventions actively worked to reduce the cost of voting among those less likely to participate, simultaneously altering the landscape of election administration.

The 1993 National Voter Registration Act (also known as the "NVRA" or "motor voter law") sought to ease the voter registration for the most likely to be disenfranchised by creating voter registration requirements for federal elections, consequently increasing voter turnout (Brown and Wedeking 2006). The National Voter Registration Act of 1993 requires that states offer voter registration opportunities at State motor vehicle agencies (Section 5), voter registration opportunities by mail-in application (Section 6), and voter registration opportunities at certain State and local offices, including public assistance and disability offices (Section 7). Section 8 of the NVRA requires states to implement procedures to maintain accurate and current voter registration lists. Election officials use data from various sources to ensure voter registration lists are accurate, including state vital statistics and death records, reports/notices from other states that a former resident has registered to vote, requests from voters for removal, Social Security Administration death records, mailed ballots returned as undeliverable, and data from interstate data-sharing compacts.[13] The NVRA also limits the conditions under which a voter can be removed from the voter registration list. These include the death of the registrant, the registrant's written confirmation that their address has changed to a location outside the registrar's jurisdiction, the request of the registrant, and the registrant's failure to respond to specific confirmation mailings along with failure to appear to vote in two consecutive federal general elec-

---

11 The provisions listed include those in subsequent amendments and reauthorizations of 1970, 1975, 1982, 1992, and 2006.

12 The VRA also includes provisions for individuals who are disabled. Section 208 allows voters who are blind, disabled, or unable to read or write to be assisted by a person of the voter's choice. Additional requirements are contained in the 1984 Voting Accessibility for the Elderly and Handicapped, 1990 Americans with Disabilities Act (ADA), 1993 National Voter Registration Act (NVRA), and 2002 Help America Vote Act (HAVA).

13 For a comprehensive list, see US Election Assistance Commission Election Administration and Voter Survey (2022) Table 2.

tions after the mailing.[14] Although the NVRA did increase "the pool of individuals legally qualified to vote, it also modified the pool to include more individuals that in all likelihood are less inclined to participate" (Brown and Wedeking 2006, 493).

Attention was expressly turned to the administration of elections following the 2000 presidential election. The winner of the Electoral College and the presidency came down to Florida's twenty-five electors. Although Katherine Harris (R), Florida Secretary of State, responsible for certifying winners in any statewide election, had initially announced that George W. Bush was the winner, because the margins between George W. Bush and Al Gore were so close, it was unclear who had won the popular vote in the state.[15,16] What followed was five weeks of uncertainty about who would become the forty-second President of the US while the Bush and Gore campaigns battled over the ballots, rules, and administrative procedures. Because the margin of victory was less than 0.5 percent, a mandatory machine recount was required by Florida Election Code 102.141. Following the machine recount, the Gore campaign requested a manual hand recount in Miami-Dade, Broward, Palm Beach, and Volusia Counties. During the manual hand recounts, varied interpretations of voter intention on the ballots led to inconsistent returns. "There were punch-card ballots where the voters' attempt to make their choice had only succeeded in detaching a portion of the perforated paper ("hanging chads") or merely denting – rather than removing – the punch-out ("dimpled chads")" (Elving 2018, n.p.). As the hand recounts continued, the Bush campaign actively argued in the courts that the manual recount should stop. After the Florida Supreme Court ruled that the manual recounts could continue, the Bush campaign appealed the ruling. On December 12, the US Supreme Court ruled in *Bush v. Gore* that the recount must stop as there was no uniform statewide methodology, and the state had insufficient time to create one and complete the recount.

Following the 2000 election, The Help America Vote Act (HAVA) of 2002 was passed by the US Congress to reform the nation's voting process. HAVA expressly addresses improvements to voting systems and voter access identified following the 2000 election (US Election Assistance Commission 2023). Key provisions of HAVA include providing funding to make polling locations accessible and to purchase new voting equipment, requiring voter identification for first-time voters, mandating that states create centralized computerized voter registration databases, requiring access to provisional voting, requiring states to identify the chief

---

14 Registrants can also be removed for mental incapacity or criminal conviction as provided by state law.
15 By the end of the election, the margin was 537 votes out of six million cast (Elving 2018).
16 Harris was also an ally of Republican Gov. Jeb Bush, George Bush's brother, and had been the co-chair of George W. Bush's campaign in Florida.

election official in each state, and establishing the US Election Assistance Commission, an independent, bipartisan commission charged with developing guidance to meet HAVA requirements. Since HAVA's passing in 2002, many federal bills governing elections and mandating stronger federal controls have failed, even with one-party control of the presidency and Congress (for example, the John Lewis Voting Rights Advancement Act of 2021/2023 and the Freedom to Vote Act 2023–2024).[17]

Although many lessons were learned after the 2000 election and federal remedies were implemented to address many challenges, Hasen (2012) notes, "Florida mainly taught political operatives the benefits of manipulating the rules, controlling election machinery, and litigating early and often." Additionally, "Election law has become a part of a political strategy" (5). Given the limited federal intervention in election administration, changes to the rules, policies, procedures, and structure of US elections remain dominated by state institutions.

10.3 The Structure of Election Administration in the States

The NVRA and HAVA require the designation of a Chief Election Official (CEO). In most states, the CEO is an elected Secretary of State, but it can also be the Lieutenant Governor or another appointed official (Table 10.1). Whether elected or appointed, the selection process in many states involves partisan influence (Table 10.2).

Given the partisan nature of most selection procedures, there have been inquiries about the potential for partisan influence on state CEOs. Hale et al. (2015, 38) suggest there are mechanisms to "limit the arbitrary use of power, including the courts and public opinion." A recent comprehensive analysis of secretaries of state partisan activity lends support to this observation. Johnson et al. (2020) find that "egregious, highly consequential incidences of partisan bias by secretaries of state

---

17 Other notable federal interventions address the ability of military personnel and overseas citizens to vote. These include the Soldiers Voting Act of 1942, Federal Voting Assistance Act of 1955 and 1968, Overseas Citizen Voting Rights Act of 1975, Uniformed and Overseas Citizens Absentee Voting Act (UOCAVA) of 1986, and Military and Overseas Voter Empowerment (MOVE) Act of 2009.

Table 10.1: Election administration at the state level.[18]

Secretary of State		Lieutenant Governor	State Commission of Elections	Executive Director
Alabama*	Missouri*	Alaska*	Delaware^	District of Columbia^
Arizona*	Montana*	Utah*		Illinois^
Arkansas*	Nebraska*			North Carolina^
California*	Nevada*			South Carolina^
Colorado*	New Hampshire^			
Connecticut*	New Jersey^			
Florida^	New Mexico*			
Georgia*	North Dakota*			
Idaho*	Ohio*			
Indiana*	Oregon*			
Iowa*	Pennsylvaia^[19]			
Kansas*	Rhode Island*			
Kentucky*	South Dakota*			
Louisiana*	Tennessee^			
Maine^	Texas^			
Massachusetts*	Vermont*			
Michigan*	Washington*			
Minnesota*	West Virginia*			
Mississippi*	Wyoming*			

---

18 In Arkansas, Georgia, Indiana, Kentucky, Rhode Island, Tennessee, and West Virginia, election responsibilities are shared between the secretary of state and a State board or commission. In Delaware, Hawaii, Illinois, Maryland, New York, North Carolina, Oklahoma, South Carolina, Virginia and Wisconsin, and Washington, D.C., a board or commission oversees elections, and the state chief election official is a member of the board or commission (National Conference of State Legislatures 2023).

19 The Chief Election Official is formally referred to as the Secretary of the Commonwealth

Table 10.1 (continued)

Chief Election Officer	Administrator of Elections	Co-Directors	Secretary of State Election Board	Commissioner
Hawaii^	Maryland^ Wisconsin^	New York^	Oklahoma^	Virginia^

*Elected
^Appointed
Source: National Conference of State Legislatures (2025).

Table 10.2: Partisanship and selection process of state chief election officials.

	Elected	Appointed
Partisan	Alabama, Alaska, Arizona, Arkansas, California, Colorado, Connecticut, Georgia, Idaho, Indiana, Iowa, Kansas, Kentucky, Maine, Massachusetts, Michigan, Minnesota, Mississippi, Missouri, Montana, Nebraska, Nevada, New Hampshire, New Mexico, North Dakota, Ohio, Oregon, Rhode Island, South Dakota, Utah, Vermont, Washington, West Virginia, Wyoming	Florida, New Jersey, Oklahoma, Pennsylvania, Tennessee, Texas, Virginia
Nonpartisan		Delaware, District of Columbia, Hawaii, Illinois, Maryland, New York, North Carolina, South Carolina, Wisconsin

Source: Hale, Montjoy, and Brown (2015).

are rare.[20] [However], less dramatic acts of partisanship have taken place more frequently" (5). For example, 29 percent of secretaries serving from 2000 to 2020 took partisan positions, such as publicly endorsing candidates, 30 percent have endorsed a candidate running in a race under their supervision, twelve of 137 served as co-chair (or equivalent) of a presidential election campaign, and approximately 20 percent have lost in court in lawsuits arising from circumstances where the secretaries' actions appeared to favor their political party (Johnson et al. 2020; Johnson 2022). Johnson et al. (2020) and Johnson (2022) also found that while approval rat-

---

20 Across states and jurisdictions managing elections may be the majority or a portion of a larger scope of responsibility for LEOs. Thirty-three percent of LEOs report that elections or election-related matters constitute all or almost all of their workload (Adona et al. 2020)

ings for election officials in general are high, partisanship among secretaries of state hurts voter confidence. On a positive note, from 2010 to 2020, the number of secretaries of state with election backgrounds increased and fewer partisan endorsements occurred during the 2020 presidential election cycle.

While secretaries of state and other state-level officials serve as the CEO, they are removed from the day-to-day operation of election offices, which are managed by local election offices that implement the policies established by states in more than 10,000 jurisdictions across the United States. The responsibilities of local election officials vary across and within states. Generally, LEOs are responsible for registering voters; selecting polling locations for early voting and Election Day; purchasing, testing, and storing voting machines; designing ballots and confirming their accuracy; mailing, receiving, and processing absentee ballots; recruiting, training, and supervising poll workers; and tabulating results.[21] CEOs, in turn, can impact the work of local election officials by using discretion to issue directives or interpret election laws and procedures into specific instructions (Johnson et al. 2020; Johnson 2022).

The administrative structure of local election offices may vary, with each jurisdiction managed by a single elected or appointed individual, a board, or a combination. Although there is no comprehensive list of the selection procedures for local election officials, the 2020 and 2022 Local Election Official Survey suggests that Local Election Officials (LEOs) are primarily elected (Gronke and Manson 2020, 2022).[22] LEOs differ across some policy preferences by selection process. Elected officials are less likely to support convenience measures like making election day a holiday, increasing internet voting, and running all elections by mail (Ferrer and Geyn 2024).

The opportunity for partisan influence to affect the behavior and decision-making of local election officials has received some, albeit limited, attention, generally finding that the party affiliation of LEOs *can* affect how they navigate the myriad statutes and decisions they are required to make when managing an election office. Local election official party affiliation can affect the casting and counting of provisional ballots, the location of polling locations, the removal of individuals believed ineligible due to felony convictions, and responsiveness to constituents (Stuart 2004; Hasen 2005, 2012; Kimball et al. 2006; Merivaki and Smith 2016; Porter and Rogowski 2018; McBrayer et al. 2020). The behavior of LEOs may also be affected by the partisan composition of the jurisdiction in which they work (Kimball

---

21 The percent elected in 2020 and 2022 was 56.7 percent and 56.6 percent, respectively (Gronke and Manson, 2020, 2022)
22 Absentee voting is also referred to as vote by mail.

et al. 2006; Kropf et al. 2013). Partisan differences also emerge regarding perceptions of the culture of election administration. Democratic and Independent LEOs are more likely to support a voter-centric participatory culture that values improving access to the ballot and voter experiences. Republican LEOs are more likely to support an integrity-centric participatory culture that limits voter access but makes the process more secure or more manageable for their workload (Suttman-Lea and Groke 2024). While these partisan preferences may exist, local election officials are not using their discretion to overtly advantage their party or ensure partisan victories in their jurisdictions (Ferrer et al. 2023).

10.4 Controversies in Election Administration

Parties have increasingly tried to leverage election policy to increase or limit access to registration and voting; partisan legislatures have actively worked, as they did in early America, to create a system that favors those most likely to support their party or candidates (Bentele and O'Brien 2013). Partisan notions of integrity and access often drive arguments that support or oppose changes in election administration. For example, following the 2020 presidential election, Republican legislators in Pennsylvania argued that changing election laws in the state to require all voters to show identification, among other policies, will increase voters' trust in elections (Caruso 2021). Georgia Republicans made similar arguments to justify SB 202, which changed election law in Georgia and redistributed administrative power. Among other things, SB 202 "removes authority from the secretary of state, making him a nonvoting member of the State Elections Board, and allows lawmakers to initiate takeovers of local election boards" (Corbett 2021, n.p.). Following the signing of the bill, Governor Brian Kemp, a Republican, noted that the bill was "another step toward ensuring our elections are secure, accessible, and fair" (Corbett, 2021, n.p.). Arguments related to confidence and integrity have also been used to limit voter access to absentee voting, drop boxes, early voting days, and other convenience measures that Democrats argue reduce the cost of voting and make participation more accessible (Brennan Center 2024).[23] When discussing a bill that would automatically send absentee ballots to active voters, former Nevada Assembly Speaker Jason Frierson, a Democrat, stated, "The more options that we give our voters, the better off we are as states, and the more we're advancing democracy" (Izaguirre 2021, n.p.).

---

23 Examples include voting more than once, non-citizen voting, absentee ballot fraud, impersonating another voter, changing the vote count, and fraudulent voter registration.

Research, however, suggests that many of the election policy reforms adopted by states do not have a demonstrable effect on voter confidence or trust (Bowler and Donovan 2016). Consistently, research suggests that the most impactful factors on confidence are the voter's personal experience and affiliation with partisan winners (Alvarez et al. 2021; Atkeson and Saunders 2007; Bryant 2020; Clark 2021; Gronke 2014; Claassen et al. 2012; King 2017, 2020; King and Barnes 2019; Stein and Vonhamme 2012; Sances and Stewart 2015; Atkeson et al. 2024; Sances 2023). Despite this, state legislators continue to work to reshape election policy in the United States actively.

Partisan perspectives are not limited to partisan elites but also extend to the general public. For example, Republican voters are more likely to support requiring all voters to show a government identification to vote, removing voters from the registration lists if they have not recently voted or confirmed their registration, and hand-counting paper ballots. They are also less likely to support automatic voter registration, allowing people with felony convictions to vote after completing their sentences, making early, in-person voting accessible for all voters for at least two weeks before Election Day, making Election Day a national holiday, Election Day or Same Day Voter Registration (Pew Research Center 2021; Stewart 2023). Republicans are more likely to believe various forms of fraud occur more frequently (Stewart 2023).[24]

The quality of voter registration rolls has also been used to call into question the integrity of US elections. The NVRA requires that states maintain an up-to-date list of eligible voters. Section 8 of the NVRA addresses the administration of voter registration by states and requires procedures to maintain accurate and current voter registration lists. Section 8(a)(4) requires that states "conduct a general program that makes a reasonable effort to remove from the voter rolls people who are ineligible by reason of death or change in residence to a location outside the jurisdiction." The NVRA also limits when states can conduct list maintenance. Under Section 8(c)(2), states must complete their maintenance programs to remove the names of ineligible voters from the official list of eligible voters no later than ninety days before a primary or general election for federal office. These ninety days are known as the "quiet period."

The use of voter list maintenance as a partisan tool, coupled with the timing of voter removals and the potential to remove eligible voters incorrectly, has been scrutinized in recent elections. On August 7, 2024, ninety days before the general election, Virginia's Republican Governor, Glen Youngkin, signed an executive order to expedite the removal of noncitizens from the state's voter rolls,

---

24 Liberal Justices Kagan, Sotomayor, and Jackson, dissenting.

maintaining that the program would only remove those who were ineligible due to lack of citizenship. The state was sued by the Department of Justice and advocacy groups who argued that the maintenance program, which removed 1,600 voters, violated the "quiet period" and demonstrated that the program removed eligible citizens from the rolls. Although a federal district court initially agreed, the state appealed the ruling to the US Supreme Court. Along ideological lines, in a 6–3 decision, the Supreme Court sided with the state.[25] Youngkin called the order "a victory for commonsense and election fairness" (Totenberg and Dutton 2024; Garber and O'Conner 2024). A similar program was implemented in Alabama by Republican Secretary of State Wes Allen. The Alabama program removed 3,000 voters who were alleged to be non-citizens. However, no one on the list was found to be a non-citizen, and the program was blocked by a federal judge (Totenberg and Dutton 2024; Garber and O'Conner 2024). In addition, before the November 2024 election, there were at least thirty-six cases related to voter rolls and their maintenance pending in nineteen US states, a noticeable increase from previous election years (Cole 2024). Although reports of noncitizen voting are rare (Lieb 2024), many of the lawsuits were based on the belief that noncitizens are illegally voting for Democrats.

Citizens often understand these and other controversies through the lens of partisanship. Partisans may disagree over matters of fact (Bartels 2002) or agree on facts but have different interpretations of the same conditions (Bisgaard 2015; Gaines et al. 2007). Where there is disagreement, partisans are more likely to align their beliefs and perceptions with those of their political party. For example, Sinclair et al. (2019) evaluate the effect of pre-election claims on election rigging. They find that before the election, elite cues from Clinton boosted the confidence of her supporters, and elite cues from Trump, which often included claims about illegal voting and election rigging, depressed Trump supporters' confidence (865). Similar findings are reported by Carter et al. (2024) in an investigation of vote-by-mail and exposure to election fraud rhetoric in 2020. And, while election officials and others may engage in fact-checking, Berlinski et al. (2021) find that the effect of unsubstantiated claims on confidence cannot be ameliorated through fact-checks that show the claims to be false.

Ever-evolving qualifications, rules, technology, processes, structure, and discretion have continuously characterized US elections and election administration. Although the administrative work of state and local election administration has

---

25 The National Association of Secretaries of State (NASS), the National Association of State Election Directors (NASED), the National Association of Election Administrators (also known as the Election Center), and state associations provide election officials with opportunities for professional development.

become increasingly professionalized, the individuals who run our elections are often selected by partisan processes.[26] While they may not overtly use their positions and discretion to ensure election outcomes that align with their partisan preferences, their decisions are scrutinized by the public, parties, voter integrity, and voter access groups alike. This, coupled with the authority of legislatures to make rules for registration and voting and restructure who has administrative authority over elections, the involvement of other state actors who execute processes, increased adjudication by the courts, and partisan elite messaging, continually put the professionals who run our elections in the crosshairs of partisan politics.

10.5 Conclusion

The administration of elections in the United States has long been a source of controversy and complexity, largely due to the country's unique federalist structure. Unlike many nations with centralized electoral management, the US allows individual states significant autonomy in shaping how elections are conducted. This autonomy manifests in diverse practices across states, such as varying voter registration deadlines, different voting technologies, and unique procedures for selecting local election administrators. Historically, these variations trace back to the colonial era and have evolved amidst debates over voter eligibility and access. The patchwork nature of US election laws has been a breeding ground for disputes, as both state autonomy and federal interventions—such as the Voting Rights Act and subsequent reforms—have often collided, reflecting enduring tensions over who should control and influence election processes.

Despite numerous federal interventions and reforms aimed at standardizing and securing elections, the administration of elections remains a contentious and partisan issue. Efforts to reform or manipulate election laws are frequently driven by the perceived electoral advantages they offer to particular parties or candidates, continuing a tradition that stretches back to the nation's founding. In recent years, controversies stemming from partisan-driven changes to election laws, varying interpretations of voter rights, and the influence of political rhetoric have highlighted the persistent fractures within the election administration landscape. As long as state autonomy underpins the US electoral system, and partisan interests are at play, the contention surrounding election administration is likely to persist, shaping the democratic process in complex and often divisive ways.

Discussion Questions

1 Are there parallels between the early American arguments for expanding and restricting the franchise that persist in contemporary discussions of voting and elections?

2 Given the contemporary challenges of election administration, what areas should future federal legislation prioritize?

3 What administrative reforms could remove partisan influence from election administration at both the state and local levels? Do you see such reforms as necessary?

4 How might the increasing involvement of state and federal courts in resolving election disputes shape election administration in the future?

5 What processes or policies should the US adopt to combat the effect of messaging from partisan elites, which can impact confidence and trust in elections?

References

Adona, Natalie, Paul Gronke, Paul Manson, and Sarah Cole. 2020. *Stewards of Democracy: The Views of American Local Election Officials. Democracy Fund*. https://evic.reed.edu/wp-content/uploads/2020/09/2019_DemocracyFund_StewardsOfDemocracy.pdf.

Alvarez, R. Michael, Jian Cao, and Yimeng Li. 2021. "Voting Experiences, Perceptions of Fraud, and Voter Confidence." *Social Science Quarterly* 102: 1225–38. https://doi.org/10.1111/ssqu.12940.

Atkeson, Lonna Rae, and Kyle L. Saunders. 2007. "The Effect of Election Administration on Voter Confidence: A Local Matter?" *PS: Political Science & Politics* 40 (4): 655–60.

Atkeson, Lonna Rae, Eli McKown-Dawson, and Robert M. Stein. 2024. "The Costs of Voting and Voter Confidence." *Political Research Quarterly*. https://doi.org/10.1177/10659129241283169

Bartels, Larry M. 2002. "Beyond the Running Tally: Partisan Bias in Political Perceptions." *Political Behavior* 24 (2): 117–50. http://www.jstor.org/stable/1558352.

Bauer, John R. 1990. "Patterns of voter participation in the American states." *Social Science Quarterly* 71 (4): 824–34.

Bentele, Keith G., and Erin E. O' Brien. 2013. "Jim Crow 2.0? Why states consider and adopt restrictive voter access policies." *Perspectives on Politics* 11 (4): 1088–16.

Berlinski, Nicolas et al. 2021. "The Effects of Unsubstantiated Claims of Voter Fraud on Confidence in Elections." *Journal of Experimental Political Science* 10 (1): 34–49.

Bisgaard, Martin. 2015. "Bias will find a way: Economic perceptions, attributions of blame, and partisan-motivated reasoning during crisis." *The Journal of Politics* 77 (3): 849–860. https://doi.org/10.1086/681591.

Blacks Law Dictionary. 12th ed. 2024.

Bowler, Shaun, and Todd Donovan. 2016. "A Partisan Model of Electoral Reform: Voter Identification Laws and Confidence in State Elections." *State Politics & Policy Quarterly* 16 (3): 340–61. https://doi.org/10.1177/1532440015624102.

Brennan Center for Justice. 2024. "Voting Laws Roundup: September 2024." https://www.brennancenter.org/our-work/research-reports/voting-laws-roundup-september-2024.

Brown, Robert D., and Justin Wedeking. 2006. "People Who Have Their Tickets But Do Not Use Them: "Motor Voter," Registration, and Turnout Revisited." *American Politics Research* 34 (4): 479–504. https://doi.org/10.1177/1532673X05281122.

Bryant, Lisa. A. 2020. "Seeing Is Believing: An Experiment on Absentee Ballots and Voter Confidence: Part of Special Symposium on Election Sciences." *American Politics Research* 48 (6): 700–704. https://doi.org/10.1177/1532673X20922529.

Carter, Luke, Ashlan Gruwell, J. Quin Monson, and Kelly D Patterson. 2024. "From Confidence to Convenience: Changes in Voting Systems, Donald Trump, and Voter Confidence." *Public Opinion Quarterly* 88 (SI): 516–35. https://doi.org/10.1093/poq/nfae034.

Caruso, Stephen. 2021, December 8. "Republicans say voter ID will increase voters' trust in elections; researchers say otherwise." *Pennsylvania Capital-Star*. https://penncapital-star.com/civil-rights-social-justice/republicans-say-voter-id-will-increase-voters-trust-in-elections-researchers-say-otherwise/.

Civil Rights Act of 1957. Public Law 85–315.

Civil Rights Act of 1960. Pub. L. 86–449 (74 Stat. 89).

Civil Rights Act of 1964. Public Law 88–352 (78 Stat. 241).

Claassen, Ryan L., David B. Magleby, J. Quin Monson, and Kelly D. Patterson. 2012. "Voter Confidence and the Election-Day Voting Experience." *Political Behavior* 35 (2): 215–35. https://doi.org/10.1007/s11109-012-9202-4.

Clark, Jesse T. 2021. "Lost in the mail? Vote by mail and voter confidence." *Election Law Journal: Rules, Politics, and Policy* 20 (4): 382–94.

Cole, Devan. 2024, September 20. "Republicans are suing more election officials over voter rolls in several battleground states." *CNN*. https://www.cnn.com/2024/09/20/politics/attempts-to-purge-voter-rolls-increase-as-election-nears/index.html.

Corbett, Jessica. 2021, March 25. "'Vicious Attack on Voting Rights': Georgia Governor Signs GOP Suppression Bill. Common Dreams." https://www.commondreams.org/news/2021/03/25/vicious-attack-voting-rights-georgia-governor-signs-gop-suppression-bill.

Downs, Anthony. 1957. *An Economic Theory of Democracy*. Harper and Row Publishers.

Elving, R. 2018. "The Florida Recount of 2000: A Nightmare that Goes on Haunting. National Public Radio." https://www.npr.org/2018/11/12/666812854/the-florida-recount-of-2000-a-nightmare-that-goes-on-haunting.

Ferrer, Joshua, and Igor Geyn. 2024. "Election America's Election Officials." In *Local Election Administrators in the United States: The Frontline of Democracy*, edited by P. Gronke, D. Kimball, T. Merivaki, M. Suttman-Lea, C. Gross and B. King, 57–99. Palgrave MacMillan.

Ferrer, Joshua, Igor Geyn, and Daniel M. Thompson. 2024. "How Partisan Is Local Election Administration?" *American Political Science Review* 118 (2): 956–71. https://doi.org/10.1017/S0003055423000631.

Gaines, Brian J., James H. Kuklinski, Paul J. Quirk, Buddy Peyton, and Jay Verkuilen. 2007. "Same Facts, Different Interpretations: Partisan Motivation and Opinion on Iraq." *Journal of Politics* 69: 957–74. https://doi.org/10.1111/j.1468-2508.2007.00601.x.

Garber, Andrew, and Eileen O'Connor. 2024, October 31. "Supreme Court Helps Virginia Illegally Purge Voters." Brennan Center for Justice. https://www.brennancenter.org/our-work/analysis-opinion/supreme-court-helps-virginia-illegally-purge-voters.

Gronke, Paul. 2014. "Voter Confidence as a Metric of Election Performance." In *The Measure of American Elections*, edited by Barry C. Burden and Charles Stewart III, 248–270. Cambridge Studies in Election Law and Democracy. Cambridge University Press.

Gronke, Paul, and Paul Manson. 2020. "2020 Local Election Official Survey Crosstabs." Elections & Voting Information Center. https://evic.reed.edu/wp-content/uploads/2024/12/crosstab_2020-1.html.

Gronke, Paul, and Paul Manson. 2022. "2022 Local Election Official Survey Crosstabs." Elections & Voting Information Center. https://evic.reed.edu/wp-content/uploads/2024/12/crosstabs_2022.html.

Hale, Kathleen, Robert Montjoy, and Mitchell Brown. 2015. *Administering Elections: How American Elections Work*. Palgrave Macmillan.

Harris, Joseph, P. 1934. *Election Administration in the United States*. Brookings Institution.

Hasen, Richard L. 2005. "Beyond the Margin of Litigation: Reforming U.S. Election Administration to Avoid Electoral Meltdown." *Washington and Lee Law Review* 62 (3): 937–99. https://scholarlycommons.law.wlu.edu/wlulr/vol62/iss3/4.

Hasen, Richard L. 2012. *The Voting Wars*. Yale University Press.

Help America Vote Act of 2002. Public Law 107–252.

Izaguirre, Anthony. 2021, May 16. "As GOP restricts voting, Democrats move to expand access." *Associated Press*. https://apnews.com/article/donald-trump-election-2020-voting-voting-rights-health-3f46e438bf9368d9b3535824e8c6c911.

Johnson, Kevin. 2022. "New Models for Keeping Partisan out of Election Administration. The Carter Center and Election Reformers Network." https://www.cartercenter.org/resources/pdfs/news/peace_publications/democracy/new-models-keeping-partisans-out-election-admin-013122.pdf.

Johnson, Kevin, Larry Garber, Edward McMahon, and Alexander Vanderklipp. 2020. "Guardrails for the Guardians: Reducing Secretary of State Conflict of Interest and Building More Impartial U.S. Election Administration." The Election Reformers Network. https://cdn.prod.website-files.com/642dcbc53f522476efc85893/6465544850ec72c5d7d894f0_Guardrails_Guardians.pdf.

Key, V. O. 1949. *Southern politics: In state and nation*. Random House, Inc.

Keyssar, Alexander. 2000. *The Right to Vote: The Contested History of Democracy in the United States*. Basic Books.

Kimball, David, Martha C., Kropf, and Lindsay Battles. 2006. "Helping America Vote? Election Administration, Partisanship, and Provisional Voting in the 2004 Election." *Election Law Journal: Rules, Politics, and Policy* 5 (4): 447–61.

King, Bridgett. 2020. "Waiting to Vote: The Effect of Administrative Irregularities at Polling Locations and Voter Confidence." *Policy Studies* 41 (2–3): 190–209.

King, Bridgett. 2017. "Policy and Precinct: Citizen Evaluations and Electoral Confidence." *Social Science Quarterly* 98 (2): 672–89.

King, Bridgett, and Alicia Barnes. 2019. "Descriptive Representation among Poll Workers and Citizen Confidence in Election Administration." *Election Law Journal* 18 (1): 16–30.

Kropf, Martha, Timothy Vercellotti, and David C. Kimball. 2013. "Representative Bureaucracy and Partisanship: The Implementation of Election Law." *Public Administration Review* 73 (2): 242–52. http://www.jstor.org/stable/23355468.

Lieb, David. 2024, September 2. "Noncitizen voting is extremely rare, yet Republicans are making it a major election concern." *Associated Press*. https://www.pbs.org/newshour/politics/noncitizen-voting-is-extremely-rare-yet-republicans-are-making-it-a-major-election-concern.

McBrayer, Markie, Williams, R. Lucas, and Andrea Eckelman. 2020. "Local Officials as Partisan Operatives: The Effect of County Officials on Early Voting Administration." *Social Science Quarterly* 101: 1475–88. https://doi.org/10.1111/ssqu.12815.

Merivaki, Thessalia, and Daniel A. Smith. 2016. "Casting and Verifying Provisional Ballots in Florida." *Social Science Quarterly* 97 (3): 729–47. https://www.jstor.org/stable/26612348.

National Conference of State Legislatures. 2025. "Election Administration at the State and Local Levels." https://www.ncsl.org/elections-and-campaigns/election-administration-at-state-and-local-levels.

National Voter Registration Act of 1993. Public Law 103–31(107 Stat. 77).

Pew Research Center. 2021, April 22. "Republicans and Democrats move further apart in views of voting access." https://www.pewresearch.org/politics/2021/04/22/republicans-and-democrats-move-further-apart-in-views-of-voting-access/.

Porter, Ehtan, and Jon C Rogowski. 2018. "Partisanship, Bureaucratic Responsiveness, and Election Administration: Evidence from a Field Experiment." *Journal of Public Administration Research and Theory* 28 (4): 602–617. https://doi.org/10.1093/jopart/muy025

Sances, Michael W. 2023. "Legitimate questions: Public perceptions of the legitimacy of US presidential election outcomes." *Research & Politics* 10 (4). https://doi.org/10.1177/20531680231206987.

Sances, Michael W., and Charles Stewart. 2015. "Partisanship and confidence in the vote count: Evidence for U.S. national election since 2000." *Electoral Studies* 40: 176–88.

Shelby County v. Holder, 570 U.S. 529 (2013).

Sinclair, Betsy, Steven S. Smith, and Patrick D. Tucker. 2018. "It's Largely a Rigged System": Voter Confidence and the Winner Effect in 2016." *Political Research Quarterly* 71 (4): 854–68. https://doi.org/10.1177/1065912918768006.

Stein, Robert M., and Greg Vonnahme. 2012. "When, Where, and How We Vote: Does It Matter?" *Social Science Quarterly* 93 (3): 692–712. http://www.jstor.org/stable/42864093.

Stewart, Charles. 2023. "How we voted in 2022. MIT Election Data and Science Lab." https://electionlab.mit.edu/sites/default/files/2023-05/How-We-Voted-In-2022.pdf.

Stuart, Gury. 2004. "Databases, Felons, and Voting: Bias and Partisanship of the Florida Felons List in the 2000 Elections." *Political Science Quarterly* 119 (3): 453–75. https://doi.org/10.2307/20202391.

Suttman-Lea, Mara, and Paul Gronke. 2024. "The Ethos of Local Election Administration." In *Local Election Administrators in the United States: The Frontline of Democracy*, edited by P. Gronke, D. Kimball, T. Merivaki, M. Suttman-Lea, C. Gross and B. King, 57–99. Palgrave MacMillan.

Thomas, Morgan. 2023, November 8. "Election Technology Through the Years. Council of State Governments: Lexington, Kentucky." https://www.csg.org/2023/11/08/election-technology-through-the-years/.

Totenberg, Nina, and Ilana Dutton. 2024, October 30. "Supreme Court allows Virginia to purge individuals from voter rolls." *National Public Radio*. https://www.npr.org/2024/10/30/g-s1-30644/supreme-court-virginia-elections.

US Election Assistance Commission Election Administration and Voter Survey. 2022. https://www.eac.gov/sites/default/files/2023-06/2022_EAVS_Report_508c.pdf.

US Election Assistance Commission Election Administration and Voter Survey. 2023. "Help America Vote Act." https://www.eac.gov/about/help_america_vote_act.aspx.

Voting Rights Act of 1965. Public Law 89–110 (79 Stat. 437).

Joel Sievert, Stephanie Mathiasen and Abby Miller

11 National Waves in Local Waters: The Impact of National Issues on Down-Ballot Elections

The association between the partisan outcome of presidential and subpresidential elections has increased considerably over the last several decades. We can see this clearly when we compare the state-level outcome of presidential and U.S. Senate elections. During the 1980s, the same party won the statewide vote in nearly half of the presidential and Senate contests (Sievert and McKee 2019). By the 1990s and 2000s, the congruence between the partisan outcome of presidential and Senate elections increased to around 60 and 70 percent, respectively. In the 2010s, the proportion of races won by the same party was routinely around 90 percent, and, in some years, the same party carried both contests in each state (Jacobson 2017). Election scholars refer to this increased correspondence between presidential and subpresidential elections as nationalization.

The intrusion of national issues and political forces into elections at all levels of government is a defining characteristic of American politics in the early twenty-first century. Whether it is driven by presidential politics (Abramowitz and Webster 2016; Jacobson 2015; Sievert and McKee 2019), partisanship (Davis and Mason 2016; Sievert and Banda 2024), or salient and divisive issues (Das et al. 2022; Hopkins 2018), down-ballot elections are less insulated from national politics than they once were. While prior studies have outlined several ways to conceptualize the nationalization of elections (Carson et al. 2024; Hopkins 2018), our focus in this chapter is on the nationalization of election outcomes and vote choice.

With respect to vote choice and election outcomes, nationalization is typically thought of as a process in which top-down forces exert greater influence on vote choice and election outcomes than do candidate-specific characteristics or local forces. By top-down forces, we mean that factors like presidential vote choice, presidential approval, and/or partisan identification drive vote choice rather than do attributes of subpresidential candidates, such as incumbency or candidate ideology. During the 2024 election, for example, incumbent US Senator Jon Tester, a Democrat from Montana, lost to Tim Sheehy, a Republican with no prior electoral experience. Tester, who was first elected in 2006, had defied political gravity in 2012 and 2018 when he won reelection in a state where Democrats have only won the statewide presidential vote once in the last fifty years. Sheehy's defeat of a three-term,

Joel Sievert, Stephanie Mathiasen, Abby Miller, Texas Tech University

https://doi.org/10.1515/9783111591902-011

moderate Democrat highlights how one of the primary consequences of nationalization is the increased importance of partisanship and national issues for voter decision-making in offices up and down the ballot (Sievert and Banda 2024).

11.1 What are Nationalized Elections?

The nationalization of elections implies that "voters use the same criteria to choose candidates across the federal system" (Hopkins 2018, 3). Under this framework, prior research has conceptualized nationalization as a process in which top-down forces exert greater influence on vote choice and election outcomes than do candidate-specific characteristics or local forces. These top-down forces can include factors like presidential vote choice or presidential approval (Carson and Sievert 2017; Carson et al. 2024; Hopkins 2018; Jacobson 2019; Rogers 2016; Sievert and McKee 2019) or partisanship (Abramowitz and Webster 2016; Davis and Mason 2016; Jacobson 2015; Zingher 2022; Zingher and Richman 2019). When elections become more nationalized, these factors are given greater weight in voter decision-making at the expense of local context or candidate-specific traits, like incumbency or ideology. The 2024 Texas Republican primary provides a notable example of this development. President Donald Trump endorsed a total of eighteen Republican state legislative primary candidates in Texas, which included a challenger who sought to unseat the incumbent Texas Speaker of the House, Dade Phelan. These candidates were largely successful as fourteen of the Trump-backed candidates secured the Republican nomination and of these six defeated an incumbent state legislator (Johnson 2024; Svitek 2024).

The growing body of research on the nationalization of elections has produced considerable evidence about its consequences for voter behavior. First, the propensity of voters to cast a split- or straight-ticket vote is an important source of more nationalized elections. When voters cast a split-ticket vote, they employ different criteria in assessing the candidates in the presidential and subpresidential contest (Born 2000). In contrast, the rise in straight-ticket voting in both congressional and state-level elections has led to the historic levels of partisan loyalty that have been a defining feature of our more nationalized electoral politics in recent decades (Jacobson 2015). An important consequence of these increases in partisan loyalty is the diminished role for local context (Hopkins 2018), candidate-specific attributes (Carson and Sievert 2017; Jacobson 2015), and incumbency in both congressional and gubernatorial contests, which has been one of the more notable results of increased nationalization (Abramowitz and Webster 2016; Carson et al. 2024; Sievert and McKee 2019).

In addition to increased partisan loyalty, voters' attitudes toward the president have played a more prominent role in vote choice and election outcomes. The correlation between presidential vote share at either the state or district-level and subpresidential election outcomes has strengthened over time in both federal (Carson et al. 2020; Jacobson 2015) and gubernatorial contests (Hopkins 2018; Sievert and McKee 2019). As a result, the ability of congressional campaigns to impact vote choice is at least in part a function of evaluations of the incumbent president (Carson et al. 2024; Sievert and Williamson 2022). Candidates for down-ballot races, like state legislature and judicial offices, also find that their electoral fortunes are tied to presidential election outcomes (Jacobson 2019; Weinschenk et al. 2020) and even presidential approval (Rogers 2016). Even retrospective voting in response to local economic conditions can be viewed as "president-centric" at nearly every level of government (de Benedictis-Kessner and Warshaw 2020).

With respect to voter behavior, increased nationalization has renewed attention to the connection between presidential approval or vote choice and partisan loyalty in subpresidential contests. Although several decades of evidence indicate that assessments of the president or presidential candidates can inform vote choice (Atkeson and Partin 1995; Simon 1989), these effects have increased over time (Jacobson 2019; Sievert and McKee 2019). Not only is it now increasingly rare for voters to defect and support a different party in subpresidential contests (Davis and Mason 2016), but there is also greater stability in vote choice across elections (Smidt 2017). If we know who a voter supported in the presidential contest, we can predict with increasing accuracy who they will support in midterm elections for Congress and gubernatorial contests. To be sure, there are still voters who switch their partisan vote choice across time, but the probability of such changes in behavior is still likely to be a function of how a voter evaluates the president (Sievert and Banda 2024; Carson et al. 2024; Carson et al. 2024; Rogers 2016; Jacobson 2015, 2019; Sievert and McKee 2019; Sievert and Williamson 2022; Weinschenk et al 2020).

11.2 Nationalization in Congressional Elections

During the 2024 election, Representative Marie Gluesenkamp Perez, a first-term Democratic incumbent from Washington's 3rd Congressional district, found herself in a rematch against Republican Joe Kent, who was endorsed by President Donald Trump (Fuentes 2024). Gluesenkamp Perez won the 2022 contest by less than 3,000 votes in a district that had historically leaned Republican.[1] The two candidates adopted dramatically different campaign strategies for the 2024 general election contests. "Gluesenkamp Perez says her proven commitment to the district, including its rural, working-class voters, makes her worthy of another term. Kent, meanwhile, focused on national issues, criticizing Democrats' handling of the U.S.-Mexico border and the economy" (Fuentes 2024, n.p.). The campaigns' respective messaging strategy highlights the contrast between a localized and nationalized electoral contest. By linking himself with the national Republican's policy priorities, Kent hoped to nationalize the race and get voters to cue on partisanship or presidential politics when casting a voting in this House race. By contrast, Gluesenkamp Perez emphasized both local issues and her legislative record to encourage voters to think about candidate attributes rather than purely partisan concerns.

As the foregoing example suggests, a more nationalized electoral environment has the potential to profoundly reshape the dynamics of modern congressional elections. While congressional elections were long viewed as localized contests where candidate attributes informed election outcomes (Born 2000; Carson et al. 2020), congressional elections now turn on partisan factors and presidential politics (Carson et al. 2024; Jacobson 2015). The incumbency advantage is one candidate-specific attribute that has diminished in this more nationalized electoral environment (Carson et al. 2020; Jacobson 2015). Over time, the electoral benefits of incumbency have shrunk, making way for factors like partisanship and presidential approval to become more impactful (Carson et al. 2020; Jacobson 2015). While incumbents still tend to win reelection over challengers, the size of the electoral advantage is moderated by the levels of nationalization (Carson et al. 2020). Nationalization's influence can also be seen in Senate elections (Sievert and McKee 2019). A surge in straight-ticket voting has not only weakened the electoral returns of incumbency, but it has also led to a stronger correlation between the outcome of Senate and presidential contests (Sievert and McKee 2019).

As vote choice becomes more congruent with voter's opinions on the president's job performance, members of Congress have less of an opportunity to insulate themselves from national partisan forces (Jacobson 2015). Strengthened partisanship among the electorate can lead to increasingly partisan behavior, despite many voters identifying as independent (Abramowitz and Webster 2016; Davis and Mason 2016; Zingher 2022). Voters who view their choice through the lens of partisanship make their choice based on preventing the opposing party from

---

1 The Republican incumbent in 2022, Jamie Herrera Beutler, failed to advance out of the blanket primary as Kent received just over 1,000 more voters than Beutler.

gaining power rather than their stances on issues (Abramowitz and Webster 2016). Similarly, voters who are better sorted, which is to say their partisan and ideological identifications are closely aligned, will be more reliably partisan regardless of the candidates on the ballot (Davis and Mason 2016). In short, partisanship is another top-down force that has informed voter's decisions, thus leading to nationalization and increasing party loyalty in elections for lower-level offices.

A more nationalized political environment also has implications for campaign contributions through candidates' increased reliance on out-of-state donations (Jacobs and Imboywa 2024; Sievert and Mathiasen 2023). Jacobs and Imboywa (2024) argue that the nationalization of campaign money challenged the representative structure of the Senate, while also democratizing campaign donations by allowing a wider array of people to participate. However, out-of-state donations have the ability to shift legislators preferences to appeal to this more nationalized donor base and away from constituents' interests (Barber 2016; Canes-Wrone and Miller 2022). Keena (2024) suggests that out-of-state donors act in a way to invest in the collective success of the party, when giving to senators who are on the campaign trail. For senators who are off cycle, they can use bill sponsorship as a way to attract and develop relationships with future out-of-state donors who will reward them for the position they have taken (Keena 2024). It is in these cases, where members of Congress are working to court a national donor base, that nationalization can have policy implications.

Lastly, it is important to note that the level of nationalization observed in contemporary congressional elections is not without precedent. During the nineteenth century, elections were contested under the party ballot, which included candidates for all offices from one party on a single, party-supplied ballot (Engstrom and Kernell 2005). Under this arrangement, voters cast their votes through the party ballot, which meant their only option was to vote for the party's entire slate of candidates. It was difficult, if not impossible, for voters to split their ticket and support candidates from different parties, especially in view of party workers stationed to monitor the polling place, a practice that is unheard of in today's era of the secret ballot (Carson and Roberts 2013). House candidates' electoral fortunes were therefore tied to their party and presidential candidate (Engstrom and Kernell 2005), which created a party-centered electoral environment akin to our current nationalized elections. That is not to say that candidate-attributes were inconsequential in this period (Carson and Sievert 2017), but their influence was weaker due to the electoral institutions in place (Carson and Roberts 2013; Carson et al. 2020).

These historical differences are important because they highlight key distinctions between the causes of more nationalized elections. In earlier eras, nationalization of down-ballot races was the result of electoral institutions, like the party ballot (Engstrom and Kernell 2005; Carson et al. 2024). In more recent decades, voter behavior is the mechanism that drives nationalization rather than electoral institutions (Davis and Mason 2016; Sievert and Banda 2024). Our modern electoral institutions are highly candidate-centered and should encourage a more localized electoral environment, but instead we observe that voters now choose to behave in highly nationalized manner. Our current levels of nationalization are therefore unlikely to ebb without major changes to either the party system or vote behavior.

11.3 Nationalization in State and Local Elections

In the fall of 2020, candidates for elected office not only had to find new ways to campaign during a global pandemic but also had to navigate a contentious presidential election and issues like economic inequality, racial injustice, and abortion politics. While these topics are commonly featured in congressional campaigns, they also found their way into local elections in cities of all sizes. The nonpartisan mayoral race in Montevallo, Alabama—a town of less than 7000 people—exemplified this dynamic. During a candidate forum, Joyce Jones, who was running to be the town's first Black mayor, responded to a question about how she would work with the town's police department that as mayor she would "consider adding social programs to help the town not just respond to crime (of which there is little in Montevallo) but prevent it, too" (Plott 2020, n.p.). By the next morning, Jones was accused of wanting to "defund the police" and some citizens claimed her language was akin to that used by the Black Lives Matter movement. Rusty Nix, a City Council member who was running against Jones, did not shy away from these issues and made the fight against "identity politics" and "progressives" a central part of his campaign (Plott 2020).

While the issues of race and inequality became the flashpoint in the Montevallo mayoral campaign, two West Texas mayoral candidates found themselves clashing over an entirely different issue—presidential politics. The race featured Dan Pope, the incumbent mayor of Lubbock, against political newcomer Stephen Sanders. Like Montevallo, the Lubbock mayoral race is a nonpartisan contest, but what made this contest different was that both candidates were running as conservatives. To differentiate himself from Pope, Sanders adopted an unconventional campaign strategy for a local office and campaigned on being the more pro-Trump option (Dotray 2020). Sanders not only spoke at local rallies in support of President Trump but was vocal about and unapologetic for his support of the president throughout the campaign. In response, Pope sought to argue that the election "doesn't need to be about what's going on in (Washington) D.C., it needs to be about what's going on in Lubbock, Texas" and that as mayor he would continue to provide "common-sense leadership, fiscal discipline, conservative decision making" (Dotray 2020, n.p.).

Candidates for down-ballot elections have historically focused on issues closely tethered to state and local governance. The origins of these developments can be traced back to the mid-1990s with the rise of polarization where parties made social issues, like abortion, a major part of their platform while regional issues, like agriculture, were no longer points of conversation (Hopkins et al. 2022). State politics started to focus on national issues and thus began adopting national party narratives. The shift away from state politics towards more national conversations has serious consequences for state elections and representation. For example, state legislative incumbents of the same party as the president, particularly during unpopular presidencies, are more likely to be challenged in an election (Rogers 2016). This is regardless of the incumbent's policies and positions, which indicates that voters are taking partisan cues directly from national level presidential elections and applying them to how they vote in their state elections, thus making state level voting behavior more of a national party heuristic.

Historically speaking, party politics at the national level may be too extreme for state politics, leading state candidates try to moderate their positions (Zingher and Richman 2019). For example, from 2010 to 2012, the Hawaii and Massachusetts state parties did not mention abortion in their party platform as the issue, while important in national politics, did not reflect the views of Republican voters from their state (Hopkins et al. 2022). The degree to which candidates successfully try to moderate state and national party positions is dependent upon how polarized national politics are (Zingher and Richman 2019). A rise in national polarization may induce a nationalized responses from state voters.

The public may enjoy more polarized politics, rather than more moderated politics, since they feel that they most identify with a party when their options are very distinct from one another (Levendusky 2009; Zingher and Richman 2019). When it comes to state elections, many people do not even know who the candidates are, and often see limited media coverage on state and local politics (Hopkins et al. 2022). Since information is very limited, voters tend to rely on party ID as a heuristic to decide, which is often easier and clearer when parties are dramatically polarized (Zingher and Richman 2019). This then incentivizes candidates to emphasize issues and narratives that resonate broadly, making national social issues the best platform to cue party IDs, despite their lack of relevance to the state election. State politics then begins to focus on national issues, often choosing to adopt national party platforms (Hopkins et al. 2022). It is not surprising then that increased polarization in national politics leads to state level presidential voting patterns predicting the partisan balance of state legislators (Zingher and Richman 2019). As a result, the political agendas of state and local parties tend to reflect those advanced by their respective national party. Hopkins et al. (2022) conclude that the unification of political agendas across various levels of government is a sign that "parties that were once local retailers are now national brands—more McDonalds than mom and pop" (n.p.).

Similar to state politics, local politics are often more impactful to citizens than national politics due to their "close to home" nature. For example, mayors tend to focus on public goods like streets and sanitation which directly affect the everyday lives of citizens (Oliver, Ha, and Callen 2012; Das et al. 2022). This means that a nationalized version of local politics often comes at the expense of local issues like sanitation and city planning (Das et al. 2022). In Florida, for example, a slate of candidates in nonpartisan, county-level elections campaigned on an "America First" platform, a term that has been closely associated with President Trump since his 2016 presidential campaign (Sabino 2024). The use of the term "America First" is notable because it is associated with President Trump's foreign policy agenda, an issue that would has no relevance for a candidate seeking a county-level office.

This does not mean though that all local governments take their cues from national party behavior. For example, Trounstine (2018) found that voters in one out of every three counties selected politicians from different parties in the local and federal elections. Trounstine offers three explanations for this disconnect: incomplete realignment, local contextual factors, and differentials in party strength. Incomplete realignment occurs when people vote for a different candidate than they normally would in a presidential election, which begins to change their voting behavior at the local level. Local contextual factors then play a role where residents have long-standing local loyalties and will tend to vote for the incumbent in local races, regardless of their party identification. Differentials in party strength can skew a local election where one local party is very strong in terms of capacity to organize and campaign, which leaves no real alternative at the local level, even when the national election is more evenly matched. Southern Republicans in the mid-twentieth century fit this mold as they lacked the institutional capacity to organize and challenge the dominant Democratic Party (Heersink and Jenkins 2020). Indeed, it took decades of extensive and consistent investments in state-level party building before the Southern Republican parties could achieve organizational parity with their Democratic counterparts (Galvin 2013).

Even though local elections may be slower to conform to national party behavior, it does not mean that nationalization has not occurred. In the last decade, large national donors have begun to play a significant role in school board elections (Henig et al. 2019; Shah et al. 2023). During the 2022 Wisconsin school board elections, for instance, Republican presidential vote share was positively related to the chances that a school district had a "conflict election," which Shah et al. (2023) defined as race, in which the campaign focused on national concerns. A candidate who ran on a national platform was also more likely to win in areas where President Trump performed better in 2020, but these candidates performed more poorly in areas where Trump support was lower (Shah et al. 2023).

It is important to note that election timing can also impact the extent of nationalization. When local and presidential elections are held at the same time, local candidates receive less attention, which makes people more likely to cast a vote in their local contest according to the presidential vote choice (Trounstine 2018).[2] For example, presidential politics became more central to the 2020 Lubbock mayoral race in part because the race was contested in November, instead of its usual May date, due to the COVID-19 pandemic. Additionally, the size of a city is also important. As the size of a city increases, mayoral rhetoric echoes that of congressional rhetoric; however, the longer that someone has been in office, the less that they sound like a member of Congress (Das et al. 2022). This is noteworthy because the candidates themselves can influence certain voter behaviors. For example, elites that condone harsh racial language can embolden citizens to act on prejudices (Shah et al. 2023). In sum, local elections may seem slow to follow nationalization, but national funding, national debate issues, and candidate cues can initiate nationalization at the local level. At both the state and local level, nationalized politics has serious consequences for representation, political discourse, and agenda setting.

11.4 Implications for Governance

A more partisan, nationally focused electorate and political environment has several notable implications for governance. First, nationalized elections have the potential to undermine political accountability. When vote choice is driven by top-down forces instead of evaluations of an individual elected official, it means that candidate-specific factors and office-based judgements of political perfor-

---

2 Carson and Sievert (2017) uncovered a similar dynamic during nineteenth century congressional elections when every party candidate ran on the same party ballot. Congressional elections in this era were not all contested on the same date, which allowed them to examine how candidates performed when they shared the ballot with the president versus when the presidential candidate was not on the ballot. They found that election timing moderated the magnitude of any incumbency or candidate quality effects for congressional candidates.

mance take a back seat. For example, constituents' evaluations of their representatives are remarkably stable across time (Carson et al. 2024; Sievert and Williamson 2022), which means electoral contests may do little to update or alter voters' attitudes about their representatives. We may also observe greater stability in partisan vote choice across elections even when the candidates voters are selecting among are not the same (Smidt 2017).

These electoral patterns have important consequences for how representatives behave in office. If elected officials have little reason to expect to be punished on Election Day, it can alter their incentives while in office. If taken to an extreme, this dynamic could free politicians to make choices that run counter to constituent preferences since they need not fear electoral blowback. Indeed, partisan motivated reasoning can result in a disconnect between incumbent performance and voter beliefs (Bartels 2002; Little et al. 2022). At a minimum, the changes in incentive structures may encourage greater partisan conflict because strong partisans prefer it to compromise (Harbridge and Malhotra 2011). That is not to say that voters will prefer partisan attacks to substantive representation (Costa 2021), but it does suggest that governmental gridlock and dysfunction are not electorally costly.

Second, our current nationalized political environment has resulted in political parties being more president-centered. One way this occurs is the strengthened connection between presidential politics and subpresidential elections, which we have discussed at length above. Another avenue through which this phenomenon emerges is a strengthened connection between public attitudes toward the president and political parties. For example, presidential approval and approval of congressional parties are now more strongly correlated than they were in earlier, less nationalized eras (Jacobson 2019). Presidents also exert greater influence over voters' beliefs about the parties' ideological positions and their affective attitudes toward the parties (Jacobson 2019; Sievert and Hinojosa 2022).

As parties and the president become more closely linked in the public's mind, elected officials' incentives to compromise or work with the president are altered. In Congress, this means that out-partisans are increasingly motivated to deny the president a win or to use the oversight process to score political points against a presidential administration (Lee 2016). The long-term consequence of these developments is an increase in what Lee refers to as partisan team play, which occurs when legislative behavior is informed by political considerations rather than just a legislator's ideological position.

We see these dynamics outside of Congress where governors are increasingly likely to take public actions to counter presidential policy agendas or blame the president for certain policy outcomes. In 2021, Republican Texas Governor Greg

Abbott launched "Operation Lone Star"—the deployment of Texas National Guard Troops to the Texas-Mexico border—which was intended to highlight what Abbott viewed as the failures of Democratic President Joe Biden's border policy (Choi and Downen 2024). Democratic governors and state attorney generals have also acted to oppose presidential actions when Republicans controlled the White House. By the end of 2020, then Washington Attorney General Bob Ferguson had sued the Trump administration over eighty times to combat policies ranging from the U.S. Census to 3-D printed guns (Gutman 2020). In the immediate aftermath of President Trump's electoral victory in 2024, several Democratic governors pledged that they would not cooperate with the federal government on mass deportations, which was one of Trump's key campaign pledges (Rahman 2024).

Third, politicians may change their policy focus and rhetoric in response to the more nationalized electoral environment. When national policies underlie political competition, then politics are organized around national matters and partisan divisions. If, however, local considerations are central, then politics are shaped by more parochial factors, such as candidate attributes or local policy concerns. There is growing evidence that politics at both the state and local level increasingly reflect this national orientation (Hopkins 2018; Das et al. 2022). The opinions of both state and local elected officials and citizens reflect the national partisan divides (Lee et al. 2023; Schaffner et al. 2024). Notably, the divides among local political actors cannot be explained by voter preferences alone as they tend to be more polarized along partisan lines than would be expected based on their respective constituencies (Lee et al. 2023).

In addition to changing the nature of political contestation, nationalization can also impact the policymaking process. Burke (2021) shows that an increase in election nationalization is associated with a change in state legislative issue focus. When the electorate nationalizes, state legislators dedicate more attention to national issues (e.g. abortion) and less to local issues (e.g. education and transportation), and a state government's policy agenda becomes more attentive to national political conditions. When a new party captures control of the federal government, state governments controlled by the national-out party move policy further in their preferred direction to counteract the loss of political power at the national level (Miras and Rouse 2022). Notably, this state-level counter balancing did not emerge until the mid-1990s when partisan competition returned to national politics (Miras and Rouse 2022, 584).

11.5 Conclusion

In this chapter, we have identified several factors that contribute to and foster the nationalization of American elections. First, partisanship, especially the strengthening of individual-level partisan attachments (Davis and Mason 2016), results in higher levels of partisan loyalty in elections up and down the ballot (Abramowitz and Webster 2015; Sievert and Banda 2024). Partisanship also influences voters' ideological and affective evaluations of candidates, with the public viewing co-partisan candidates in increasingly similar terms over time (Carson et al. 2024). An important consequence of this development is that public evaluations of a candidate are not only more polarized along partisan lines, but they are also more stable over time (Sievert and Williamson 2022).

Second, presidential politics plays a more central role in down-ballot elections in our nationalized electoral environment. We observe this both with respect to voter behavior and political messaging strategies. There is a robust relationship between presidential approval and vote choice in elections at both the federal, state, and local levels (Sievert and Banda 2024; Carson et al. 2024; Carson et al. 2024; Rogers 2016; Jacobson 2019; Sievert and McKee 2019; Sievert and Williamson 2022; Weinschenk et al. 2020). The president also features prominently in state and local politics through the campaign messages and official communications of candidates and elected officials (Das et al. 2022; Dotray 2020; Hopkins et al. 2022; Plott 2020).

While most research focuses on how nationalization influences elections and voting, it can also have important consequences for governance. Elected officials in more nationalized electoral environments may opt to shift their issue focus from localized policies, such as roads and education, to more nationally salient issues (Burke 2021; Hopkins et al. 2022). Nationalization may also encourage state policymaking to be more responsive to national conditions. Miras and Rouse (2022) observe that a change in partisan control of the federal government leads the state parties who are in the national minority to move policy further in their preferred direction to counteract the loss of political power at the national level. During the start of his second term, for example, President Trump and Congressional Republicans acted quickly to change federal policy. In response, states, such as California, with Democratically controlled governments passed legislation to defend or bolster their more liberal state policies (Austin 2025).

In sum, the folk wisdom that "all politics is local" no longer accurately describes American politics. Instead, national politics informs both elections and governance at all levels of government. It is important to remember though that American politics was highly nationalized throughout the nineteenth century (Carson et al. 2024). A key difference though is that nationalization in this earlier period was the result of our electoral institutions (Carson and Sievert 2017), while today's nationalization is a product of voter choice and candidate messaging. As such, the potential return to a less nationalized electoral environment is unclear since our electoral rules and governmental structures are designed to bolster local over national politics

Discussion Questions

1   How has the concept of "nationalized elections" changed the landscape of local and state elections in the United States?
2   What are the potential consequences of a more nationalized electorate for political accountability at the local and state level?
3   How does the increased role of out-of-state campaign donations reflect the nationalization of elections, and what effects might this have on local representation?
4   Discuss the impact of nationalized political environments on the behavior and policy outcomes of elected officials once they are in office.
5   What steps could be taken to encourage more localized decision-making in elections, and is this desirable in the current political climate?

References

Abramowitz, Alan I., and Steven Webster. 2016. "The Rise of Negative Partisanship and the Nationalization of U.S. Elections in the 21st Century." *Electoral Studies* 41: 12–22.

Atkeson, Lonna Rae, and Randall W. Partin. 1995. "Economic and Referendum Voting: A Comparison of Gubernatorial and Senatorial Elections." *American Political Science Review* 89 (1): 99–107.

Austin, Sophie. 2025. "California Assembly Approves $50M to Protect State Policies from Trump Plans." *Associate Press*. February 4.

Barber, Michael. 2016. "Donation Motivations: Testing Theories of Access and Ideology." *Political Research Quarterly* 69 (1): 148–59.

Bartels, Larry M. 2002. "Beyond the Running Tally: Partisan Bias in Political Perceptions." *Political Behavior* 24 (1): 117–50.

Born, Richard. 2000. "Congressional Incumbency and the Rise of Split-Ticket Voting." *Legislative Studies Quarterly* 25 (3): 365–87.

Burke, Richard. 2021. "Nationalization and Its Consequences for State Legislatures." *Social Science Quarterly* 102 (1): 269–80.

Canes-Wrone, Brandice, and Kenneth M. Miller. 2022. "Out-of-District Donors and Representation in the US House." *Legislative Studies Quarterly* 47 (2): 361–95.

Carson, Jamie L., Damon Cann, Jeffrey L. Yates, and Ronald F. Wright. 2024. "The Increasing Nationalization of Local Elections: The Case of Prosecutors." *Political Research Quarterly* 77 (3): 1026–36.

Carson, Jamie L., and Jason M. Roberts. 2013. *Ambition, Competition, and Electoral Reform: The Politics of Congressional Elections Across Time*. University of Michigan Press.

Carson, Jamie L., and Joel Sievert. 2017. "Congressional Candidates in the Era of Party Ballots." *Journal of Politics* 79 (2): 534–45.

Carson, Jamie L., Joel Sievert, and Ryan D. Williamson. 2020. "Nationalization and the Incumbency Advantage." *Political Research Quarterly* 73 (1): 156–68.

Carson, Jamie L., Joel Sievert, and Ryan D. Williamson. 2024. *Nationalized Politics: Evaluating Electoral Politics Across Time*. Oxford University Press.

Choi, Matthew, and Robert Downen. 2024. "'Hold the Line': Republicans Rally to Abbott's Defense in Border Standoff with Biden." *Texas Tribune*. January 25.

Costa, Mia. 2021. "Ideology, not Affect: What Americans Want from Political Representation." *American Journal of Political Science* 65 (2): 342–58.

Das, Sanmay, Betsy Sinclair, Steven W. Webster, and Hao Yan. 2022. "All (Mayoral) Politics is Local?" *Journal of Politics* 84 (2): 1021–34.

Davis, Nicholas T., and Lilliana Mason. 2016. "Sorting and the Split-Ticket: Evidence from Presidential and Subpresidential Elections." *Political Behavior* 38 (2): 337–54.

de Benedictis-Kessner, Justin, and Christopher Warshaw. 2020. "Accountability for the Economy at All Levels of Government in United States Elections." *American Political Science Review* 114 (3): 660–76.

Dotray, Matt. 2020. "The Evolution, Politicization of Lubbock's Mayoral Race." *Lubbock Avalanche-Journal*. October 17.

Engstrom, Erik J., and Samuel Kernell. 2005. "Manufactured Responsiveness: The Impact of State Electoral Laws on Unified Party Control of the Presidency and House of Representatives, 1840–1940." *American Journal of Political Science* 49 (3): 531–49.

Fuentes, Carlos. 2024. "National Spotlight Shines on SW Washington Congressional Race between Incumbent Marie Gluesenkamp Perez and Joe Kemp." *The Oregonian*. October 7.

Galvin, Daniel J. 2013. "Presidential Partisanship Reconsidered: Eisenhower, Nixon, Ford, and the Rise of Polarized Politics." *Political Research Quarterly* 66 (1): 46–60.

Gutman, David. 2020. "Bob Ferguson Sued the Trump Administration 82 Times. What's He Going to Do Now?" *Seattle Times*. November 14.

Harbridge, Laurel, and Neil Malhotra. 2011. "Electoral Incentives and Partisan Conflict in Congress: Evidence from Survey Experiments." *American Journal of Political Science* 55 (3): 494–510.

Heersink, Boris, and Jeffery A. Jenkins. 2020. *Republican Party Politics and the American South, 1865–1968*. Cambridge University Press.

Henig, Jeffrey R., Rebecca Jacobsen, and Sarah Reckhow. 2019. *Outside Money in School Board Elections: The Nationalization of Education Politics*. Harvard Education Press.

Hopkins, Daniel J. 2018. *The Increasingly United States: How and Why American Political Behavior Nationalized*. The University of Chicago Press.

Hopkins, Daniel J., Eric Schickler, and David L. Azizi. 2022. "From Many Divides, One? The Polarization and Nationalization of American State Party Platforms, 1918–2017." *Studies in American Political Development* 36 (1): 1–20.

Jacobs, Nicholas, and Wasike Gil Imboywa. 2024. "The Nationalization of Individual Campaign Contributions in US Senate Elections, 1984–2020." *American Politics Research* 52 (3): 239–48.

Jacobson, Gary. 2015. "It's Nothing Personal: The Decline of the Incumbency Advantage in US House Elections." *Journal of Politics* 77 (3): 861–73.

Jacobson, Gary C. 2017. "The Triumph of Polarized Partisanship in 2016: Donald Trump's Improbable Victory." *Political Science Quarterly* 132 (1): 9–41.

Jacobson, Gary C. 2019. *Presidents and Parties in the Public Mind*. University of Chicago Press.

Johnson, Brad. 2024. "Here's a List of Donald Trump's 2024 Texas Endorsements." *The Texan*. February 12.

Keena, Alex. 2024. "Out-Of-State Donors and Legislative Surrogacy in the US Senate." *Political Research Quarterly*, forthcoming.

Lee, Frances E. 2016. *Insecure Majorities: Congress and the Perpetual Campaign*. University of Chicago Press.

Lee, Nathan, Michelangelo Landgrave, and Kirk Bansak. 2023. "Are Subnational Policymakers' Policy Preferences Nationalized? Evidence from Surveys of Township, Municipal, County, and State Officials." *Legislative Studies Quarterly* 48 (2): 441–44.

Levendusky, Matthew. 2009. *The Partisan Sort: How Liberals Became Democrats and Conservatives Became Republicans*. University Chicago Press.

Little, Andrew T., Keith E. Schnakenberg, and Ian R. Turner. 2022. "Motivated Reasoning and Democratic Accountability." *American Political Science Review* 116 (2): 751–67.

Miras, Nicholas S., and Stella M. Rouse. 2022. "Partisan Misalignment and the Counter-Partisan Response: How National Politics Conditions Majority-Party Policy Making in the American States." *British Journal of Political Science* 52 (2): 573–92.

Oliver, J. Eric, Shang E. Ha, and Zachary Callen. 2012. *Local Elections and the Politics of Small-Scale Democracy*. Princeton University Press.

Plott, Elaina. 2020. "In a Small Alabama Town, Suddenly All Politics is National." *The New York Times*. October 11.

Rahman, Khaleda. 2024. "Donald Trump's Deportation Plan Faces Rebellion from Democratic Governors." *Newsweek*. November 7.

Rogers, Steven. 2016. "National Forces in State Legislative Elections." *Annals of the American Academy of Political and Social Science* 667 (1): 207–25.

Sabino, Pascal. 2024. "Six 'America First' Candidates, Vying to Take Over Florida Elections, Advance to November." *Bolts*, August 23.

Schaffner, Brian F., Jesse H. Rhodes, and Raymond J. La Raja. 2024. "Are Local Policy Attitudes Distinct?" *Political Science Research and Methods*, forthcoming.

Shah, Paru, Aaron C. Weinschenk, and Alexander Yiannias. 2023. "Schoolhouse Rocked: Pandemic Politics and the Nationalization of School Board Elections." *State Politics & Policy Quarterly* 24 (2): 207–17.

Sievert, Joel, and Kevin K. Banda. 2024. "All Politics are National: Partisan Defection in National and Subnational Elections." *Social Science Quarterly* 105 (2): 180–92.

Sievert, Joel, and Victor Hinojosa. 2022. "Whose Party is It?: Lame Ducks, Presidential Candidates, and Evaluations of the Party." *American Politics Research* 50 (4): 539–44.

Sievert, Joel, and Stephanie Mathiasen. 2023. "Out-of-State Donors and Nationalized Politics in US Senate Elections." *The Forum* 21 (2): 309–28.

Sievert, Joel, and Seth McKee. 2019. "Nationalization in U.S. Senate and Gubernatorial Elections." *American Politics Research* 47 (5): 1055–80.

Sievert, Joel, and Ryan D. Williamson. 2022. "Elections, Competition, and Constituent Evaluations of US Senators." *Electoral Studies*: 75102424.

Simon, Dennis M. 1989. "Presidents, Governors, and Electoral Accountability." *Journal of Politics* 51 (2): 286–304.

Smidt, Corwin D. 2017. "Polarization and the Decline of the American Floating Voter." *American Journal of Political Science* 61 (2): 365–81.

Svitek, Patrick. 2024. "Trump Seeks to Unseat Texas House Speaker in Incursion Into State Politics," *Washington Post*. May 28.

Trounstine, Jessica. 2018. "Political Schizophrenics? Factors Affecting Aggregate Partisan Choice at the Local Versus National Level." *American Politics Research* 46 (1): 26–46.

Weinschenk, Aaron, Mandi Baker, Zoe Betancourt, Vanessa Depies, Nathan Erck, Quinne Herolt, Amanda Loehrke 2020. "Have State Supreme Court Elections Nationalized?" *Justice System Journal* 41 (3): 313–22.

Zingher, Joshua N. 2022. *Political Choice in a Polarized America: How Elite Polarization Shapes Mass Behavior*.

Zingher, Joshua N., and Jesse Richman. 2019. "Polarization and the Nationalization of State Legislative Elections." *American Politics Research* 47 (5): 1036–54.

Enrijeta Shino and Seth C. McKee

12 Voting Behavior and Participation: What Drives Us to the Polls

From 1960 to 1996, presidential elections were not as competitive as they have been since the turn of the new century in 2000. Interestingly, however, 1960 and 2000 were two of the closest contests in American history. In 1960, the Democrat John F. Kennedy defeated the Republican Richard Nixon with a popular vote margin of 0.17. Four decades later, the Republican George W. Bush defeated the Democrat Al Gore because he won an Electoral College majority even though he lost the popular vote by a 0.54 margin. Spanning 1960 to 1996, the average two-party popular presidential vote margin was 10.2 percentage points, and turnout of the eligible American population in these contests averaged just over 57 percent. In contrast, from 2000 to 2024 the average two-party popular presidential vote margin was a mere 3.2 percentage points, and turnout in these contests averaged over 60 percent.

This quick look at two fairly lengthy periods of presidential elections strongly suggests that competitiveness plays a role in whether Americans participate in voting. Of course, we should not be surprised by this—although most voters are not under the illusion that their single ballot will determine an election (Cox and Munger 1989)—competitiveness has the indirect effect of incentivizing campaigns to mobilize their supporters (Aldrich 1993). For example, until the votes were cast and then tallied, even political experts were uncertain who would prevail in the 2024 presidential election. Hence, most of the media coverage focused narrowly on the seven so-called battleground states that would ultimately decide the outcome, with all seven shifting slightly in favor of the victor, Republican Donald Trump. To be sure, a multitude of factors influence the decision of whether to vote, with competitiveness likely drawing outsized attention because it increases our interest in campaigns. In addition to competitiveness, this chapter will highlight several other features related to voter turnout.

12.1 Chapter Outline

For the remainder of the chapter, we highlight different factors associated with voter turnout. We begin with a figure displaying the historical pattern of voter turnout in federal elections for president and midterm contests for the United

https://doi.org/10.1515/9783111591902-012

States Congress.[1] Except for the first few decades of the American republic, the electorate is much more participatory in presidential cycles than midterms, which means a smaller subset of politically engaged citizens participate in the latter contests when Americans cannot select a president. Further, while all U.S. House Representatives are up for election in midterm years, just a third of U.S. Senators are on the ballot. Hence, for the sake of uniformity, with all Americans having the same major party (Democrat versus Republican) candidates at the top of their ballot, we examine voter turnout in detail in the last two presidential elections of 2020 and 2024.

We will show more data on the 2020 presidential election because of the availability of a large survey that validates whether its respondents voted: the 2020 Cooperative Election Study (CES). Nevertheless, we make use of state-level data from 2024 that likely will not change that much with respect to general turnout patterns.[2] It is imperative that our data is based on actual, validated turnout because self-reported turnout is always notably higher, and there is variation in the types of people who are more (or less) likely to claim voting (Ansolabehere and Hersh 2012). For instance, in the 2020 CES, whereas 74.9 percent of respondents reported voting, the validated rate was 64.3 percent.

Described as a low-cost/low-benefit activity (Aldrich 1993), there are a multitude of factors that influence whether someone votes, including the weather on Election Day (Gomez et al. 2007). However, we will limit ourselves to four domains that exhibit substantial variation in voter turnout and are fairly stable from one election cycle to the next. First, we show variation in the propensity to vote according to some common demographic characteristics: educational attainment, household income, race and ethnicity, gender, and age. Second, we then examine expressly political factors and civic engagement measures, such as party identification (PID) strength, ideological strength, whether one voted in the 2016 election, political knowledge, and interest in the news. Next, we look at how differences in voting laws, as well as historic statutory alterations to the right to vote, have impacted participation. Finally, we consider the role of political context, specifically how competitiveness influences voter turnout.

---

1 This data is from Michael P. McDonald (available here: https://election.lab.ufl.edu/data-archive/national/) and it shows the estimated number of votes cast in presidential and congressional races (Senate and House) based on the number of eligible voters (those allowed to vote, including those registered and those who can register to cast a ballot). The turnout data reported in the chapter introduction comes from the aforementioned source.
2 We have most of the 2024 state-level data at this time, even if for many states the numbers are not yet finalized (they will not change very much).

12.2 American Voter Turnout in Presidential and Midterm Elections, 1789–2024

Figure 12.1 displays the historical pattern of voter turnout in federal elections for president and midterm contests for the U.S. Congress. This lengthy time span, from the first election of President George Washington in 1789 to the second election of President Donald Trump in 2024, shows remarkable variation in Americans' political participation. We highlight the entirety of voter turnout in these American federal elections because there are notable changes in participation rates. First, the right to vote was extremely limited in the early years of the American republic. Suffrage was essentially confined to White males who, depending on the state where they lived, faced considerable restrictions based on things like wealth, property ownership, and even religious qualifications (Keyssar 2009). Also noticeable is that midterm turnout was always *higher* than in presidential cycles until the election of President Andrew Jackson in 1828.

President Jackson ushered in a new and nationally competitive two-party system with Democrats facing off against Whigs from 1836 to 1856 (Aldrich 2011). Voting qualifications were loosened among the still very small electorate of White males and participation among this select group soared. For instance, in the 1824 presidential contest, which Jackson lost to John Quincy Adams, there was a total of 365,928 votes cast with a 27 percent turnout rate.[3] Bitter from a contest in which he won the most popular and electoral votes but nonetheless lost the presidency after the U.S. House of Representatives decided the outcome for Adams, Jackson and his supporters expanded the electorate four years later when his 1828 victory was accompanied by more than a tripling in the number of votes cast (1,283,720) and a turnout of 57 percent.[4]

Voter turnout rises to all-time highs starting in the 1840s, after which the midterm rate never again surpasses presidential participation. In 1860, as the Whig Party gave way to the Grand Old Party (GOP) and the nation stood divided between northern Republicans and southern Democrats on the brink of the Civil War, voter participation reached an impressive 82 percent. Voter turnout reached historic highs consistently in the latter half of the 1800s (Kleppner 2010), with powerful party machines particularly in large urban centers (e.g., Boston, Chi-

---

3 The number of presidential votes is from *Dave Leip's Atlas of U.S. Presidential Elections* (https://uselectionatlas.org/RESULTS/).
4 If no one wins a majority of the Electoral College vote (as occurred in 1824), then the U.S. House of Representatives, with each state delegation having one vote, decides the outcome with a simple majority.

cago, and New York City) mobilizing local populations through an effective political patronage system that offered services and employment in exchange for votes. At almost 83 percent, voter turnout reached its all-time high in the disputed 1876 presidential election, a Republican victory settled upon via a bipartisan commission that offset this outcome by ending military reconstruction in the soon-to-be Solid Democratic South (Foner 1988).[5]

A populist revolt (Goodwyn 1978) took hold for a brief time in the mid-1890s, as farmers attempted to counter the monopolistic power of the captains of industry, and in particular the railroads. More lasting was the direct conflict between party machines and the progressive movement (Wiebe 1966), which had success in weakening partisan influence over elections with widespread passage of the secret ballot, direct primaries (many were nonpartisan for local races, like mayor), and voters' self-registration. As these reforms took hold in the late 1800s, party machines were greatly weakened—with a decline in their mobilizing capacity substantially raising the cost of participation. Consequently, voter turnout began a long descent; in presidential contests it dropped from almost 80 percent in 1896 to 49 percent in 1924 (and from 60 percent in the 1898 midterm to 33 percent in the 1926 midterm).

Though nowhere near the turnout levels attained before the aforementioned progressive reforms took hold at the turn of the twentieth century, voter participation did generally rise during the Great Depression years of the 1930s and America's involvement in World War II (1941–1945). This said, turnout plunged to 34 percent in 1942, the first midterm during the war, and while it rose to 52 percent in 1948, the first presidential contest after the war, this did not match earlier years. In the following three presidential elections (1952–1960), turnout exceeded 60 percent and peaked at nearly 64 percent in 1960. As noted, the 1960 presidential election produced one of the closest popular vote margins in American history, and in hindsight became a focal point for participation scholars because turnout never reached the 1960 mark until the next millennium.[6] In fact, from the 1970s to 2000, turnout never reached 60 percent, and in 1996 it bottomed out at less than 52 percent.

Starting in the twenty-first century, turnout rebounded considerably versus the notable decline spanning 1960 to 1996. In this last period, from 2000 to 2024,

---

5 In the Electoral College, the Republican candidate Rutherford Hayes defeated the Democratic candidate Samuel Tilden by a single vote (185 to 184). From 1876 to 1944, none of the eleven former Confederate southern states (AL, AR, FL, GA, LA, MS, NC, SC, TN, TX, and VA) voted Republican for president more than twice (Key 1949).
6 The popular vote total for the Democrat John F. Kennedy and the Republican Richard Nixon was 68,329,141, and Kennedy's margin of victory was 112,827 votes.

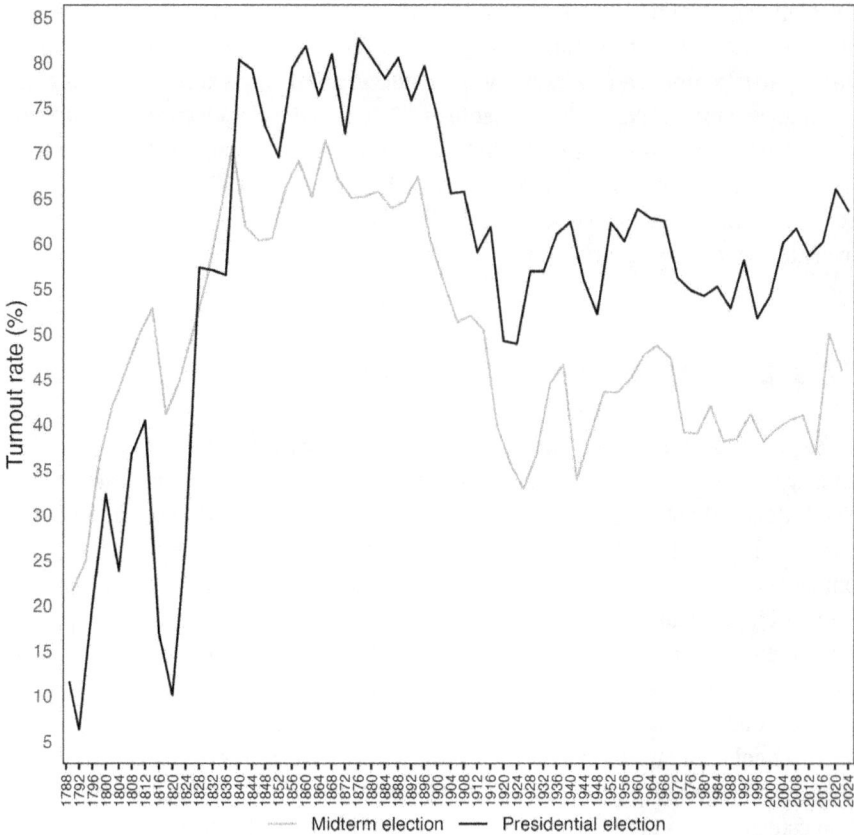

Figure 12.1: Voter turnout among the eligible American electorate, 1789–2024.
Note: Data replicated from the UF Election Lab website (with the 2024 estimate added) found here:
https://election.lab.ufl.edu/voter-turnout/.

factors boosting turnout include the long-term increase in partisan identifiers in the American electorate, their fairly balanced numbers, and how this results in close elections for the White House and Congress (Shafer 2016).[7] Most recently,

---

7 We can partition the electorate into pure independents, independent leaners (leaning toward Democratic/Republican Party), weak partisans (not so strong Democrat/Republican), and strong partisans (strong Democrat/Republican). In 1960, there were more weak partisans (38.7 percent) than strong partisans (36 percent). In 2020, strong partisans were the most prevalent group (44.2 percent), and more than double the number of weak partisans (22 percent) (Data from the American National Election Study, and available here: https://electionstudies.org/data-tools/anes-guide/anes-guide.html?chart=strength_of_pid).

the high degree of partisan polarization among Democrats and Republicans, especially during the first Trump administration (2016–2020), resulted in very high voter participation. In the 2018 midterm, the turnout rate exceeded 50 percent, the highest since 1914. In the subsequent 2020 presidential election, the turnout rate of 66 percent was the highest in 120 years. By comparison, turnout was lower in the 2022 midterm (over 45 percent) and 2024 presidential election (over 63 percent), but these rates were still relatively high compared to what we have seen over the last quarter-century.

12.3 Demographics and Voter Turnout

Table 12.1 shows the rate of abstention and voting, as validated among 2020 CES survey respondents based on the above-mentioned demographic characteristics. The influential book *Who Votes?* by the authors Wolfinger and Rosenstone (1980) stressed the significance of socioeconomic status (SES) with respect to voter turnout. Socioeconomic status' component parts, consisting of education, income, and occupation, all showed a strong relationship with the likelihood of voting. Here we forego a demonstration of the relationship between various occupations and turnout but highlight how much greater the act of voting is, according to education level and one's household income. Starting with education, ranging from a high school diploma or less to a graduate degree (e.g., master's, doctorate), it shows a 35-point disparity—going from 39 percent turnout for the lowest education category to 74 percent in the highest. By comparison, there is an even slightly larger turnout gap of thirty-seven points from the lowest income category (annual income under $10,000) at 36 percent to the highest income bracket at 73 percent (annual income exceeding $150,000).

Race and ethnicity also show a long-term and generally consistent ordered pattern of differences in participation. However, this arrangement is sometimes altered, depending on the profile of candidates seeking office. For instance, the 2008 pathbreaking election of Democratic presidential candidate Barack Obama saw a surge in Black turnout (McKee et al. 2012), especially with regard to African American women (Ansolabehere and Hersh 2013). The 2020 CES data, however, shows a more typical pattern with participation the highest among non-Hispanic Whites (65 percent), followed by African Americans (51 percent), and no real difference among Hispanics (of any racial classification) at 45 percent, compared to respondents claiming some other racial classification at 46 percent. We would also report Asian turnout (America's fourth largest racial group), but the survey sample size is not large enough to get a reliable estimate.

Table 12.1: Demographic characteristics and voter turnout in the 2020 election.

Characteristic	Category	Did Not Vote (%)	Voted (%)
Education	Less than high school	61	39
	High school degree	51	49
	Some college	38	62
	College degree	28	72
	Graduate degree	26	74
Income	Less than 10K	64	36
	10K–29K	49	51
	30K–49K	43	57
	50K–69K	38	62
	70K–99K	32	68
	100K–149K	27	73
	150K+	27	73
Race/ethnicity	White	35	65
	African American	49	51
	Hispanic	55	45
	Other race	54	46
Gender	Male	40	60
	Female	40	60
Age	18–29	62	38
	30–44	47	53
	45–64	33	67
	65+	23	77

Note: Data computed by authors from the 2020 CES.

Interestingly, we do not find a gender gap associated with turnout in the 2020 CES data. This is surprising because women have consistently been more participatory than men all the way back to the 1980 presidential election.[8] Nevertheless, we find that both women and men voted at a rate of 60 percent in the 2020 CES.[9] Finally, we display voter turnout rates on the basis of age, as partitioned across four age groups: 18 to 29, 30 to 44, 45 to 64, and 65 years old or higher. Here we see the greatest disparity in political participation, a thirty-nine-point difference between the youngest cohort of voters (18–29) at 38 percent and the oldest group of seniors (65+) at 77 percent turnout in the 2020 election. Some principal reasons why age is so strongly and positively associated with voting is because older citizens are more settled into their communities (e.g., they are less likely to have moved from their place of residence), they have developed a habit of voting over time (Plutzer 2002), and they see themselves as having more at stake in the outcome (e.g., they are keenly interested in policies affecting their financial status as it relates to things like healthcare and taxes).

12.4 Political Views, Civic Engagement, and Voter Turnout

The oldest running survey of the American electorate, the American National Election Study (ANES), recorded the highest percentage of strong partisans in 2020 (at 44.2 percent), going all the way back to the first documented data reported on the strength of PID in its 1952 survey. This finding is in line with the tenor of this book, which has repeatedly shown an increase in party-based polarization with respect to the political behavior and attitudes of contemporary Americans. Indeed, as more Americans have come to view their PID as a social identity (Green et al. 2002; Greene 1999; Mason 2018), we would expect those citizens to be

---

8 The Center for American Women and Politics (CAWP) documents women's and men's self-reported turnout from 1980 to 2020, and the data can be found here: https://cawp.rutgers.edu/facts/voters/gender-differences-voter-turnout. There is a possibility that these self-reported numbers are quite different from validated data like what we report in Table 12.1. That said, our assessment (not shown) of self-reported versus validated turnout rates demonstrates that men are usually significantly more likely to report voting when they have not (on this point, see also Ansolabehere and Hersh 2012).

9 In contrast, the 2020 Fox News Voter analysis (partnering with the Associated Press) had the following participation distribution based on gender: 47 percent men and 53 percent women. This participation gap appears to be significant, but this survey did not validate turnout.

more engaged in the political process and hence show a greater inclination to vote.

In Table 12.2, we begin by displaying the relationship between PID strength and voter turnout. Pure independents, those who express no affiliation with either major party (Democratic/Republican), show the lowest turnout at 40 percent in the 2020 election. Although we have long known that the vote choices of independent leaners and weak partisans typically do not vary that much (Keith et al. 1992), it is still a surprise to see that the former group voted at a considerably higher rate (64 percent) compared to those expressing a weak (not so strong) identification with one of the major parties (56 percent turnout). Finally, as expected, the most participatory segment of the American electorate is found among strong partisans, who voted at a 70 percent clip in 2020.

Table 12.2: Political views, civic engagement, and voter turnout in the 2020 election.

Characteristic	Category	Did Not Vote (%)	Voted (%)
PID strength	Pure independent	60	40
	Independent leaner	36	64
	Weak partisan	44	56
	Strong partisan	30	70
Ideology strength	Moderate	50	50
	Somewhat conservative/liberal	38	62
	Conservative/liberal	31	69
	Very conservative/liberal	31	69
Voted in 2016	No	64	36
	Yes	25	75
Political knowledge	Low	63	37
	Medium	55	45
	High	26	74
News interest	Hardly at all	71	29
	Only now and then	59	41
	Some of the time	46	54
	Most of the time	25	75

Note: Data computed by authors from the 2020 CES. The response to whether one voted in 2016 is self-reported.

Closely related to PID is political ideology, i.e., one's political worldview (Converse 1964). For decades now, more Americans have come to align their ideology with their PID (Abramowitz 2022), so that there is a growing share of liberal Democrats and conservative Republicans (McKee 2024). This long-term dynamic of partisan sorting according to political ideology (Levendusky 2009) leads us to anticipate that those holding ideological positions nearer the poles of this measure (very conservative/liberal) are also more participatory. There is a twelve-point jump in turnout from the moderate (middle-of-the-road) category at 50 percent to the next category for somewhat conservative/liberal, with a 62 percent rate of voting. We see no difference in the next two categories, which Converse (1964) referred to as near-ideologues (conservative/liberal) and ideologues (very conservative/liberal), with both groups exhibiting the highest turnout at 69 percent.

Although it is true that we rely on the respondent's self-report of voting in 2016, we find a very strong relationship with validated turnout in 2020. Simply put, those respondents who reported abstaining from voting in 2016 were markedly less likely to participate in 2020—only 36 percent of them did. By comparison, respondents who claimed to have voted in 2016 voted at a rate of 75 percent in 2020. This suggests evidence of a demarcation among sporadic voters versus habitual voters, with the latter more likely to cast a ballot in any given election (Shino et al. 2023).

Participation scholars have long recognized that one of the most powerful predictors of voting is whether the individual finds politics interesting (Luskin 1990). Hence, it is expected that a greater knowledge of politics indicates more interest in the subject, which should spur turnout. Here, we measure political knowledge based on correct answers regarding which party had the majority in the U.S. House and U.S. Senate after the 2020 election. The House was controlled by Democrats and the Senate by Republicans.[10] Low political knowledge captures respondents who were incorrect about party control of both legislative chambers, and their turnout rate was a notably low 37 percent. Turnout was eight points higher, at 45 percent, among respondents who were correct about party control of one legislative chamber. Turnout shoots up to 74 percent among respondents who knew which party had the majority in both legislative chambers.

Finally, interest in the news is strongly correlated with participation. The more closely citizens pay attention to current events, the more likely they are to vote. People who hardly follow the news at all voted at a paltry 29 percent. In contrast, simply following the news only now and then increased turnout to 41 percent. For those following the news some of the time, their turnout rate was 54 percent. Lastly, the segment of citizens most engaged with current events, i.e., those following the news most of the time, had a turnout rate of 75 percent.

---

10 Chamber control was the same before and after the election but was later altered in the Senate once Democrats won both runoff elections in Georgia on January 5, 2021, which gave the party majority control with incoming Democratic Vice President Kamala Harris' tie-breaking vote.

12.5 Variation in Voting Laws, Historic Statutory Changes to Suffrage, and Voter Turnout

According to the basic principle that lowering the cost of voting should increase participation (Downs 1957), making voting more convenient (easier to do) should be positively associated with turnout (Shino and Smith 2020; McDonald et al. 2024a, 2024b). We begin with Table 12.3, which shows the turnout rate on the basis of two distinguishing state-level features of voter participation: (1) whether the resident needs an excuse to vote by mail; and (2) whether the individual resides in a state that allows for registration on Election Day (same day registration).[11]

The differences in turnout do not appear substantial but they are at least detectable. First, for respondents living in states where they need an excuse to vote by mail, their turnout rate was 56 percent in 2020, whereas for individuals residing in states where no excuse is necessary to vote by mail (or they can only vote by mail), their rate of voting was 61 percent. Second, the turnout gap is smaller regarding whether citizens can register on the same day they cast a ballot. In states without same-day voter registration, 59 percent of these residents voted in the 2020 election. By comparison, respondents living in states with same-day voter registration participated at the higher rate of 62 percent.

Table 12.3: Variation in voting laws and voter turnout in the 2020 election.

Characteristic	Category	Did Not Vote (%)	Voted (%)
Vote by mail	Excuse required	44	56
	No-excuse/all mail	39	61
Same-day registration	No	41	59
	Yes	38	62

Note: Data computed by authors from the 2020 CES.

Table 12.4 presents data similar to Table 12.3, except it is based on state-level rates of voter turnout in 2020 and 2024. Once again, starting with differences based on whether an excuse is needed to vote by mail, we see that the state-level voting eligible turnout rate is lower. In 2020, turnout was 61 percent in states requiring an excuse to vote by mail, seven points less than the 68 percent turnout rate in states with either all-mail voting or no excuse needed to cast a mail ballot. The turnout disparity was slightly smaller in 2024, the first post-pandemic presidential

---

11 North Dakota does not have voter registration and thus we treat individuals residing in this state as having same-day voter registration.

election that saw a marked reduction in mail voting versus 2020. Here, the turnout rate is 60 percent in states requiring an excuse to vote by mail, whereas the rate of voting is 66 percent in states that only vote by mail, or no excuse is needed to do so.

In the bottom half of Table 12.4 we again find differences in voter turnout depending on whether there is same-day registration. In 2020, the turnout rate was 65 percent in states not providing a same-day voter registration option. In contrast, states with a same-day voter registration option notched a turnout rate of 70 percent in 2020. These differences narrow a bit in 2024—we find that turnout was 63 percent in states lacking same-day voter registration versus 66 percent in states providing same-day voter registration.

Table 12.4: Variation in voting laws and voter turnout in the 2020 and 2024 elections.

Characteristic	Category	2020		2024	
		Did Not Vote (%)	Voted (%)	Did Not Vote (%)	Voted (%)
Vote by mail	Excuse required	39	61	40	60
	No-excuse/all mail	32	68	34	66
Same-day registration	No	35	65	37	63
	Yes	30	70	34	66

Note: State-level voter turnout rates computed by authors from the UF Election Lab (https://election.lab.ufl.edu/voter-turnout/).

We conclude this section with an interesting look at the association between a large-scale change in voter eligibility and the subsequent turnout rate. Specifically, we document the turnout rate in years before and after an alteration to suffrage on four historic occasions: (1) expansion of the right to vote as granted to males regardless of their race, with passage of the 15th Amendment (February 3, 1870); (2) women granted the right to vote in all states with passage of the 19th Amendment (August 18, 1920); (3) greater protection of the right to vote for African Americans residing in certain southern states, with passage of the 1965 Voting Rights Act (August 6, 1965); and (4) lowering the right to vote to the age of eighteen in all states, with passage of the 26th Amendment (July 1, 1971).

We expect the general pattern is one of a decline in voter participation following such a large expansion of the franchise. However, there is one exception to this dynamic, and it concerns the 1965 Voting Rights Act. In this case, African Americans in the South were actively demonstrating for their right to suffrage, taking to the streets in mass protests and even holding mock elections to show their desire to vote (Black and Black 1987; McKee 2012; Woodward 2002). And although the 1965 Voting Rights Act's provisions did not blanket the eleven ex-Confederate states of the South, we will display the turnout rate for this entire region because we claim that Black citizens in southern states with laxer laws (e.g., Arkansas and Tennessee) were still likely to be mobilized.[12] Further, in displaying the turnout rate before and after passage of the 1965 Voting Rights Act, we show data based on the voting age population as estimated by the U.S. Census for 1964 and 1968. In the other three cases, we show the national turnout rate and are able to present it according to the voting eligible population (data we lack for the American South in 1964 and 1968).[13]

As anticipated, with such a large influx of eligible voters who previously were barred from voting in most states/localities, the major suffrage amendments (15th, 19th, and 26th) all indicate a drop in turnout in the initial election after their enactment. First, the 15th Amendment's expansion of the franchise to males irrespective of their race finds midterm turnout going from 71 percent in 1866 to 67 percent in 1870. Next, essentially doubling the electorate with passage of the 19th Amendment in the immediate term shows the greatest decline in turnout. The 1916 turnout rate was almost 62 percent, which plummets to 49 percent in 1920 with women's suffrage secured. Likewise, there is a drop in turnout after enactment of the 26th Amendment lowered the minimum voting age to 18. In 1968 the turnout rate was close to 63 percent, which then subsequently declined to 56 percent in 1972. Another contributing factor to the lower participation rate in 1972 was a lack of competitiveness in the presidential election (more on this in the next section)—Republican President Richard Nixon won reelection in a landslide, with his Democratic challenger George McGovern winning only the electoral votes of Massachusetts and Washington, D.C.

Finally, as expected, the 1965 Voting Rights Act exhibits a rise in participation after its passage. Limiting the data to the eleven states of the American South, in the 1964 presidential election the turnout rate for the estimated voting age population was 45 percent. Four years later, with the possibility of federal involvement

---

12 In the eleven-state South, before the expansion of its coverage, the 1965 Voting Rights Act contained provisions protecting the right to vote in Alabama, Georgia, Louisiana, Mississippi, North Carolina (covering 40 of its 100 counties), South Carolina, and Virginia (Davidson and Grofman 1994). We acknowledge that turnout increased in 1968 not just because of Black mobilization but also due to a counter-mobilization exhibited by racially conservative White southerners (see Hood et al. 2012; McKee 2017).

13 The turnout rates displayed in Figure 12.2 for the three constitutional amendment cases (15th, 19th, and 26th) are the same as those presented for the same years in Figure 12.1.

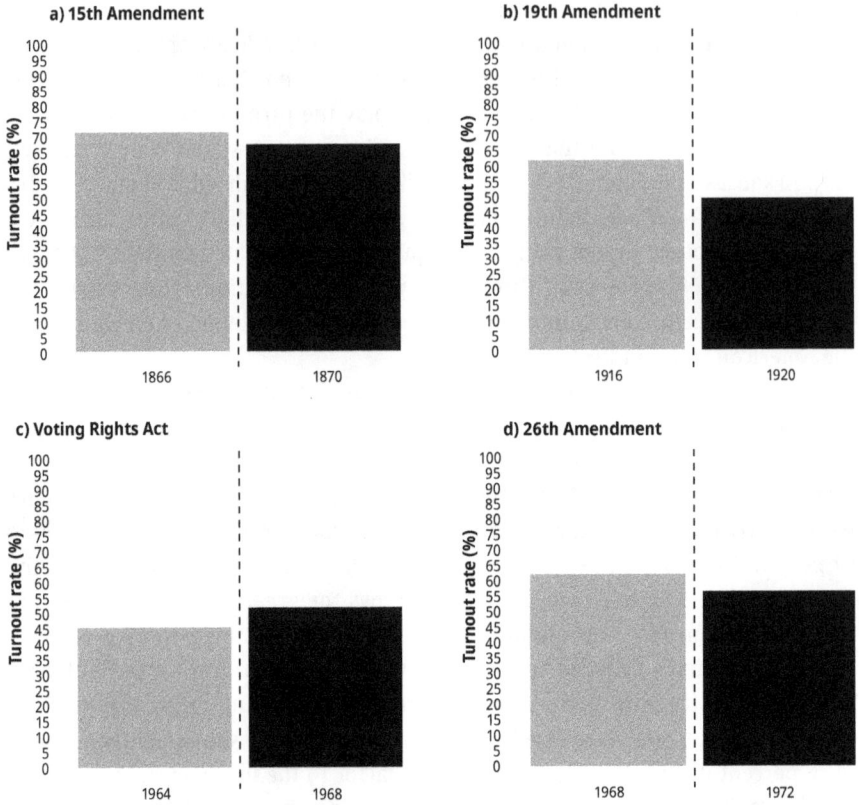

Figure 12.2: Voter turnout in presidential years before and after suffrage expansion.
Note: Data computed by the authors from the UF Election Lab (https://election.lab.ufl.edu/voter-turn
out/) for the 15th, 19th, 26th Amendment cases, and from the U.S. Census Bureau for the 1965 Voting
Rights case.

in jurisdictions reluctant to comply with the voting protections established by the
1965 Voting Rights Act, voting age turnout in the South went up to almost 52 percent. Also, this turnout was not isolated to a handful of southern states. In fact,
compared to 1964, the voting age turnout in 1968 only *declined* in one state, Georgia: 43.2 percent in 1964 and 41.7 percent in 1968.

12.6 Competitiveness and Voter Turnout

As remarked upon at the start of the chapter, participation typically rises in more competitive electoral contexts. Again, it is not necessarily because the chances of casting a pivotal ballot improve somewhat (Downs 1957) but rather because candidates and their campaigns invest more resources (e.g., candidate visits and money spent on political ads) into getting their supporters to the polls (Aldrich 1993). Hence, closeness, per se, does not drive higher turnout (Cox and Munger 1989); it is the investment in campaign resources that lowers the cost of voting (McKee 2008) and thus spurs mobilization (Hill and McKee 2005). This dynamic comes into stark relief in presidential elections because in recent cycles only a handful of states are deemed winnable by both major parties. Indeed, the same seven states were thought to be battlegrounds in 2020 and 2024: Arizona, Georgia, Michigan, Nevada, North Carolina, Pennsylvania, and Wisconsin. Florida was viewed as a swing state in 2020 (Sides et al. 2023) but dropped out of the mix in 2024 when Trump ended up winning the two-party vote by more than thirteen percentage points.

We classify the presidential battleground states as the aforementioned seven, which both major parties viewed as such in 2020 and 2024. Although we do not show this data, the bulk of campaign resources (candidate visits and political ads) were poured into these states, which is a pattern with a long history because of the strategic rationality of devoting the most effort in states with the greatest likelihood of breaking toward either party (Shaw 2006; Shaw et al. 2024).

This outsized attention given to a small number of states perceived as winnable by both major party presidential nominees produces a discernible dichotomy of battleground states versus blackout states (Gimpel et al. 2007).[14] For instance, in a blackout state like Oklahoma, its residents are exposed to hardly any political ads, except those aired nationally, and not targeted to the state's specific media markets (e.g., Oklahoma City or Tulsa).[15] Additionally, there is simply no reason outside of fundraising for either major party presidential/vice presidential nominee to pay the Sooner State a visit. The showering of campaign resources in a swing state has the effect of raising turnout (Gimpel et al. 2007; Hill and McKee 2005), but blackout state residents are not motivated to vote based on the excitement and attention created by a close contest because this electoral milieu is absent.

---

14 The term blackout means a lack of (television) exposure to a political campaign.
15 In 2016, 2020, and 2024, Trump won a majority of the popular vote in all of Oklahoma's seventy-seven counties.

Table 12.5 shows turnout data from the 2020 CES based on whether a respondent resided in a battleground state and whether they were contacted by a campaign. Contrary to expectations, we see no difference in the turnout rate according to battleground status—60 percent voting in swing states and blackout states. However, by homing in on a proxy for mobilization, whether a respondent was contacted by a campaign, we find this variable is strongly correlated with participation. Specifically, turnout was just 43 percent among respondents not contacted by a campaign, while turnout vaults to 73 percent for respondents who were contacted.

Table 12.5: Turnout according to state type and whether contacted by a campaign.

Characteristic	Category	Did Not Vote (%)	Voted (%)
Battleground state	No	40	60
	Yes	40	60
Contacted by campaign	No	57	43
	Yes	27	73

Note: Data computed by authors from the 2020 CES.

We also present state-level turnout data in Table 12.6 to see if it captures a difference in participation at this aggregate level, on the basis of competitiveness. The state-level data reveals some notable disparities in turnout according to competitiveness. In 2020, the turnout rate was 66 percent in blackout states. In contrast, the 2020 turnout rate in battleground states was 70 percent: four points higher than participation in the blackout states. In 2024, the turnout rate in battleground states holds steady at 70 percent, but it declines to 63 percent in the blackout states—producing a substantial seven-point turnout gap.

Table 12.6: State-level turnout in 2020 and 2024, based on battleground state status.

		2020		2024	
		Did Not Vote (%)	Voted (%)	Did Not Vote (%)	Voted (%)
Battleground state	No	34	66	37	63
	Yes	30	70	30	70

Note: Data computed by the authors from the UF Election Lab (https://election.lab.ufl.edu/voter-turnout/).

Although we did not find a participation difference with the 2020 CES data, depending on residence in a battleground state versus blackout state, the state-level data comports with our expectations in the 2020 and 2024 elections. Recall that presidential turnout in 2020 was the highest since 1900 and that it dropped a few percentage points in 2024 (see the discussion of Figure 12.1). Nevertheless, in the battleground states the turnout rate stayed at the same high rate registered in 2020, while it experienced a drop in the forty-three other blackout states, which were never in doubt as to which party's candidate would win them.

12.7 Conclusion

As we have shown in this chapter, a multitude of factors affect voter turnout. We believe this is the case because, in line with Aldrich (1993), voting is a low-cost/low-benefit political activity. For example, equipped with a single ballot and only one vote for a given elective office, we do not know of anyone who can claim their participation determined a political outcome. Even the 2000 presidential election in Florida came down to a 537-vote margin between the winner George W. Bush and his opponent Al Gore. Hence, competitiveness (or lack thereof) is only one of many variables related to participation. Instead, regardless of the competitiveness of the place where an individual resides, we see that their demographic and political characteristics have a strong association with the likelihood of voting. For example, citizens of greater means, and those with more education and higher incomes, are much more likely to vote. We also find considerable variation in turnout according to one's race, ethnicity, and age. Although we show these turnout differences with respect to a single survey, they are longstanding from one election to the next (Wolfinger and Rosenstone 1980).

Similarly, political views and civic engagement both exhibit substantial variation in the probability of casting a ballot. Citizens who express more polarized positions with respect to their affiliation with a major party or their alignment with a political ideology are both more participatory. We also find evidence of greater turnout among those who voted in the last presidential election—indicating a much higher rate of participation among habitual voters (Plutzer 2002). And not surprisingly, individuals who demonstrate more knowledge of politics and those who pay closer attention to current events both vote at markedly higher rates. The convenience of voting also impacts turnout. Making participation easier via laws that allow voting by mail without having to provide a reason, and states that allow citizens to register at the same time they cast their ballot, consistently show a positive relationship with voting. Nevertheless, massive expansions to suffrage (15th, 19th, and 26th Amendments) usually reduce participation in the immediate aftermath because it takes some time to get familiar with exercising the franchise.

The United States is currently experiencing a period of historically heightened partisan polarization (Abramowitz 2022). Most scholars studying this phenomenon lament the degree of partisan vitriol expressed by our elected representatives and sometimes by rank-and-file voters in the mass electorate. Indeed, there is widespread consensus that lowering the political temperature would likely result in a healthier democracy. Surveys repeatedly show that most Americans would prefer our leaders to adopt a more unifying posture in the political arena. Despite this expressed desire, the U.S. remains a divided country with two major parties of roughly equally sized coalitions that decide whether it is Democrats or Republicans who control the levers of power in our governing institutions. One thing is certain, because the political stakes appear weighty to most Americans in this contentious electoral environment, it has contributed to elevated turnout rates since the dawn of the twenty-first century.

Discussion Questions

1 As opposed to the turnout decline after passage of the 15th, 19th, and 26th Amendments, why did turnout actually show an increase after passage of the 1965 Voting Rights Act?

2 Looking back at Figure 12.1, which shows voter turnout in presidential and midterm elections from 1789 to 2024, in what period was turnout the highest, and why was this the case?

3 Looking back at Table 12.1, it shows that age has a strong positive association with turnout. What are some reasons why the oldest category of voters (65+) is so much more participatory than the youngest 18–29 cohort?

4 As the authors caution, why is it preferable to analyze survey data that validates turnout as opposed to examining survey data that relies on a respondent's self-reported claim of voting?

5 Why is it expected that competitiveness, in this case whether a state is a so-called battleground state or blackout state, will influence voter turnout?

References

Abramowitz, Alan I. 2022. "The Polarized American Electorate: The Rise of Partisan-Ideological Consistency and Its Consequences." *Political Science Quarterly* 137 (4): 645–74.

Aldrich, John H. 1993. "Rational Choice and Turnout." *American Journal of Political Science* 37 (1): 246–78.

Aldrich, John H. 2011. *Why Parties? A Second Look*. University of Chicago Press.

Ansolabehere, Stephen, and Eitan Hersh. 2012. "Validation: What Big Data Reveal About Survey Misreporting and the Real Electorate." *Political Analysis* 20 (4): 437–59.

Ansolabehere, Stephen, and Eitan Hersh. 2013. "Gender, Race, Age, and Voting: A Research Note." *Politics and Governance* 1 (2): 132–37.

Black, Earl, and Merle Black. 1987. *Politics and Society in the South*. Harvard University Press.

Converse, Philip E. 1964. "The Nature of Belief Systems in Mass Publics." In *Ideology and Discontent*, edited by David E. Apter. The Free Press of Glencoe.

Cox, Gary W., and Michael C. Munger. 1989. "Closeness, Expenditures, and Turnout in the 1982 U.S. House Elections." *American Political Science Review* 83 (1): 217–31.

Davidson, Chandler, and Bernard Grofman, eds. 1994. *Quiet Revolution in the South: The Impact of the Voting Rights Act, 1965-1990*. Princeton University Press.

Downs, Anthony. 1957. *An Economic Theory of Democracy*. Harper & Row.

Foner, Eric. 1988. *Reconstruction: America's Unfinished Revolution, 1863-1877*. Harper & Row.

Gimpel, James G., Karen M. Kaufmann, and Shanna Pearson-Merkowitz. 2007. "Battleground States versus Blackout States: The Behavioral Implications of Modern Presidential Campaigns." *Journal of Politics* 69 (3): 786–77.

Gomez, Brad T., Thomas G. Hansford, and George A. Krause. 2007. "The Republicans Should Pray for Rain: Weather, Turnout, and Voting in U.S. Presidential Elections." *Journal of Politics* 69 (3): 649–63.

Goodwyn, Lawrence. 1978. *The Populist Moment: A Short History of the Agrarian Revolt in America*. Oxford University Press.

Green, Donald, Bradley Palmquist, and Eric Schickler. 2002. *Partisan Hearts and Minds: Political Parties and the Social Identities of Voters*. Yale University Press.

Greene, Steven. 1999. "Understanding Party Identification: A Social Identity Approach." *Political Psychology* 20 (2): 393–403.

Hill, David, and Seth C. McKee. 2005. "The Electoral College, Mobilization, and Turnout in the 2000 Presidential Election." *American Politics Research* 33 (5): 700–25.

Hood, M.V.III, Quentin Kidd, and Irwin L. Morris. 2012. *The Rational Southerner: Black Mobilization, Republican Growth, and the Partisan Transformation of the American South*. Oxford University Press.

Keith, Bruce E., David B. Magleby, Candice J. Nelson, Elizabeth Orr, Mark C. Westlye, and Raymond E. Wolfinger. 1992. *The Myth of the Independent Voter*. University of California Press.

Key, V.O.Jr. 1949. *Southern Politics in State and Nation*. Alfred A. Knopf.

Keyssar, Alexander. 2009. *The Right to Vote: The Contested History of Democracy in the United States*. Basic Books.

Kleppner, Paul. 2010. *The Third Electoral System, 1853-1892: Parties, Voters, and Political Cultures*. University of North Carolina Press.

Levendusky, Matthew. 2009. *The Partisan Sort: How Liberals Became Democrats and Conservatives Became Republicans*. University of Chicago Press.

Luskin, Robert C. 1990. "Explaining Political Sophistication." *Political Behavior* 12 (4): 331–61.

Mason, Lilliana. 2018. *Uncivil Agreement: How Politics Became Our Identity*. University of Chicago Press.

McDonald, Michael P., Juliana K. Mucci, Enrijeta Shino, and Daniel A. Smith. 2024a. "Mail Voting and Voter Turnout." *Election Law Journal: Rules, Politics, and Policy* 23 (1): 1–18.

McDonald, Michael, Enrijeta Shino, Daniel A. Smith, Payton Lussier, and Danielle Dietz. 2024b. "Campus Voting During the COVID-19 Pandemic." *American Politics Research* 52 (3): 225–38.

McKee, Seth C. 2008. "Closeness, Expenditures, and Turnout in the 2000 Presidential Election." *Journal of Political Marketing* 7 (1): 69–91.

McKee, Seth C. 2012. "Demanding Deliverance in Dixie: Race, The Civil Rights Movement, and Southern Politics." In *The Oxford Handbook of Southern Politics*, edited by Charles S. Bullock III and Mark J. Rozell. Oxford University Press.

McKee, Seth C. 2017. "Race and Subregional Persistence in a Changing South." *Southern Cultures* 23 (2): 134–59.

McKee, Seth C. 2024. "Changes in Voting and Elections." In *The Routledge International Handbook of Changes in Human Perceptions and Behaviors*, edited by Kanako Taku and Todd K. Shackelford. Routledge.

McKee, Seth C., M. V. Hood III, and David Hill. 2012. "Achieving Validation: Barack Obama and Black Turnout in 2008." *State Politics and Policy Quarterly* 12 (1): 3–22.

Plutzer. Eric. 2002. "Becoming a Habitual Voter: Inertia, Resources, and Growth in Young Adulthood." *American Political Science Review* 96 (1): 41–56.

Shafer, Byron E. 2016. *The American Political Pattern: Stability and Change, 1932–2016*. University Press of Kansas.

Shaw, Daron R. 2006. *The Race to 270: The Electoral College and the Campaign Strategies of 2000 and 2004*. University of Chicago Press.

Shaw, Daron, Scott L. Althaus, and Costas Panagopoulos. 2024. *Battleground: Electoral College Strategies, Execution, and Impact in the Modern Era*. Oxford University Press.

Shino, Enrijeta, and Daniel A. Smith. 2020. "Mobilizing the Youth Vote? Early Voting on College Campuses." *Election Law Journal: Rules, Politics, and Policy* 19 (4): 524–41.

Shino, Enrijeta, Seth C. McKee, and Michael Binder. 2023. "Voter Habituation and Opinion Activation in Misreporting Voting Behavior in the 2020 Presidential Election." *The Social Science Journal*. https://doi.org/10.1080/03623319.2023.2277030.

Sides, John, Daron Shaw, Matt Grossmann, and Keena Lipsitz. 2023. *Campaigns and Elections: Rules, Reality, Strategy, Choice*. W. W. Norton and Company.

Wiebe, Robert H. 1966. *The Search for Order, 1877–1920*. Macmillan Publishers.

Wolfinger, Raymond E., and Steven J. Rosenstone. 1980. *Who Votes?* Yale University Press.

Woodward, C. Vann. 2002. *The Strange Career of Jim Crow*. Oxford University Press.

Joshua McCrain

13 From Local News to Polarized Views: The Nationalization of the American Media

Two trends characterize the modern media environment in the United States. First, local media consumption is consistently declining among the general public, and sources of local news are disappearing (Hayes and Lawless 2021; McCrain and Peterson 2023). Second, the *type* of media individuals consume is strongly predictive of their partisanship and the way people vote (see Figure 13.1 below). The decline of local media, combined with increasing demand for nonpolitical media and/or partisan media, paints a worrying picture for the future of American democracy. In a representative democracy, it is imperative that voters are able to hold their elected officials accountable. In this equilibrium, elected officials behave "better" in order to be reelected. When voters know less about their elected officials, they are unable to reward the good ones with reelection and punish the bad ones by removing them from office. Through these mechanisms, the media environment directly shapes the quality of representative democracy and the material lives of American voters (Snyder and Stromberg 2010; Hayes and Lawless 2015).

At first glance, Figure 13.1 tells a compelling and straightforward story about the modern state of politics. Individuals who consume traditional "hard news" from sources such as newspapers and national nightly broadcasts are more liberal. Individuals who consume no political news, or news from social media or cable, are more conservative. A conclusion one might draw, as many in the media have since the 2024 election, is that the information content of these different types of news sources is changing the way people vote. In other words, the causal story is that if more people (e.g.) read more newspapers, Biden would have won more votes. This chapter will explain in detail why such a conclusion would be overly simplistic at best and entirely misleading at worst. It is not that the type of media being consumed is changing voting behavior—it is that Americans are increasingly siloed into different media diets, and political ideology is a strong predictor of an individual's media diet.

Joshua McCrain, University of Utah

https://doi.org/10.1515/9783111591902-013

NEWS SOURCES AND VOTING

▨Joe Biden (%)   ▪Donald Trump (%)

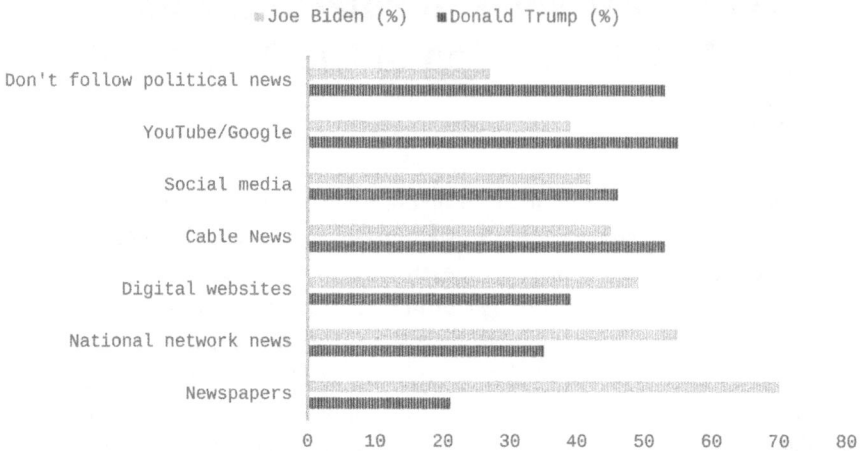

Figure 13.1: News source by 2024 presidential candidate preference.
Source: https://www.documentcloud.org/documents/24614251-240126-nbc-april-2024-poll-4-26-2024-release.

13.1 The Modern Media Environment

Historically, American citizens' largest source for political information, and how they develop political ideas, is the news media. Zaller (1992) describes a process of public opinion formation where individuals are on a spectrum of low to high political interest. Those with low interest and/or knowledge of politics are less likely to receive information about politics (given they are not keen on paying attention to it), but when they do receive information, they are more likely to update their prior beliefs about a particular political issue. On the other hand, those who have high interest and/or knowledge in politics are more likely to receive information about politics (because they are interested in it). However, these individuals, due to having high existing knowledge about politics, are *unlikely* to update their existing views.

As many scholars have noted since Zaller, most Americans are not particularly interested in politics. To varying degrees, this position is "rational" (Lupia and McCubbins 1998). Why? Paying attention to politics is *costly* because it is complex, technical, and frequently changing. It takes a lot of time and expertise to fully understand political issues, which is of course why we elect people to do this for us. Thus, a little new political information could potentially move public opinion in meaningful ways, especially on important issues. This story, however, re-lies not only on a source of political information to exist but also that individuals with low-to-no interest in politics will see that information.

In this context, Prior (2007) explains how the evolving media landscape has fundamentally altered the way individuals form opinions on political issues, and why it is increasingly easy to avoid news about politics at all. As Prior details, in the era of radio and then early television, if you wanted to consume *any* media you had very few options. In particular, because the government permits broad-cast companies to use the airwaves, the government (through the Federal Com-munications Commission) regulates that over-the-air broadcasts must contain sig-nificant news content.[1] As a result, two things happened. First, broadcasts explicitly competed with each other to deliver the "best" nightly news broadcasts (in order win viewers and advertising revenue). Second, and most importantly, even if you were not someone who was interested in politics, if you wanted to watch *any television at all,* you were necessarily exposed to some news content.

Of course, in the 1980s and into the 1990s the United States saw the expansion and proliferation of cable television. This evolution in entertainment media, com-bined with the affordability of both televisions and cable subscriptions, resulted in two things. First, individuals with strong preferences for only entertainment media (e.g., sports, comedy) could easily select to view only that kind of media. One no longer had to sit through the news, because it was the only thing on, and could now avoid it entirely. In other words, many of these low information voters were no longer incidentally exposed to some news content. The second conse-quence, the inverse of this, is that individuals with a strong preference for politi-cal content can now absorb as much as they want. In the last section of this chap-ter, I discuss specific effects of this shift in the media environment on political attitudes and behavior.

This discussion so far has only focused on television media. Obviously, the proliferation of the internet, especially high-speed internet, exacerbated the trends just described. Imagine, prior to the existence of the internet, you were primarily interested in entertainment media and avidly watched TV. In this con-text, you may still be incidentally exposed to some news content either through flipping through channels (more on this later) or through something like watch-ing your local news broadcast to get local weather and sports. In the high-speed internet era, and in the current era of ubiquitous internet entertainment media

---

1 From 1949 to 1987, the so-called "fairness doctrine" was also in place. This stated that stations using public airwaves also had an obligation to present both sides of controversial issues. It is worth noting that today a) this no longer exists and b) if it did exist, it would not apply to cable or internet news sources.

(i.e., smart phones), it is increasingly possible to avoid any real exposure to hard news. This has been documented by scholars as either intentional or unintentional "news avoidance"—a trend that has markedly increased since the 2010s (Zerba 2011; Skovsgaard and Andersen 2020). On the other hand, it has led to more individuals who are politically interested consuming increasingly more *nationalized* political content (Hopkins 2018). In sum, the modern media environment is characterized by a proliferation of media choices available to consumers.

So what does the modern landscape actually look like? In many ways, this is difficult to study. Self-reports of media diets (in, for instance, surveys) are notoriously poor measures of capturing what media sources individuals consume and from where they get their political information (Zaller 1992; Bartels 1993). What is known is that newspapers are no longer a major source of information for Americans, with circulation numbers lower than they've ever been (Hayes and Lawless 2021). Local TV news remains the "most trusted" source for news among Americans (Figure 13.2) but is primarily watched by older populations (Martin and McCrain 2019) and its overall viewership is consistently declining (Martin et al. 2024). For younger populations, the internet and especially the internet on mobile devices is the most prominent source for news—though it is nearly impossible to capture actual, behavioral consumption patterns (Guess 2021). Considerably more is known, however, about cable news consumption: Broockman and Kalla (2023, 3) combine comprehensive datasets of individual-level television viewership and find that "approximately 1 in 7 Americans consume over 8 hours of partisan media per month." They also find that consumption of cable news is highly segregated by partisan alignment (that is, Republicans consuming Fox News and Democrats consuming MSNBC).

What are the consequences of these viewership and consumption patterns? Why is local news declining while national political media—especially the partisan sort—remains a robust source of political news? In the next section, I discuss how this high choice environment, through market forces, shapes the current media landscape, explains the rise of partisan media sources, and portends the end of robust local journalism in the United States.

13.2 Supply and Demand for Local and National Media

The competition for viewers/readers among media producers is not unlike other markets and industries that compete for consumers (Mullainathan and Shleifer 2005; Gentzkow and Shapiro 2010). In the world of media production, more view-

TRUST IN LOCAL NEWS

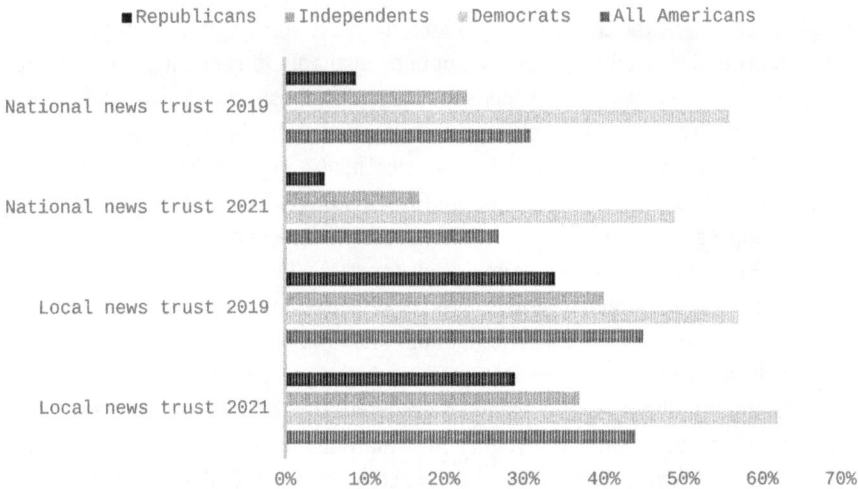

■ Republicans   ▧ Independents   ▨ Democrats   ■ All Americans

National news trust 2019

National news trust 2021

Local news trust 2019

Local news trust 2021

0%   10%   20%   30%   40%   50%   60%   70%

Figure 13.2: Trust in local news by political party.
Source: https://www.pewresearch.org/journalism/2024/05/07/americans-changing-relationship-with-local-news/.

ers and readers means more eyeballs on the content and the ability to sell more advertising. While somewhat obvious as an observation, the implications of what it means for media producers to compete among themselves for viewers has subtle and important consequences for what kind of media is produced. As previously discussed, the media that is produced, and what consumers consume, shapes the kind, quality, and quantity of information voters receive about politics.

A demand-side explanation for production of media content simply means that media producers create the content that they think consumers want. This is the typical explanation one would learn in an introductory economics course. In a functioning marketplace, the production of content, its news content, its national or local focus, and its partisan slant would in equilibrium match what consumers in that market want. On the reverse side is a supply-side explanation for the production of news content. Here, media producers have substantial influence over the production of content and shape what consumers can view based on the owners' idiosyncratic preferences. In particular, they may be willing to trade off revenues for some other objective, such as altering political outcomes. Ultimately, whether media content is produced by supply and/or demand mechanisms is an empirical question, which I examine next.

13.2.1 Consequences for National Media

As discussed above, the transition to ubiquitous cable subscriptions and then high-speed internet drastically changed the options available to consumers. Those who decide to consume news can now consume a lot of it; those who want strictly entertainment media can now entirely avoid news content. In the supply and demand framework, this means that in a high choice media environment producers of news media are now strictly competing for consumers with high preference for news (as opposed to the broadcast era where all TV viewers watched some news).

Starting in the 2000s, this competition for cable TV news viewers led to the expansion of partisan media outlets, specifically Fox News and then MSNBC.[2] The proliferation of partisan media is a demand story: as Zaller (1992) argues, people will sort into viewing content that agrees with the prior political viewpoints. In an environment where news consumers are primarily those who actually want to consume news, this means that higher information voters are explicitly rejecting content that *challenges* their political perspective. In the United States, these political viewpoints are increasingly divided along partisan lines (Abramowitz and Webster 2016). In other words, as the country becomes more partisan, the competition for cable TV news viewers is largely on the partisan dimension (Kim et al. 2022).

This preference for politicized national news creates a feedback loop. National news is, in general, more polarized and contains information that further triggers viewers' partisan identification (Hetherington 2001; Arceneaux and Johnson 2013) and increases viewers' awareness of the primacy of partisan conflict in American politics (Levendusky and Malhotra 2016). This partisan news content then creates additional awareness of and interest in partisan-specific stories that, with the rise of high-speed internet, created increasing demand for highly polarized sources of news (Lelkes et al. 2017). It is also likely that consumption of polarized content on strictly digital media platforms creates particular communities where individuals do not have their prior views challenged, only hardened (Törnberg 2022).

Another way of framing this discussion is that the reason there exists biased or slanted media[3] is *because it is what consumers want*, and producers are simply

---

2 In this time period, CNN fell soundly in the middle of the ideological spectrum on average (Martin and Yurukoglu 2017). However, new research measuring the slant of the big three cable news channels since 2010 finds that CNN sharply shifted towards the left, largely matching MSNBC, while Fox News took a stronger turn to the right (Kim et al. 2022)

3 The literature broadly uses these terms interchangeably, though there is a large and growing literature on the measure of media slant outside the scope of this chapter (e.g., Kim et al. 2022).

matching that demand. However, there is still potential for supply-side mechanisms in the production of polarized political media on cable TV news. Owners of
major media outlets are frequently political actors and/or have political objectives; they might then change the content of their broadcasts in such a way to
influence public opinion towards these objectives. This is a concept known as
"media power" (Prat 2018) and captures the idea that a) the media has the ability
to influence public opinion and b) media producers could choose to alter their
content in such a way to maximize this goal (relative to maximizing profits). In
groundbreaking work on this topic, Martin and Yurukoglu (2017) find that cable
news channels are indeed partisan (Fox News the most conservative, MSNBC the
most liberal) and that the degree of partisan slant demonstrated by Fox News in
the 2000s–2010s is such that they are potentially trying to alter election outcomes
rather than purely maximizing profits. Martin and Yurukoglu also document that
channels such as MSNBC could potentially behave the same way, on the reverse
side, but do not appear to be doing so. As I discuss next, the concept of media
power is particularly important in the discussion of local media.

13.2.2 Consequences for Local Media

Local media in the United States is facing disaster. Newspapers across the country
are cutting staff, cutting beats, reducing the size of their "news hole" (the space
for news after advertising is sold), or shuttering completely. Hayes and Lawless
(2021) extensively document the decline of the newspaper industry in the United
States; for instance, they find that "in 2004, there were on average 8.1 newsroom
staff for every newspaper operating in the United States. Today, that number is
down to just 5.5" (20). Peterson (2021) finds that when newspapers cut staff, their
reporters are forced to cover additional beats, with the implication of less quality
coverage across each beat. But what is driving this well-documented decimation
of the local newspaper industry?

Increasing evidence suggests that the increase in interest in national politics
(Hopkins 2018) is substituting for an interest in local politics (Martin and McCrain
2019). For newspapers, that during the height of the print era made the bulk of
their revenues from advertisers (Hayes and Lawless 2021), the potential lack of
demand for local news means both fewer subscribers and fewer advertisers.[4]

---

4 A primary driver for the reduction in advertising revenue was the industry-wide shift in much
more efficient and cost effective internet advertising, which drove advertisers to platforms other
than newspapers.

Some evidence suggests that, in a survey setting, Americans will state their support for local newspapers when told about the importance of local government (Hayes and Lawless 2021). However, there is no empirical evidence that, on average, Americans are willing to financially support local newspapers. Hopkins and Gorton (2024) randomly handed out free subscriptions to a well-known local newspaper and found, out of 2,529 individuals given the free subscription, only forty-four actually subscribed. In an observational setting using behavioral data, McCrain and Peterson (2023) find that there is no apparent increase in consumption of local news surrounding high-profile local elections. These findings are important because they suggest that simply shifting to a non-profit model for local news outlets is not a panacea, as non-profits still need to generate revenue. In short, there is no good news for local newspapers.

The other primary source for local news is local television news, which is broadcast over the air but typically consumed as part of cable packages.[5] Local TV news viewership attracts roughly an order of magnitude more viewers on a nightly basis than cable TV news (Martin and McCrain 2019). Local TV news is also widely the most trusted source Americans report for news (Fioroni 2022). Local TV news viewership, however, is also gradually declining, though at a less precipitous rate than newspaper circulation (McCrain and Peterson 2023).

There is substantially less research on how the forces of supply and demand change local TV news content. What is well-documented, and gives us insight into these forces, is the changing economic landscape of media ownership. In both newspapers and local television, outlets are increasingly being bought by large, nationwide media conglomerates. In the newspaper industry, Gannet owns and/ or operates one-sixth of US daily newspapers (Doctor 2019) while the three largest local TV conglomerates own over 40 percent of US local television stations (Martin et al. 2024). The consolidation of local media among major conglomerates is important for two reasons: first, it suggests that many outlets are struggling financially and are cheap to acquire; second, it suggests very specific economic forces are operating that have important *supply-side* effects on local television news.

The consolidation of local television among major nationwide conglomerates suggests that *economies of scale* should be operating for these ownership groups. This means that as these ownership groups acquire more stations, it will become cost effective for them to reduce the number of local journalists in each station (who are expensive) and centralize the production of content, pushing out the centralized content to their local affiliates. Martin and McCrain (2019) study this

---

5 The FCC mandates that cable providers include a market's local broadcast news as part of their cable packages.

idea specifically, analyzing what happens when Sinclair—one of the largest media ownership groups—acquires local TV stations. They find that, relative to non-acquired stations in the same media market, Sinclair stations begin to cover less local content. This is strong evidence of the economies of scale argument. However, they also find that these stations cover more *national* political content while simultaneously cutting local content. Importantly, and likely unique to the Sinclair context,[6] Sinclair stations also shift the slant of their national political content to the right.

These trends are potentially consistent with a *demand*-driven story of changes in media content. Sinclair executives could argue, for instance, that these changes in coverage post-acquisition are purely driven by meeting consumers where they are at; indeed, as previously discussed, there is ample evidence that consumers of local news are more interested in national politics than local politics. In the local TV setting, the evidence for this is mixed. The content changes uncovered by Martin and McCrain (2019) do *not* result in an increase in viewership (nor do they result in a decrease). In other words, consumers are not obviously tuning in or out based on these changes. In new research on this topic, Martin et al. (2024) find more broadly that consumers do not seem to have aggregate preferences towards the balance of content displayed on local news broadcast—overall viewership remains unchanged despite the fact that conglomerate-acquired stations spend less time on local news and more time on advertising.[7] While some changes to content are likely supply-driven (Sinclair changing slant), others *could* be demand-driven. The bottom line, however, is that the changes produced by media conglomeration are not obviously reflected in viewership—meaning that there is substantial potential for media power among owners of local media outlets.

This discussion leads to a set of important questions for citizens and scholars alike: what is the effect of these changes in consumption patterns, in local news coverage, in the decline of newspapers, on political outcomes? Does slanted media change voter preferences? Does it *matter* that Sinclair stations exhibit more right-leaning coverage relative to same-market stations? Is the disappearance of substantial local reporting altering political knowledge and the behavior of elected officials? I turn to these questions next.

---

6 Sinclair is a particular case in that its ownership is very prominently Republican-leaning and supports Republican candidates. Indeed, high level Sinclair employees served in the first Trump White House (Atkinson 2019).

7 It is worth emphasizing that these results are in the *aggregate*; in other words, it could be possible that the audience composition changes but not the overall viewership numbers.

13.3 Media Effects

The prior discussion has emphasized a few features of the modern media land-scape in the US. First, consumers have many choices available to them. The prolif-eration of choices allows people to *select* the kind of content they like, whether it is a purely non-news media diet, a heavy partisan news media diet, or something in between. Second, evidence suggests consumers of news media have preferen-ces for national political content relative to local content. Third, sources for reli-able local news are disappearing. Each of these trends implies the potential for meaningful effects on politics. This section will discuss what academic research finds on "media effects" and why these questions are difficult to study.

A primary mechanism through which media can affect politics is changing the accountability relationship between voters and elected officials. In represen-tative democracies, citizens must have some knowledge over the actions of their elected representatives in order to reward the good ones and punish the bad ones. The media is the primary source of that information. However, this is diffi-cult to study. The ideal setting for a study on this relationship would be to ran-domly assign different amounts of media coverage to different politicians. Of course, this is impossible, leaving open the possibility of spurious relationships brought about by different features of places, politicians, and the interaction of these two things. To solve this, scholars have come up with two general solutions.

First, scholars take advantage of the arbitrary nature of geography, primarily in how *media markets* overlap with legislative districts. Snyder and Stromberg (2010) note that congressional districts have varying degrees of overlap with newspaper markets; some districts are perfectly contained within a newspaper market, some are in multiple markets, and some markets have to cover many congressional districts (for instance, New York city is geographically small and contains many members of Congress). Exploiting this variation, Snyder and Stromberg find that when members of Congress are subject to more coverage by local media, they behave better. They deliver more federal funds to their district, they vote more in line with district preferences, and voters know more about their behavior. Other research takes advantage of the difference between elec-toral geography and media geography, finding that more local coverage of politi-cians reduces the nationalization of politics for those races (the candidates are more locally focused and less nationally focused; Moskowitz 2021).

The other approach to studying the media's effect on accountability is through exploiting changes in the media environment. In one strand of this re-search, scholars find that when local newspapers close, voters are less likely to engage in split-ticket voting (Darr et al. 2018), cities get worse municipal bond rat-ings (Gao et al. 2020), and local businesses get away with more corporate misconduct (Heese et al. 2022). Other research takes advantage of the previously discussed changes to local media ownership, finding that when conglomerates buy stations, voters know less about local politics (Martin et al. 2024) and, in the Sinclair case specifically, are less supportive of Democratic politicians (Levendusky 2022). Mastrorocco and Ornaghi (2022) find that municipal police behave worse due to Sinclair's reduction of local political content, clearing fewer crimes.

The second question of interest in media effects research is: how does media consumption affect political attitudes and polarization? This question is very difficult to answer in a causal way. As previously discussed, we know that consumers have strong preferences for ideological media. Thus, the challenge is in disentangling the direction of the causal process. Is it that partisan media produce partisan attitudes, or that voters with already developed partisan attitudes *select* to consume partisan media? There is plenty of evidence for the latter (e.g., Broockman and Kalla 2023), making answering the former question difficult.

In an ideal research design, the researcher would randomly assign voters to be forced to consume, e.g., only Fox News or MSNBC. This of course is not how media diets work in reality, and even if resources for doing such an experiment were not a problem, it is impossible to perfectly recreate how individuals naturally consume partisan media.[8] Some research attempts to tackle this issue through survey experiments, where participants are randomly assigned to consume a partisan news article, a non-partisan article, or no news at all. They are then asked questions about their political attitudes. This style of research is fraught because it does not generalize how people consume media in reality (they select congenial media; Wittenberg et al. 2023).

To get around these questions, scholars have found sources of exogenous variation that can be thought of as an as-if random assignment in consuming partisan media. For example, Lelkes et al. (2017) exploit features of geography and policy environments that make it easier or harder to install broadband internet. They find that in places that broadband internet installation was easier (around the initial rollout of broadband internet), people developed more polarized partisan attitudes because it became easier for them to consume more partisan media via the internet. Other research in this vein takes advantage of the staggered rollout of Fox News in the 1990s (Arceneaux and Johnson 2013) and the acquisition of local TV stations by political owners (Levendusky 2022).

A particularly creative approach to studying the effects of partisan media on voting and attitudes takes advantage of differential channel lineups across media

---

8 However, see Broockman and Kalla (2025) for a very promising approach to this exact type of experimental design.

markets. The idea is that when Fox News (or any partisan outlet) appears *lower* (i.e., the channel number is lower) in the channel lineup, people who are flipping through channels are more likely to see more of that partisan outlet. Martin and Yurukoglu (2017) demonstrate that channel position: a) predicts increased viewership of partisan news; and b) when Fox News is lower in the channel lineup it also predicts increased Republican vote share in presidential elections in the 2000s. Others have used this approach to show that as-if random Fox News viewership increases Republican vote share across most elections (Ash et al. 2022) and worsened the effects of the COVID-19 pandemic due to Fox News downplaying the seriousness of the pandemic (Ash et al. 2024).[9]

This section is not meant to be an exhaustive review of the academic literature on these topics. Rather, the point of this section is to indicate that there is substantial evidence that the media in general and the contemporary environment specifically do have effects on political outcomes. At the same time, I want to emphasize that the effects of the media on political outcomes *are not obvious*. Precisely because the media is a marketplace, and consumers have particular demands for particular content, the causal effects of media consumption are inextricably linked to people selecting a media diet that they want to consume—including because it serves to confirm their already held political viewpoints. Even the most creative research designs, such as the use of channel alignment, are limited in that they only apply to the kinds of people who will watch more Fox News (or MSNBC) when incidentally flipping through channels.[10] In other words, it is empirically not well established what the effect of Fox News/MSNBC viewership "does" to people who already agree with those channels' political perspectives.

13.4 The Future of Media's Role in American Politics

We can now return to the motivating example at the beginning of this chapter, that in the 2020 (and 2024) presidential election the type of media voters con-

---

9 Another creative approach to get around selection of congenial media takes advantage of the appearance of the television show *The Apprentice* after other popular programs. In places where *The Apprentice* appeared after a popular program, Kim and Patterson Jr (2024) find that Donald Trump performed better in the 2016 Republican primary.
10 This a subtle but important point. These designs identify a *local* treatment effect, and they cannot and do not try to say anything about, for example, hardened partisans who already have strong predispositions for partisan media.

sumed was highly correlated with vote share. The discussion in this chapter allows us to interpret such snapshots of the American electorate. Because people select the kind of media they want to consume, one cannot simply "blame" the media for the outcomes of elections. Nor should people necessarily suggest that media consumption patterns are the "cause" of one candidate winning or losing. Any discussion of media effects must take this selection story into account.

What does the future hold for media's role in American politics? The clearest conclusion is that the role of partisan media will continue, whether it is on TV or on the internet. All available evidence points to declining demand for traditional "non-partisan" media sources. What does this mean for politics? Largely, it suggests that strong partisans will continue to get their news from very different media ecosystems. Insofar as consumption of partisan media entrenches polarized politics, there is no reason to think these trends will reverse in the near future.

The most worrying trend in the modern media environment, however, is the disappearance of local news. While this trend may be hastened by the rise of conglomerate media ownership groups, it is also being exacerbated by regulatory changes that facilitate these changes. Most problematic, though, is that all empirical evidence available points to the fact that consumers are no longer willing to pay enough for local media to sustain it. While there will always be outliers to this situation, the local news industry must deal with the fact that subscriptions are simply not enough. If you are a voter that cares about effective and responsive government, the best thing you can do is continue to support your local news outlets.

Discussion questions

1   What role did national media outlets play in the 2024 election cycle?
2   What are some options for "saving" local news?
3   How does the disappearance of local media affect the behavior of local politicians?
4   Do you agree with the pessimistic conclusion of this chapter? Why or why not?
5   How do your political views affect the type of news media you see and seek out?

References

Abramowitz, Alan I., and Steven Webster. 2016. "The rise of negative partisanship and the nationalization of US elections in the 21st century." *Electoral Studies* 41: 12–22.

Arceneaux, Kevin, and Martin Johnson. 2013. *Changing Minds or Changing Channels?: Partisan News in an Age of Choice*. University of Chicago Press.

Ash, Elliott, Sergio Galletta, Dominik Hangartner, Yotam Margalit, and Matteo Pinna. 2024. "The effect of Fox News on health behavior during COVID-19." *Political Analysis* 32 (2): 275–84.

Ash, Elliott, Sergio Galletta, Matteo Pinna, and Christopher Warshaw. 2022. "The effect of Fox News channel on US elections: 2000–2020." SSRN 3837457.

Atkinson, Claire. 2019. "Sinclair drops Boris Epshteyn and other political analysts." *NBC News* Accessed December 18, 2024. https://www.nbcnews.com/business/business-news/sinclair-drops-boris-epshteynother-political-analysts-n1099796.

Bartels, Larry M. 1993. "Messages received: The political impact of media exposure." *American political science review* 87 (2): 267–85.

Broockman, David E., and Joshua L Kalla. 2025. "Consuming cross-cutting media causes learning and moderates attitudes: A field experiment with Fox News viewers." *The Journal of Politics* 87 (1).

Broockman, David, and Joshua Kalla. 2023. "Selective exposure and partisan echo chambers in television news consumption: Evidence from linked viewership, administrative, and survey data." *OSF Preprints*. April 14.

Darr, Joshua, Matthew Hitt, and Johanna Dunaway. 2018. "Newspaper Closures Polarize Voting Behavior." *Journal of Communication* 68 (6): 1007–28.

Doctor, Ken. 2019. "Newsonomics: The potential GateHouse/Gannett merger shows "more scale!" is still the newspaper industry's top strategy." *Nieman Journalism Lab*. Accessed December 18, 2024. https://www.niemanlab.org/2019/05/newsonomics-the-potential-gatehousegannett-merger-shows-more-scale-is-still-the-newspaper-industrys-real-strategy/.

Fioroni, Sarah. 2022. "Local News Most Trusted in Keeping Americans Informed About Their Communities." *Knight Foundation*. Accessed December 18. 2024.https://knightfoundation.org/articles/local-news-most-trusted-in-keepingamericans-informed-about-their-communities/.

Gao, Pengjie, Chang Lee, and Dermot Murphy. 2020. "Financing dies in darkness? The impact of newspaper closures on public finance." *Journal of Financial Economics* 135 (2): 445–67.

Gentzkow, Matthew, and Jesse M. Shapiro. 2010. "What Drives Media Slant? Evidence From U.S. Daily Newspapers." *Econometrica* 78 (1): 35–71.

Guess, Andrew M. 2021. "(Almost) everything in moderation: new evidence on Americans' online media diets." *American Journal of Political Science* 65 (4): 1007–22.

Hayes, Danny, and Jennifer L. Lawless. 2015. "As Local News Goes, So Goes Citizen Engagement: Media, Knowledge and Participation in US House Elections." *Journal of Politics* 77 (2): 447–62.

Hayes, Danny, and Jennifer Lawless. 2021. *News Hole: The Demise of Local Journalism and Political Engagement*. Cambridge University Press.

Heese, Jonas, Gerardo P´erez-Cavazos, andCaspar David Peter. 2022. "When the local newspaper leaves town: The effects of local newspaper closures on corporate misconduct." *Journal of Financial Economics* 145 (2): 445–63.

Hetherington, Marc J. 2001. "Resurgent mass partisanship: The role of elite polarization." *American political science review* 95 (3): 619–31.

Hopkins, Daniel J. 2018. *The Increasingly United States: How and Why American Political Behavior Nationalized*. University of Chicago Press.

Hopkins, Daniel J., and Tori Gorton. 2024. "Unsubscribed and undemanding: Partisanship and the minimal effects of a field experiment encouraging local news consumption." *American Journal of Political Science.*

Kim, Eunji, and Shawn Patterson Jr. 2024. "The American viewer: political consequences of entertainment media." *American Political Science Review*, 1–15.

Kim, Eunji, Yphtach Lelkes, and Joshua McCrain. 2022. "Measuring dynamic media bias." *Proceedings of the National Academy of Sciences* 119 (32): e2202197119.

Lelkes, Yphtach, Gaurav Sood, and Shanto Iyengar. 2017. "The hostile audience: The effect of access to broadband internet on partisan affect." *American Journal of Political Science* 61 (1): 5–20.

Levendusky, Matthew, and Neil Malhotra. 2016. "Does media coverage of partisan polarization affect political attitudes?" *Political Communication* 33 (2): 283–301.

Levendusky, Matthew S. 2022. "How does local TV news change viewers' attitudes? The case of Sinclair broadcasting." *Political Communication* 39 (1): 23–38.

Lupia, Arthur, and Mathew D. McCubbins. 1998. *The Democratic Dilemma: Can Citizens Learn What They Need to Know?* Cambridge University Press.

Martin, Gregory J., and Ali Yurukoglu. 2017. "Bias in Cable News: Persuasion and Polarization." *American Economic Review* 107 (9): 2565–99.

Martin, Gregory, and Josh McCrain. 2019. "Local News and National Politics." *American Political Science Review* 113 (2): 372–84.

Martin, Gregory, Nicola Mastrorocco, Joshua McCrain, and Arianna Ornaghi. 2024. *Media Consolidation.* Kilts Center at Chicago Booth Marketing Data Center Paper.

Mastrorocco, Nicola, and Arianna Ornaghi. 2022. *DP17756 Who Watches the Watchmen? Local News and Police Behavior in the United States.* Technical report. CEPR Press.

McCrain, Joshua, and Erik Peterson. 2023. "Local elections do not increase local news demand." *Political Science Research and Methods*, 1–11.

Moskowitz, Daniel. 2021. "Local News, Information, and the Nationalization of US Elections." *American Political Science Review* 115 (1): 114–29.

Mullainathan, Sendhil, and Andrei Shleifer. 2005. "The market for news." *American Economic Review* 95 (4): 1031–53.

Peterson, Erik. 2021. "Paper Cuts: How Reporting Resources Affect Political News Coverage." *American Journal of Political Science* 65 (2): 443–59.

Prat, Andrea. 2018. "Media power." *Journal of Political Economy* 126 (4): 1747–83.

Prior, Markus. 2007. *Post-Broadcast Democracy: How media choice increases inequality in political involvement and polarizes elections.* Cambridge University Press.

Skovsgaard, Morten, and Kim Andersen. 2020. "Conceptualizing news avoidance: Towards a shared understanding of different causes and potential solutions." *Journalism Studies* 21 (4): 459–76.

Snyder, James M., and David Stromberg. 2010. "Press Coverage and Political Accountability." *Journal of Political Economy* 118 (2): 355–408.

Törnberg, Petter. 2022. "How digital media drive affective polarization through partisan sorting." *Proceedings of the National Academy of Sciences* 119 (42): e2207159119.

Wittenberg, Chloe, Matthew A Baum, Adam J. Berinsky, Justin de Benedictis-Kessner, and Teppei Yamamoto. 2023. "Media Measurement Matters: Estimating the Persuasive Effects of Partisan Media with Survey and Behavioral Data." *The Journal of Politics* 85 (4): 1275–90.

Zaller, John. 1992. *The Nature and Origins of Mass Opinion.* Cambridge University Press.

Zerba, Amy. 2011. "Young adults' reasons behind avoidances of daily print newspapers and their ideas for change." *Journalism & Mass Communication Quarterly* 88 (3): 597–614.

Teena Wilhelm

14 Redefining Reproductive Rights: Policy Evolution from *Roe* to *Dobbs*

14.1 Introduction

The politics of "reproductive rights" refers to the political debate surrounding the legality, accessibility, and moral implications of (primarily) abortion.[1] Although not limited to the United States, the politics of reproduction are a deeply polarizing topic in contemporary American society. While the issue involves legal and health-related considerations, it also involves ideological and ethical considerations. The issue reflects a tension between individual rights and societal values. It is both a prominent and divisive issue in American politics.

Reproductive rights in the United States are shaped by legal decisions, congressional and state legislative policies, partisan platforms, and interest group perspectives. Given the alignment of the issue with political parties, reproductive politics can directly affect elections, judicial appointments, and legislative priorities at both state and federal levels. An extensive network of activists, advocacy groups, and nonprofits exist that lobby policymakers, educate the public, and mobilize citizens to support their positions on the issue.

Despite the intensity of the issue, reproductive rights have not always been a fault line in American politics. In fact, throughout most of American history, the abortion procedure itself was not politicized. Prior to the late 1900s, the American electorate did not sort itself based on support for abortion, and neither party viewed the issue as defining. To understand how reproductive rights became one of the most highly salient issues in American politics, it is important to consider the history of abortion law in the United States and those factors that shifted political discourse around the issue.

---

1 Abortion is defined as the termination of a pregnancy, whether through inducement (pharmacological or surgical) or spontaneous, also known as miscarriage. See https://www.oxfordbibliog raphies.com/display/document/obo-9780199756797/obo-9780199756797-0090.xml?rskey=tygpVh&re sult=1

Teena Wilhelm, University of Georgia

https://doi.org/10.1515/9783111591902-014

14.2 History of Abortion Law in the US

Prior to 1840, the choice to have an abortion was a "widespread, largely stigma-free experience for American women" (Holland n.d.). The abortion timetable was measured by quickening, which is the point in the pregnancy when a pregnant woman can feel the fetus move. Abortions after quickening were criminalized only as misdemeanor offenses, and there were few prosecutions. Given all this, abortion access was best classified as discreet but legal throughout most of early American history.

By 1900, a physician-led anti-abortion movement began that was primarily concerned with regulation of the medical procedure. The movement also responded to cultural concerns over increasing education, rights, and general autonomy of women (Mohr 1979). As a result of the movement, every state had a law forbidding abortion by the early 1900s with exceptions to preserve the life of the mother. Over the next sixty years, abortion access through medical channels was dictated by physician discretion, but a sizeable black market for the procedure was also created.

In the 1960s, an abortion reform movement began that coincided with a larger cultural shift in attitudes about reproductive rights. The reform movement was partly motivated by medical concerns. The 1960s were marked by higher infant mortality and fetal deformity across both Europe and the United States, due in part to the side effects of a widely used sleeping pill, Thalidomide, and an outbreak of German measles that resulted in many stillbirths and babies born with major abnormalities (Reagan 2010). The American Law Institute created model legislation in 1959 that advocated for abortion reform to include exceptions for women that were rape victims, whose fetuses were deformed, or who were at risk for mental or physical health issues. Another motivation was an emerging feminist sentiment which argued that women should control their own reproductive healthcare. These combined forces pushed some state legislatures to reform abortion laws. By 1971, five states had legalized abortion on demand while fourteen others allowed it under certain circumstances (Holland 2020). The genesis of the modern anti-abortion political movement was also born during this time, when a consortium of Catholic professionals and housewives emerged with a "right-to-life" argument to push back on abortion reforms (Holland 2020).

While the abortion issue was inarguably becoming more salient in the late 1960s and early 1970s, it was not measurably divisive. The Catholic church opposed abortion, but it was generally not an issue that resonated with religious voters. Moreover, there were not obvious partisan differences in opinions about abortion at the time.[2]

14.3 Reproductive Rights become Political

In the 1970s and 1980s, several historical developments were instrumental as the abortion issue evolved from a non-politicized medical procedure to a polarizing focal point about reproductive rights in American politics. These include the U.S. Supreme Court's decision in *Roe v. Wade* (1973),[3] the emergence of the New Right in conservative politics, and the partisan response to the reproductive rights platform that forced politicians and voters to pick sides.

14.3.1 Roe v. Wade

Roe v. Wade involved a challenge to a restrictive law in Texas that made it a criminal offense to perform or attempt to perform an abortion, with the singular exception of saving the life of a pregnant woman. In its decision, the Court overturned the Texas law and recognized more broadly the concept of a constitutional right to privacy that gave protection for a woman's right to choose abortion. Two things about the Court's legal analysis were most significant.

First, while the Court asserted that a right to privacy existed in the Constitution, it acknowledged that this right was *implied* rather than explicitly mentioned in the text. Justice Blackmun's majority opinion reasoned:

> *This right of privacy, whether it be founded in the Fourteenth Amendment's concept of personal liberty and restrictions upon state action, as we feel it is, or, as the District Court determined, in the Ninth Amendment's reservation of rights to the people, is broad enough to encompass a woman's decision whether to terminate her pregnancy.*[4]

Second, the Court recognized that a woman's right to choose to have an abortion would have to be balanced against the interests of the government to protect maternal health and unborn life.

---

2 For example, consider bipartisan Congressional voting on HR15580 in 1974 that prohibited public spending on abortion. The voting breakdown can be found at https://voteview.com/rollcall/RH0930783
3 Roe v. Wade, 410 U.S. 113 (1973).
4 *Roe*, 410 U.S. at 153.

> *A State may properly assert important interests in safeguarding health, maintaining medical standards, and in protecting potential life. At some point in pregnancy, these respective interests become sufficiently compelling to sustain regulation of the factors that govern the abortion decision. . . . We, therefore, conclude that the right of personal privacy includes the abortion decision, but that this right is not unqualified and must be considered against important state interests in regulation.*[5]

When would a state's interests outweigh a woman's ability to choose abortion without restriction? To address this timetable, the Court created a trimester regulatory framework. In its simplest form, the framework allowed little regulation in the first trimester and regulation in the second semester only to protect maternal health. In the third trimester, which the Court identified as the point of "viability" (when life could be maintained outside the womb), the Court reasoned that the state's interest was most compelling and therefore legal prohibitions were allowed except where necessary to protect maternal health.

Political reaction to the Court's decision was not immediate. Even though the decision overturned abortion laws in forty-five states, most Americans in the immediate aftermath were preoccupied with other political issues such as the ending of the Vietnam War or the Watergate scandal. Reaction to the Court's decision had little, if any impact on the 1974 midterm elections or the 1976 presidential election. Moreover, the platforms of both political parties acknowledged the division of opinion about abortion within their own ranks (Elvin 2022). Betty Ford, wife of Republican president Gerald Ford, remarked on the program *60 Minutes* in 1975 that *Roe v. Wade* was a "great, great decision" (Bonk 2024). Meanwhile, a young Democratic Senator named Joe Biden gave an interview in 1974 in which he claimed "I don't like the Supreme Court decision on abortion. I think it went too far" (Kelley 1974, n.p.).

Beyond political parties, pro-life and pro-choice activists did not cease efforts to identify areas of agreement after the Court's decision. In fact, some evidence suggests that *Roe* intensified the dialogue for compromise on both sides, even though profound division both predated and remained after (Ziegler 2014). For these reasons, *Roe v. Wade* is best understood for its part in the eventual politicization of the abortion issue rather than activating an immediate political backlash. The decision established the legal parameters of abortion in a right to privacy, and over time became a symbol for social-movement strategy and Supreme Court politics.

---

5 *Roe*, 410 U.S. at 154.

14.3.2 The New (Religious) Right

If *Roe v. Wade* did not escalate conflict around reproductive rights with immediacy, there were forces outside the Court's decision that did. According to historian Mary Ziegler, some "movement members, politicians, and political operatives" created political strategy that "*deliberately* and *consistently* . . . intensified abortion conflict" during the late 1970s (2014, 1005). Even though abortion policy was not a significant concern for most voters at the time, there were some who understood the potential electoral consequences of mobilization around the issue. For these prescient individuals, abortion policy presented a strategic political opportunity.

Who were these strategists that intensified conflict around the abortion issue? Leaders of an emerging political movement known as the "New Right" saw abortion as a promising wedge issue to draw voters that conventionally voted with Democrats into the Republican fold. The New Right movement began as a response to perceived excesses of the liberalism of the 1960s. It emphasized traditional conservative values and was conceived as the voice of a silent "moral majority" of Americans who deserved a political voice. Leaders of the movement saw the potential for a formidable voting bloc in white evangelicals who might share their political vision but who had largely been absent from American politics as an organized group. New Right leaders understood that activating this group would require a rallying cause and chose the abortion issue for this purpose.

While the pro-life movement may be synonymous with evangelicals today, this was not the case prior to 1980. Evangelicals were largely indifferent, considering abortion primarily a "Catholic issue." In 1968, the magazine *Christianity Today* cited justifications for abortion that included "health, family welfare, and social responsibility." According to Balmer (2014), delegates to the Southern Baptist Convention in 1971 passed a resolution encouraging its members to work for legislation that supported abortion. This position was reaffirmed after the passage of *Roe*, in 1974 and 1976.

To encourage (and create) evangelical opposition to abortion, New Right strategists produced a series of films with graphic representations of abortion and abortion imagery. They orchestrated an evangelical-targeted film tour in early 1979 that largely succeeded in mobilizing anti-abortion sentiment in places where it did not exist, as well as strengthening it in places where it did. Beyond films, the group used direct mailings and promoted the anti-abortion message with radio and television sermons. As a result, the Southern Baptist Convention reversed its position and passed a resolution that opposed abortion less than one year later (Sullivan 2022). Leaders of the New Right also helped fund new pro-life organizations and a pro-life political action committee that "worked to put abortion at the top of the national political agenda" (Ziegler 2014, p. 1007). Finally, they communicated to Republican political hopefuls that commitments to pro-life voters would bring them a large and energetic share of the electorate.

The successful wedge-issue strategy of the New Right pushed the abortion issue into mainstream politics, and evangelicals were mobilized to vote for pro-life candidates in 1980. In this way, conservative evangelicals saw a stark difference between the Democratic incumbent Jimmy Carter, who refused to support a constitutional amendment to overturn *Roe*, and Republican candidate Ronald Reagan, who campaigned as a pro-life resolute.[6] At this time, the pro-life movement itself became decidedly conservative, political, and allied with the Republican Party. This did not mean that all Republican voters cared equally about abortion, but those who prioritized the issue found support in the Republican platform.

14.3.3 Parties and Politicians Pick Sides, and Voters Follow

As the anti-abortion movement began to coalesce on the Right, activists also began to push the Democratic Party towards a platform that embraced reproductive rights, and women's rights more generally. Polarization of the parties on gender issues was both rapid and dramatic during the 1970s (Wolbrecht 2000). For feminist advocates, reproductive rights overlapped with workplace equity and equal protection before the law. Leaders within the Coalition for Women's Rights were successful in securing planks at the 1980 Democratic convention that supported ratification of the Equal Rights Amendment (ERA) and opposed a constitutional amendment to ban abortion (Rosenfeld 2017). Further, groups like *NARAL Pro-Choice America* and *Planned Parenthood* aligned with Democrats, and the party increasingly identified itself as the party defending abortion rights. Democratic strategists used this to appeal to women and young voters who were concerned about protecting reproductive rights.

But even as advocates mobilized around reproductive rights and influenced party platforms, most voters did not think of abortion as an important problem facing the nation in the 1980s, and opinion on abortion did not sort around party lines (Granberg and Burleson 1983). The prominence of reproductive rights as a

---

6 To be fair, fundamentalist Cristian voters were also discouraged by Carter's decision to withdraw tax-exempt status from segregated church schools, as well as Supreme Court decisions to ban school prayer.

political division within the electorate happened quite gradually, and only after polarization in the parties forced politicians to choose sides.

As the 1980s gave way to the 1990s, activists within both parties required loyalty for their respective platforms, and fewer "pro-choice Republicans" or "pro-life Democrats" survived in prominent roles in the parties. In this climate, political candidates found it increasingly necessary to align with one side or the other. Republican George H.W. Bush, an earlier supporter of abortion rights, won the presidency in 1988 as an abortion opponent. In 1992 he was defeated by Democrat Bill Clinton, an abortion rights supporter who had been opposed to abortion earlier in his career. Clinton campaigned on "safe, legal, and rare" abortions in an appeal to moderate swing voters while maintaining support from pro-choice Democrats. Beyond the presidency, the elite polarization occurred in Congress as well. Over 80 percent of Democrats voted pro-choice on abortion disputes by the mid-1990s with the same percentage of Republicans voting pro-life (Adams 1997).

Polarization of the issue shaped the judicial branch as well, as both parties recognized the Supreme Court's pivotal role in shaping reproductive rights. Judicial appointment and confirmation hearings began to reflect this strategy. Despite conservative appointments by Reagan and Bush, the Court's decision in *Planned Parenthood v. Casey* (1992)[7] upheld the constitutionality of abortion rights and was a significant affirmation for pro-choice activists. However, the decision also allowed states to restrict abortion as long as restrictions did not place an "undue burden" on women seeking the procedure. The decision mobilized anti-abortion activists to push for state-level regulations and abortion-rights activists to resist their efforts.

Public discourse was shaped by the abortion issue during the 1990s too. The debate over reproductive rights became a cultural flashpoint, discussed in the media and movies. Issues like "partial birth abortion" brought intense public debate and legislative battles.[8] Pro-life groups like Operation Rescue and the Christian Coalition made protests outside abortion clinics common, and "Marches for Women's Lives" drew attention to abortion rights. Violence at abortion clinics, including arson, firebombing, and the murder of abortion doctors, also brought national attention to abortion issue extremists (Miller 2024). As activism intensified, legislative battles and judicial rulings became more high-profile, in both Congress and the states.

---

7 505 U.S. 833,1991.

8 The reference to "partial birth abortion" is not medical terminology. Rather, it refers to a rare form of late-term abortion that is done in the case of severe fetal abnormalities or serious risk to a woman's health. The language choice was intentionally graphic and used by anti-abortion groups as a debate framing strategy.

As reproductive rights polarized parties, political elites, and public dialogue, voters gradually sorted over the issue. There were stark divides in this sorting based on geography, religion, gender, and party affiliation. By the early 2000s, the issue was no longer a policy debate. Instead, position-taking on abortion itself had become synonymous with cultural and political identity (Hout et al. 2022).

14.4 Abortion and the 2016 Election

Abortion was an important issue during U.S. presidential elections between 2000 and 2012, but it was not particularly salient for presidential campaigns.[9] The winning candidates, George W. Bush (2000 and 2004) and Barack Obama (2008 and 2012), delivered traditional party verbiage in their platforms, as did their opponents. This changed in 2016, as escalating political and cultural battles over reproductive rights and the future of the Supreme Court resulted in provocative differences between the campaign platforms of Donald Trump and Hillary Clinton.

Several reasons help explain why abortion politics took center stage in the 2016 presidential election. The most significant is that the election represented the opportunity to change the composition of the U.S. Supreme Court, which was closely divided on support for the constitutionality of abortion rights. The Court had become increasingly conservative in the last decade and had experienced an unexpected vacancy during the election cycle with the death of Justice Antonin Scalia. This, combined with potential departures in the next four years, heightened electoral stakes.

A second reason is that while both candidates framed their positions on judicial nominations as critical for the future of abortion access, Trump accentuated the issue. Beyond his promise to appoint justices that would overturn *Roe v. Wade*, he used rhetoric that described abortions with vivid and inflammatory language and remarked that women who had abortions "should face some sort of punishment" (Krieg 2016). He also promised to defund Planned Parenthood unless it ceased providing abortion services. This was a particularly salient point for many Republicans, following intense efforts to curb the organization after controversial (and later discredited) videos surfaced in 2015 that claimed the organiza-

---

9 There is an argument to be made that abortion was salient in 2012 U.S. presidential campaigning. A key difference between 2012 and 2016, however, is that both Barack Obama and Mitt Romney made concerted efforts in their campaign dialogue to side with their respective base voters without alienating minority viewpoints in their parties. See https://www.npr.org/sections/health-shots/2012/11/05/164185767/why-abortion-has-become-such-a-prominent-campaign-issue

tion profited from the sale of fetal tissue (Ludden 2015). Clinton continued to argue that the organization was a vital provider of women's healthcare services. Her overall messaging defended *Roe v. Wade* and emphasized personal choice.

Finally, by 2016 many Republican-controlled states had enacted abortion restrictions that included mandatory waiting periods and ultrasound requirements. Many abortion clinics had closed due to stringent regulations about provider qualifications to the point that some states only had one single clinic. In this climate, the importance of the Supreme Court for abortion access was reaffirmed in June 2016 when a restrictive Texas law was struck down in *Whole Woman's Health v. Hellerstedt.*[10] The decision motivated activists on both sides to invest heavily in the campaigns of both candidates.

The abortion issue became an important driver of turnout in the 2016 presidential election, especially for social conservatives and progressive, pro-choice voters (Aldrich et al. 2019). Many voters prioritized the future of the Supreme Court and made abortion a crucial factor in their decision-making.[11] Beyond the campaigns, the 2016 election also had a lasting impact on abortion policy itself. After assuming office, Trump fulfilled his promise to appoint judicial candidates that would overturn *Roe v. Wade*. His appointment of three Supreme Court justices over the course of his first term shifted the overall ideological balance of the Court and impacted reproductive rights almost immediately. Specifically, the conservative majority on the Court had the opportunity to revisit the constitutionality of abortion itself.

14.5 Reproductive Rights Upended

In 2022, nearly fifty years after the U.S. Supreme Court's landmark decision in *Roe v. Wade*, the court reversed itself on the constitutionality of abortion rights in *Dobbs v. Jackson Women's Health Organization* (2022).[12] In its decision, the Court upheld a Mississippi law that made abortions illegal after fifteen weeks (previability). In doing so, a five-person majority found that there was no Constitutional protection for abortion, thereby overturning the central holding of *Roe* and

---

10 597 U.S. 582 (2016).
11 See polling results at https://www.pewresearch.org/politics/2016/07/07/4-top-voting-issues-in-2016-election/
12 597 U.S. 215 (2022).

Planned Parenthood v. Casey.[13] Justice Alito's majority opinion held, "The Constitution makes no reference to abortion, and no such right is implicitly protected by any constitutional provision."[14] The majority decision also emphasized that states should make final decisions about abortion policy, thereby recognizing that states could regulate abortion or prevent it entirely without federal or judicial interference.

The *Dobbs* decision was a watershed moment in American law. It also reshaped the landscape of reproductive rights across the country. In many Republican-led states, "trigger laws" existed that pre-dated the *Dobbs* decision, intended to ban abortion entirely if the Supreme Court limited or overturned *Roe*. Once this happened, abortion bans went into effect immediately in these states. Similarly, some Democratic-led states immediately passed laws or constitutional amendments to protect abortion rights.

Unlike the prominent but cursory media coverage of the *Roe* decision, the American public was inundated with news about *Dobbs* before and after the Court's opinion was formally released. Abortion politics dominated the news cycle in an unprecedented way in June 2022.[15] Public reaction to the Court's decision was largely negative. Opinion polls suggested that anywhere between 56 and 63 percent of Americans disagreed with the decision to overturn *Roe* (Norrander and Wilcox 2023). Perhaps more instructive, public opinion polling found that institutional trust in the Court declined as much as twenty-two points, from 68 percent in 2019 to 46 percent after the *Dobbs* decision.[16]

14.6 Reproductive Rights Today

The status of reproductive rights today is best analyzed by examining the post-*Dobbs* policy environment across the states. Here I include analysis of abortion access across the states, legislative and electoral action undertaken in the states,

---

13 While the Mississippi law was upheld by a 6 to 3 majority, Chief Justice Roberts declined to join the majority opinion that overturned *Roe v. Wade*. Instead, Roberts wrote a concurring opinion that agreed with the decision outcome but not with the Court's reasoning.

14 *Dobbs*, 597 U.S. 215 (2022).

15 At the time, a Pew Research Center survey found that 60 percent of respondents indicated that they heard "a lot" about the decision, with another 31 percent indicating they heard "a little," and only 3 percent saying they heard "nothing at all." See Norrander and Wilcox (2023).

16 AIOD Survey, May and August 2024, Annenburg Public Policy Center, https://www.annenberg publicpolicycenter.org/trust-in-us-supreme-court-continues-to-sink/

and reproductive healthcare issues beyond abortion impacted by state policy responses to *Dobbs*.

14.6.1 Geographic Disparities in Abortion Access

The Supreme Court recognized in *Dobbs* that states could regulate abortion without federal constitutional protection for reproductive rights. This means that states may pass abortion laws with whatever level of protection or restriction is deemed appropriate by their legislature or electorate. Like other policy areas in which states have primary authority such as minimum wage laws, death penalty sentencing, and legalization of marijuana, abortion access in the post-*Dobbs* environment is currently dependent on location. As illustrated in Figure 14.1, abortion is not accessible or nearly inaccessible in much of the South and Midwest but available in much of the West and Northeast. Table 14.1 describes the status of abortion access in each state. Currently, nineteen states restrict abortion before viability, and the remaining thirty-one states permit abortion to the point of viability or beyond.

14.6.2 Legislative and Electoral Responses to Dobbs

Since *Dobbs* was handed down in June 2022, twenty-three state legislatures have tried to implement abortion regulation that is more restrictive than the *Roe* viability timetable. While these attempts have largely succeeded, litigation has blocked some attempts, including challenges to "heartbeat bills" and bans with no exceptions for rape or incest.[17] Beyond action by state legislatures, several unsuccessful ballot measures have also attempted to restrict abortion access. Voters in Kentucky and Kansas rejected a constitutional amendment that would deny constitutional protection for abortion in 2022. That same year, voters in Montana rejected LR-131, an initiative known as the "Born-Alive Infant Protection Act" that had previously failed in the state legislature.[18]

State legislatures have also acted to protect reproductive rights in the years since the *Dobbs* decision. Table 14.2 summarizes these actions. Since 2022, fifteen

---

17 "Heartbeat bills" are laws that prohibit abortions once a fetal heartbeat can be detected. They often do not make exceptions for rape or incest but may allow exceptions for medical emergencies. States with current (2024) enforced "Heartbeat bills" are Texas, Ohio, and Georgia.
18 See https://ballotpedia.org/Montana_LR-131,_Medical_Care_Requirements_for_Born-Alive_Infants_Measure_(2022)

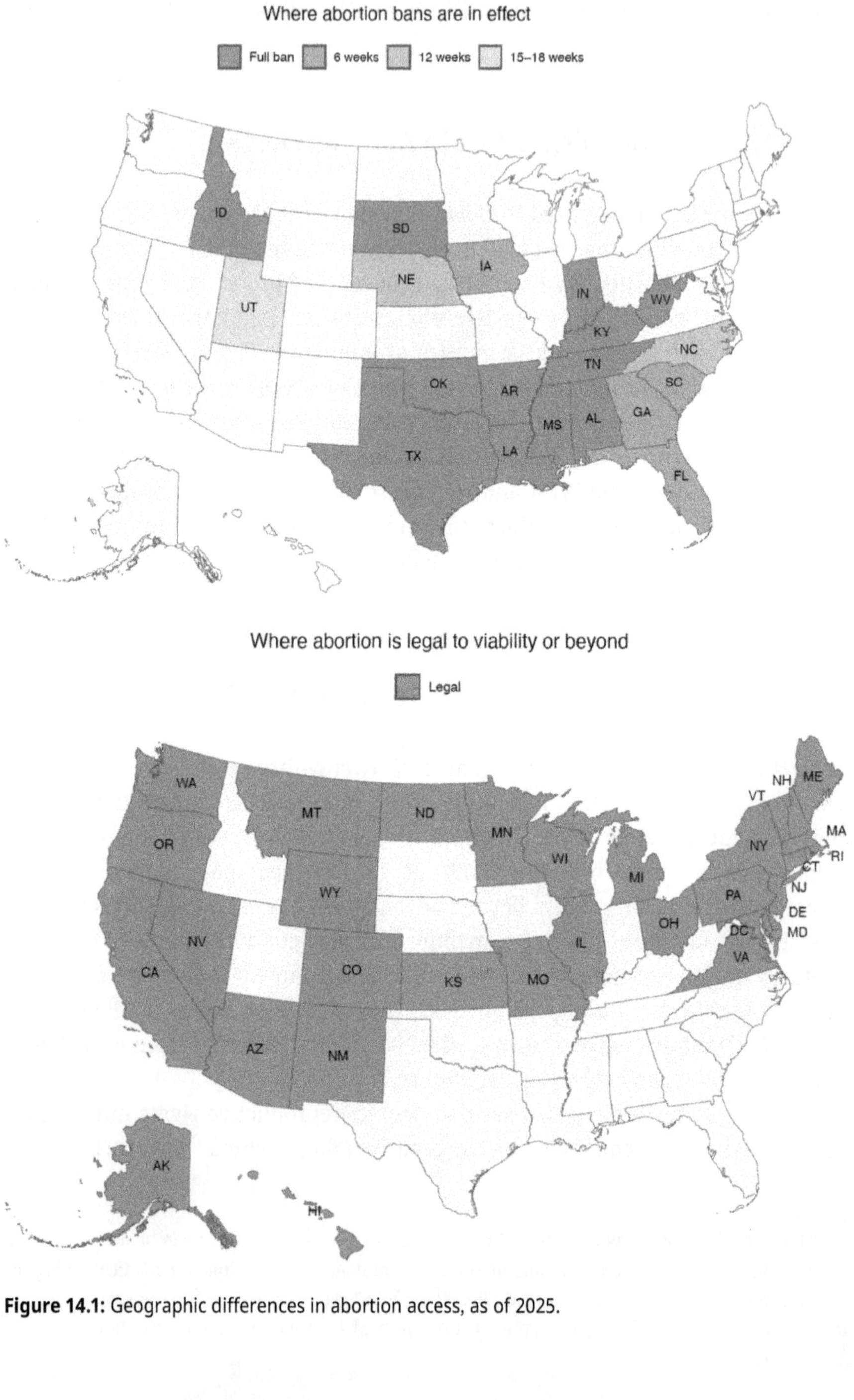
Where abortion bans are in effect
Full ban
6 weeks
12 weeks
15–18 weeks
ID
SD
NE
IA
UT
IN
WV
KY
NC
TN
OK
AR
SC
GA
MS
AL
TX
LA
FL
Where abortion is legal to viability or beyond
Legal
WA
MT
ND
MN
OR
WI
MI
WY
NV
CA
CO
KS
MO
IL
OH
PA
NY
VT
NH
ME
MA
RI
CT
NJ
DE
MD
DC
VA
AZ
NM
AK
HI

Figure 14.1: Geographic differences in abortion access, as of 2025.

Table 14.1: Post-*Dobbs* status of state abortion access.

States where abortion is legal to viability (or beyond)		States with total or pre-viability ban			
		Total Ban	6 weeks	12 weeks	18 weeks
AK	ND	AL	FL	NC	UT*
AZ	NH	AR	GA	NE	
CA	NJ	ID	IA		
CO	NM	IN	SD		
CT	NV	KY			
DE	NY	LA			
HI	OH	MS			
IL	OR	OK			
KS	PA	TN			
MA	RI	TX			
MD	VA	SD			
ME	VT	WV			
MI	WA				
MN	WI				
MO	WY*				
MT					

Source: Abortion in the United States Dashboard, KFF November 6, 2024,
https://www.kff.org/womens-health-policy/dashboard/abortion-in-the-u-s-dash
board/ and Center for Reproductive Rights.
*State abortion ban currently blocked by courts.

states have passed abortion "shield laws" designed to protect individuals and organizations involved in abortion services. More specifically, these laws offer civil and criminal prosecution protection for abortion providers and can prevent extradition of providers to a state where abortion is prosecuted. They can also protect out-of-state patients who travel for abortions from prosecution and may give protection to networks that assist and offer support to individuals to access abortion services. Such laws are intended to counter the effects of restrictive abortion laws in other states and protect the constitutional right to interstate travel for medical care. Beyond shield laws, states have also passed laws that lower barriers to abortion access or expand state health funds to cover abortion.[19]

Protection for reproductive rights has also been accomplished by direct electoral action. In eleven states, protections for reproductive rights have been added

---

19 These include Rhode Island's expansion of Medicaid and state health insurance in 2023, Minnesota's repealing of restrictions in 2023, and Michigan's "Reproductive Health Act" passed in 2024. See Crowley (2024).

Table 14.2: Post-*Dobbs* abortion-related legislative and electoral actions.

"Shield Laws"	Ballot Measures to Protect Abortion Access		Ballot Measures to Restrict Abortion Access	
CA	CA	Passed 2022	KS	Defeated 2022
CO	MI	Passed 2022	KY	Defeated 2022
CT	VT	Passed 2022	MT	Defeated 2022
DE	OH	Passed 2023	NE	Passed 2024
HI	AZ	Passed 2024		
IL	CO	Passed 2024		
ME	FL	Defeated 2024		
MA	MD	Passed 2024		
NV	MO	Passed 2024		
NM	MT	Passed 2024		
NY	NE	Defeated 2024		
OR	NV	Passed 2024		
PA*	NY	Passed 2024		
VT	SD	Defeated 2024		
WA				

Source: After Roe Fell, Abortion Laws by State, Center for Reproductive Rights, https://reproductive rights.org/maps/abortion-laws-by-state/, excludes state "trigger" laws and other legislative action to restrict abortion right.
*.Action taken by Executive Order.

to the state constitution through the ballot initiative process. While most of these amendments were passed in states where abortions were legal, ballot measures in Ohio, Arizona, and Missouri overturned existing pre-viability bans previously adopted by their state legislature. Similar initiatives were defeated in Florida, Nebraska, and South Dakota. In two years since the *Dobbs* decision, a total of eighteen abortion-related measures have appeared on ballots: six in 2022, one in 2023, and eleven in 2024. Fourteen have offered increased protection for reproductive rights, and four proposed increased limits. Of those that enhanced protections for abortion, most were successful (eleven of fourteen). Of those that increased limits, most were defeated (three of four).[20]

14.6.3 Beyond Abortion

While the primary impact of the *Dobbs* decision relates to abortion rights and access, it is nonetheless true that there are broader healthcare implications. In an

---

20 See https://ballotpedia.org/2023_and_2024_abortion-related_ballot_measures

analysis of public health impacts, Manian (2023) reveals several areas of reproductive healthcare that have been impacted by the *Dobbs* decision. The first is contraception. While emergency contraceptives (EC) and intrauterine devices (IUDs) work to prevent pregnancy, many people (including state lawmakers) mistakenly believe that they work to end pregnancy. Given this, the wording of abortion bans in some states may be used to limit contraceptives. For example, Texas law currently excludes emergency contraceptives from its Medicaid-funded family planning program. Additionally, the University of Idaho complied with its state abortion ban by discontinuing birth control medication access in student health care, and dispensing condoms only for prevention of disease transmission, not birth control (Durkee 2022).

Fertility treatments including in vitro fertilization (IVF) have also been impacted by state laws that define personhood as beginning at fertilization, as these can be construed to limit such reproductive technology. The most high-profile example of this occurred in Alabama in 2024, when the Alabama Supreme Court ruled that embryos created through IVF should be considered "unborn children" for the purposes of civil liability under Alabama's wrongful death statute.[21] The practical impact of the decision is that it would allow legal action to be taken against physicians who performed IVF procedures. The Alabama legislature took narrow action to protect physicians, but several of the state's IVF clinics paused services and have not resumed them.

Women have also faced increased difficulty when trying to access pregnancy-related medical care in states where abortion access is severely limited. Miscarriage management and ectopic pregnancy treatment are two conditions that require medical intervention during pregnancy. State laws were passed in Texas and Louisiana to limit access to mifepristone, one of two drugs approved by the FDA for medication abortion, which have impacted treatment of miscarriage management and ectopic pregnancy (Arey et al. 2022). When access to mifepristone is limited or delayed, other medications must be used, which can lead to higher rates of incomplete miscarriage that require additional medical intervention. Specifically, delays in accessing mifepristone have been shown to prolong the emotional and physical toll of miscarriage treatment, and in some cases necessitate surgical intervention.

---

21 *Lepage v. The Ctr. for Reprod. Med.*, No. SC-2022–0515 (Ala. May. 3, 2024)

14.7 Conclusion

The politics of reproductive rights have been said to represent a "clash of absolutes" with no room for compromise (Tribe 1992). As this chapter has illustrated, opinions about reproductive rights and abortion have evolved into a sorting mechanism for American political identity, with individuals belonging to one side (pro-life) or the other (pro-choice). Abortion became contentious in American politics over time, as interest groups and political parties made a concerted effort to shape public opinion on the issue. Advocacy efforts resulted in the constitutional recognition of reproductive rights, and the eventual overturning of that recognition nearly fifty years later.

While analysis of historical events and policy developments certainly demonstrates polarization around reproductive rights, it is worth considering the extent to which American public opinion is truly divided. Surprisingly, there is less disagreement than contemporary politics suggests. Instead, polling consistently demonstrates that most Americans agree that abortion itself should be legal. Figure 14.2 shows trends in public opinion over time. As the graph shows, support for overturning *Roe* has generally decreased over time, and hovered below or around 30 percent since 1990. Support for keeping *Roe* has gradually increased over time, with public support around 60 percent at the time of the *Dobbs* decision. As a general trend, a stable majority of Americans have favored keeping the protections for abortion rights offered by *Roe* since the decision was handed down.

Given this, it is not surprising that *Dobbs* has increased momentum for abortion-related ballot initiatives. Ballot measures in 2022 were the most in a single year until 2024, when that total nearly doubled. Moreover, citizen-led activity has been primarily aimed at expanding reproductive rights. This is important to consider since state legislatures have been as consequential for restricting reproductive rights as expanding them. It is also important to consider that protecting abortion access is popular in most states where the issue appears on the ballot—including those with recent legislative activity restricting abortion. Even in Florida, where the ballot measure to protect reproductive rights was defeated, a majority of voters (57.17 percent) approved the measure.[22]

The success of abortion-related ballot measures suggests that protection for reproductive rights may depend more on citizen-initiated policy change than legislative action in the future. Ultimately, public opinion may be more consequential for deciding the abortion issue than ever before. If this results in a policy en-

---

22 See https://ballotpedia.org/Florida_Amendment_4,_Right_to_Abortion_Initiative_(2024). State constitutional changes in Florida require a 60 percent supermajority approval of voters.

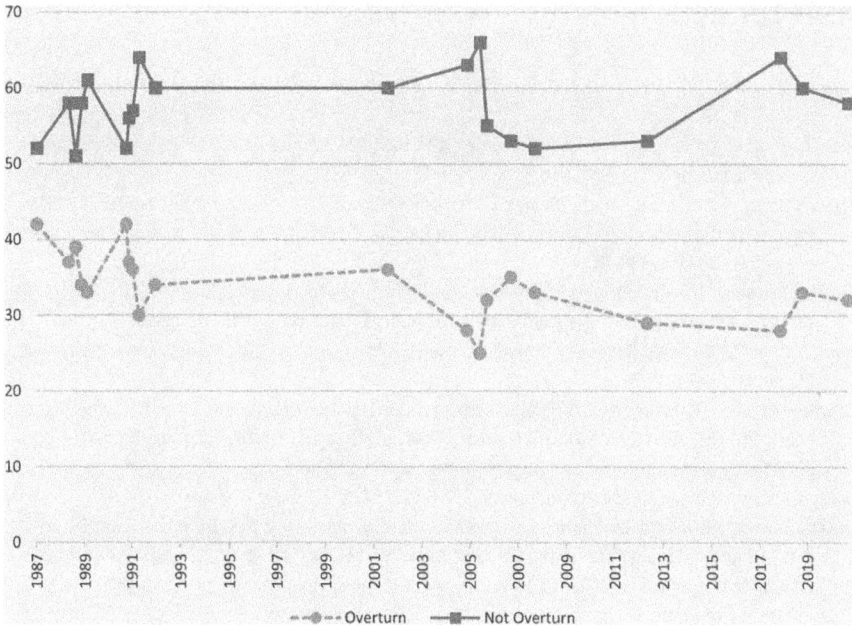

Figure 14.2: Approval of *Roe v. Wade*, Gallup Polls 1987–2019.
Source: Norrander and Wilcox (2023).

vironment where activists, politicians, and judges play a less significant role in abortion policy, it does beg an important question: Will reproductive rights become less "political" if American citizens take a leading role?

Discussion Questions
1   What is meant by "reproductive rights" and "abortion politics"?
2   What is the legal foundation for the *Roe v. Wade* decision?
3   What forces shaped the partisan divide on reproductive rights?
4   Why was abortion a prominent issue in the 2016 presidential election?
5   What healthcare issues are impacted by the *Dobbs* decision other than abortion?

References

Adams, Greg D. 1997. "Abortion: Evidence of an Issue Evolution." *American Journal of Political Science* 41 (3): 718–737.

Aldrich, John H., Jamie L. Carson, Brad T. Gomez, and David W. Rohde. 2019. *Change and Continuity in the 2016 Elections*. CQ Press/Sage.

Arey, Whitney, KlairaLerma, AnitraBeasley, LorieHarper, GhazalehMoayedi, and KariWhite. 2022. "A Preview of the Dangerous Future of Abortion Bans — Texas Senate Bill 8." *New England Journal of Medicine* 387 (5): 388–90.

Balmer. Randall. "The Real Origins of the Religious Right." *Politico Magazine*. May 27, 2014. https://www.politico.com/magazine/story/2014/05/religious-right-real-origins-107133/.

Bonk, Kathy. "Celebrating First Lady Betty Ford and Her Work for the Equal Rights Amendment." *Ms. Magazine*. April 4, 2024.

Crowley, Kinsey. "Two years ago, SCOTUS overturned the right to an abortion. Here is how each state changed." *USA TODAY*, June 23, 2024. https://www.usatoday.com/story/news/politics/2024/06/23/state-by-state-abortion-laws-dobbs-anniversary/73769814007/.

Dobbs v. Jackson Women's Health Organization, 597 U.S. 215 (2022).

Durkee, Alison. "University Of Idaho Says New Abortion Guidance Isn't That Different From Before — But Faculty Could Still Face Criminal Prosecution." *Forbes*. October 6, 2022. https://www.forbes.com/sites/alisondurkee/2022/10/06/university-of-idaho-says-new-abortion-guidance-isnt-that-different-from-before—but-faculty-could-still-face-criminal-prosecution/?sh=1c79b2003b04.

Elving, Ron. "The leaked abortion decision blew up overnight. In 1973, Roe had a longer fuse." National Public Radio (NPR). May 8, 2022. https://www.npr.org/2022/05/08/1097118409/the-leaked-abortion-decision-blew-up-overnight-in-1973-roe-had-a-longer-fuse.

Granberg, Donald, and James Burlison. 1983. "The Abortion issue in the 1980 Elections." *Family Planning Perspectives* 15 (5): 231–38.

Holland, Jennifer. "Abolishing Abortion: The History of the Pro-Life Movement in America." *The American Historian: The Politics of Motherhood*. November 2024. https://www.oah.org/tah/november-3/abolishing-abortion-the-history-of-the-pro-life-movement-in-america/.

Holland, Jennifer. 2020. *Tiny You: A Western History of the Anti-abortion Movement*. University of California Press.

Hout, Michael, Stuart Perrett, and Sarah K. Cowan. 2022."Stasis and Sorting of Americans' Abortion Opinions: Political Polarization Added to Religious and Other Differences." *Socius*, 8.

Kelley, Kitty. "Death and the All-American Boy." *Washingtonian*. June 1, 1974. https://www.washingtonian.com/1974/06/01/joe-biden-kitty-kelley-1974-profile-death-and-the-all-american-boy/.

Krieg, Greg. "Donald Trump's 3 Abortion Positions in 3 Hours." *CNN Politics*. March 31, 2016. https://www.cnn.com/2016/03/30/politics/donald-trump-abortion-positions/index.html.

Ludden, Jennifer. "Undercover Video Targets Planned Parenthood." *National Public Radio (NPR)*. July 15, 2015. https://www.npr.org/sections/thetwo-way/2015/07/15/423212004/undercover-video-targets-planned-parenthood.

Manian, Maya. 2023. "The Impact of *Dobbs* on Health Care Beyond Wanted Abortion Care." *Journal of Law, Medicine & Ethics* 51 (3): 592–600.

Miller, Cassie. "The Violent History of the Anti-Abortion Movement." *Southern Poverty Law Center*. June 13, 2024. https://www.splcenter.org/anti-abortion-movement/violent-history.

Mohr, James C. 1979. *Abortion in America: The Origins and Evolutions of National Policy, 1800–1900*. Oxford University Press.

Norrander, Barbara, and Clyde Wilcox. 2023. "Trends in Abortion Attitudes: From *Roe* to *Dobbs*."
Public Opinion Quarterly 87 (2): 427–58.

Reagan, Leslie. 2010. *Dangerous Pregnancies: Mothers, Disabilities, and Abortion in Modern America*.
University of California Press.

Planned Parenthood of Southeastern Pennsylvania v. Casey, 505 U.S. 831 (1991).

Roe v. Wade, 410 U.S. 113 (1973).

Rosenfeld, Sam. 2017. *The Polarizers: Postwar Architects of Our Partisan Era*. University of Chicago
Press.

Sullivan, Andy. "Explainer: How Abortion Became a Divisive Issue in U.S. Politics." *Reuters*. June 24,
2022. https://www.reuters.com/world/us/how-abortion-became-divisive-issue-us-politics-2022-
06-24/.

Tribe, Lawrence. 1992. *Abortion: The Clash of Absolutes*. W. W. Norton.

Whole Woman's Health v. Hellerstedt, 579 U.S. 582 (2016).

Wolbrecht, Christine. 2000. *The Politics of Women's Rights: Parties, Positions, and Change*. Princeton
University Press.

Ziegler, Mary. 2014. "Beyond Backlash: Legal History, Polarization, and *Roe v. Wade*." *Washington and
Lee Law Review* 71 (2): 969–1021. https://scholarlycommons.law.wlu.edu/cgi/viewcontent.cgi?arti
cle=4395&context=wlulr.

James N. Druckman and Dot Sawler

15 Democratic Backsliding in the United States

A purpose of government is to provide public goods such as roads, schools, a military, health care, clean air, and more. But how should governments decide which and how many of these goods to provide? In a democracy, such decisions ideally reflect citizens' preferences. Of course, what "democracy" entails is contested and ranges from a minimal requirement of regularly scheduled competitive elections to deliberative forums where randomly selected citizens inform policy decisions. All modern variants of democracy, though, involve delegation (e.g., from voters to representatives, from representatives to bureaucrats) and coordination (e.g., on how to transfer power, distribute knowledge). Democracy is unimaginable without some division of labor across "experts" and widespread agreement to respect that expertise. For example, legislators create laws, the executive implements laws and oversees the military, the judiciary interprets laws, scientists produce new technologies, educators teach young citizens, the media reports on politics and society, and so on.

This reality requires formal institutions that establish entities charged with administering governance (Ostrom 1990) as well as informal institutions or norms where members of a polity coordinate on expected behaviors (Weingast 1997). In this chapter, we explore the status of formal institutions and norms in the United States. We do so with the goal of providing insight into contemporary American democracy.

Evaluating institutions and norms can be done in a variety of ways. For example, one can assess over-time trends as to whether they move in a normatively desirable or undesirable direction. This is the approach we take in our evaluation of formal institutions such as the press, the military, and the Supreme Court. Alternatively, one can investigate the level of an outcome or behavior that is preferred relative to another outcome or behavior that is less optimal. We take this approach in evaluating norms, specifically studying whether citizens support norms long seen as democratic (preferred) or personal/partisan goals regardless of whether they are democratic (not preferred). Our choice of evaluative ap-

Note: The authors contributed equally to this chapter. We thank Jamie Carson and Ryan Williamson for very helpful comments, and Jonathan Schulman for graciously generating the figures.

James N. Druckman, Dot Sawler, University of Rochester

https://doi.org/10.1515/9783111591902-015

proach is driven partially by data availability. Even so, as will become clear, American democracy is clearly at a point of stress when it comes to trust and norms.

This kind of stress is referred to as "democratic backsliding," or the process by which institutions and norms conducive to a well-functioning democracy erode and produce conditions ripe for authoritarian elites to behave undemocratically. To demonstrate this, we present a framework for conceptualizing the process of democratic backsliding. We provide some examples of how citizens' levels of trust in institutions and discoordination on norms offer elites leeway for non-democratic power grabs—that is, actions that violate laws or norms so as to accumulate power (e.g., ignoring court rulings, limiting voting, censoring media). We additionally discuss the emergent cleavage over democratic institutions and how this divide has come to shape American politics.

15.1 Trust In Formal Institutions

Formal institutions include actors governed by a set of rules (Crawford and Ostrom 1995). In the U.S., the most prominent institutions are the branches of government (i.e., political institutions) including the executive/president, Congress, and the judiciary. Functioning democracy, however, requires more, including economic institutions (e.g., banks, labor, companies), knowledge institutions (e.g., science, education, the press), and norm-enforcement institutions (e.g., military, police, religion) (Brady and Kent 2022).

These different kinds of institutions provide services and goods to citizens, and thus in essence function only if citizens trust them. *"Trust exists when one party to the relation believes the other party has incentive to act in his or her interest or to take his or her interests to heart . . . we trust you because we think you take our interests to heart and encapsulate our interests as your own"* (Cook et al. 2005, 2, 5, italics in the original; also see, e.g., Coleman 1990; Cook 2001; Hardin 2002). When people lack trust in an institution, they will be less likely to rely upon it. For instance, they will not consume material from entities that produce information such as scientific and educational organizations; they will be less likely to support the allocation of resources to institutions that provide order such as the military and police; and they will be less likely to rely on organizations that stabilize the economy such as banks. Carson and Williamson explain in Chapter 1 that "the erosion of public trust in political institutions [is] a fundamental pillar of democracy in any setting."

To be clear, blind trust is also problematic. Nonetheless, low trust creates two potential problems. First, if trust is too low, then the predictability provided by these entities is challenged and chaos can ensue. For instance, when people reject scientific advice, it can cause a public health crisis; when they refuse to delegate to law enforcement, it can result in perpetual crime and vigilantism; and when they distrust electoral institutions, it can undermine participation (see King's chapter). In Figure 15.1, we display trends in trust in institutions with data from the General Social Survey, which has regularly asked, since 1973: "I am going to name some institutions in this country. As far as the people running these institutions are concerned, would you say you have a great deal of confidence, only some confidence, or hardly any confidence at all in them?" The question is followed by the names of the institutions listed in Figure 15.1, which divides up political institutions, economic institutions, knowledge institutions, and norm-enforcement institutions (Brady and Kent 2022).[1] Overall, the picture is one of decline. We see sizeable drops in trust in banks and financial institutions, education, the press, medicine, and organized religion. The only institution with some increase in trust is the military; the others either stay flat or decline somewhat.

Second, if trust in institutions divides along party lines such that Democrats have high (low) trust and Republicans have low (high) trust, it can create coordination problems. Political parties are involved in governance, which requires coordination; if they cannot agree on which institutions to rely and/or to invest in, then public policy radically shifts each time a new party gains power. Investment in education, science, or the military goes up and down, creating instability, or economic and communication regulation becomes inconsistent, making it difficult for actors to adapt. As Carson and Williamson discussed in Chapter 1, when trust polarizes, "Essential policy areas including education, healthcare, and infrastructure are caught in ideological battles, where pragmatic decision-making takes a backseat to partisan agenda." In Figure 15.2, we present polarization in trust in institutions over time. The x-axis shows time. The y-axis is the difference between the percentage of Democrats who express "a great deal" of confidence in the institution minus the percent of Republicans who express "a great deal" of confidence.[2] If trust is not polarized—that is, if Democrats and Republicans equally (dis)trust an institution—over time, then the line should hover around 0. When it is above (below) 0, it means Democrats (Republicans) exhibit more trust.

---

1 On the low score of Congress, see the chapter by Williamson and Windham. We do not include the executive in the figure as that largely is a proxy for partisanship such that trust depends largely on whichever party controls the presidency.
2 We include independents who lean toward the Democratic or Republican party as partisans.

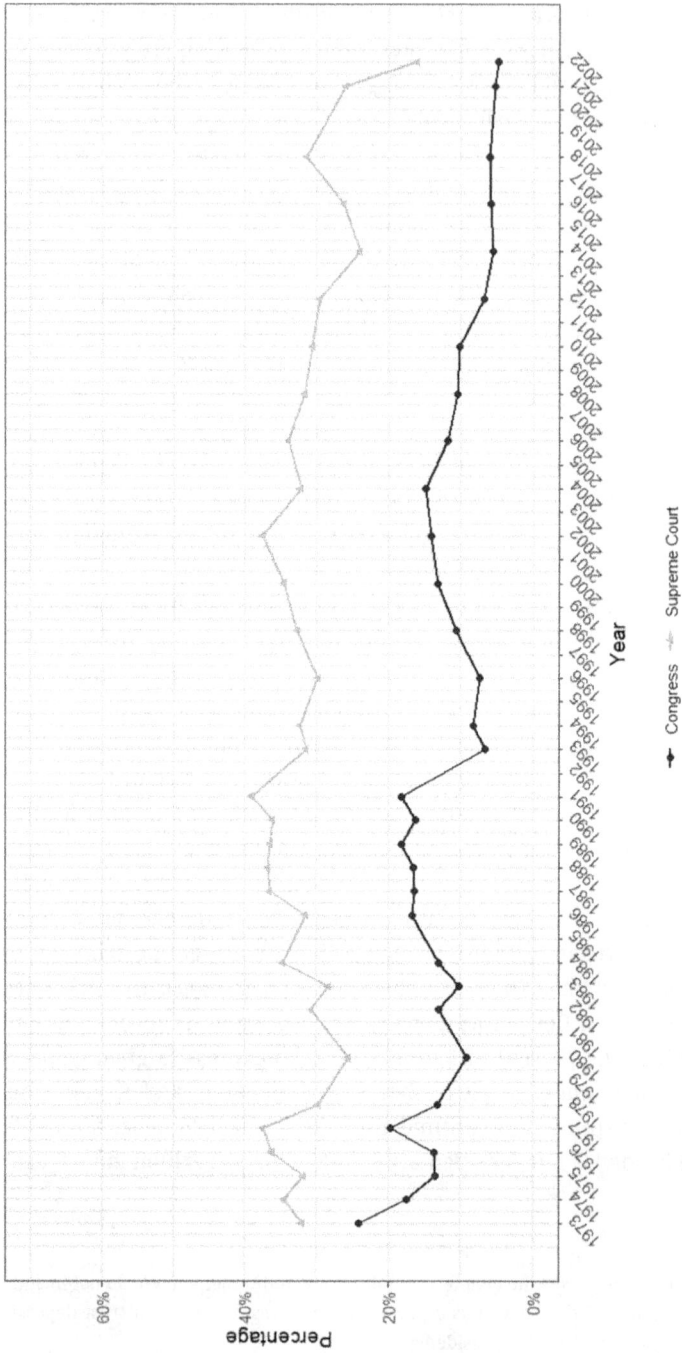

Figure 15.1: Confidence in institutions over time.

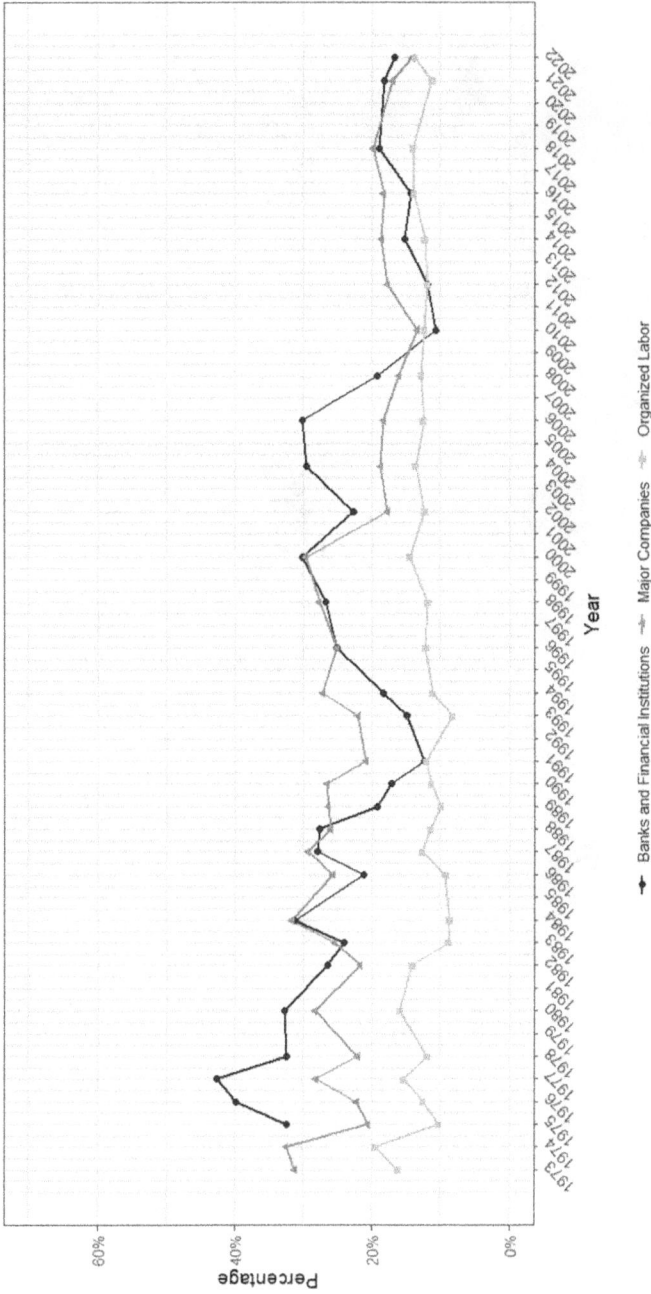

Figure 15.1 (continued)

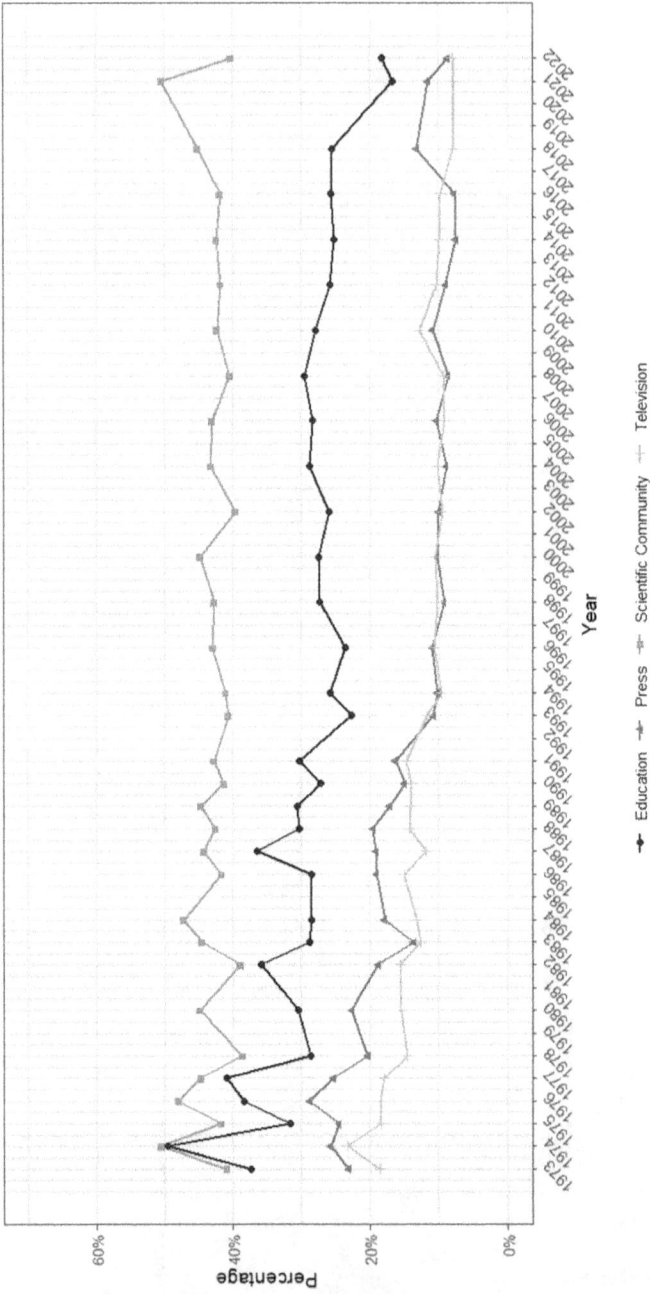

Figure 15.1 (continued)

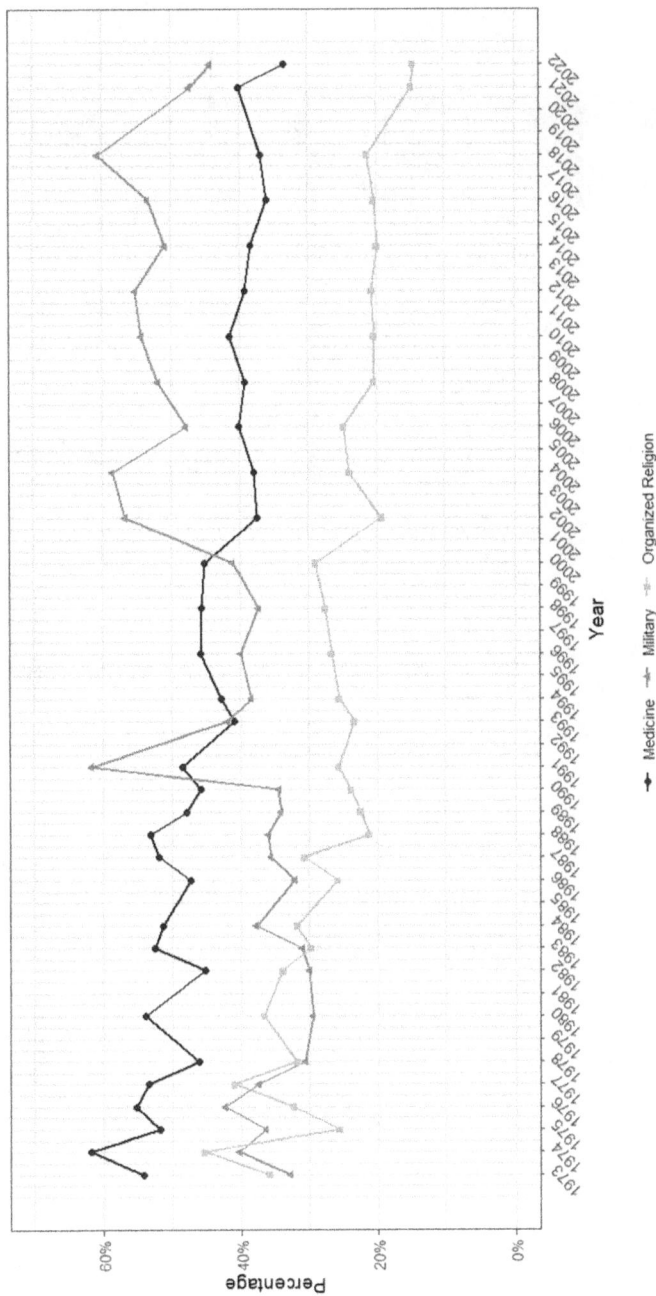

Figure 15.1 (continued)

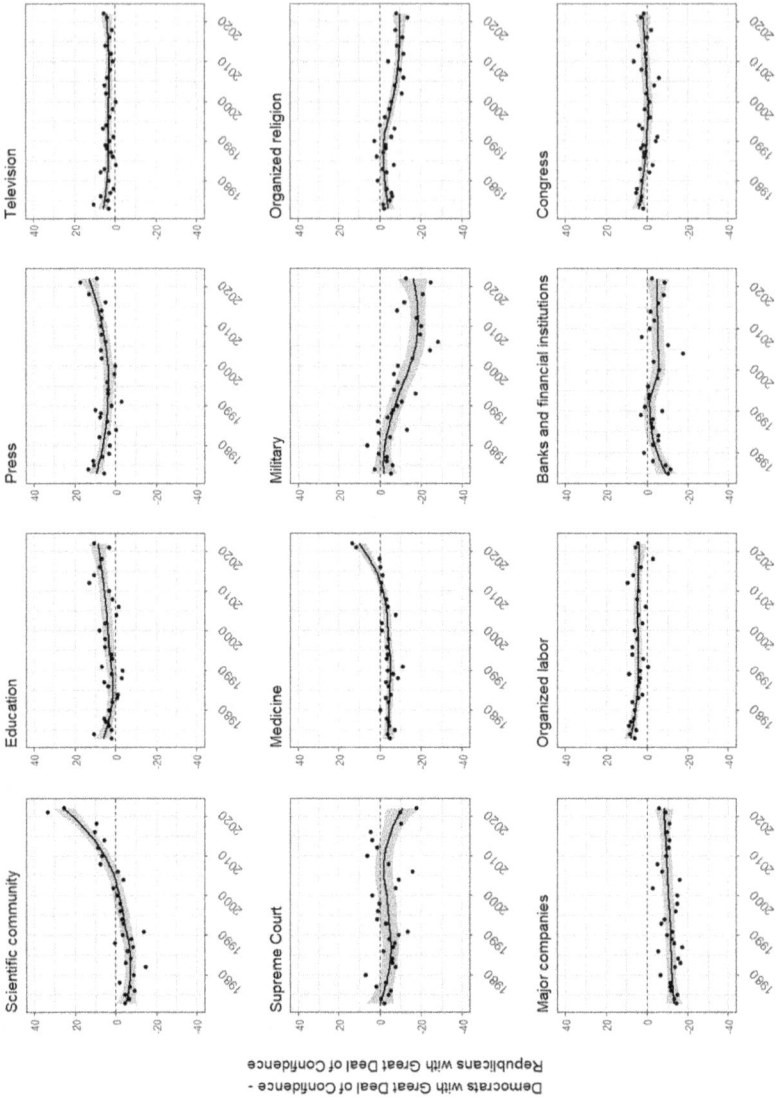

Figure 15.2: Partisan gaps in confidence in institutions over time.

The results show increased over-time polarization when it comes to a large number of institutions (even some that showed stability in trust in Figure 15.1), including the scientific community, education, the press, the Supreme Court, medicine, the military, and organized religion. The only institutions that show signs of depolarization are banks and financial institutions. These trends present a challenge to democracy: lower and/or polarized trust means that undemocratic elites could leverage the situation to obtain power for themselves—such as when populists leaders seek to move power away from institutions toward themselves. Keefer et al. (2021, 253–254) explain that "Populist leaders attempt to undermine the influence of institutions that aggregate individual demands and to identify themselves as the authentic and sole interpreters of popular will . . . Leaders who are not bound by institutions are free to execute government polices unconstrained by law."

In the U.S., President Donald J. Trump engaged in such tactics. Examples include intentionally undermining the legitimacy of the 2020 Presidential Election, reprogramming Department of Defense funding to build a wall on the southern border after failing to persuade Congress to appropriate more funds to the project, unilaterally appropriating additional Department of Defense funding to send aid to Ukraine, disallowing executive branch employees from testifying during his impeachment investigation, calling for the Attorney General to indict former-President Obama and former Vice President Joe Biden, threatening to use the presidential pardon to pardon himself if convicted of a crime, and calling on the military to remove peaceful protestors from Lafayette Square in Washington D.C. (Pfiffner 2022).

15.2 Coordinating on Democratic Norms

Governance, and more generally societal functioning, also requires coordination on informal institutions or norms. These are not written into constitutions or laws and do not involve organizations (such as the entities discussed above) per se (Gretchen and Helmke 2025). Instead, they govern:

> how citizens interact with one another and with the community's symbols and institutions. Such norms translate abstract and contested democratic values—like equality and reciprocity—into useable ethical guidance (Chapman 2020). They also enable citizens to coordinate in sanctioning antidemocratic behavior. Because of the role of norms in coordinating behavior amid uncertainty and disagreement, we have reasons for complying with a democratic norm even when we believe it ought not exist. Transgressing democratic norms, therefore, typically requires justification . . . (Chapman 2024, 148).

For instance, norms work to limit executive power by normalizing practices where the executive respects checks from other institutions (e.g., courts, the media), and does not challenge the transfer of power after an election (Levitsky and Ziblatt 2018; Carey et al. 2019; Lieberman et al. 2019; Graham and Svolik 2020; Ahmed 2023). Norms encompass what Levitsky and Ziblatt (2018) term *forbearance*: restraint when a leader has the legal right to do something but precedent suggests they should not. Forbearance acts, in effect, as a self-imposed limit on power, reflecting the fact that norms, unlike laws, depend on actors voluntarily agreeing to abide by them. Crucially, norms require that individuals follow practices even when they are counter to their short-term self-interest (Weingast 1997).

Identifying the full set of relevant norms that sustain democratic contestation and participation (Helmke and Levitsky 2004) is nearly impossible. Carey et al. (2019, 700) explain, "the potential set of rights and principles a political leader might violate is vast." While the most notable include free and fair elections, power transition, civil liberty protections, and expansive voting rights and representation, this is far from complete.[3] Two primary threats to the maintenance of norms are the privileging of partisan or policy position over democratic norms, and misperceptions that others will not abide by the norm.

Graham and Svolik's (2020) study exemplifies the former, focusing on voting for candidates who violate norms (also see Voelkel et al. 2024). They present a nationally representative sample of Americans with the opportunity to choose between candidates who are randomly assigned issue positions, including positions that violate democratic norms (concerning free and fair elections, civil liberties, and checks and balances). Support for democracy is measured by whether the respondents opt for the pro-democracy candidates. The authors find that "just over 10 percent of Americans value democracy enough to punish an otherwise-favored candidate for violating a democratic principle by voting against him" (Graham and Svolik 2020, 399). In short, partisans prefer candidates from their own party even if they violate democratic norms (also see Kalmoe and Mason 2022 on partisan violence). In a similar experiment, Gidengil et al. (2022) show that voters are willing to support candidates who would weaken legislative and judicial checks on the executive if the candidate shares their position on abortion (also see, e.g., Albertus and Grossman 2021; Sasmaz et al. 2022, Simonovits et al. 2022, Chiopris et al. 2023; Touchton et al. 2023).

---

3 Carey et al. (2019) provide a substantial list that includes seven elements: elections, voting, rights, protections, accountability, institutions, and discourse. They also suggest that the public and experts differ on the importance of various principles for democracy.

Voters might even rationalize what they view as democratic, perceiving typical policies with which they disagree (e.g., proposing to increase everyone's taxes to spend more on unemployment benefits) as more undemocratic than objective democratic transgressions where they agree with the policy (e.g., reduce everyone's taxes and spend less on unemployment benefits and prohibit all labor union leaders from running for Congress for ten years) (Krishnarajan 2023). This suggests conditions ripe for citizens misconstruing violations of democratic norms (also see Carey et al. 2022).[4] All of this evidence suggests citizens prioritize their short-term interests (or preferences) over longer-term political/democratic stability, which potentially opens the door to democratic backsliding.

The second challenge involves misperceiving what others, particularly those from the other side of the political aisle, might do. Norms depend on expectations of what is desirable or common. For instance, partisans may be less likely to vote for an anti-democratic candidate from their party if they know members of the other party would never do so either—as all benefit in the long term from democracy. Yet, if they believe the members of the other party will elect a non-democratic leader, then there is an incentive to do so first (i.e., it is better to have an authoritarian on one's side rather than the other). The consequence is the devaluation of democratic norms.

It turns out that partisans exhibit notable misperceptions of out-partisans. Generally, they view those from the other side as more ideologically extreme and engaged (Druckman et al. 2022), more prejudiced (Moore-Berg et al. 2020), more obstructionist (Lees and Cikara 2020), and more demographically stereotypical (Ahler and Sood 2018; Busby et al. 2021) than they are. More directly, partisans vastly misperceive the anti-democratic attitudes of out-partisans. Braley et al. (2023) find that partisans, on average, view members of the other side as being "probably" or "definitely" likely to violate more than five of seven democratic norms (e.g., ignoring controversial court rulings by judges from the other party, reducing polling stations in towns that support the other party), even though the actual average is approximately 1.35 of seven (across parties) (also see Pasek et al. 2022). The same exaggeration manifests regarding support for partisan violence, a clear violation of a norm (i.e., support for violence differs from illegally engaging in violence). Mernyk et al. (2022) report that partisans overestimate the average amount of support for partisan violence by out-partisans by between 245 percent

---

[4] That said, there are limits, as Frederiksen (2022) shows that voters do not blindly accept anti-democratic behavior. They punish in-party candidates as much as other candidates for behaving undemocratically, and they punish candidates with whom they agree on policy more than candidates with whom they disagree (even if they may end up voting for anti-democratic candidates from their party).

and 442 percent. Moreover, there exist significant relationships between these misperceptions and attitudes. Partisans' own anti-democratic attitudes and their own support for partisan violence are correlated with their perceptions of how members of the other party would act. Thus, misperceptions directly lead to anti-democratic and violent attitudes.[5]

Some work suggests that one can correct misperceptions and thus temper anti-democratic attitudes and support for partisan violence (e.g., Lees and Cikara 2020; Ruggeri et al. 2021). Yet, the robustness of these corrections is unclear (Dias et al. 2024). Druckman (2023) shows that correcting misperceptions of the out-party's propensity to behave anti-democratically does work but that when partisans are presented with competing information corrections, they choose to believe the worst about members of the other party. Thus, providing accurate information does not robustly reduce support for undemocratic practices or partisan violence.

Just as fractures in institutional trust provide leeway for authoritative elites, so does the decay of norms. Trump again provides an example—a longstanding norm in the United States is the endorsement of participatory inclusiveness such that voting should be made as easy as possible. Yet, Trump's own rhetoric led his supporters to dismiss this norm (Hall and Druckman 2023). Moreover, being exposed to claims of election fraud contributed to Republican Trump voters doubting that their 2020 vote was counted fairly and also prompted them to question electoral responsiveness and democracy overall (Justwan and Williamson 2022). Trump and his allies leveraged these beliefs about participation, responsiveness, and democracy to equate expanding voting access (e.g., early voting, drop boxes) with electoral fraud. Without norms of respect for the election process, autocratic action became possible.

15.3 Autocratic Elites

We have intimated various ways in which the trust and norms trends can influence democracy. Here, we offer a more explicit argument. Like other longstanding democracies, the central question for the U.S. is whether and/or the extent to which democracy is eroding. Druckman (2024) explains that identifying

---

5 A tangential question is whether affective polarization or partisan animosity (i.e., dislike of the other party) relates to anti-democratic attitudes or support for partisan violence. The evidence is ambiguous (e.g., Kingzette et al. 2021; Broockman et al. 2023; Voelkel et al. 2023, 2024; Druckman et al. 2024; Holliday et al. 2024). On the relationship with trust in the branches of government, see Nicholson and Lamberth's chapter.

cases of backsliding means isolating how a particular behavior by a specific actor renders the polity less democratic (i.e., less contestable, less inclusive in terms of participation).

With this in mind, we operationalize backsliding with a two-by-two framework, as displayed in Table 15.1. The rows refer to types of damage to democracy from an action—these also can be thought of as faster (hard) or slower (soft) ways to erode democracy. In each case, the act undermines contestation and/or inclusiveness/access. For instance, voter fraud, violence, and executive aggrandizement limit contestation, as does distrust in institutions that otherwise ensure varied perspectives and ideas. Many norm violations affect inclusiveness since they often involve restricting voting access (gerrymandering, fewer polling places, etc.).

The columns differentiate institutional actions, typically by elites, from attitudinal dynamics, which often come from citizens.[6] The fast actions mean a relatively quick change in regime type; the fast institutional cell captures many historic regime changes that are much less likely in contemporary times (Levitsky and Ziblatt 2018). The more proximate reasons for erosion, today, are slower institutional devolutions where elites accumulate power over time (the slow/institutional cell). As Bartels (2023) states, democracy erodes from the top (also see Bermeo 2016; Druckman et al. 2023; Hopkins 2023). Most of our discussion has centered on citizens' attitudes including distrust in institutions and opposition to democratic norms. These feed into elite-driven erosion because citizens' beliefs provide the opportunity or leeway for erosive elites to act (i.e., the attitudinal actions lead to the institutional ones).

To see how this might work, consider how low trust and polarized trust in institutions (slow/attitudinal cell) can normalize destabilizing behaviors such as ignoring public health guidance during the COVID-19 pandemic (Druckman et al. 2024) and launching an insurrection on January 6 (Baum et al. 2024b). Cleavages over how the polity should operate emerge, leading to the politicization of institutions. This dynamic can be seen in the U.S. with media (Shultziner and Stukalin 2021; Broockman and Kalla 2024), education (Oretega 2020; Safarpour et al. 2024),

---

6 Druckman (2024) points to the role of social movements in democratic erosion; these are not explicitly part of the framework we present although they could be incorporated. For examples of scholarship on each respective cell, see for the hard/institutional case: Mechkova et al. (2017), and Pérez-Liñán, Schmidt, and Vairo (2019); for the soft/institutional case: Bermeo (2016), Kaufman and Haggard (2019), and Gidengil et al. (2022); for the hard/attitudinal case, Graham and Svolik (2020), Janssen and Turkenburg (2024), Wunsch, Jacob, and Derksen (2022); and for the soft attitudinal case, Foa and Mounk (2017), Braley et al. (2023), Fossati et al. (2022), and Krishnarajan (2023).

Table 15.1: Democratic backsliding processes.

	Institutional (Elites)	Attitudinal (Citizens)
Hard (fast)	Civil wars, military coups, election-day voter fraud	Support for political violence (anticipatory or reciprocal), voting for anti-democratic candidates
Soft (slow)	Court packing, executive aggrandizement, strategic voter repression	Distrust in institutions, opposition to democratic norms, tolerance of undemocratic behavior by others

science (Druckman and Shulman 2024; Schulman et al. n.d.), health (Gadarian et al. 2022; Druckman et al. 2024), elections (Stewart 2022; Cohen and Sheagley 2024), police (Donahue 2023; Kent 2023), and more. The guardrails that supposedly stabilize the scope of conflict (contestation) become the topics of conflict themselves. Instead of institutions working for the public good they become partisan tools, providing leeway for authoritarian elites. Examples of democratically-elected leaders pursuing strategies that highlight distrust as a rationale to increase executive power and weaken legislatures, judiciaries, and professional bureaucracies (i.e., eroding democracy) include Viktor Orban in Hungary, and Recep Erdogan in Turkey; Benjamin Netanyahu in Israel, who worked to weaken judicial checks and balances; Emanuel Macron in France who bypassed parliament to push though his pension reform; and Boris Johnson in the UK with his prorogation of Parliament. And, as discussed, Donald Trump via his assertion of executive control over the judiciary and professional bureaucracies and refusal to accept an electoral loss. Here, soft threat attitudes become causes of institutional erosion (by elites).

Similarly, leaders exploit norm discoordination to accumulate power. For example, Helmke et al. (2021) show that when coordination on informal norms breaks down (i.e., citizens disagree on what norms should be followed), politicians use legal loopholes to benefit their party, which could contribute to democratic erosion. The authors show that in the U.S., democratic norms about electoral rules collapse if specific social groups are asymmetrically advantaged by their demise and those groups sort into a particular party (which then has the incentive to abandon the norm). In the U.S., the Republican party benefited from devolved electoral norms and thus engaged in legally permissible, but norm-violating, partisan gerrymandering (due to non-urban voters benefiting and becoming relatively Republican) and voter suppression (due to non-Black voters benefiting and becoming relatively Republican) (also see Grumbach 2022, 2023).

Moreover, rational authoritarian-leaning elites can manipulate what citizens view as the status quo to grab power (e.g., Luo and Przeworski 2023). Grillo and

Pratto (2023) show that if an extreme politician with anti-democratic inclinations wins office but then does not act as undemocratically as citizens expected, pro-democracy voters will offer support, ironically, because the incumbent is ostensibly more democratic than anticipated. The politician wins office and can violate laws, norms, and/or ideals or take power-consolidating actions to some extent but not enough that it will lead to an electoral loss. Erosion occurs gradually as the status quo expectation shifts to become less and less democratic. Put another way, elected officials exploit the shifting expectations among voters by slowly moving the point of reference to more undemocratic scenarios (i.e., changing what is democratically acceptable), and then citizens accept increasingly undemocratic behaviors. This can be seen in the U.S. where disagreement about the appropriate levels of censorship of hate speech (Solomon et al. 2024) enabled politicians to demand educational institutions, which are historically independent, police speech in ways that cohere with their partisan leanings (Knott 2024).

A similar trend can be found in education funding that historically has not been contingent on partisan politics. Barrett et al. (2023) find that Republican-controlled states cut higher education funding at much higher rates than would be expected based on macroeconomic conditions. The authors (2022, 797) conclude this as "declining state appropriations to higher education in Republican-controlled U.S. states as an instance of democratic backsliding, meaning the process by which elected partisans seek to destabilize independent institutions in order to increase the likelihood that they remain in power."

The hope is that there will be some electoral accountability for leaders who engage in erosive behavior. Yet, in an age of polarized trust and norm devolution, that does not seem to be the case. For instance, Holliday et al. (2024) show even though citizens in their data exhibit a relatively stable commitment to democratic norms, elites can engage in backsliding regardless of where the public stands. In fact, Bartels and Carnes (2023) find that Republican members of Congress who endorsed conspiracies that the 2020 election was stolen suffered little or no electoral penalty in contested elections and were even more likely to win primaries and run unopposed in general elections (also see Baum et al. 2024a).

In sum, when trust in formal institutions and/or coordination on informal norms break down, it provides elites with leeway to accumulate power. If all elites were committed to democracy, this may not be a problem, but the reality is that absent constraint, an authoritarian often finds a way to gain power.

15.4 Trust in Institutions, Democratic Norms, and Autocratic Elites

In this section, we draw on the ideas put forth so far to assess the contemporary state of American politics. Our starting point is that a new crucial divide in American politics is (dis)trust in institutions. We demonstrated earlier that trust in several institutions has polarized over time. The partisan nature of that trust varies depending on the institution. However, when it comes to government agencies specifically—such as the CDC, postal service, FBI, Federal Reserve, and the like—Democrats consistently exhibit more trust than Republicans. In fact, across thirteen government entities, Democrats have more confidence than Republicans in all but one (i.e., U.S. armed forces) (Guirgis and Blank 2022). This reflects a partisan divide in beliefs about the integrity and capability of governmental institutions (i.e., Democrats, relative to Republicans, view institutions as being more able to address problems and as being more efficient) (e.g., Doherty, Kiley, and Asheer 2024). Roughly, Republicans emphasize the need to change institutions, the lack of efficiency and inadequate outcomes/delivery, and the plight of constituencies that claim to be ill-served (e.g., regulated business sector, young men).[7] In contrast, Democrats tend to focus more on protecting institutions, producing policies and processes, and supporting those who work within the institutions (e.g., educated government employees). Even so, President Joe Biden's (end of term) pardon of his son Hunter Biden may indicate the exact type of norm devaluation process we discussed earlier—when one side anticipates that the other side is not following norms, they stop following them as well.

This has become an acute cleavage for a variety of reasons. First, policies that should, in theory, produce beneficial outcomes have not been maintained or updated due to polarization. For example, Mettler (2016) illustrates how education policy (e.g., student loans) have failed to evolve with the population due, in part, to polarized parties that cannot compromise. She concludes that "citizens may be aware that the federal government aims to promote educational opportunity, but also that many students leave college with high student loan debt and without degrees. In turn, this may engender a sense that government is largely ineffective in this domain and that tax dollars devoted to it are wasted . . . the deferred maintenance of the policyscape may weaken the bonds between citizens and government" (n.p.). Put another way, the inability to produce outcomes diminishes trust. Mettler demonstrates that these types of policy challenges exist across sa-

---

7 This divide produced the ostensibly awkward coalition in the 2024 election with conservative institutionalists such as Dick Cheney and Liz Cheney supporting Democrat Kamala Harris.

lient policy areas including immigration, transportation, the environment, race relations, and more. Second, the legal environment has led to many lawsuits against institutions, making them risk averse when it comes to change. Third, hiring in the institutions has long been merit-based, since the passage of the 1883 Pendleton Civil Service Act. Yet, the merit-based system did not account for structural inequities; consequently, Democrats embraced diversity considerations, that, in turn, led to calls of politicalization with Republicans advocating for the Dismantle DEI (Diversity, Equity, and Inclusion) Act of 2024 that eliminates federal funding and support for any DEI initiatives in agencies or contractors. Now, workers in institutions have become virtual pawns in a politicized battle between the parties.

The divide in fundamental institutions has come to reflect both partisan battles that have made it difficult for the institutions to deliver and cultural divides over how institutions should operate. The events of the twenty-first century reflect and contributed to these dynamics including the endless wars in Iraq and Afghanistan after 9/11, the Great Recession, COVID-19 and debates about lockdowns, a spike in crime (and gun purchasing), the Black Lives Matter (BLM) protests, and more. These events intersect with a fractured media environment, fastmoving demographic change, and hot-button social cleavages (e.g., abortion, transgender rights) to create a democratic tinderbox. It is here where a partisan asymmetry is apparent. While one could critique the left for failing to reform institutions to address contemporary ills (e.g., crime in Democratic cities), it is Republicans who have more forcefully leveraged the trust cleavage to advocate for anti-democratic—i.e., anti-contestation and participation—measures such as violating norms (as discussed), by-passing checks and balances, politicizing large swaths of government, passing restrictive voting laws, encouraging violence, and undermining electoral legitimacy without evidence. In some sense, Republicans have stronger incentive to undertake these steps since they have notably benefited from the anti-majoritarian institutions of the Senate and the Electoral College that may not last into the future (Levitsky and Ziblatt 2024). How this plays out remains to be seen and will depend on the resilience of the institutions and decisions by both parties regarding how to minimize erosion while also building institutions that deliver for the citizenry.

15.5 Conclusion

Why have these trends regarding trust and norms occurred? There is no simple answer—it depends on many factors and choices at different times (Druckman 2024). They presumably reflect a mix of social, technological, economic, and political changes. As mentioned, several notable social changes have occurred that have shifted individuals' preferences away from adhering to norms and institutions and toward protecting in-group cohesion. Specifically, the twenty-first century has witnessed substantial demographic change such that the white population is forecasted to become a minority by the 2040s. This, in turn, generates a sense of threat among white individuals and they move in an exclusionary direction (Craig et al. 2018). In some sense, the demographic transformations combined with the election of first Black president (Obama) set the stage for a backlash, exemplified by Trump. More generally, research shows that white identity and/or perceptions of ethnic diversifications contribute to anti-democratic attitudes (e.g. Bartels 2020; Jardina and Mickey 2022). Even moments of racial liberalization such as the 2020 Black Lives Matter protests are met with backlash that opens avenues for backsliding (Thompson et al. 2024).

Another key social change that compounds the first is the communication/IT revolution. When the Fairness Doctrine, which compelled all those with broadcast licenses to present issues of public importance and to do so in a manner that reflected differing viewpoints, ended in 1987, it paved the way for partisan media that potentially contribute to echo chambers. This, coupled with the 1996 Communication Act, gave internet providers *carte blanche*, resulting in a largely unregulated media marketplace from which a nontrivial proportion of Americans receive information. Consequently, people receive less credible information online and this contributes to political misperceptions and increases the difficulty of coordinating on norms. These problems become particularly pernicious for democracy when those who oversee these media companies become partisan political actors. Examples of this include Mark Zuckerberg, the owner of Facebook, who eliminated staff specifically focused on removing demonstrably false misinformation from the platform; and Elon Musk, who purchased X (formerly Twitter) and reinstated many users to the platform who had been banned for spreading misinformation and inciting violence. Moreover, Jeffrey Bezos, the owner of Amazon and *The Washington Post*, ended, in 2024, the newspaper's nearly fifty-year tradition of endorsing a presidential candidate. When those who control major media platforms use them for political ends or refuse to use them as a source of input, those platforms are no longer independent, hamstringing one foundational check against authoritarianism in democracies. The result is the lack of information needed for evaluation of trust, accountability, and coordination. This aligns with what Snyder (2017) refers to as "obeying in advance," such that individuals anticipate a consequence before it occurs and in so doing behave in a way that foments authoritarianism.

Economic inequality also has mattered. The great recession contributed to increased inequality as the country prioritized supporting banks. The overall consequence has been a rise in economic grievance, connected to less institutional trust (Wroe 2016). More generally, inequality contributes to polarization that, in turn, can influence democratic stability (Finkel et al. 2020; Chiopris et al. 2023; Jannssen and Turkenburg 2024).

Finally, several institutional changes have occurred in the political milieu—state parties, local news, and interest groups have all declined in their influence, leading to the nationalization of politics (Pierson and Schickler 2024). Consequently, geographic contexts do not provide cross-cutting cleavages that historically guard against tyrannical national majorities. This is a point emphasized in Chapter 1 as well as Chapters 11 and 13. Related to this is that the costs of politics have increased, meaning that only those who are more extreme run and hold office (Hall 2019). This leads to elite polarization that manifests in the populace as calcified identities where voters become increasingly tied to their political loyalties such that their likelihood of changing their political behavior, evaluations, or partisanship vanishes (Sides et al. 2022). This undermines political accountability via the electoral connection, because elites' approval rating is no longer tied to current events (e.g., Small and Eisinger 2020).

When combined with the seemingly high number of the aforementioned event stressors in the last quarter century—including the contested election of 2000, the attacks on 9/11, two wars, the great recession, the surprise 2016 election, the COVID-19 pandemic, the contested 2020 election, the January 6 insurrection, and the remarkable 2024 presidential election (with a candidate dropping out and two assassination attempts)—American democracy has a feeling of instability. Yet, the future is not a foregone conclusion. Political theorists have long debated whether the American constitutional design created duplicative checks by relying on a pluralistic nation but also checks and balances and federalism (e.g., Kernell 2003). The idea is that if the former are sufficient, the latter generate unnecessary gridlock. Yet, sorting over time and the nationalization of politics has raised concerns about the cross-cutting cleavages that solidify pluralism (Mason 2018). This makes formal checks and balances and federalism vital institutional checks.

Devolving trust in institutions and norms creates challenges even with these institutions but they also can provide a backstop as the legal system did during Trump's 2020 electoral challenges. More generally, evidence suggests that citizens strongly support democratic representative institutions and do not want strong single leaders (Trüdinger et al. 2024)—the ultimate question is whether such preferences combined with institutional protections and social level efforts (via civic organizations) suffice to limit elected officials who are intent on attacking institutions and norms that have defined American democracy for generations. This is an open question but one for which we maintain some optimism.

Discussion Questions

1   What is more vital—maintaining high levels of trust in institutions or preventing the polarization of trust in institutions?
2   What trust in institution trend(s) seems most concerning?
3   If voters vote for undemocratic candidates from their own party, is it the voters' fault or is it the party elites' fault for providing them/supporting them?
4   If voters knowing choose to democratically elect undemocratic leaders, is democracy working?
5   Who is more important for democratic erosion: elites or citizens, and why?
6   What changes in society seem most impactful in shaping the democratic tra-
jectory of a country?

References

Ahler, Douglas J., and Gaurav Sood. 2018. "The Parties in Our Heads: Misperceptions about Party
Composition and Their Consequences." *The Journal of Politics* 80 (3): 964–81.
Ahmed, Amel. 2023. "Is the American Public Really Turning Away from Democracy? Backsliding and
the Conceptual Challenges of Understanding Public Attitudes." *Perspectives on Politics* 21 (3):
967–78.
Albertus, Michael, and Guy Grossman. 2021. "The Americas: When Do Voters Support PowerGrabs?"
Journal of Democracy 32 (2): 116–31.
Bågenholm, A., M. Bauhr, M. Grimes, and B. Rothstein. 2021. *The Oxford Handbook of the Quality of
Government*. OUP Oxford.
Barrett, J. Taylor, Kelsey Kunkle, and Kimberly Watts. 2023. "Democratic Backsliding and the Balance
Wheel Hypothesis: Partisanship and State Funding for Higher Education in the United States."
Higher Education Policy 36: 781–803.
Bartels, Larry M. 2020. "Ethnic Antagonism Erodes Republicans' Commitment to Democracy."
Proceedings of the National Academy of Sciences 117 (37): 22752–59.
Bartels, Larry M. 2023. *Democracy Erodes From the Top: Public Opinion and the Crisis of Democracy in
Europe*. Princeton University Press.
Bartels, Larry M., and Nicholas Carnes. 2023. "House Republicans Were Rewarded for Supporting
Donald Trump's 'Stop the Steal' Efforts." *Proceedings of the National Academy of Sciences* 120 (34):
e2309072120.
Baum, Matthew A., James N. Druckman, Katherine Ognyanova, and Jonathan Schulman. 2024a.
"Misperceptions, Depression, and Voting for Election Deniers in the United States." *International
Journal of Public Opinion Research* 36 (2): edae024.
Baum, Matthew A., James N. Druckman, Matthew D. Simonson, Jennifer Lin, and Roy H. Perlis. 2024b.
"The Political Consequences of Depression: How Conspiracy Beliefs, Participatory Inclinations,
and Depression Affect Support for Political Violence." *American Journal of Political Science* 68 (2):
575–94.
Bermeo, Nancy. 2016. "On Democratic Backsliding." *Journal of Democracy* 27 (1): 5–19.

Braley, Alia, Gabriel S. Lenz, Dhaval Adjodah, Hossein Rahnama, and Alex Pentland. 2023. "Why Voters Who Value Democracy Participate in Democratic Backsliding." *Nature Human Behaviour* 7 (8): 1282–93.

Brady, Henry E., and Thomas B. Kent. 2022. "Fifty Years of Declining Confidence & Increasing Polarization in Trust in American Institutions." *Daedalus* 151 (4): 43–66.

Broockman, David E., and Joshua L. Kalla. 2024. "Selective Exposure and Echo Chambers in Partisan Television Consumption: Evidence from Linked Viewership, Administrative, and Survey Data." *American Journal of Political Science*: ajps.12886.

Broockman, David, Joshua Kalla, and Sean Westwood. 2023. "Does Affective Polarization Undermine Democratic Norms or Accountability? Maybe Not." *American Journal of Political Science* 67 (3): 808–28.

Busby, Ethan C., Adam J. Howat, Richard Shafranek, and Jacob Rothschild. 2021. *The Partisan Next Door: Stereotypes of Party Supporters and Consequences for Polarization in America*. Cambridge Elements. Cambridge University Press.

Carey, John M., Gretchen Helmke, Brendan Nyhan, Mitchell Sanders, and Susan Stokes. 2019. "Searching for Bright Lines in the Trump Presidency." *Perspectives on Politics* 17 (3): 699–718.

Carey, John M., Gretchen Helmke, Brendan Nyhan, Mitchell Sanders, Susan C. Stokes, and Shun Yamaya. 2022. "The Effect of Electoral Inversions on Democratic Legitimacy: Evidence from the United States." *British Journal of Political Science* 52 (4): 1891–1901.

Chapman, Emilee Booth. 2020. "Review of Smarter Ballots: Electoral Realism and Reform by J. S. Maloy and Rule by Multiple Majorities: A New Theory of Popular Control by Sean Ingham." *Perspectives on Politics* 18 (3): 935–37.

Chapman, Emilee Booth. 2024. "Democratic Norms and the Ethics of Resistance." *Annual Review of Political Science* 27 (1): 147–64.

Chiopris, Caterina, Monika Nalepa, and Georg Vanberg. 2023. "A Wolf in Sheep's Clothing: Citizen Uncertainty and Democratic Backsliding." Working paper. https://www.monikanalepa.com/up loads/6/6/3/1/66318923/chioprisnalepavanberg.pdf.

Cohen, Mollie J., and Geoffrey Sheagley. 2024. "Partisan Poll Watchers and Americans' Perceptions of Electoral Fairness." *Public Opinion Quarterly* 88 (SI): 536–60.

Coleman, James S. 1990. *Foundations of Social Theory*. Harvard University Press.

Cook, Karen S., ed. 2001. *Trust in Society*. Russell Sage Foundation.

Cook, Karen S., Russell Hardin, and Margaret Levi. 2005. *Cooperation Without Trust?* Russell Sage Foundation.

Craig, Maureen A., Julian M. Rucker, and Jennifer A. Richeson. 2018. "Racial and Political Dynamics of an Approaching 'Majority-Minority' United States." *The Annals of the American Academy of Political and Social Science* 677 (1): 204–14.

Crawford, Sue E. S., and Elinor Ostrom. 1995. "A Grammar of Institutions." *American Political Science Review* 89 (3): 582–600.

Dias, Nicholas C., Laurits F. Aarslew, Kristian Vrede Skaaning Frederiksen, Yphtach Lelkes, Lea Pradella, and Sean J. Westwood. 2024. "Correcting Misperceptions of Partisan Opponents Is Not Effective At Treating Democratic Ills." *PNAS Nexus* 3 (8): 304.

Doherty, Carroll, Jocelyn Kiley, and Nida Asheer. 2024. "Americans' Views of Government's Role: Persistent Divisions and Areas of Agreement." *Pew Research Center*. https://www.pewresearch.org/wp-content/uploads/sites/20/2024/06/PP_2024.6.24_role-of-government_REPORT.pdf.

Donahue, Samuel Thomas. 2023. "The Politics of Police." *American Sociological Review* 88 (4): 656–80.

Druckman, James N. 2023. "Correcting Misperceptions of the Other Political Party Does Not Robustly Reduce Support for Undemocratic Practices or Partisan Violence." *Proceedings of the National Academy of Sciences* 120 (37): e2308938120.

Druckman, James N. 2024. "How to Study Democratic Backsliding." *Advances in Political Psychology* 45 (S1): 3–42.

Druckman, James N., Suji Kang, James Chu, Michael N. Stagnaro, Jan G. Voelkel et al. 2023. "Correcting Misperceptions of Out-Partisans Decreases American Legislators' Support for Undemocratic Practices." *Proceedings of the National Academy of Sciences* 120 (23): e2301836120.

Druckman, James N., Samara Klar, Yanna Krupnikov, Matthew Levendusky, and John Barry Ryan. 2022. "(Mis)estimating Affective Polarization." *The Journal of Politics* 84 (2): 1106–17.

Druckman, James N., Samara Klar, Yanna Krupnikov, Matthew Levendusky, and John Barry Ryan. 2024. *Partisan Hostility and American Democracy: Explaining Political Divisions and When They Matter*. The University of Chicago Press.

Druckman, James N., and Jonathan Schulman. 2024. "The Polarization and Politicization of Trust in Scientists." Unpublished Paper. https://papers.ssrn.com/abstract=4906359.

Finkel, Eli J., Christopher A. Bail, Mina Cikara, Peter H. Ditto, Shanto Iyengar, et al. 2020. "Political Sectarianism in America." *Science* 370 (6516): 533–36.

Foa, Roberto Stefan, and Yascha Mounk. 2017. "The Signs of Deconsolidation." *Journal of Democracy* 28 (1): 5–15.

Fossati, Diego, Burhanuddin Muhtadi, and Eve Warburton. 2022. "Why Democrats Abandon Democracy: Evidence from Four Survey Experiments." *Party Politics* 28 (3): 554–66.

Frederiksen, K.V.S. 2022. "When Democratic Experience Distorts Democracy: Citizen Reactions to Undemocratic Incumbent Behaviour." *European Journal of Political Research* 61: 281–92.

Gadarian, Shana Kushner, Sara Wallace Goodman, and Thomas B. Pepinsky. 2022. *Pandemic Politics: The Deadly Toll of Partisanship in the Age of COVID*. Princeton University Press.

Gidengil, Elisabeth, Dietlind Stolle, and Olivier Bergeron-Boutin. 2022. "The Partisan Nature of Support for Democratic Backsliding: A Comparative Perspective." *European Journal of Political Research* 61 (4): 901–29.

Graham, Matthew H., and Milan W. Svolik. 2020. "Democracy in America? Partisanship, Polarization, and the Robustness of Support for Democracy in the United States." *American Political Science Review* 114 (2): 392–409.

Grillo, Edoardo, and Carlo Prato. 2023. "Reference Points and Democratic Backsliding." *American Journal of Political Science* 67 (1): 71–88.

Grumbach, Jacob M. 2022. *Laboratories Against Democracy: How National Parties Transformed State Politics*. Princeton University Press.

Grumbach, Jacob M. 2023. "Laboratories of Democratic Backsliding." *American Political Science Review* 117 (3): 967–84.

Guirgis, David, and Lew Blank. 2022. "Analyzing Public Trust in Government Agencies." *Data For Progress*. https://www.dataforprogress.org/blog/2022/2/16/analyzing-public-trust-in-government-agencies.

Hall, Andrew B. 2019. *Who Wants to Run? How the Devaluing of Political Office Drives Polarization*. The University of Chicago Press.

Hall, Matthew E. K., and James N. Druckman. 2023. "Norm-Violating Rhetoric Undermines Support for Participatory Inclusiveness and Political Equality among Trump Supporters." *Proceedings of the National Academy of Sciences* 120 (40): e2311005120.

Hardin, Russell. 2002. *Trust and Trustworthiness*. Russell Sage Foundation.

Helmke, Gretchen, Mary Kroeger, and Jack Paine. 2021. "Democracy by Deterrence: Norms, Constitutions, and Electoral Tilting." *American Journal of Political Science* 66 (2): 434–50.

Helmke, Gretchen, and Steven Levitsky. 2004. "Informal Institutions and Comparative Politics: A Research Agenda." *Perspectives on Politics* 2 (4): 725–40.

Helmke, Gretchen, and Josiah Rath. n.d. "Defining and Measuring Democratic Norms." *Annual Review of Political Science*. Forthcoming.

Holliday, Derek E., Shanto Iyengar, Yphtach Lelkes, and Sean J. Westwood. 2024. "Uncommon and Nonpartisan: Antidemocratic Attitudes in the American Public." *Proceedings of the National Academy of Sciences* 121 (13): e2313013121.

Hopkins, Daniel J. 2023. "Stable Views in a Time of Tumult: Assessing Trends in US Public Opinion, 2007–20." *British Journal of Political Science* 53 (1): 297–307.

Janssen, Lisa, and Emma Turkenburg. 2024. "Breaking Free from Linear Assumptions: Unravelling the Relationship between Affective Polarization and Democratic Support." *European Journal of Political Research*. https://doi.org/10.1111/1475-6765.

Jardina, Ashley, and Robert Mickey. 2022. "White Racial Solidarity and Opposition to American Democracy." *Annals of the American Academy of Political and Social Science* 699 (1): 79–89.

Justwan, Florian, and Ryan D. Williamson. 2022. "Trump and Trust: Examining the Relationship between Claims of Fraud and Citizen Attitudes." *PS: Political Science & Politics* 55 (3): 462–69.

Kalmoe, Nathan P., and Lilliana Mason. 2022. *Radical American Partisanship: Mapping Violent Hostility, Its Causes, and the Consequences for Democracy.* The University of Chicago Press.

Kaufman, Robert R., and Stephan Haggard. 2019. "Democratic Decline in the United States: What Can We Learn from Middle-Income Backsliding?" *Perspectives on Politics* 17 (2): 417–32.

Keefer, Philip, Carlos Scartascini, and Razvan Vlaicu. 2021. "Trust, Populism, and the Quality of Government." In *The Oxford Handbook of the Quality of Government*, edited by Andreas Bagenholm, Monika Bauhr, Marcia Grimes, and Bo Rothstein, 249–64. Oxford University Press.

Kent, Thomas B. 2023. "Partisan Polarization of Trust in Societal Institutions: Causes and Effects." Ph.D, University of California, Berkeley.

Kernell, Samuel. 2003. "The True Principles of Republican Government." In *James Madison: The Theory and Practice of Republican Government*, edited by Samuel Kernell, 92–125. Stanford University Press.

Kingzette, Jon, James Druckman, Samara Klar, Yanna Krupnikov, Matthew Levendusky, and John Barry Ryan. 2021. "How Affective Polarization Undermines Support for Democratic Norms." *Public Opinion Quarterly* 85 (2): 663–77.

Knott, Katherine. 2024. "Colleges Say GOP Bill to Protect Free Speech Would Do the Opposite." *Inside Higher Ed*. https://www.insidehighered.com/news/government/politics-elections/2024/09/20/bill-end-woke-higher-education-clears-house.

Krishnarajan, Suthan. 2023. "Rationalizing Democracy: the Perceptual Bias and (Un)democratic Behavior." *American Political Science Review* 117 (2): 474–96.

Lees, Jeffrey, and Mina Cikara. 2020. "Inaccurate Group Meta-Perceptions Drive Negative out-Group Attributions in Competitive Contexts." *Nature Human Behaviour* 4 (3): 279–86.

Levitsky, Steven, and Daniel Ziblatt. 2018. *How Democracies Die*. First edition. Crown.

Levitsky, Steven, and Daniel Ziblatt. 2024. *Tyranny of the Majority*. First edition. Crown.

Lieberman, Robert C., Suzanne Mettler, Thomas B. Pepinsky, Kenneth M. Roberts, and Richard Valelly. 2019. "The Trump Presidency and American Democracy: A Historical and Comparative Analysis." *Perspectives on Politics* 17 (2): 470–79.

Luo, Zhaotian, and Adam Przeworski. 2023. "Democracy and Its Vulnerabilities: Dynamics of Democratic Backsliding." *Quarterly Journal of Political Science* 18 (1): 105–30.

Mason, Lilliana. 2018. *Uncivil Agreement: How Politics Became Our Identity*. University of Chicago Press.

Mechkova, Valeriya, Anna Lührmann, and Staffan I. Lindberg. 2017. "How Much Democratic Backsliding?" *Journal of Democracy* 28 (4): 162–69.

Mernyk, Joseph S., Sophia L. Pink, James N. Druckman, and Robb Willer. 2022. "Correcting Inaccurate Metaperceptions Reduces Americans' Support for Partisan Violence." *Proceedings of the National Academy of Sciences* 119 (16): e2116851119.

Mettler, Suzanne. 2016. "The Policyscape and the Challenges of Contemporary Politics to Policy Maintenance." *Perspectives on Politics* 14 (2): 369–90.

Moore-Berg, Samantha L., Lee-Or Ankori-Karlinsky, Boaz Hameiri, and Emile Bruneau. 2020. "Exaggerated Meta-Perceptions Predict Intergroup Hostility between American Political Partisans." *Proceedings of the National Academy of Sciences* 117 (26): 14864–72.

Ortega, Alberto. 2020. "State Partisanship and Higher Education." *Economics of Education Review* 76: 101977.

Ostrom, Elinor. 1990. *Governing the Commons: The Evolution of Institutions for Collective Action*. 1st ed. Cambridge University Press.

Pasek, Michael H., Lee-Or Ankori-Karlinsky, Alex Levy-Vene, and Samantha L. Moore-Berg. 2022. "Misperceptions about Out-Partisans' Democratic Values May Erode Democracy." *Scientific Reports* 12 (1): 16284.

Pérez-Liñán, Aníbal, Nicolás Schmidt, and Daniela Vairo. 2019. "Presidential Hegemony and Democratic Backsliding in Latin America, 1925–2016." *Democratization* 26 (4): 606–25.

Pew Research Center. 2024, "Americans' Views of Government's Role: Persistent Divisions and Areas of Agreement." June 24. https://www.pewresearch.org/politics/2024/06/24/americans-views-of-governments-role-persistent-divisions-and-areas-of-agreement/.

Pfiffner, James P. 2022. "President Trump and the Shallow State: Disloyalty at the Highest Levels." *Presidential Studies Quarterly* 52 (3): 573–95.

Pierson, Paul, and Eric Schickler. 2024. *Partisan Nation: The Dangerous New Logic of American Politics in a Nationalized Era*. The University of Chicago Press.

Ruggeri, Kai, Bojana Većkalov, Lana Bojanić, Thomas L. Andersen, Sarah Ashcroft-Jones, Nélida Ayacaxli, Paula Barea-Arroyo et al. 2021. "The General Fault in Our Fault Lines." *Nature Human Behaviour* 5 (10): 1369–80.

Safarpour, Alauna, Kristin Lunz Trujillo, Jon Green, Caroline High Pippert, Jennifer Lin et al. 2024. "Divisive or Descriptive?: How Americans Understand Critical Race Theory." *The Journal of Race, Ethnicity, and Politics* 9 (1): 157–81.

Sasmaz, Aytuğ, Alper H. Yagci, and Daniel Ziblatt. 2022. "How Voters Respond to Presidential Assaults on Checks and Balances: Evidence from a Survey Experiment in Turkey." *Comparative Political Studies* 55 (11): 1947–80.

Schulman, Jonathan, Druckman, James N., Alauna C. Safarpour, Matthew Baum, Katherine Ognyanova et al. n.d.. "Continuity and Change in Trust in Scientists in the United States: Demographic Stability and Partisan Polarization." *Public Opinion Quarterly*. Forthcoming.

Shultziner, Doron, and Yelena Stukalin. 2021. "Politicizing What's News: How Partisan Media Bias Occurs in News Production." *Mass Communication and Society* 24 (3): 372–93.

Sides, John, Chris Tausanovitch, and Lynn Vavreck. 2022. *The Bitter End: The 2020 Presidential Campaign and the Challenge to American Democracy*. Princeton: Princeton University Press.

Simonovits, Gabor, Jennifer McCoy, and Levente Littvay. 2022. "Democratic Hypocrisy and Out-Group Threat: Explaining Citizen Support for Democratic Erosion." *The Journal of Politics* 84 (3): 1806–11.

Small, Raphael, and Robert M. Eisinger. 2020. "Whither Presidential Approval?" *Presidential Studies Quarterly* 50 (4): 845–63.

Snyder, Timothy. 2017. *On Tyranny: Twenty Lessons from the Twentieth Century*. Crown.

Solomon, Brittany C., Matthew E. K. Hall, Abigail Hemmen, and James N. Druckman. 2024. "Illusory Interparty Disagreement: Partisans Agree on What Hate Speech to Censor but Do Not Know It." *Proceedings of the National Academy of Sciences* 121 (39): e2402428121.

Stewart, III, Charles. 2022. "Trust in Elections." *Daedalus* 151 (4): 234–53.

Taylor, Barrett J., Kelsey Kunkle, and Kimberly Watts. 2023. "Democratic Backsliding and the Balance Wheel Hypothesis: Partisanship and State Funding for Higher Education in the United States." *Higher Education Policy* 36 (4): 781–803.

Thompson, Andrew Ifedapo et al. 2024. "Anti-Black Political Violence and the Historical Legacy of the Great Replacement Conspiracy." *Perspectives on Politics*: 1–18.

Touchton, Michael, Casey Klofstad, and Joseph Uscinski. 2023. "Does Partisanship Promote Anti-Democratic Impulses? Evidence from a Survey Experiment." *Journal of Elections, Public Opinion and Parties* 33 (2): 197–209.

Turchton, Michael, Casey Klofstad, and Joseph Uscinski. 2023. "Does Partisanship Promote Anti-Democratic Impulses? Evidence from a Survey Experiment." *Journal of Elections, Public Opinion and Parties* 33 (2): 197–209.

Trüdinger, Eva-Maria, André Bächtiger, James N. Druckman, and Mark E. Warren. 2024. "The Public's Preference for Institutional Stability and Innovation in Turbulent Times." Unpublished Paper.

Voelkel, Jan G., James Chu, Michael N. Stagnaro, Joseph S. Mernyk, Chrystal Redekopp, Sophia L. Pink, James N. Druckman, David G. Rand, and Robb Willer. 2023."Interventions Reducing Affective Polarization Do Not Necessarily Improve Anti-Democratic Attitudes." *Nature Human Behavior* 7: 55–64.

Voelkel, Jan G., Michael N. Stagnaro, James Y. Chu, Sophia L. Pink, Joseph S. Mernyk, Chrystal Redekopp, Isaias Ghezae et al. 2024. "Megastudy Testing 25 Treatments to Reduce Antidemocratic Attitudes and Partisan Animosity." *Science* 386 (6719): eadh4764.

Weingast, Barry R. 1997. "The Political Foundations of Democracy and the Rule of the Law." *American Political Science Review* 91 (2): 245–63.

Wroe, Andrew. 2016. "Economic Insecurity and Political Trust in the United States." *American Politics Research* 44 (1): 131–63.

Wunsch, Natasha, Marc S. Jacob, and Laurenz Derksen. 2022. "The Demand Side of Democratic Backsliding: How Divergent Understandings of Democracy Shape Political Choice." Working paper.

List of Contributors

Jamie L. Carson is the UGA Athletic Association Professor of Public & International Affairs II in the Department of Political Science at the University of Georgia. He studies congressional elections, separation of powers, and American political development. His most recent books are *Nationalized Politics: Evaluating Electoral Politics Across Time* and *The Politics of Congressional Elections, 11th edition*.

Lindsey Cormack is an Associate Professor in the College of Arts and Letters and Director of the Diplomacy Lab at Stevens Institute of Technology in Hoboken, New Jersey. Since 2009, she has run DCinbox, archiving and providing to the public all official e-newsletters sent by members of Congress.

James Curry is a Professor of Political Science at the University of Notre Dame. His research focuses on U.S. politics and policymaking, with a focus the U.S. Congress. He is the author of two books, *Legislating in the Dark* and *The Limits of Party*, and his research has been published in the *American Political Science Review*, the *Journal of Politics*, *Perspectives on Politics*, and more.

Stephanie Davis is an assistant professor of political science at the University of Arkansas at Little Rock. Her research interests involve American political institutions, with a particular focus on legislatures and the separation of powers. She recently coauthored an article in *Legislative Studies Quarterly* that examines senators' digital communication strategies and representational styles.

James Druckman is a Professor in the Department of Political Science at the University of Rochester. His research focuses on political preference formation and communication. His work examines how citizens make political, economic, and social decisions in various contexts. He also researches the relationship between citizens' preferences and public policy and the polarization of American society. He has published more than 150 articles and book chapters in political science, communication, economics, science, and psychology journals. He has authored, co-authored, or co-edited the books *Cambridge Handbook of Experimental Political Science*, *Who Governs? Presidents, Public Opinion, and Manipulation*, *Advances in Experimental Political Science*, and *Experimental Thinking: A Primer on Social Science Experiments*. He has served as editor of the journals *Political Psychology* and *Public Opinion Quarterly* as well as the University of Chicago Press's series in American Politics.

Charles Finocchiaro is the Associate Director of the Carl Albert Congressional Research and Studies Center and Professor of Political Science at the University of Oklahoma. His research examines the development and organization of legislative institutions as well as congressional elections, with ongoing projects analyzing the transformation of Congress in the late nineteenth and early twentieth centuries. He has published work in a range of journals including the *American Journal of Political Science*, *The Journal of Politics*, *Political Research Quarterly*, *Legislative Studies Quarterly*, and *Political Science Research and Methods*.

Abigail Hassett is a PhD student at the University of South Carolina. She studies American politics with a specific emphasis on the judiciary.

https://doi.org/10.1515/9783111591902-016

Gbemende Johnson is an Associate Professor of Political Science at the University of Georgia. Her research interests include American institutions, judicial politics, executive branch politics, and judicial diversity. She also has interests in race and politics.

Bridgett King is an Associate Professor of American Politics in the Department of Political Science at the University of Kentucky. Her research focuses on election administration, public policy, citizen voting experiences, and representation. She has received external support for her election research from the National Science Foundation, Rockefeller Family Fund, and the Democracy Fund.

Tabitha Lamberth is a PhD student at the University of Georgia. She studies American politics with specific research interests in political behavior and political psychology.

Hannah Lee is an undergraduate student at the University of Georgia.

Stephanie Mathiasen is a PhD student at Texas Tech University. Her research interests include campaigns, elections, gender and politics, and the U.S. Congress.

Joshua McCrain is an Assistant Professor of Political Science at the University of Utah. His research focuses on public policy and political institutions, lobbying, Congress, media and politics, health policy, policing and criminal justice policy, political methodology and computational social science.

Seth McKee is a Professor of Political Science at Oklahoma State University. He earned his PhD in Government from the University of Texas in 2005. He is a scholar of American politics with expertise in Southern politics, political parties, political behavior, campaigns and elections, public opinion, redistricting, and American political institutions.

Abby Miller is a PhD student at Texas Tech University. Her research interests include international relations, democratic backsliding, peace and conflict resolution, and gender politics.

Stephen P. Nicholson is the Philip H. Alston Jr. Distinguished Professor in the Department of Political Science at the University of Georgia. His research interests include mass public behavior, public opinion, political psychology and direct democracy. He is co-editor of *Advances in Political Psychology* and serves on the editorial boards of *Political Behavior* and *Journal of Experimental Political Science*. He has published numerous peer-reviewed articles in the *American Journal of Political Science*, *Journal of Politics*, *British Journal of Political Science*, *Political Research Quarterly*, *Political Behavior*, *Public Opinion Quarterly* and *State Politics and Policy Quarterly*. In 1999, he won the American Political Science Association's E.E. Schattschneider Award for the Best dissertation in American Politics, and in 2006 he was awarded the Emerging Scholar Award for the American Political Science Association's section on Elections, Public Opinion and Voting Behavior.

Anna Puente is a PhD student at the University of South Carolina. She is primarily interested in studying human security and the role that identity plays in international violent conflict.

Kirk Randazzo is a Professor in the Department of Political Science at the University of South Carolina. His research and teaching interests span the fields of American Politics, Comparative Politics, and Methodology – with a particular focus on law and judicial politics. His work focuses on legal constraints to judicial decision making, strategic behavior among judges, and aspects of judicial independence within fledgling democracies.

Dot Sawler is a PhD student at the University of Rochester. She studies American politics with a specific interest in political behavior.

Enrijeta Shino is an Assistant Professor of American Politics at the University of Alabama. She studies elections, voting behavior, public opinion, and political methodology. Her research has been published in several journals including *Public Opinion Quarterly*, *Political Science Research and Methods*, *Political Research Quarterly*, *Journal of Elections*, *Public Opinion and Parties*, *Electoral Studies*, *American Politics Research*, and *Journal of Survey Statistics and Methodology*.

Joel Sievert is an Associate Professor of Political Science at Texas Tech University. His research focuses on American political institutions with an emphasis on the presidency, congressional politics and elections, political parties, and institutional development. He has published articles in journals such as the *Journal of Politics*, *Legislative Studies Quarterly*, and *Political Research Quarterly* and two books, *Electoral Incentives in Congress*, and *Nationalized Politics: Evaluating Electoral Politics Across Time*.

Stewart Ulrich is an Assistant Professor at Sam Houston State University. He received his PhD from the University of Georgia in 2025. His primary research interests are in American politics with specialized interests in executive politics, elections, and political behavior.

Teena Wilhelm is an Associate Professor in the Department of Political Science at the University of Georgia. She received her PhD from the University of Arizona in 2005. Her research has appeared in major political and legal journals, and has been honored by the Southern Political Science Association and the National Science Foundation.

Ryan D. Williamson is an Assistant Professor of Political Science at the University of Wyoming. His research focuses on congressional elections, legislative procedure, institutional development, and public policy. He is co-author of *Nationalized Politics: Evaluating Electoral Politics Across Time* and numerous articles in political science journals such as the *Journal of Politics*, *Political Research Quarterly*, *Electoral Studies*, and *State Politics & Policy Quarterly*.

Jordan A. Windham is a graduate student at the University of Wyoming. She studies American politics with a particular interest in political parties and legislative behavior.

Yao Yao is a PhD student at the University of Georgia. She studies American politics with a specific emphasis on the executive branch.

Index

Note: Page numbers in *italics* indicate figures, **bold** indicate tables in the text, and references following "n" refer notes.

https://doi.org/10.1515/9783111591902-017

www.ingramcontent.com/pod-product-compliance
Lightning Source LLC
Chambersburg PA
CBHW031406270326
41929CB00010BA/1346